Island in a Puddle

2

Kei Sanbe

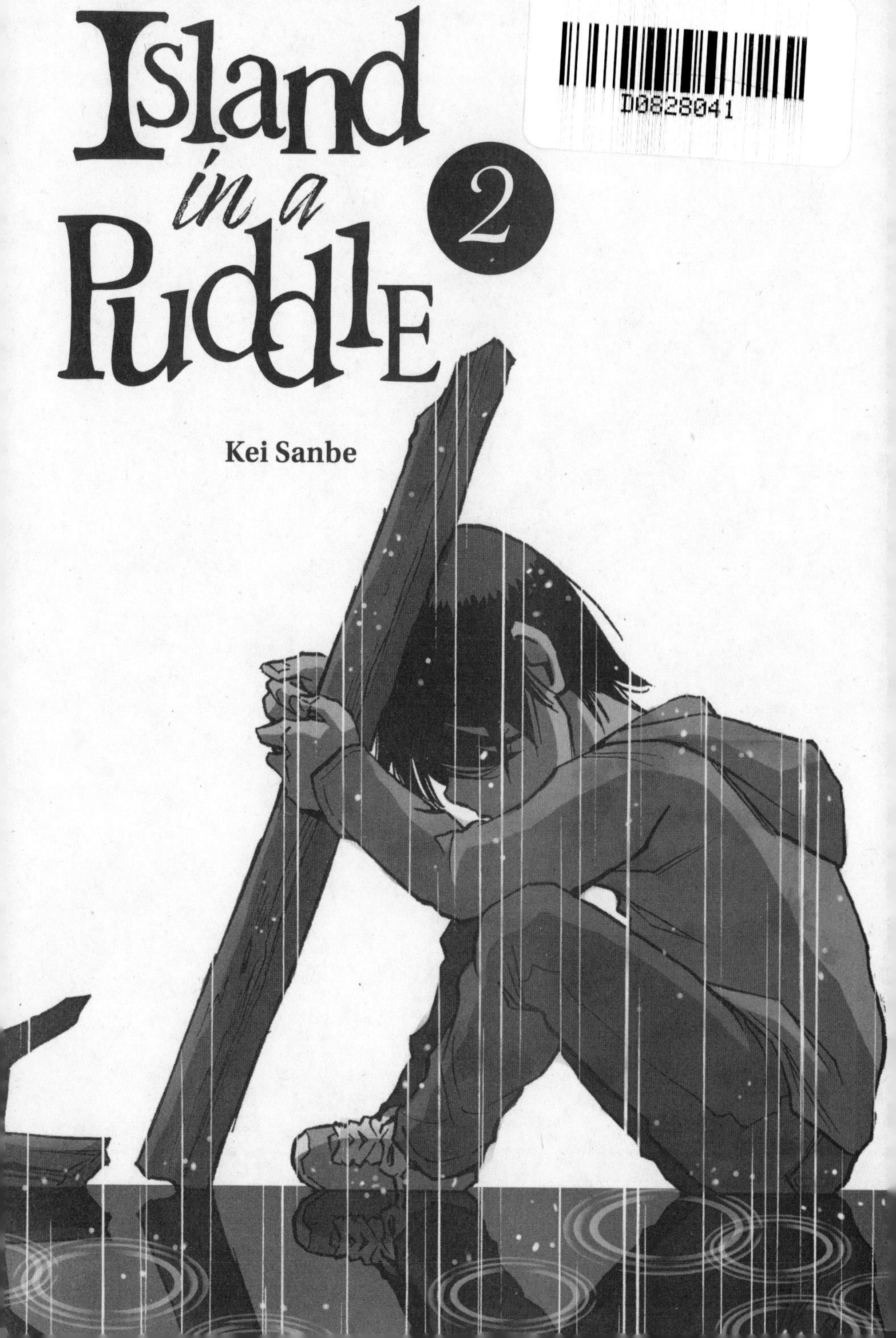

CONTENTS

CHAPTER 6

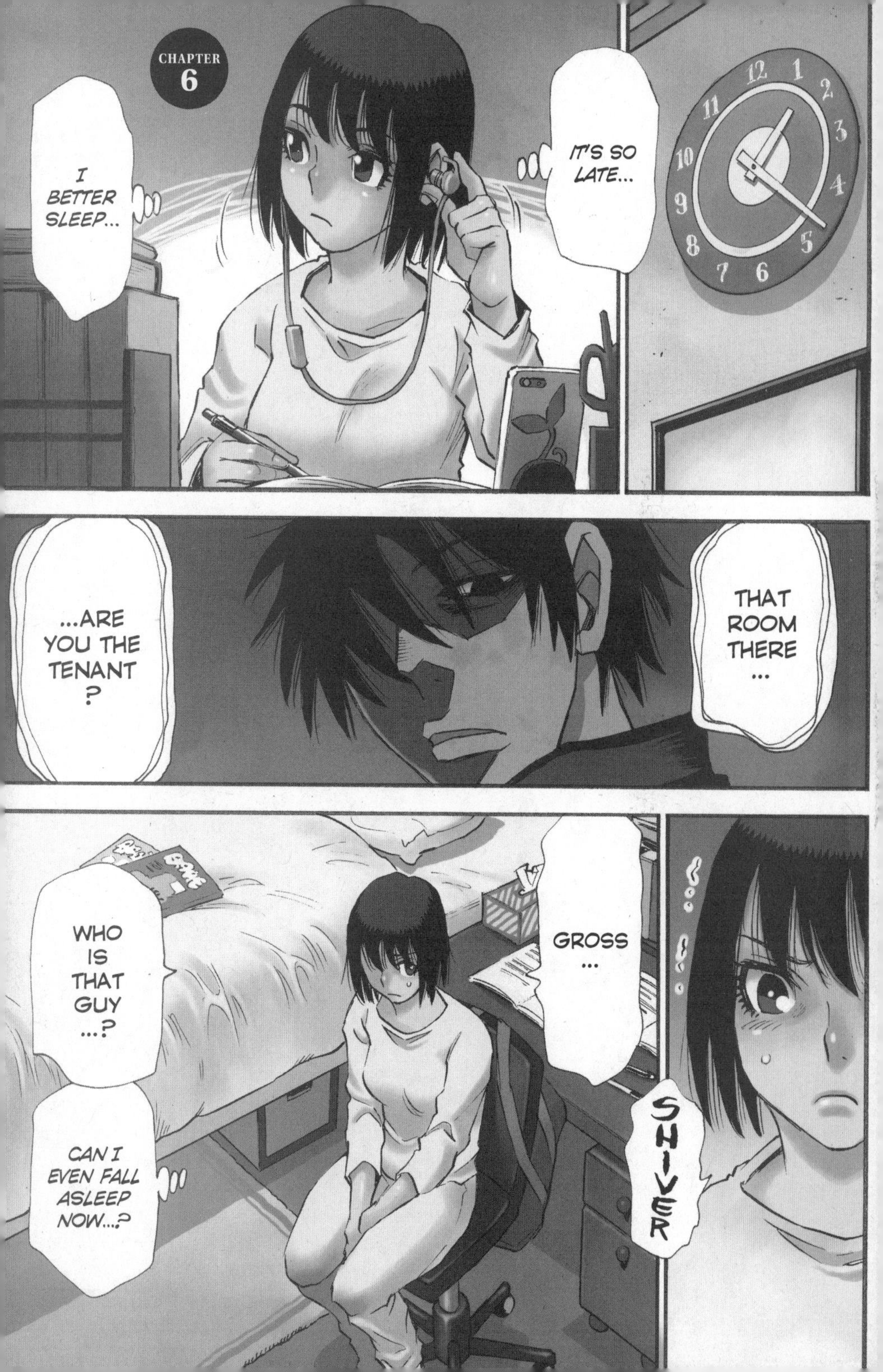
IT'S SO LATE...
I BETTER SLEEP...
THAT ROOM THERE ...
...ARE YOU THE TENANT ?
SHIVER
GROSS ...
WHO IS THAT GUY ...?
CAN I EVEN FALL ASLEEP NOW...?

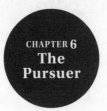

CHAPTER 6
The Pursuer

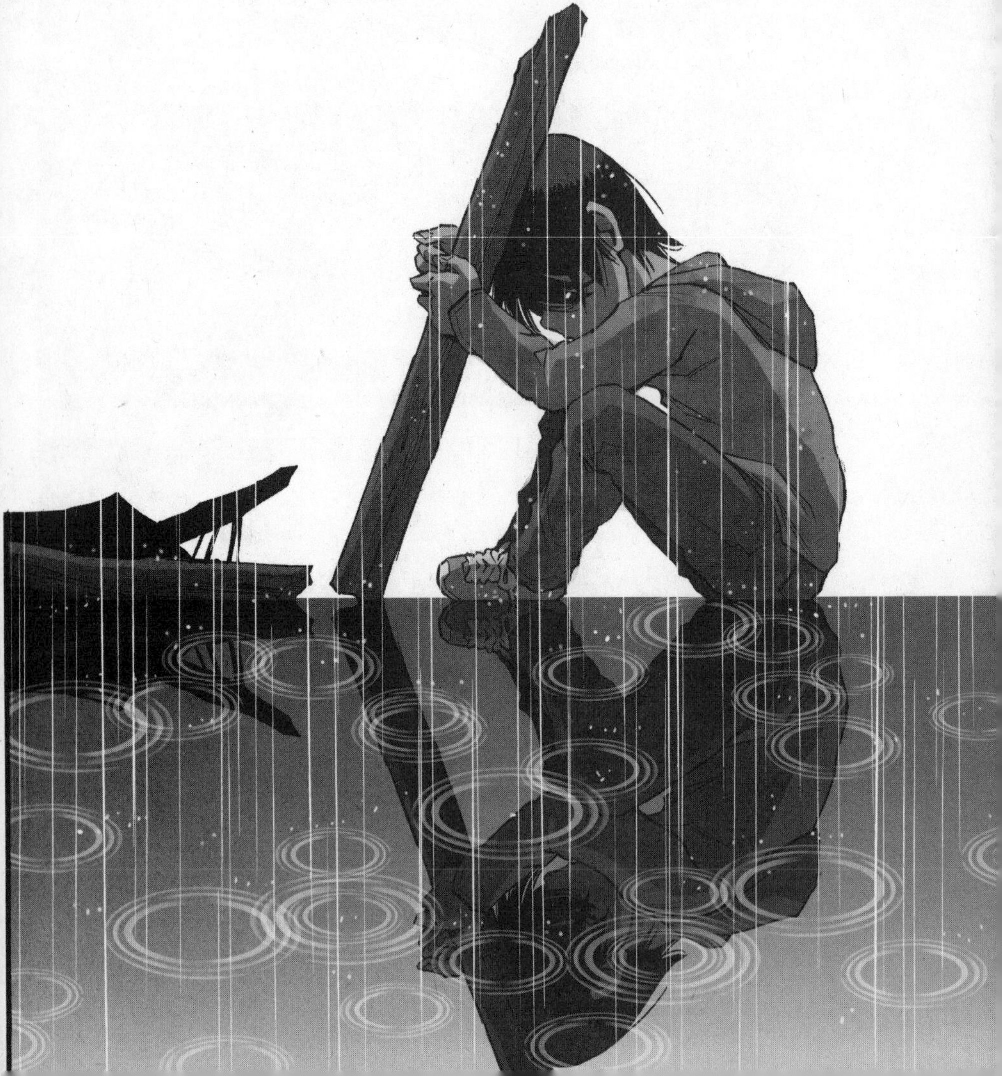

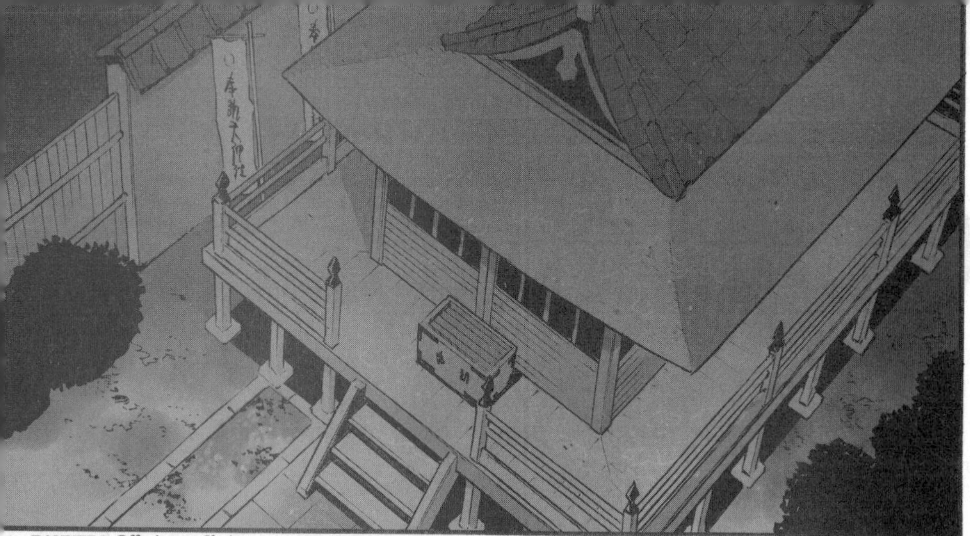

BANNERS: Offering to Shrine

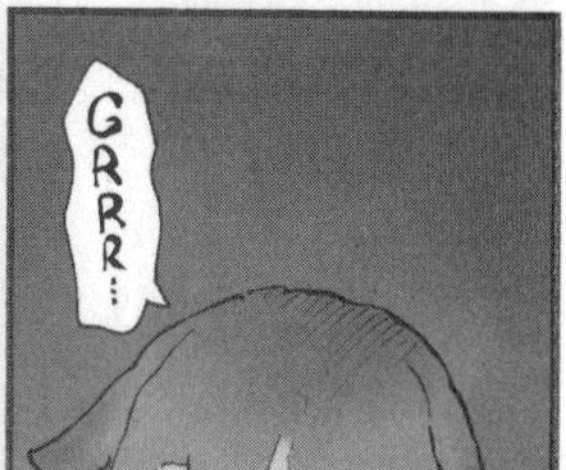
GRRR..

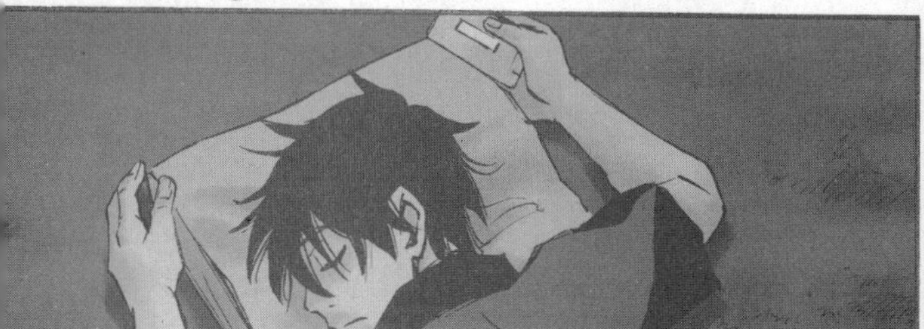

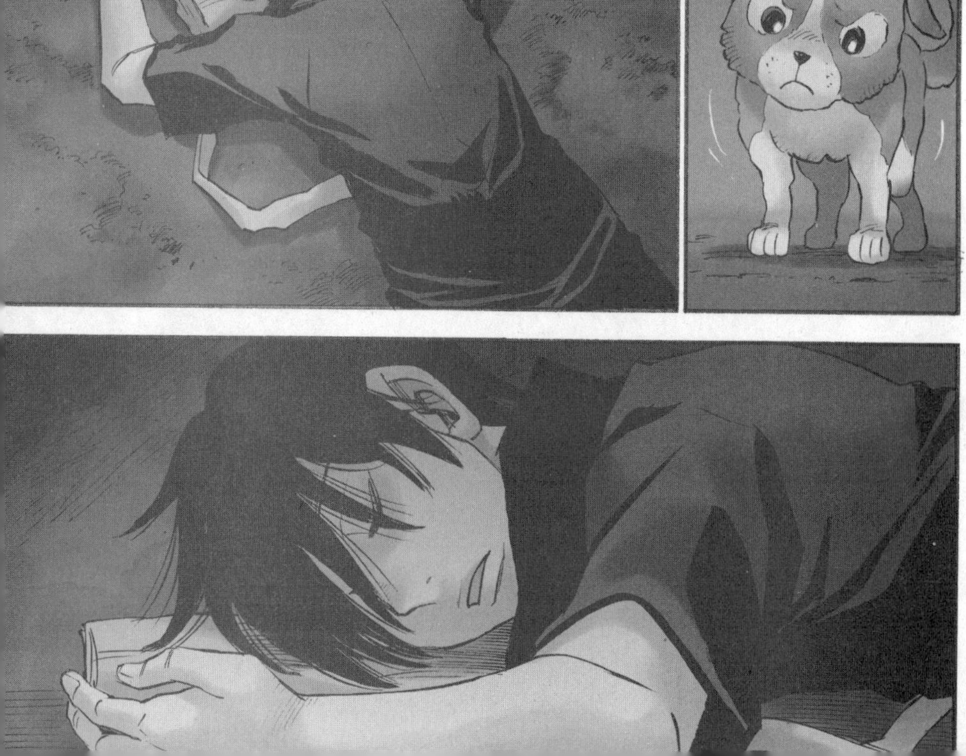

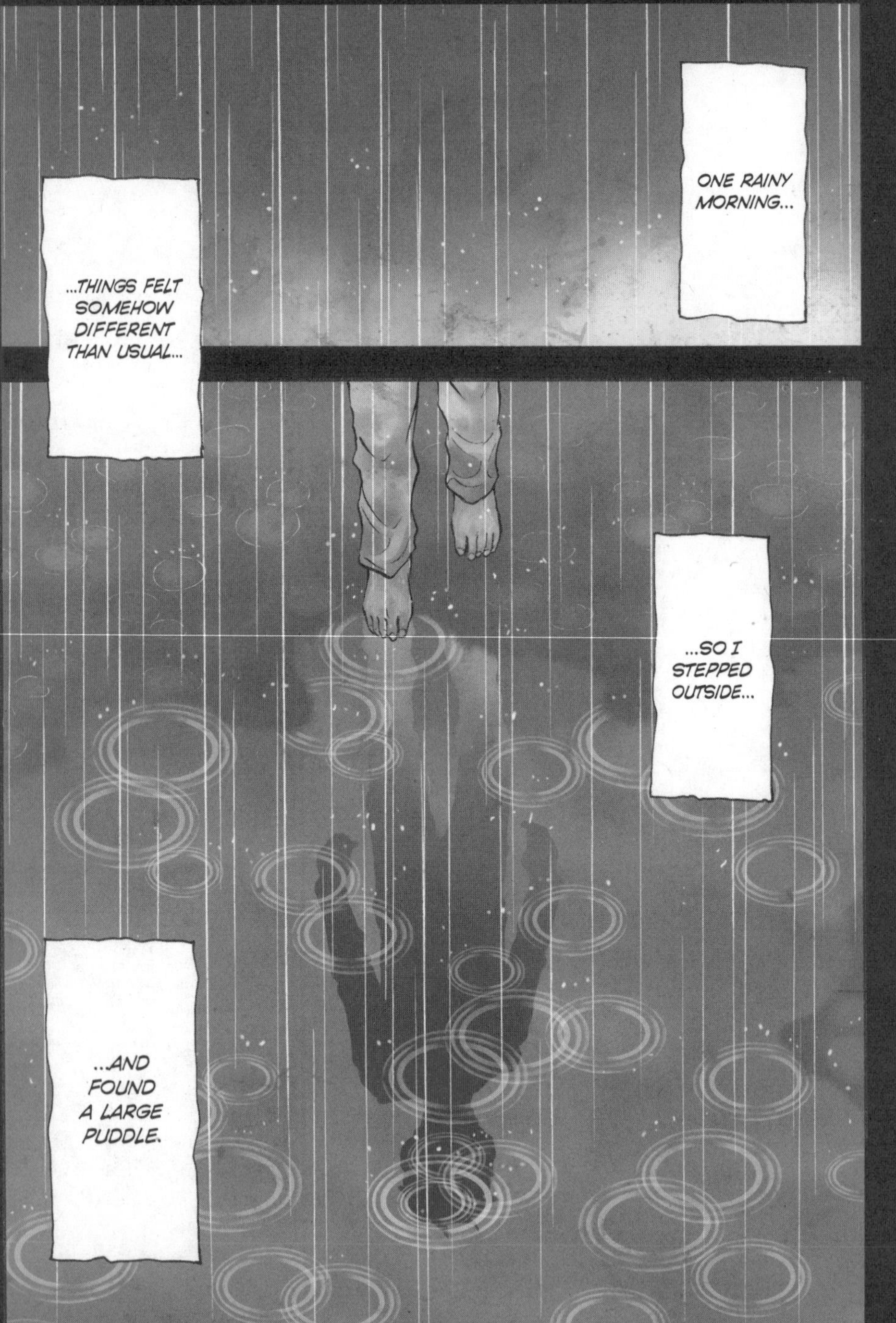
ONE RAINY MORNING...
...THINGS FELT SOMEHOW DIFFERENT THAN USUAL...
...SO I STEPPED OUTSIDE...
...AND FOUND A LARGE PUDDLE.

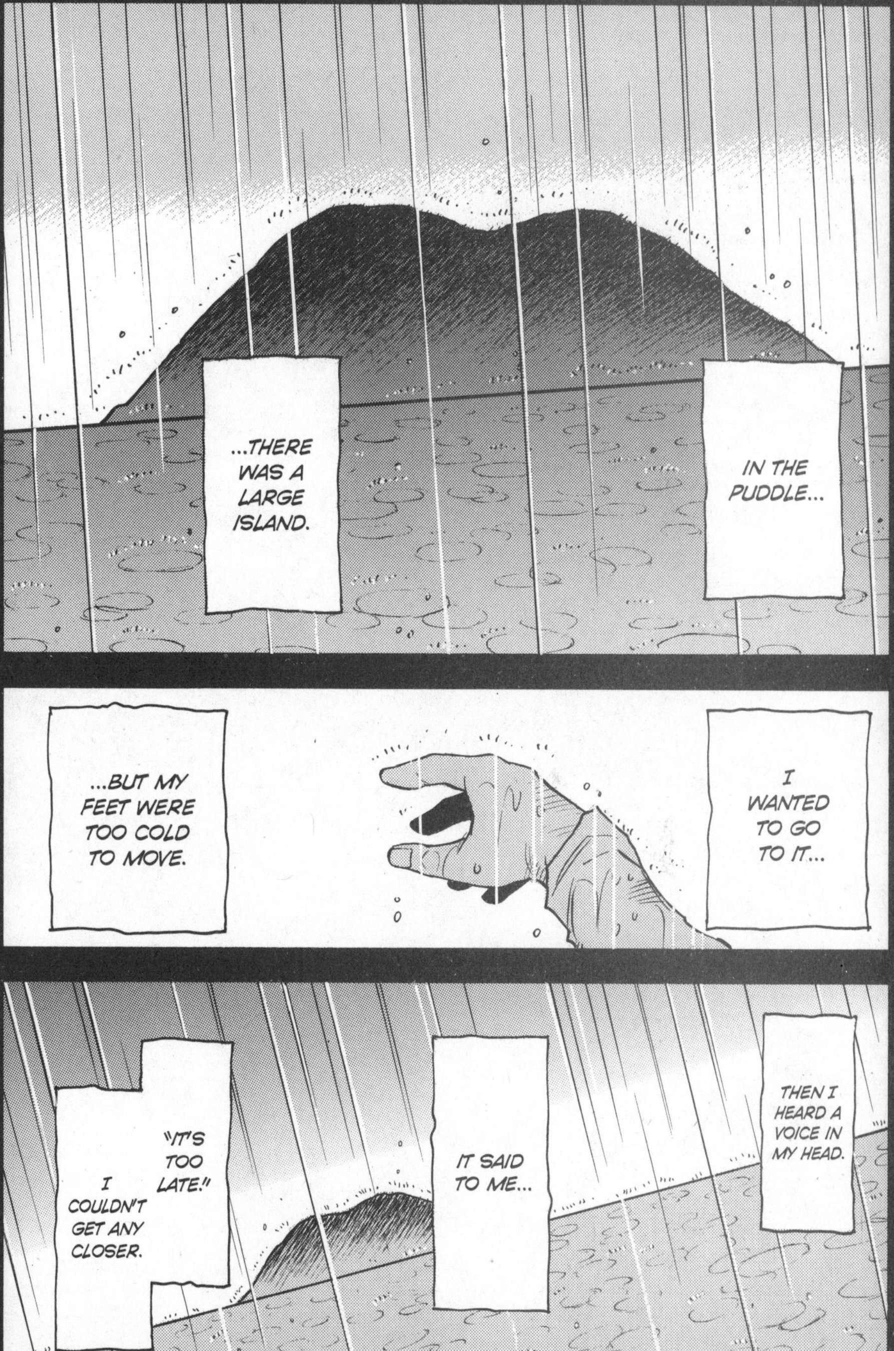
IN THE PUDDLE...
...THERE WAS A LARGE ISLAND.
I WANTED TO GO TO IT...
...BUT MY FEET WERE TOO COLD TO MOVE.
THEN I HEARD A VOICE IN MY HEAD.
IT SAID TO ME...
"IT'S TOO LATE."
I COULDN'T GET ANY CLOSER.

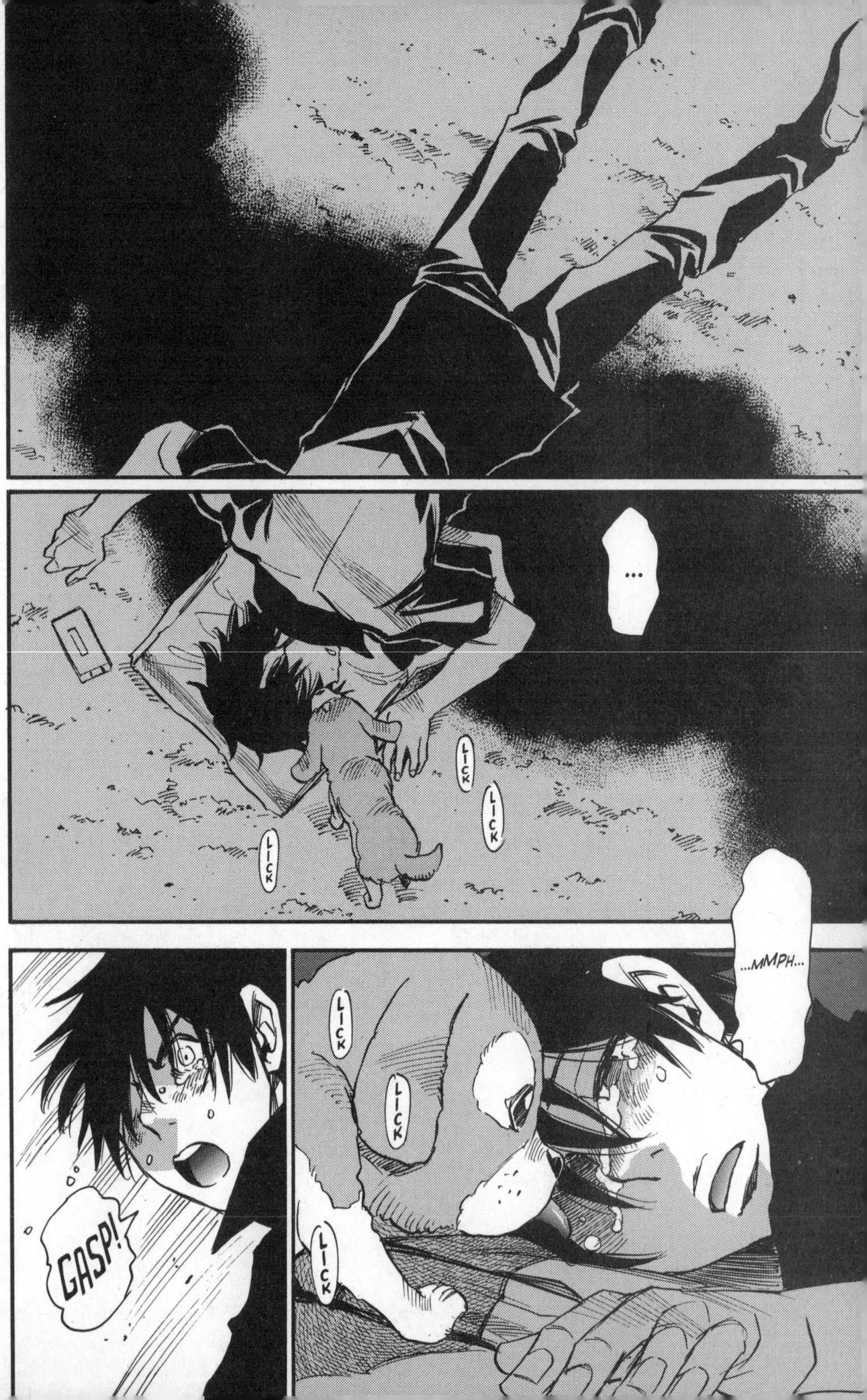
...
LICK
LICK
LICK
...MMPH...
LICK
LICK
LICK
GASP!

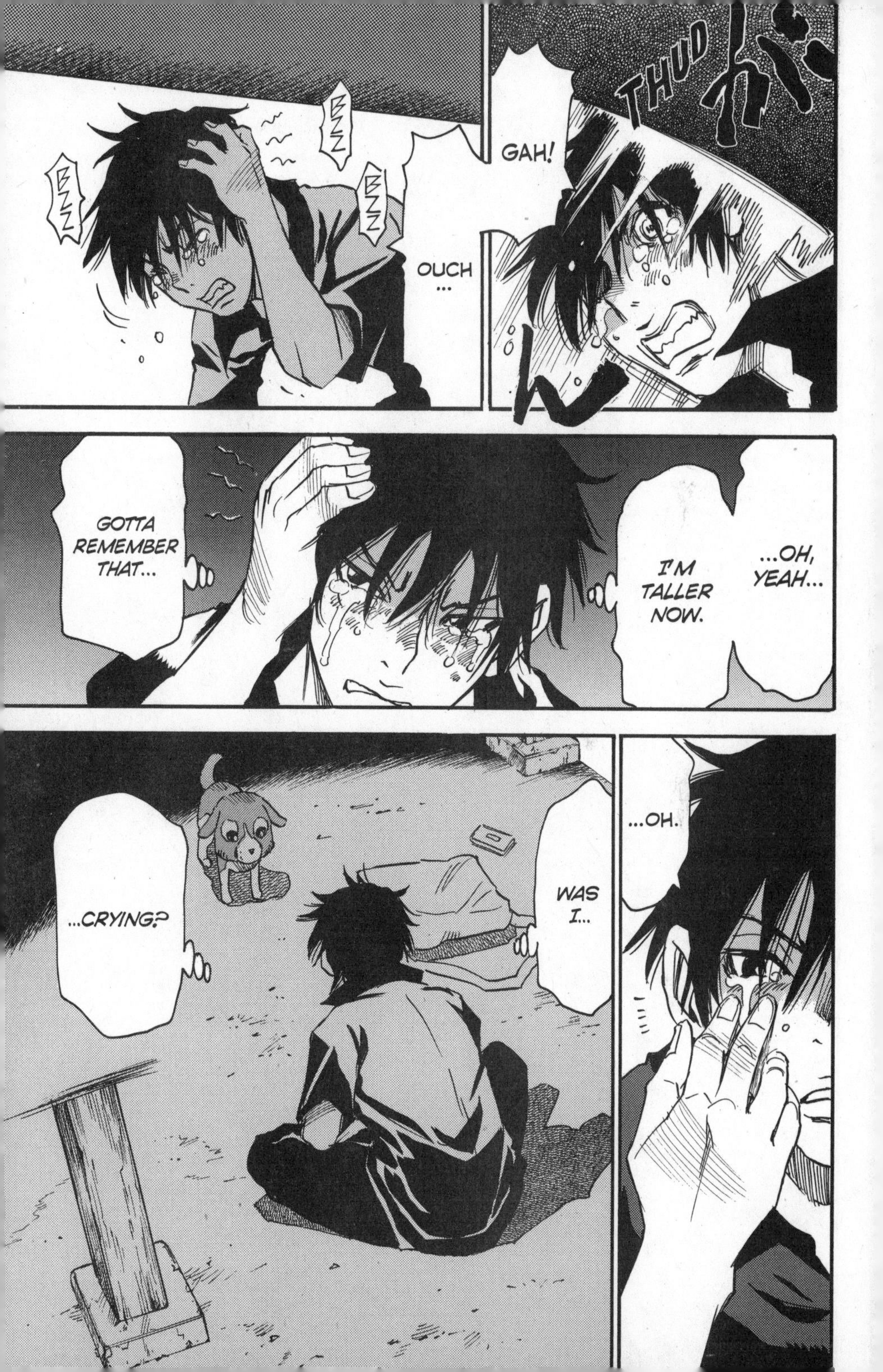
THUD
GAH!
BZZ
BZZ
OUCH ...
BZZ
...OH, YEAH...
I'M TALLER NOW.
GOTTA REMEMBER THAT...
...OH.
WAS I...
...CRYING?

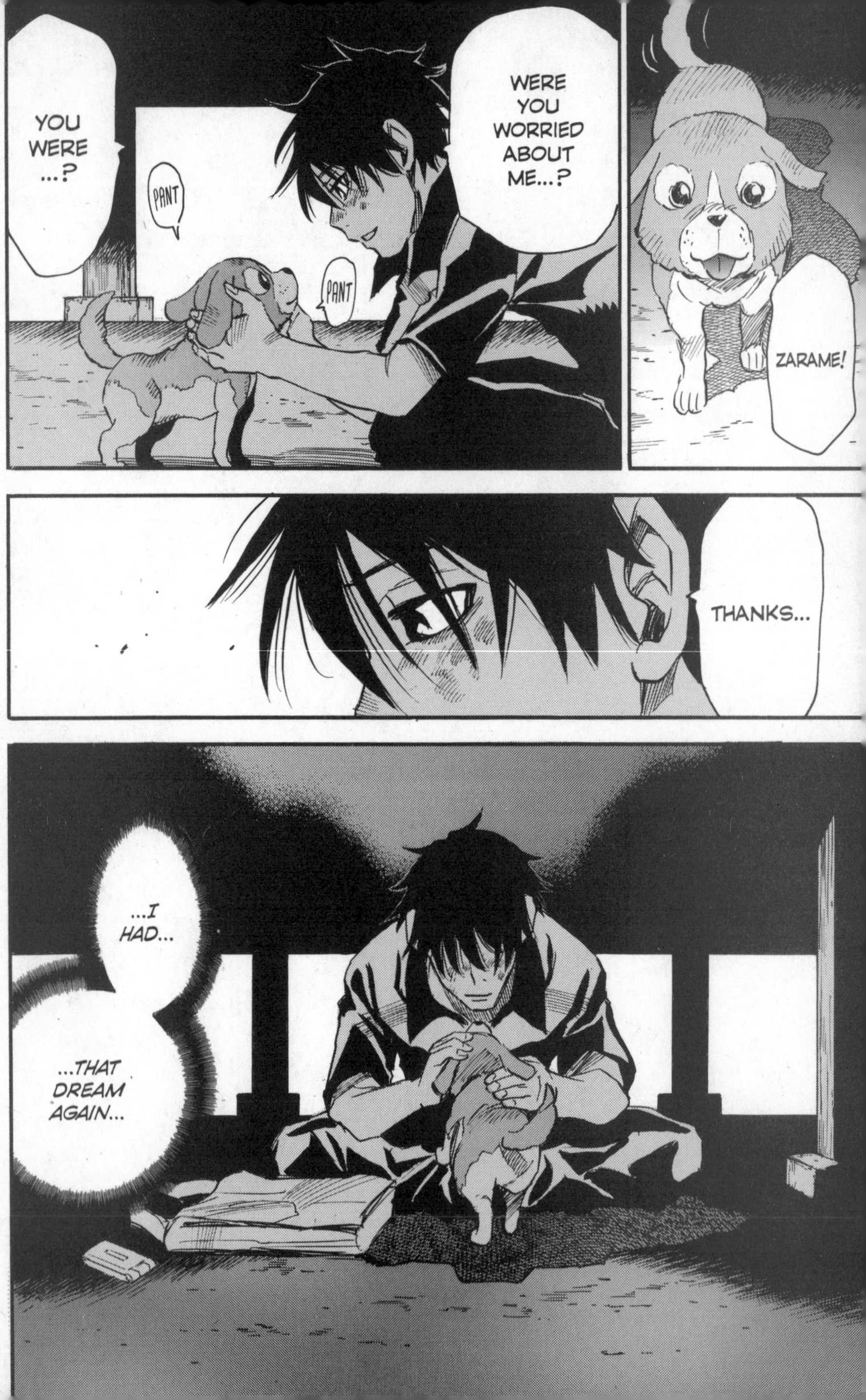
ZARAME!
WERE YOU WORRIED ABOUT ME...?
YOU WERE ...?
PANT
PANT
THANKS...
...I HAD...
...THAT DREAM AGAIN...

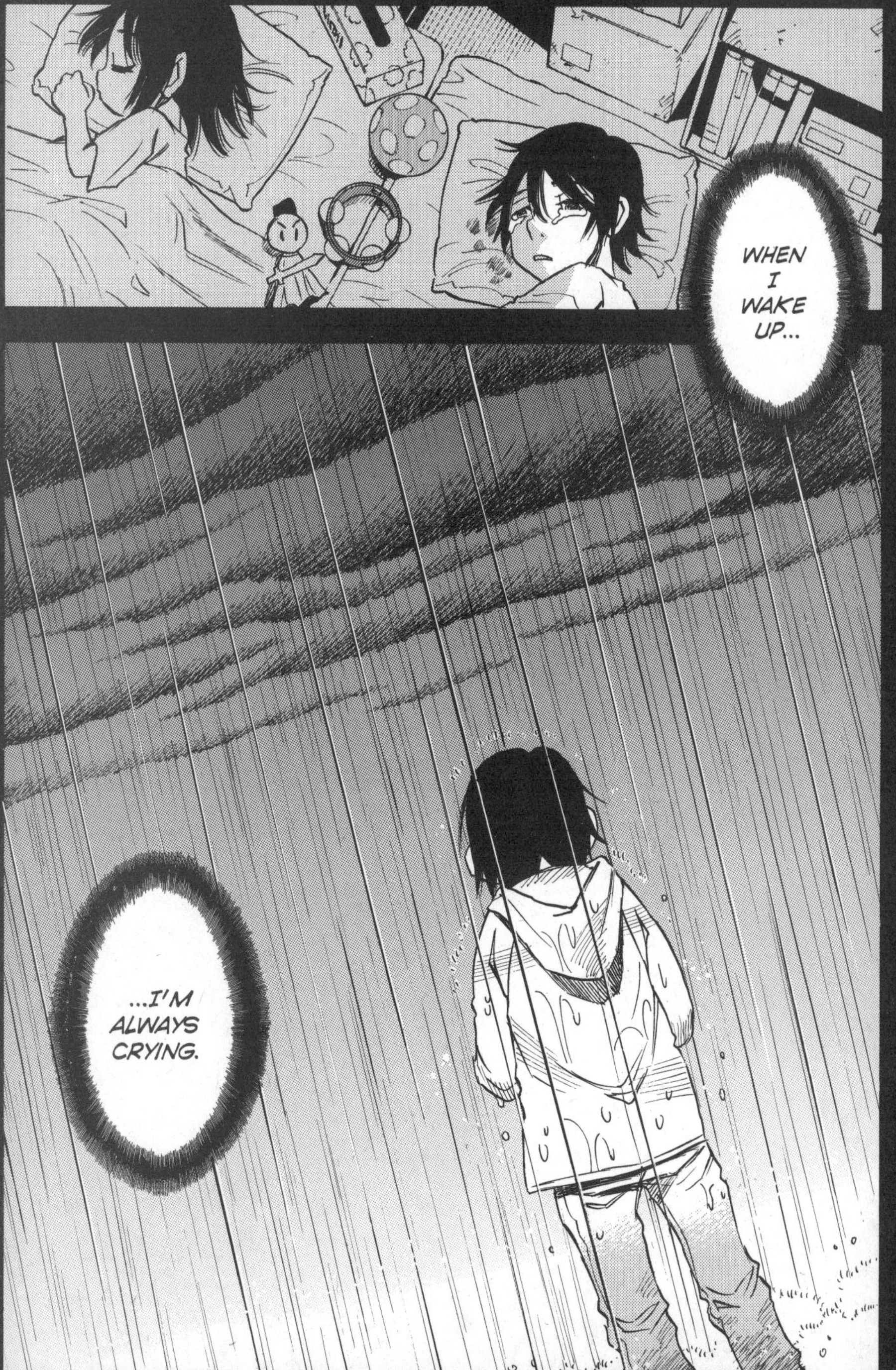
WHEN I WAKE UP...
...I'M ALWAYS CRYING.

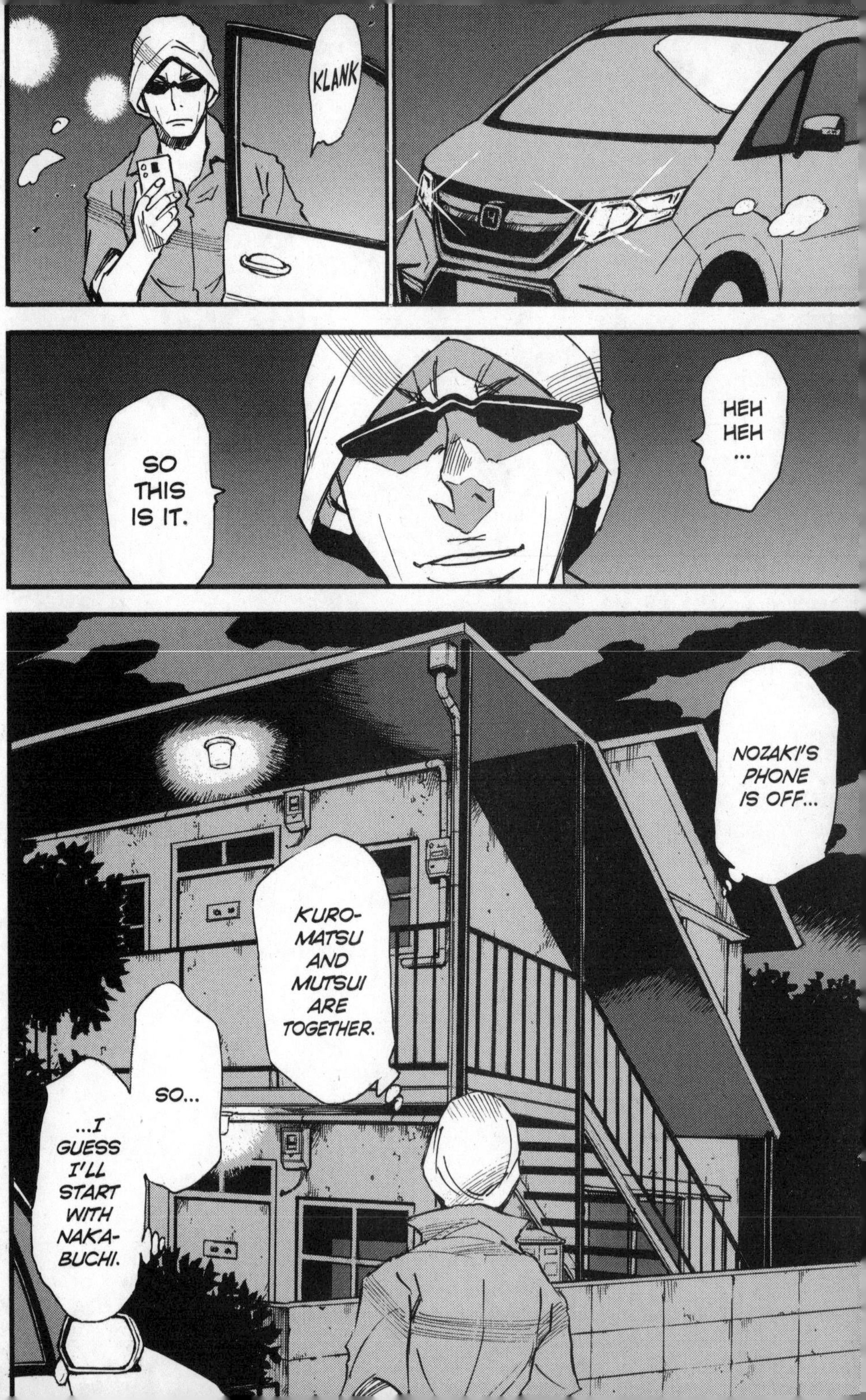
KLANK
HEH HEH ...
SO THIS IS IT.
NOZAKI'S PHONE IS OFF...
KURO-MATSU AND MUTSUI ARE TOGETHER.
SO...
...I GUESS I'LL START WITH NAKA-BUCHI.

WHAT AN IDIOT.

長渕
NAGABUCHI

...

KLANK

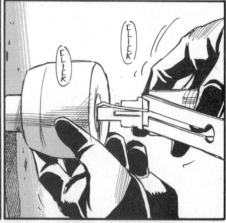
CLICK

CLICK

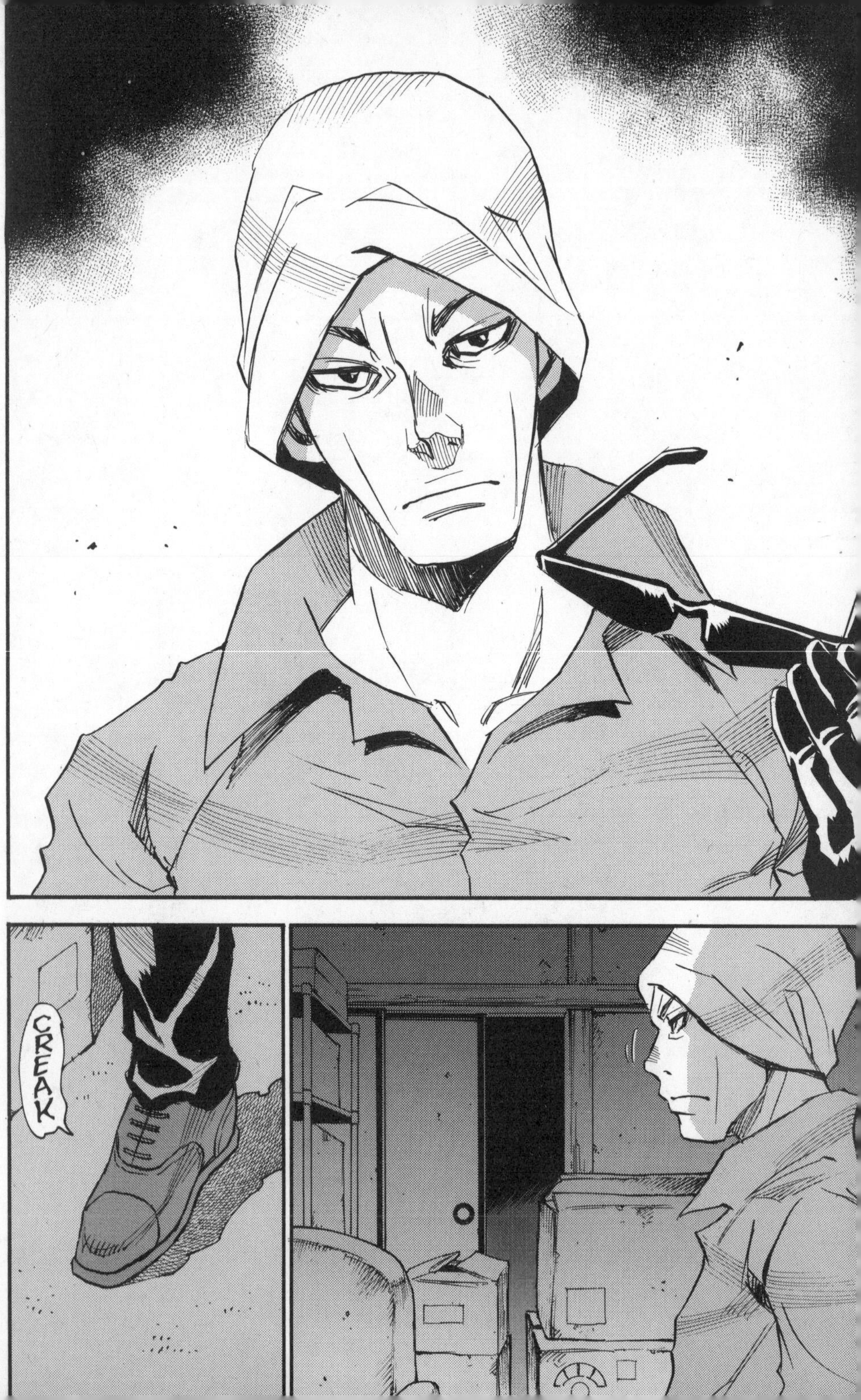
CREAK

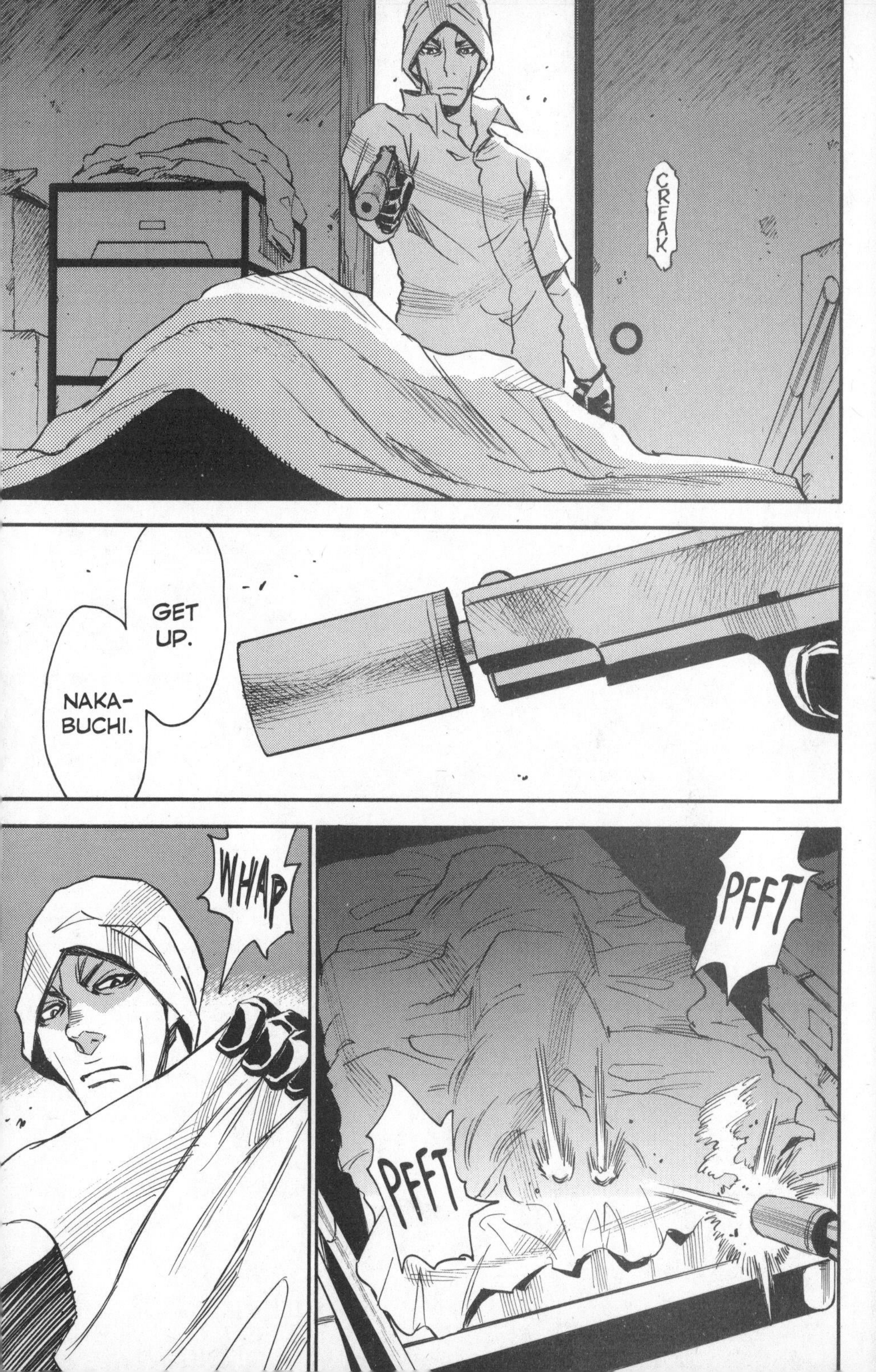
CREAK
GET UP.
NAKA-BUCHI.
PFFT
PFFT
WHAP

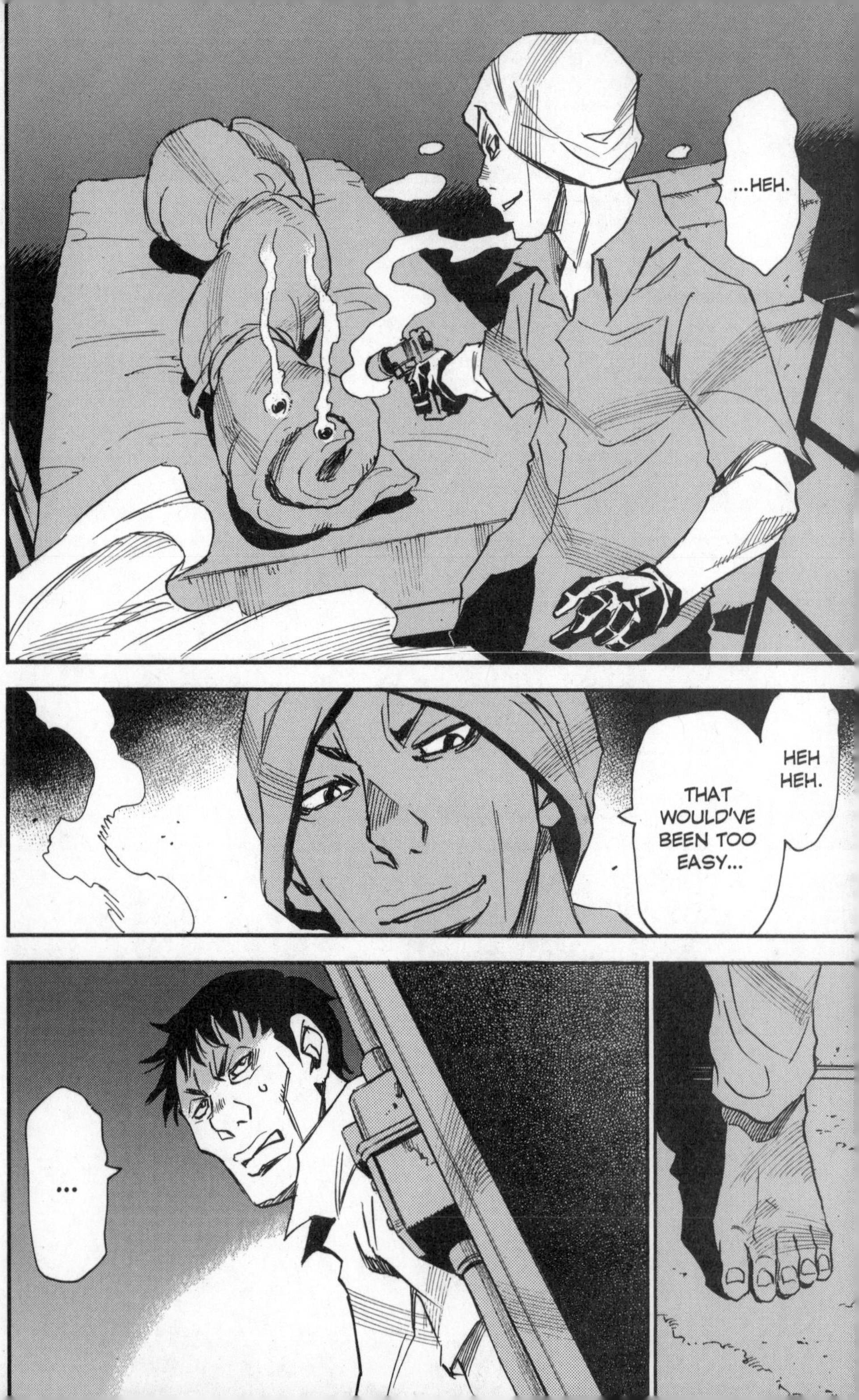
...HEH.
HEH HEH.
THAT WOULD'VE BEEN TOO EASY...
...

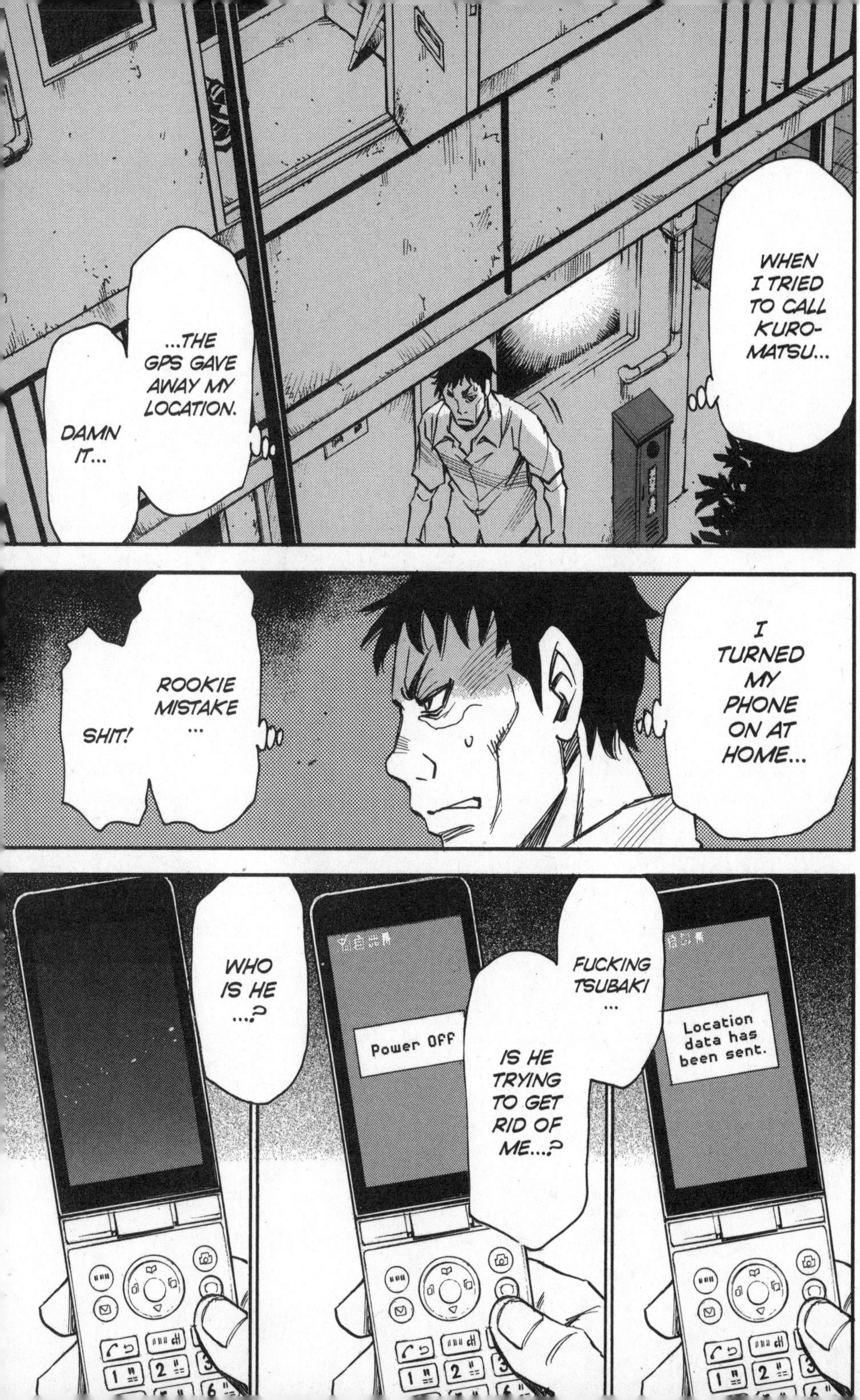
WHEN I TRIED TO CALL KURO-MATSU...
...THE GPS GAVE AWAY MY LOCATION.
DAMN IT...
I TURNED MY PHONE ON AT HOME...
ROOKIE MISTAKE...
SHIT!
Location data has been sent.
FUCKING TSUBAKI...
IS HE TRYING TO GET RID OF ME...?
Power Off
WHO IS HE...?

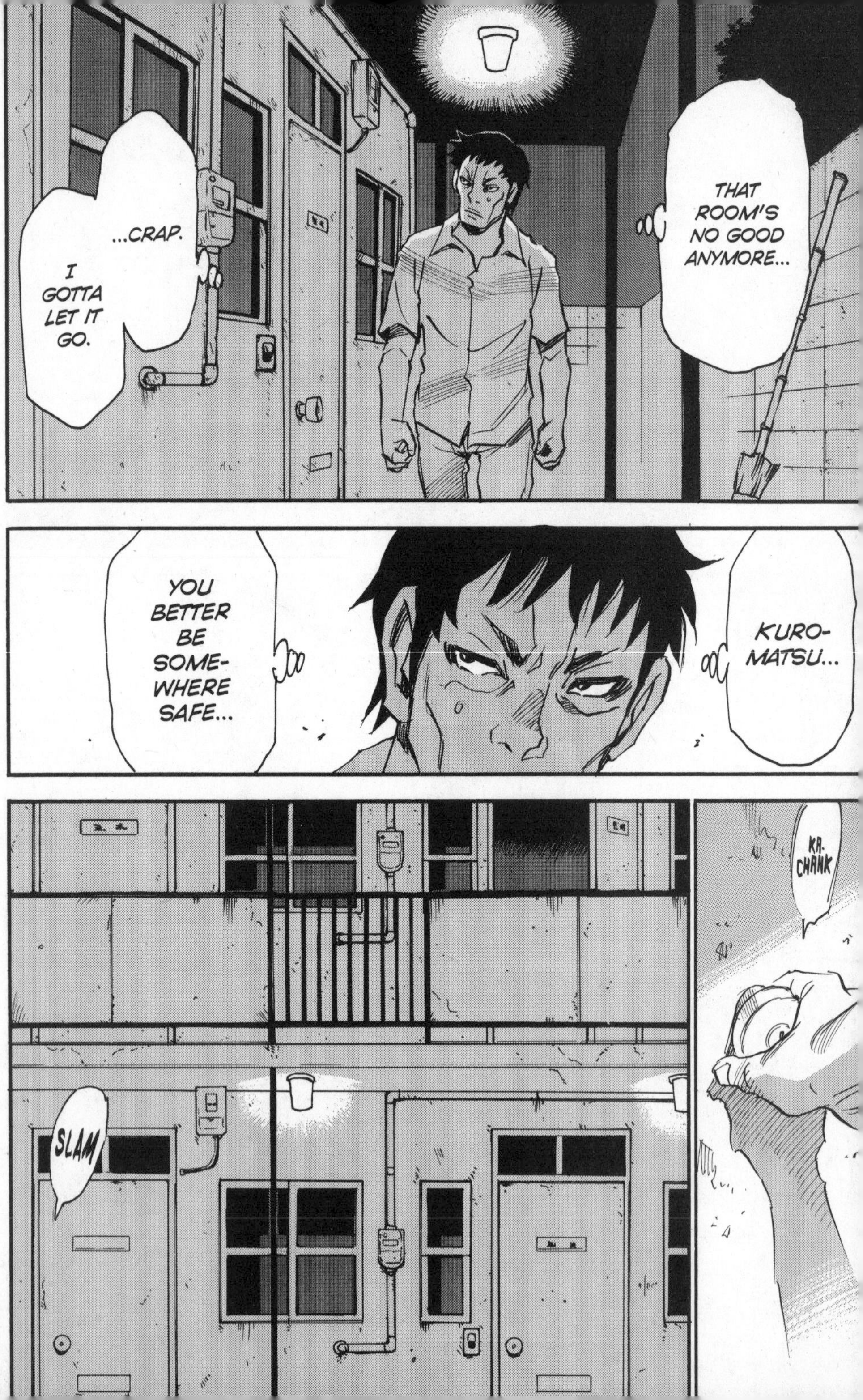
THAT ROOM'S NO GOOD ANYMORE...
...CRAP.
I GOTTA LET IT GO.
KURO-MATSU...
YOU BETTER BE SOME-WHERE SAFE...
KA-CHANK
SLAM

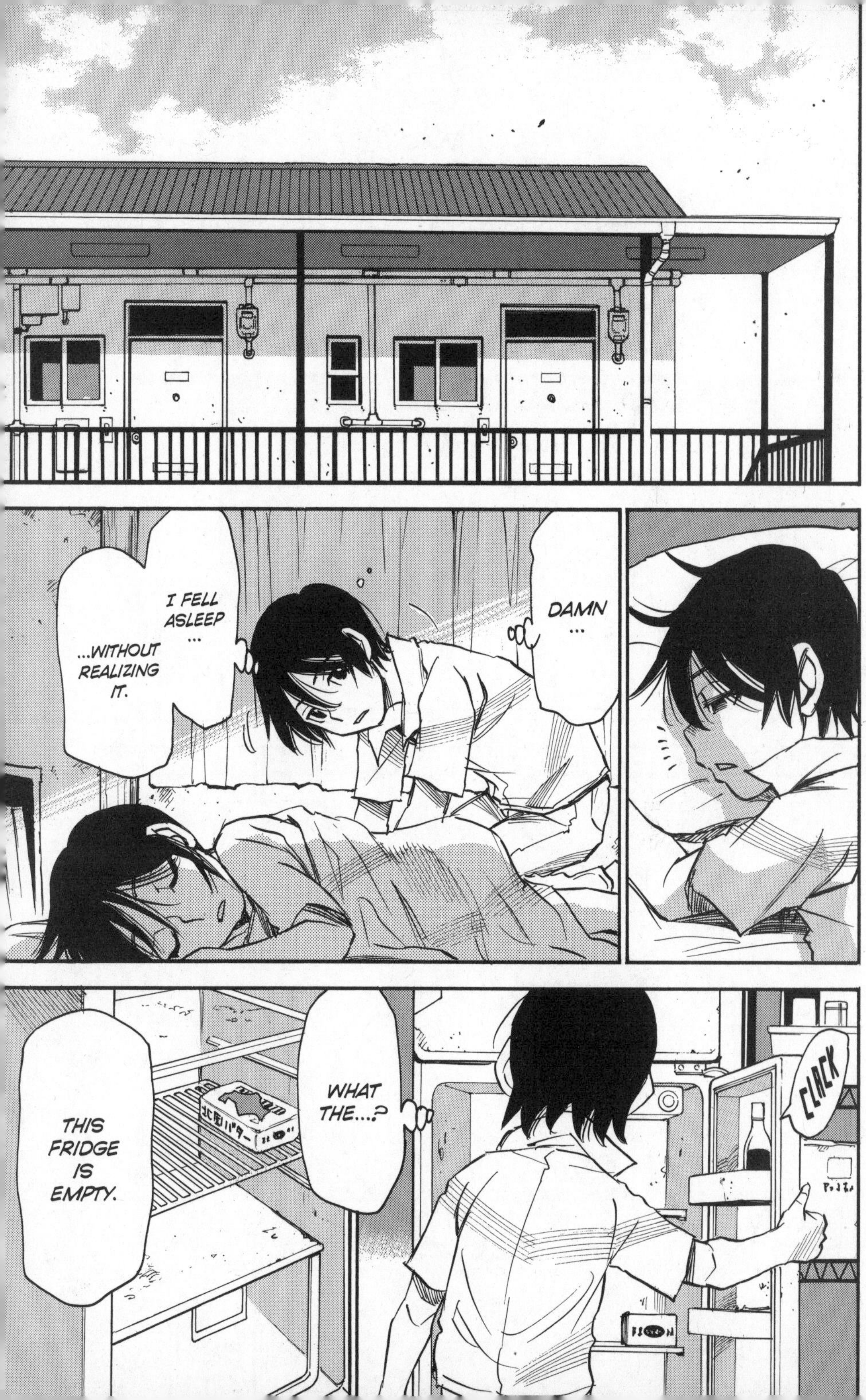
DAMN ...
I FELL ASLEEP ...
...WITHOUT REALIZING IT.
CLACK
WHAT THE...?
THIS FRIDGE IS EMPTY.

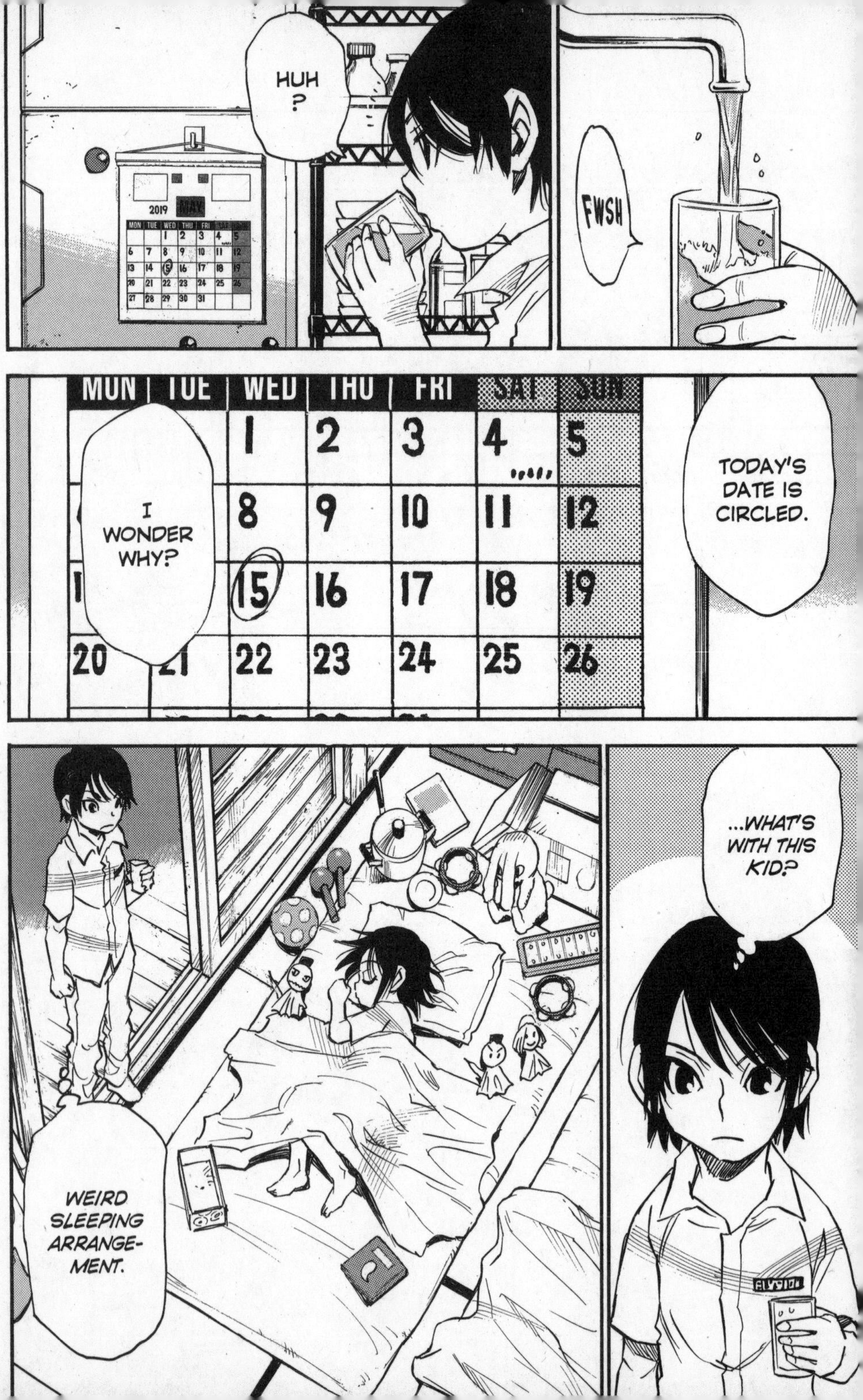
FWSH
HUH?
TODAY'S DATE IS CIRCLED.
I WONDER WHY?
...WHAT'S WITH THIS KID?
WEIRD SLEEPING ARRANGE-MENT.

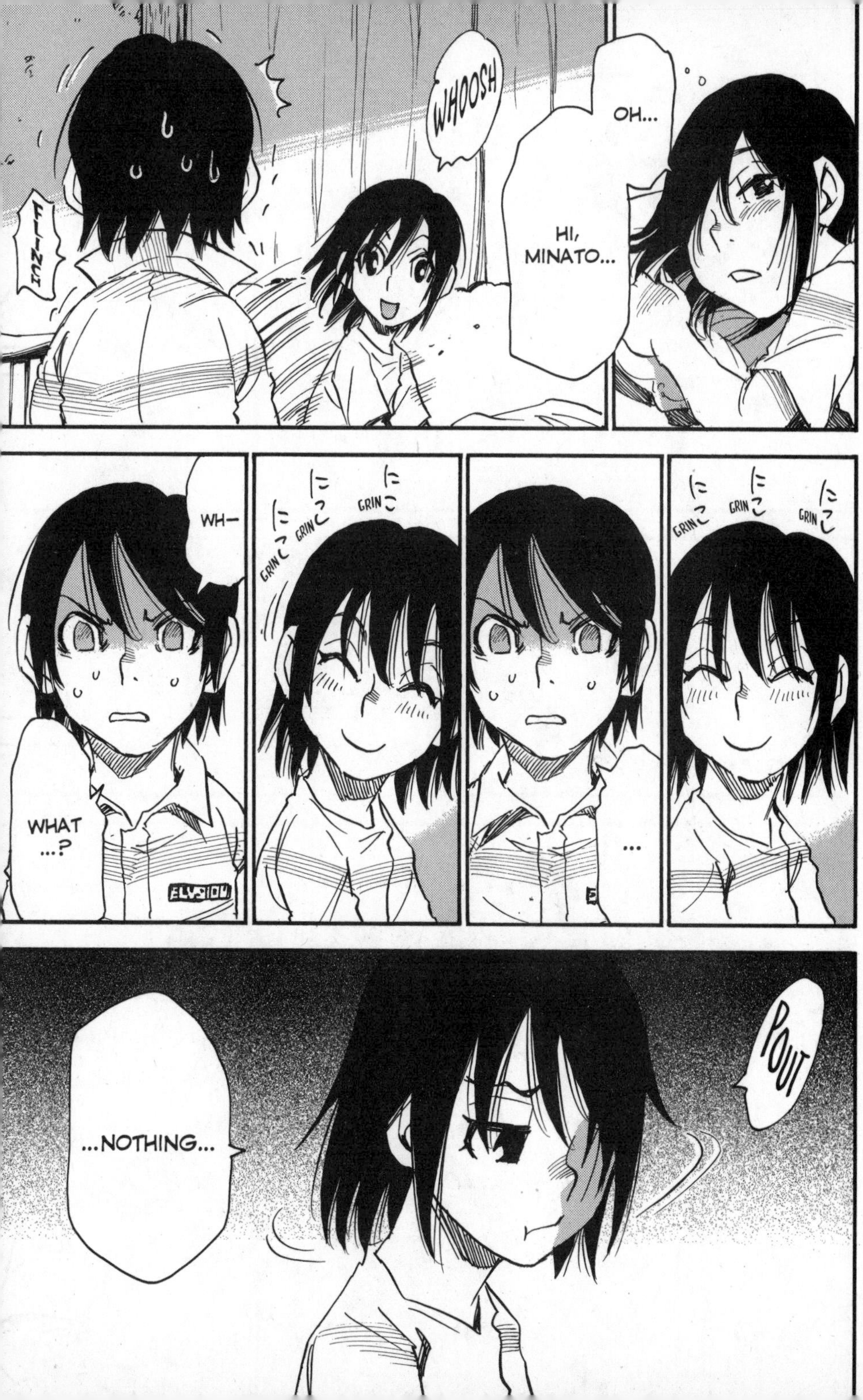
OH...
HI, MINATO...
WHOOSH
FLINCH
GRIN
GRIN
GRIN
...
GRIN
GRIN
GRIN
WH-
WHAT ...?
ELYSION
POUT
...NOTHING...

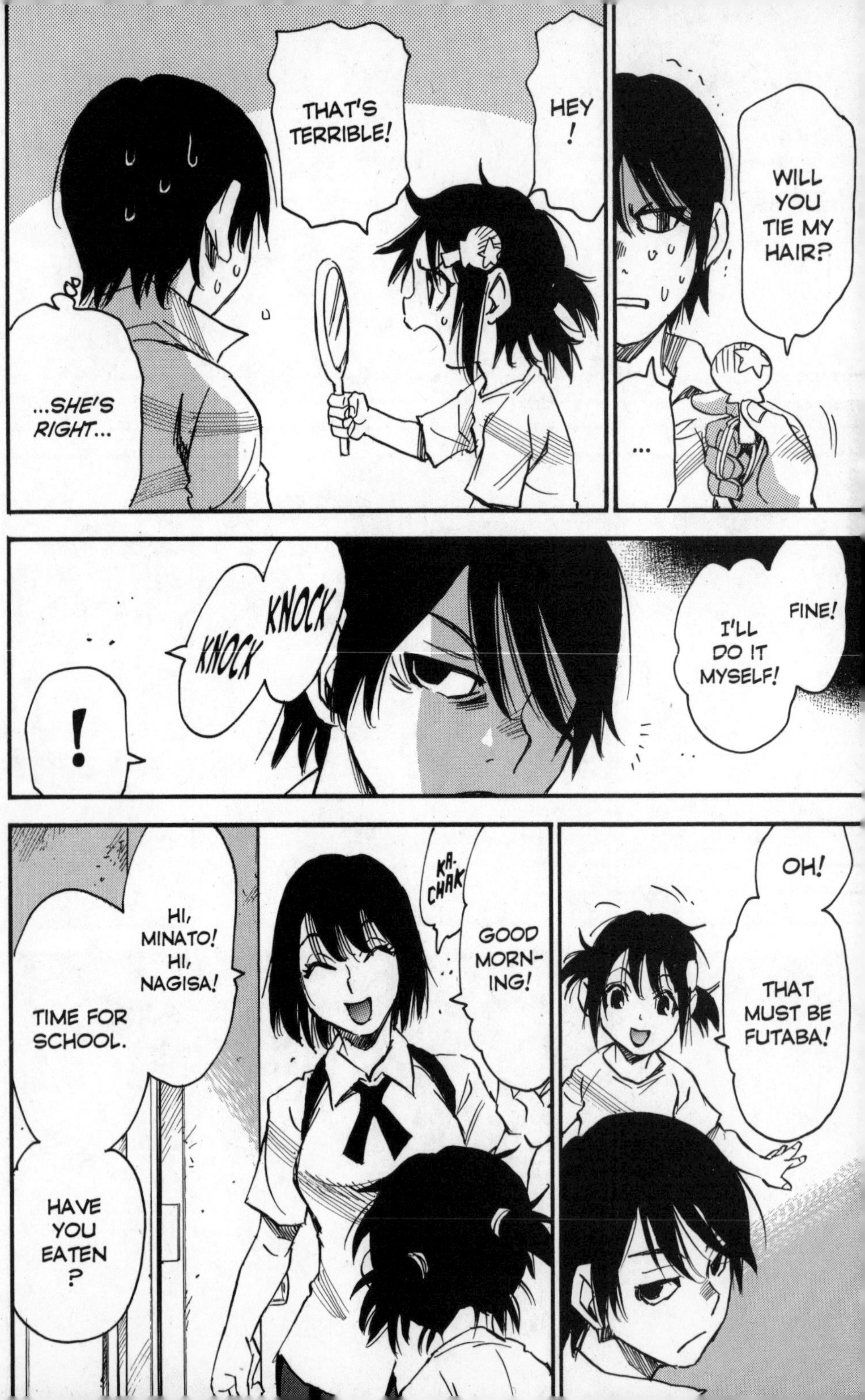
WILL YOU TIE MY HAIR?
...
HEY!
THAT'S TERRIBLE!
...SHE'S RIGHT...
FINE! I'LL DO IT MYSELF!
KNOCK KNOCK
!
OH!
THAT MUST BE FUTABA!
KA-CHAK
GOOD MORNING!
HI, MINATO! HI, NAGISA!
TIME FOR SCHOOL.
HAVE YOU EATEN?

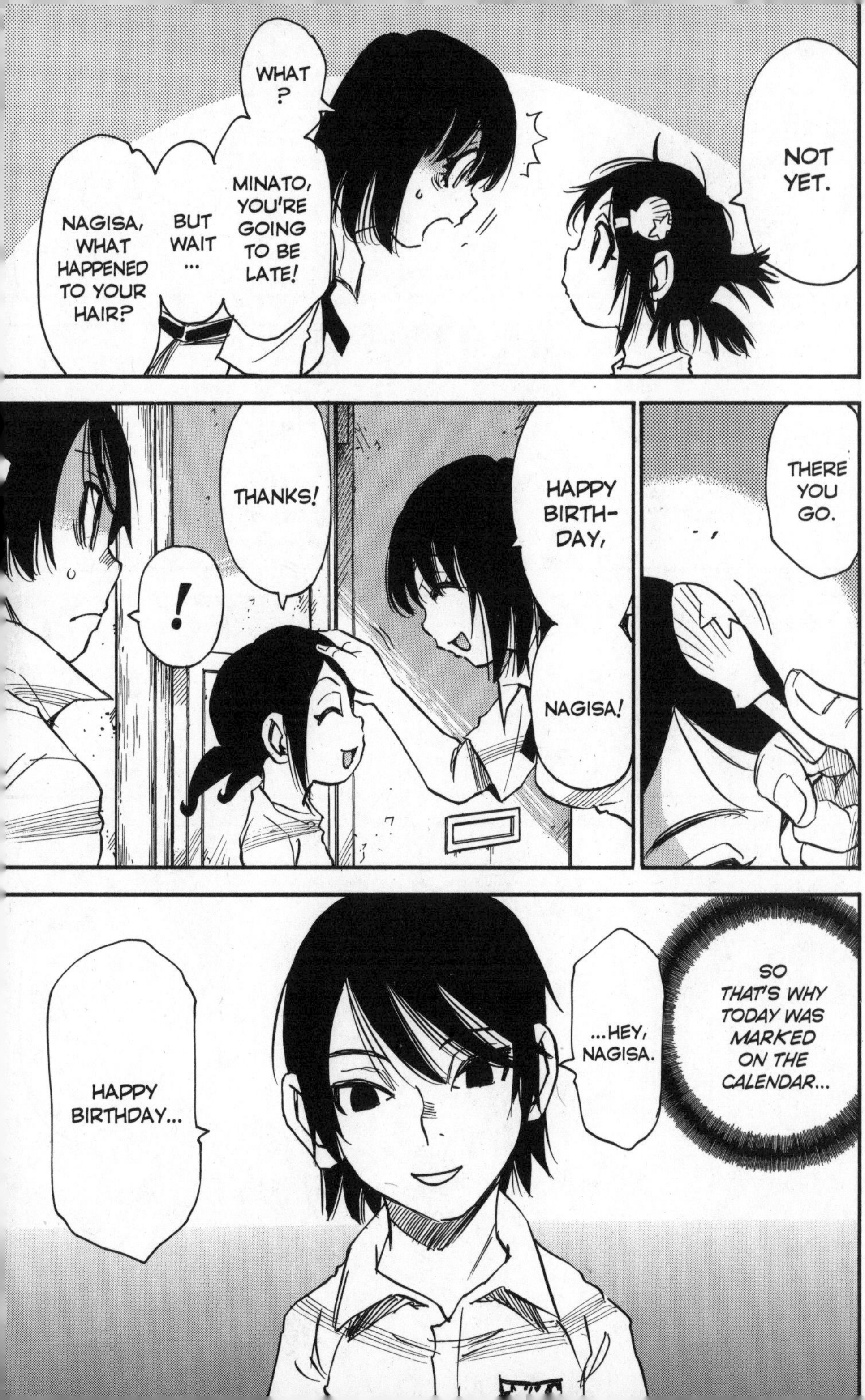
NOT YET.
WHAT ?
MINATO, YOU'RE GOING TO BE LATE!
BUT WAIT ...
NAGISA, WHAT HAPPENED TO YOUR HAIR?
THERE YOU GO.
HAPPY BIRTH-DAY,
NAGISA!
THANKS!
!
SO THAT'S WHY TODAY WAS MARKED ON THE CALENDAR...
...HEY, NAGISA.
HAPPY BIRTHDAY...

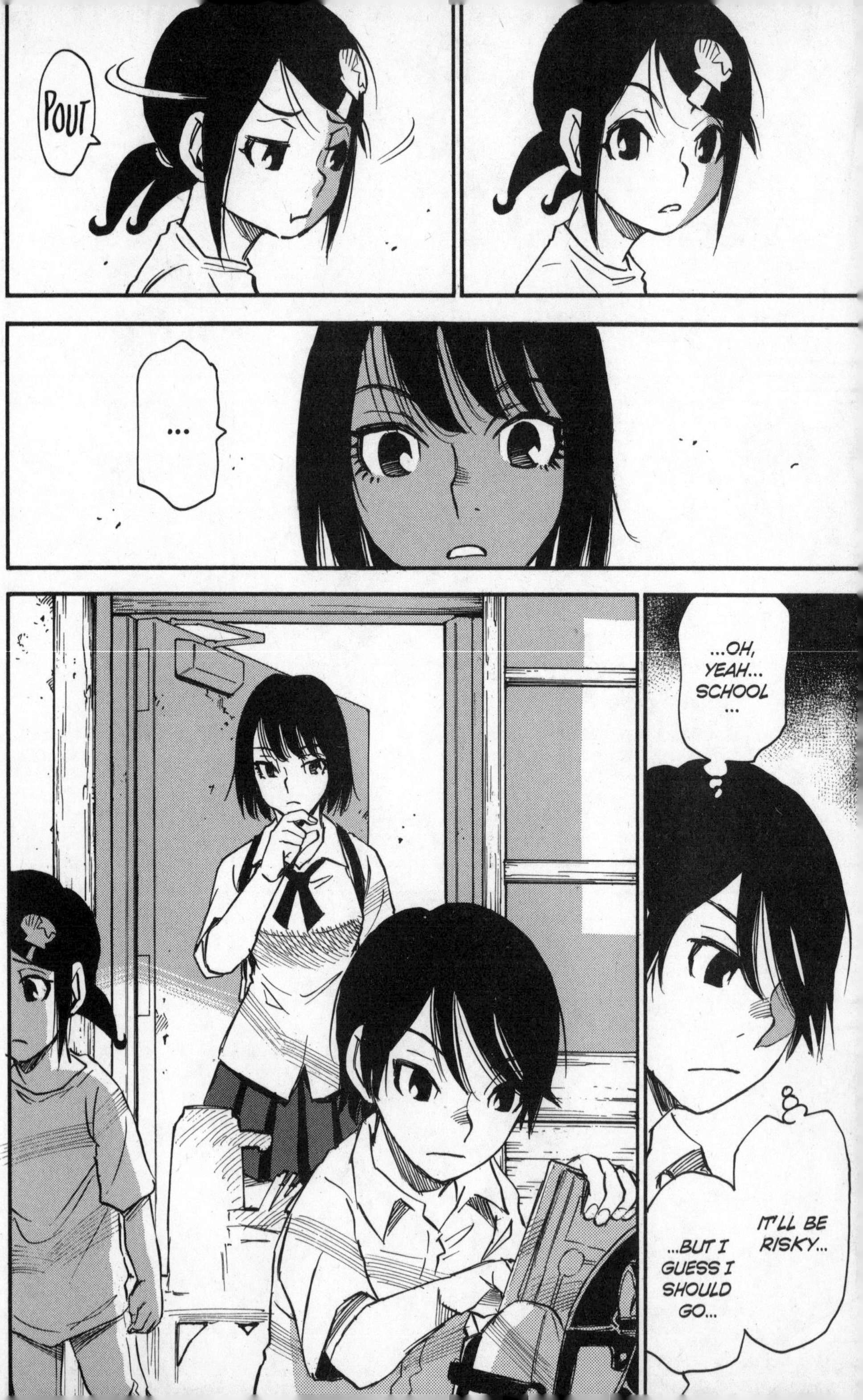
POUT
...
...OH, YEAH... SCHOOL ...
IT'LL BE RISKY...
...BUT I GUESS I SHOULD GO...

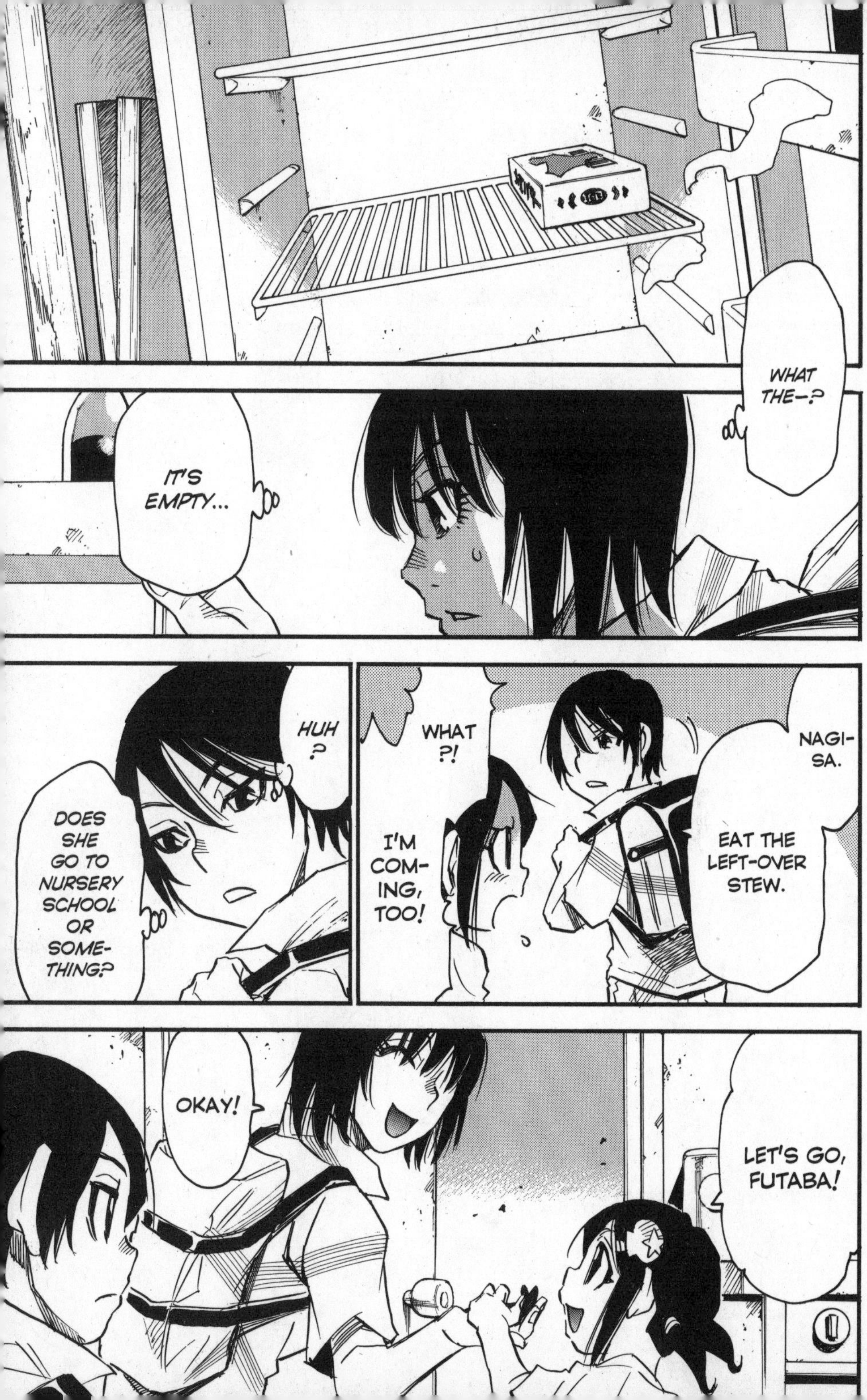

WHAT THE--?
IT'S EMPTY...
NAGI-SA.
EAT THE LEFT-OVER STEW.
WHAT?!
I'M COMING, TOO!
HUH?
DOES SHE GO TO NURSERY SCHOOL OR SOMETHING?
LET'S GO, FUTABA!
OKAY!

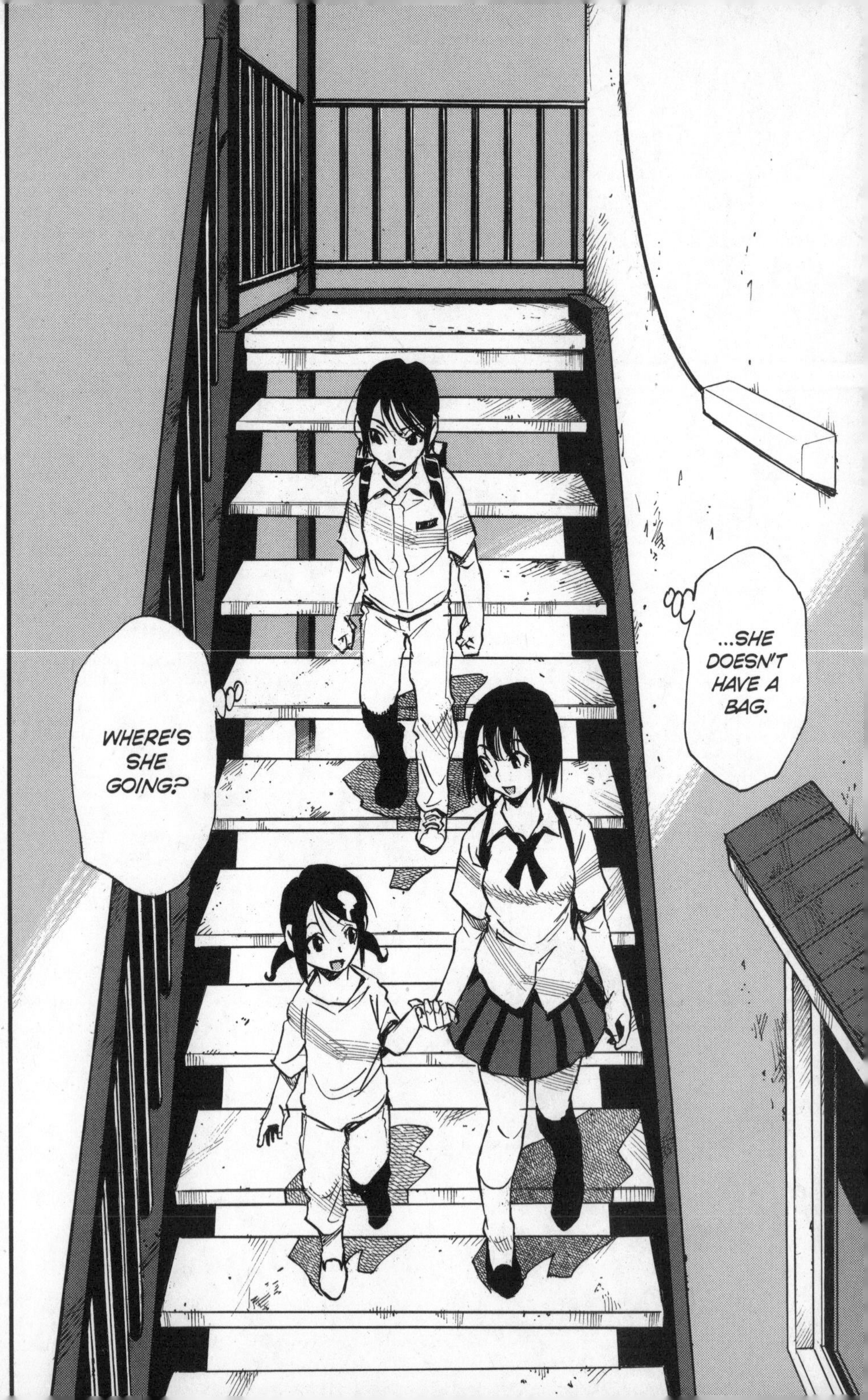
...SHE DOESN'T HAVE A BAG.
WHERE'S SHE GOING?

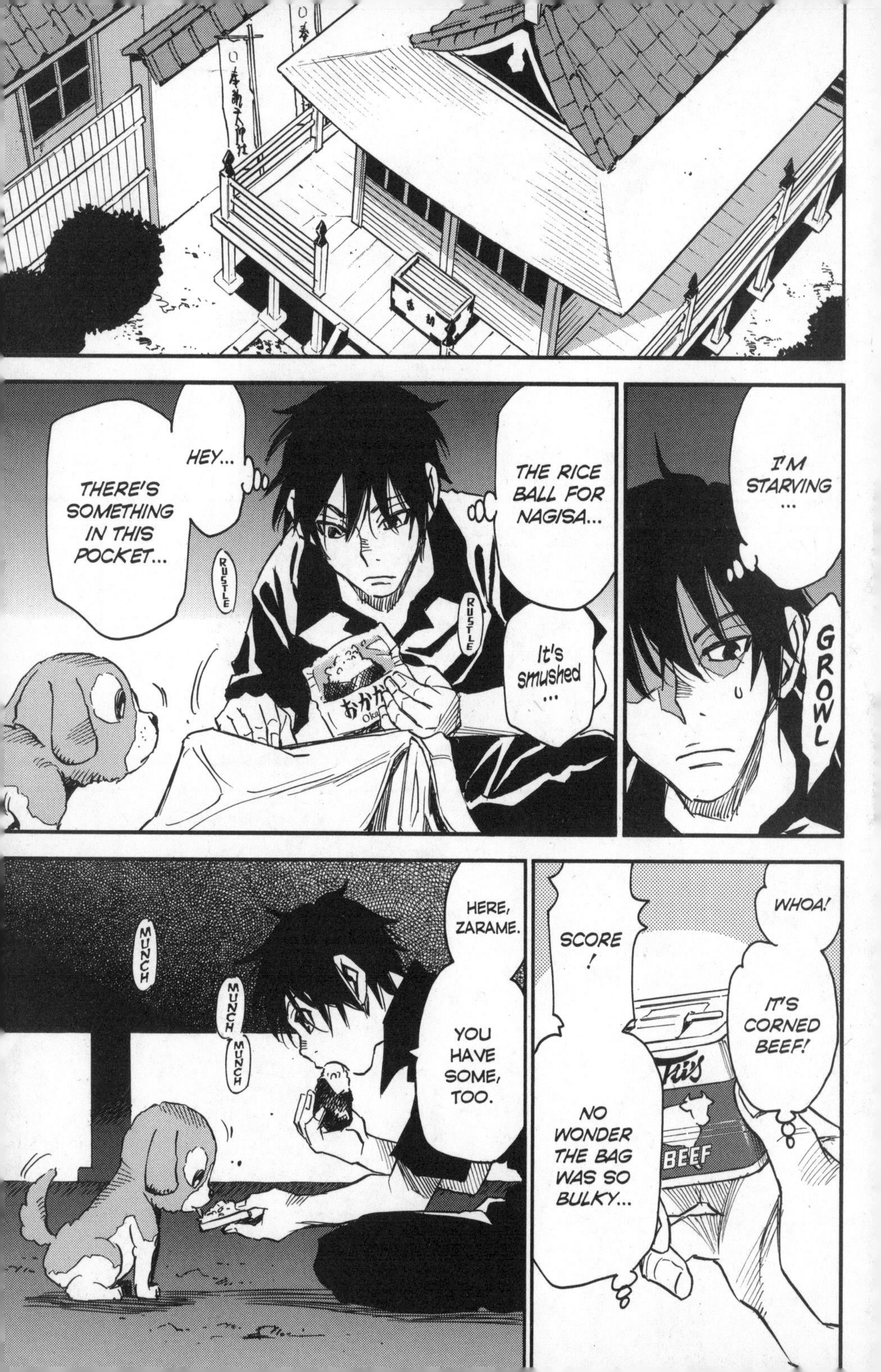

I'M STARVING ...
GROWL
THE RICE BALL FOR NAGISA...
It's smushed ...
RUSTLE
HEY...
THERE'S SOMETHING IN THIS POCKET...
RUSTLE
WHOA!
IT'S CORNED BEEF!
SCORE!
NO WONDER THE BAG WAS SO BULKY...
BEEF
HERE, ZARAME.
YOU HAVE SOME, TOO.
MUNCH MUNCH
MUNCH

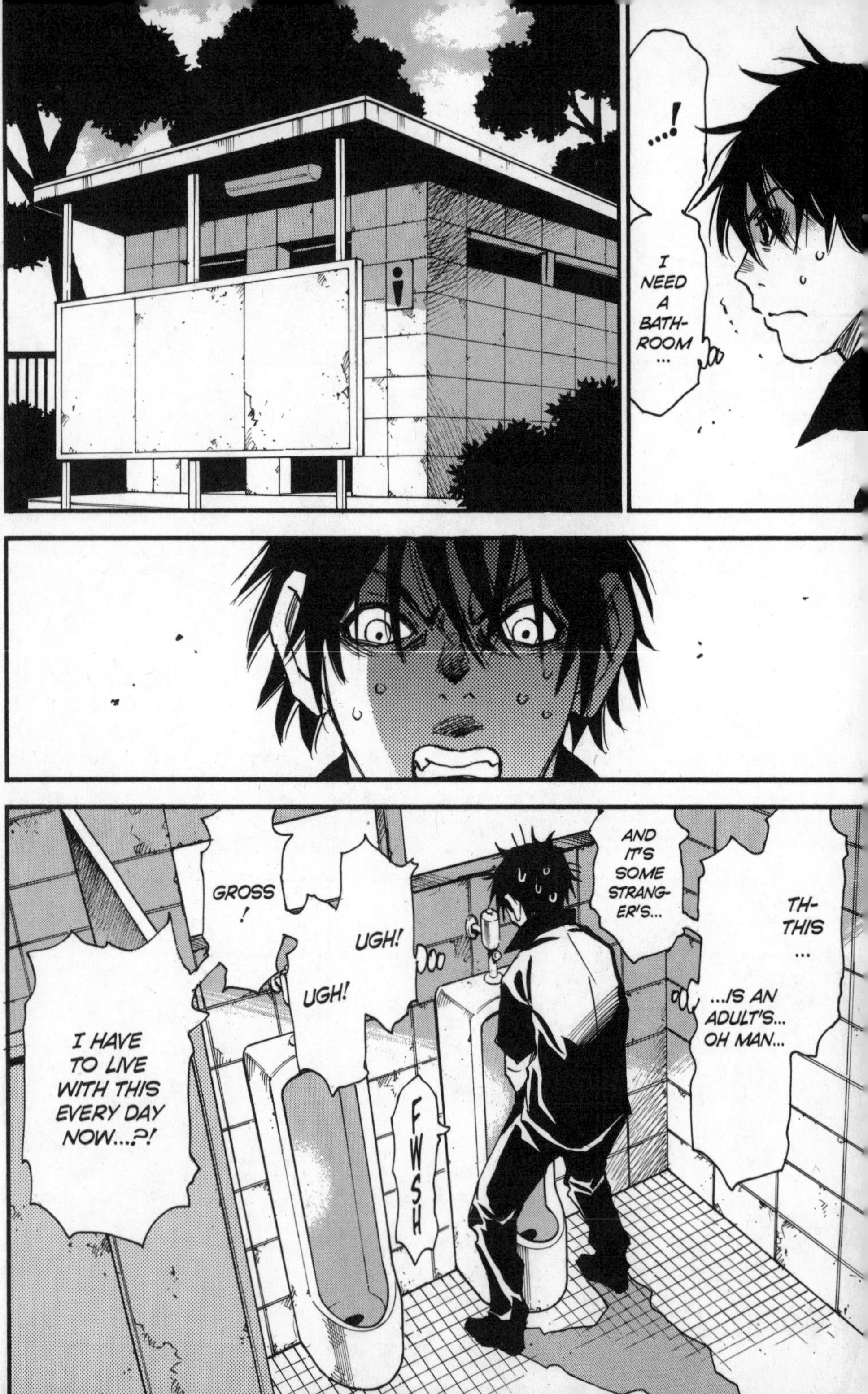
...!
I NEED A BATHROOM...
TH- THIS...
...IS AN ADULT'S... OH MAN...
AND IT'S SOME STRANGER'S...
GROSS!
UGH!
UGH!
FWSH
I HAVE TO LIVE WITH THIS EVERY DAY NOW...?!

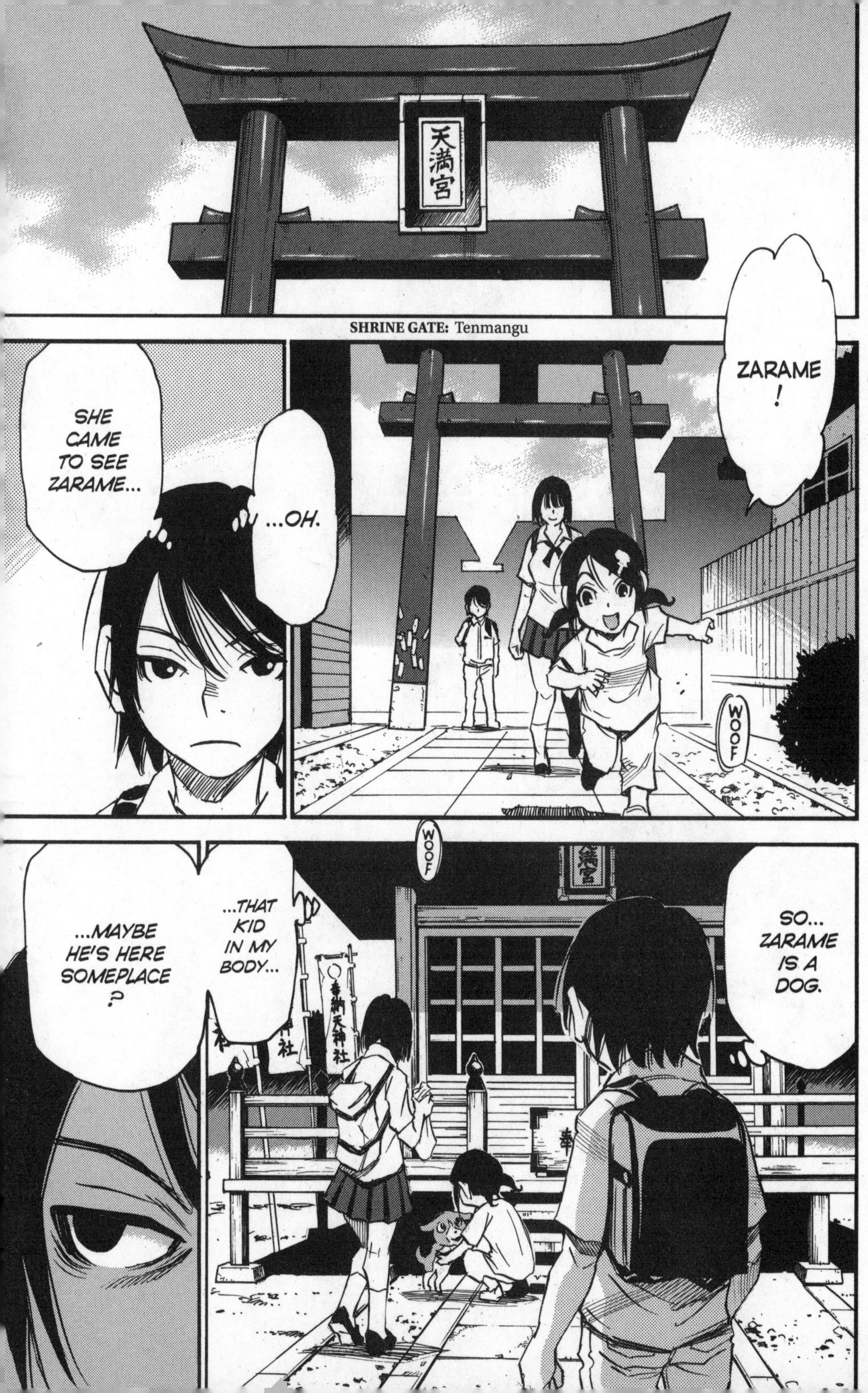
天満宮
SHRINE GATE: Tenmangu
ZARAME!
WOOF
...OH.
SHE CAME TO SEE ZARAME...
SO... ZARAME IS A DOG.
WOOF
...THAT KID IN MY BODY...
...MAYBE HE'S HERE SOMEPLACE?

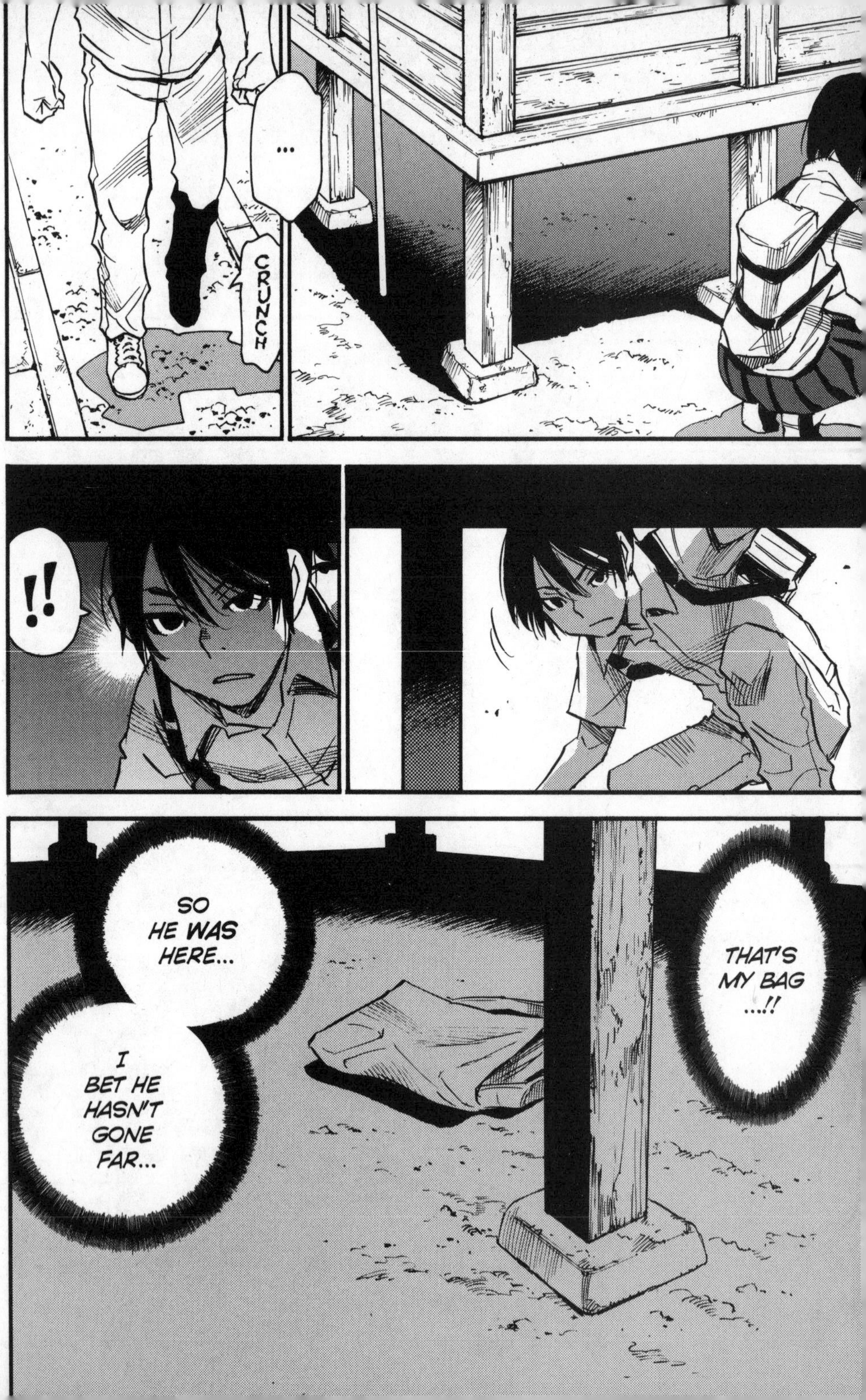
...
CRUNCH
!!
THAT'S MY BAG ...!!
SO HE WAS HERE...
I BET HE HASN'T GONE FAR...

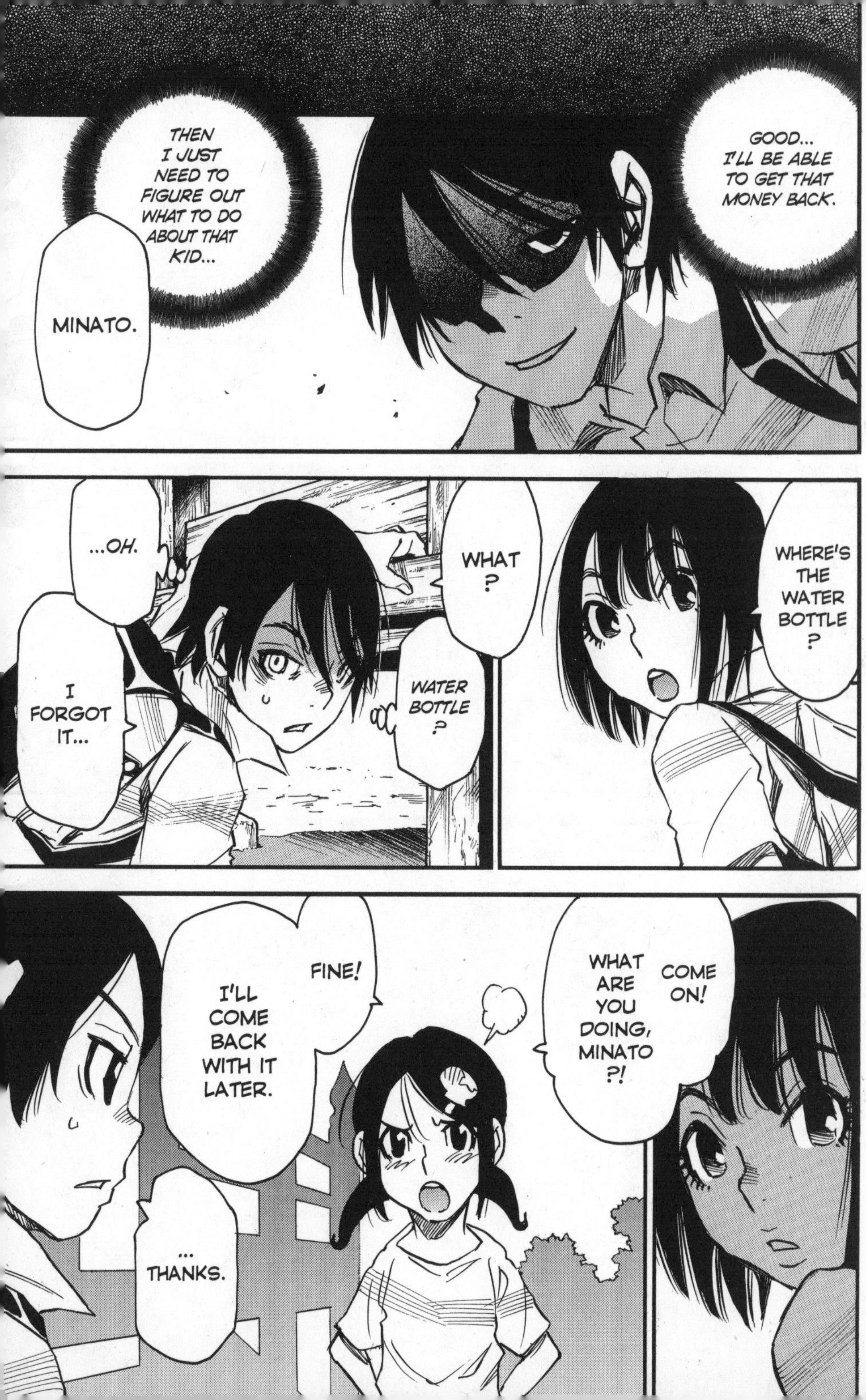
GOOD... I'LL BE ABLE TO GET THAT MONEY BACK.
THEN I JUST NEED TO FIGURE OUT WHAT TO DO ABOUT THAT KID...
MINATO.
WHERE'S THE WATER BOTTLE?
WHAT?
WATER BOTTLE?
...OH.
I FORGOT IT...
COME ON!
WHAT ARE YOU DOING, MINATO?!
FINE!
I'LL COME BACK WITH IT LATER.
...THANKS.

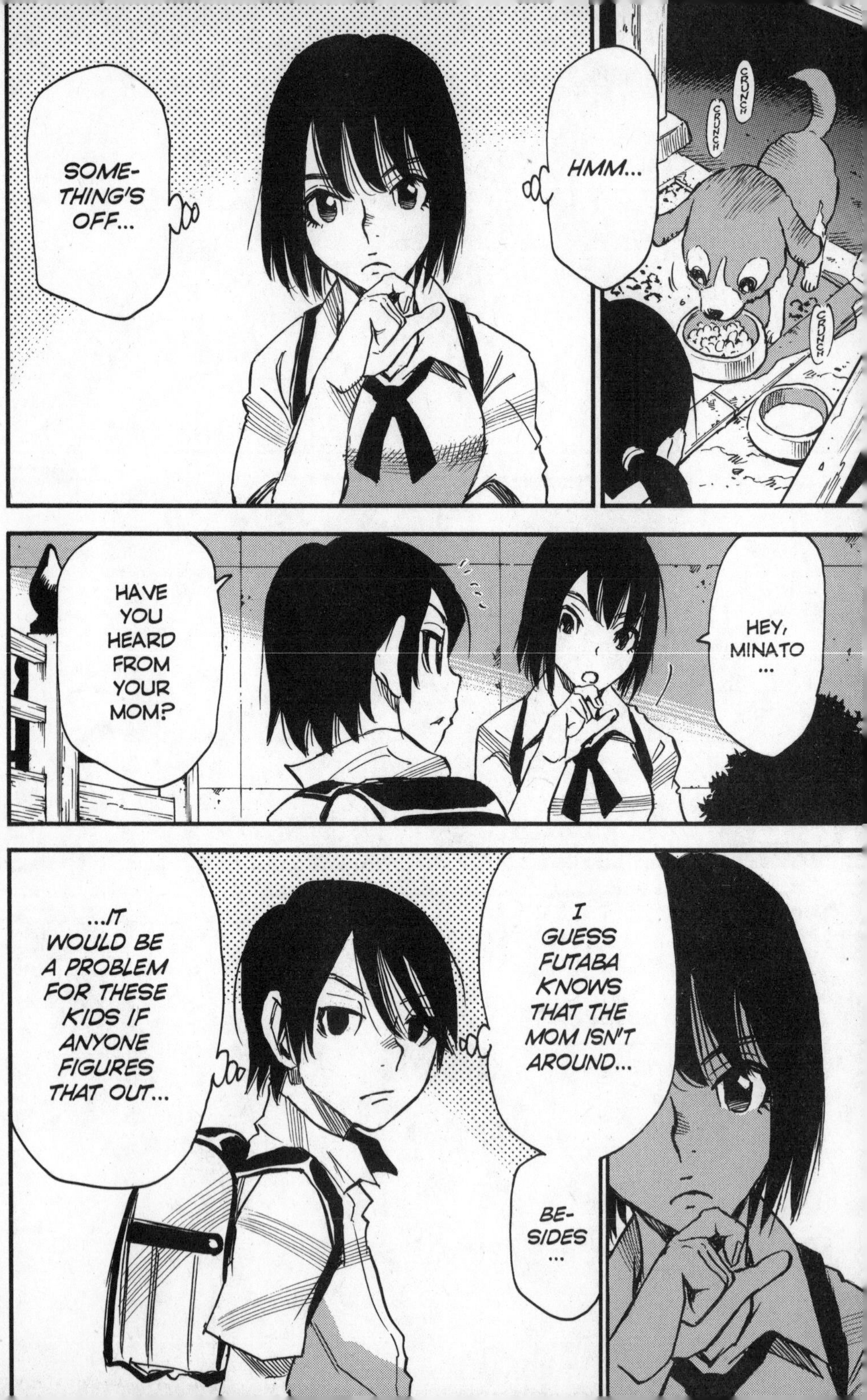
CRUNCH
CRUNCH
HMM...
CRUNCH
SOME-THING'S OFF...
HEY, MINATO...
HAVE YOU HEARD FROM YOUR MOM?
I GUESS FUTABA KNOWS THAT THE MOM ISN'T AROUND...
BE-SIDES...
...IT WOULD BE A PROBLEM FOR THESE KIDS IF ANYONE FIGURES THAT OUT...

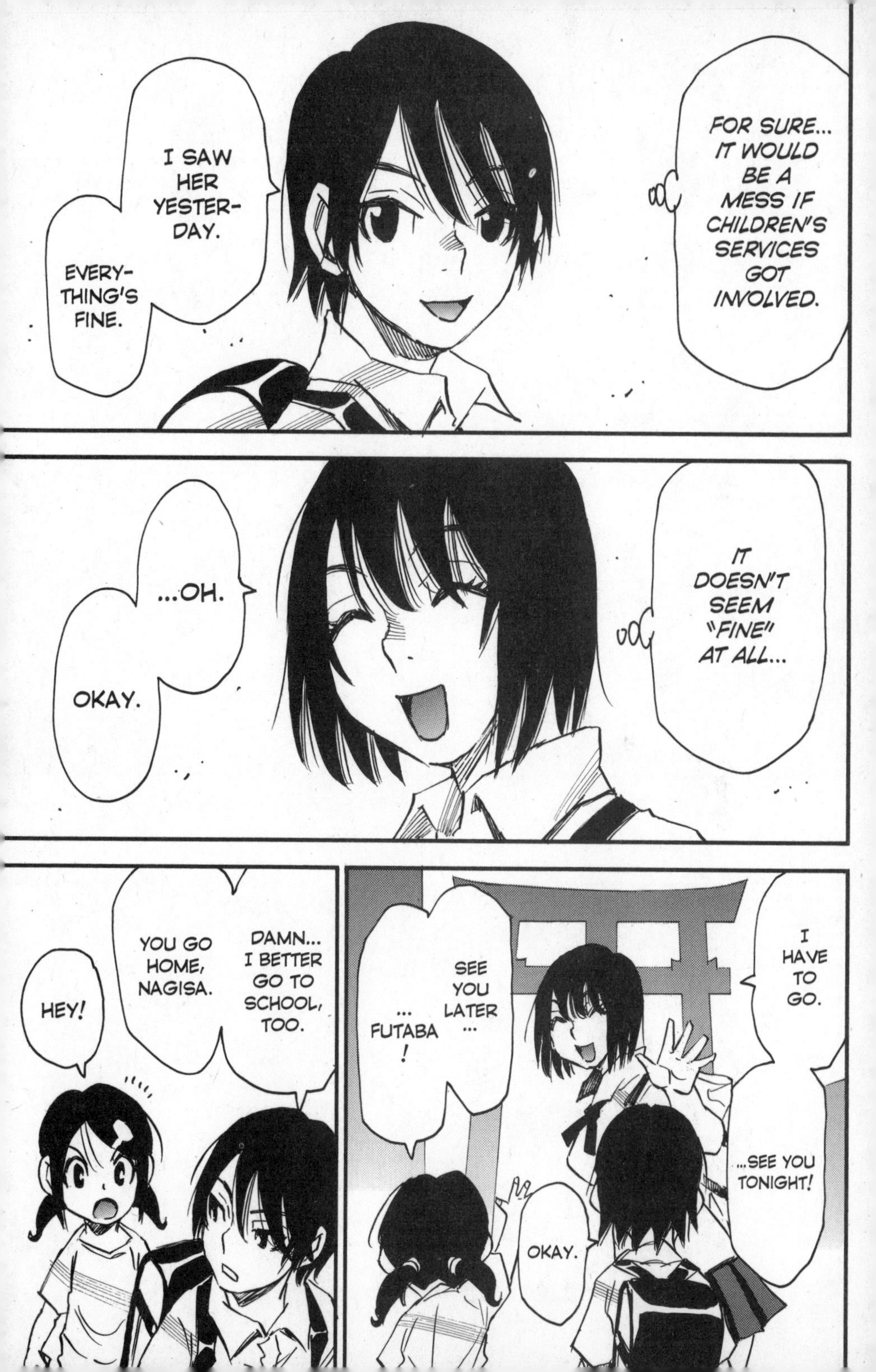
FOR SURE... IT WOULD BE A MESS IF CHILDREN'S SERVICES GOT INVOLVED.
I SAW HER YESTERDAY.
EVERYTHING'S FINE.
IT DOESN'T SEEM "FINE" AT ALL...
...OH.
OKAY.
I HAVE TO GO.
SEE YOU LATER ...
... FUTABA!
...SEE YOU TONIGHT!
OKAY.
DAMN... I BETTER GO TO SCHOOL, TOO.
YOU GO HOME, NAGISA.
HEY!

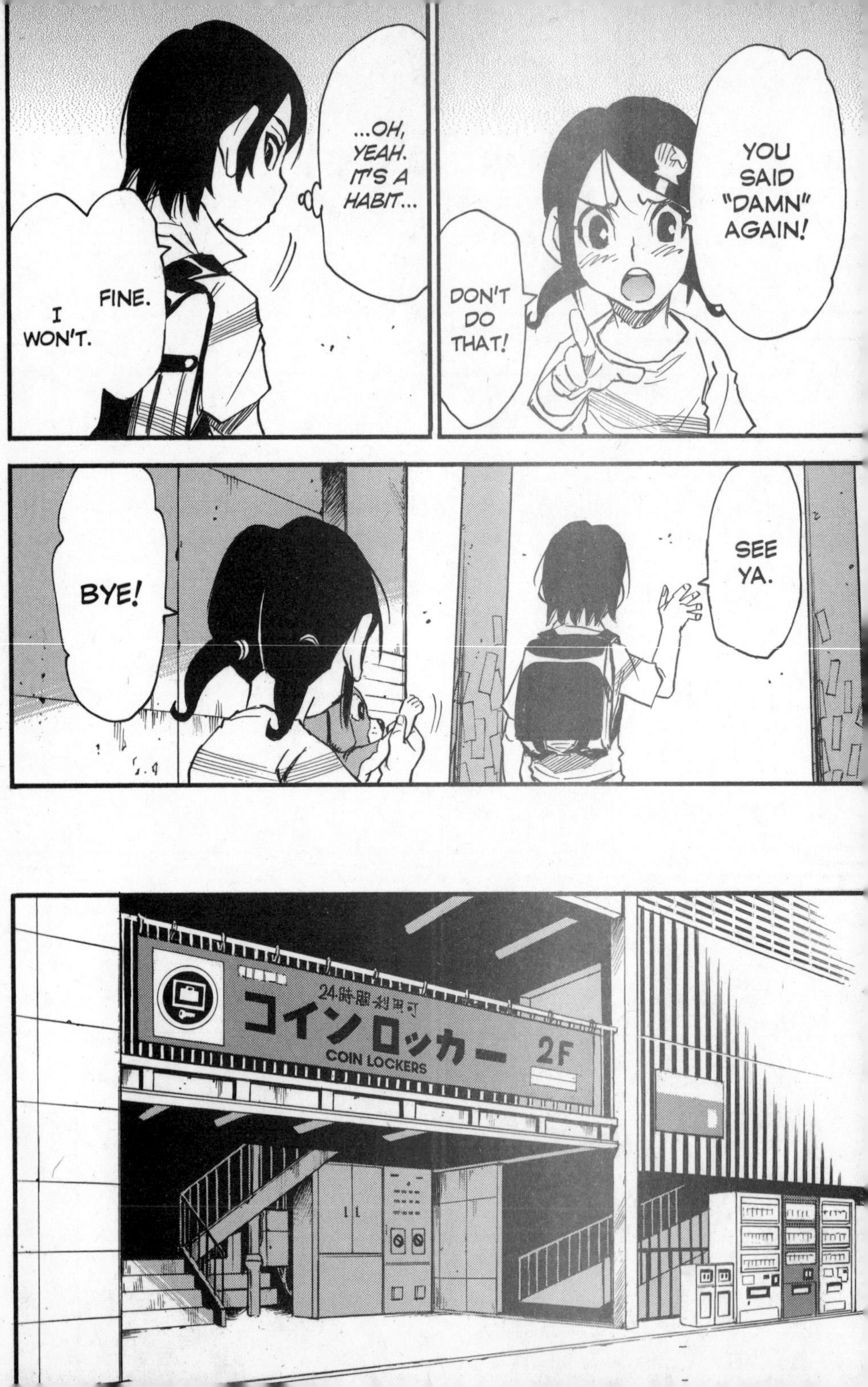
YOU SAID "DAMN" AGAIN!
DON'T DO THAT!
...OH, YEAH. IT'S A HABIT...
FINE. I WON'T.
SEE YA.
BYE!
コインロッカー
COIN LOCKERS
2F

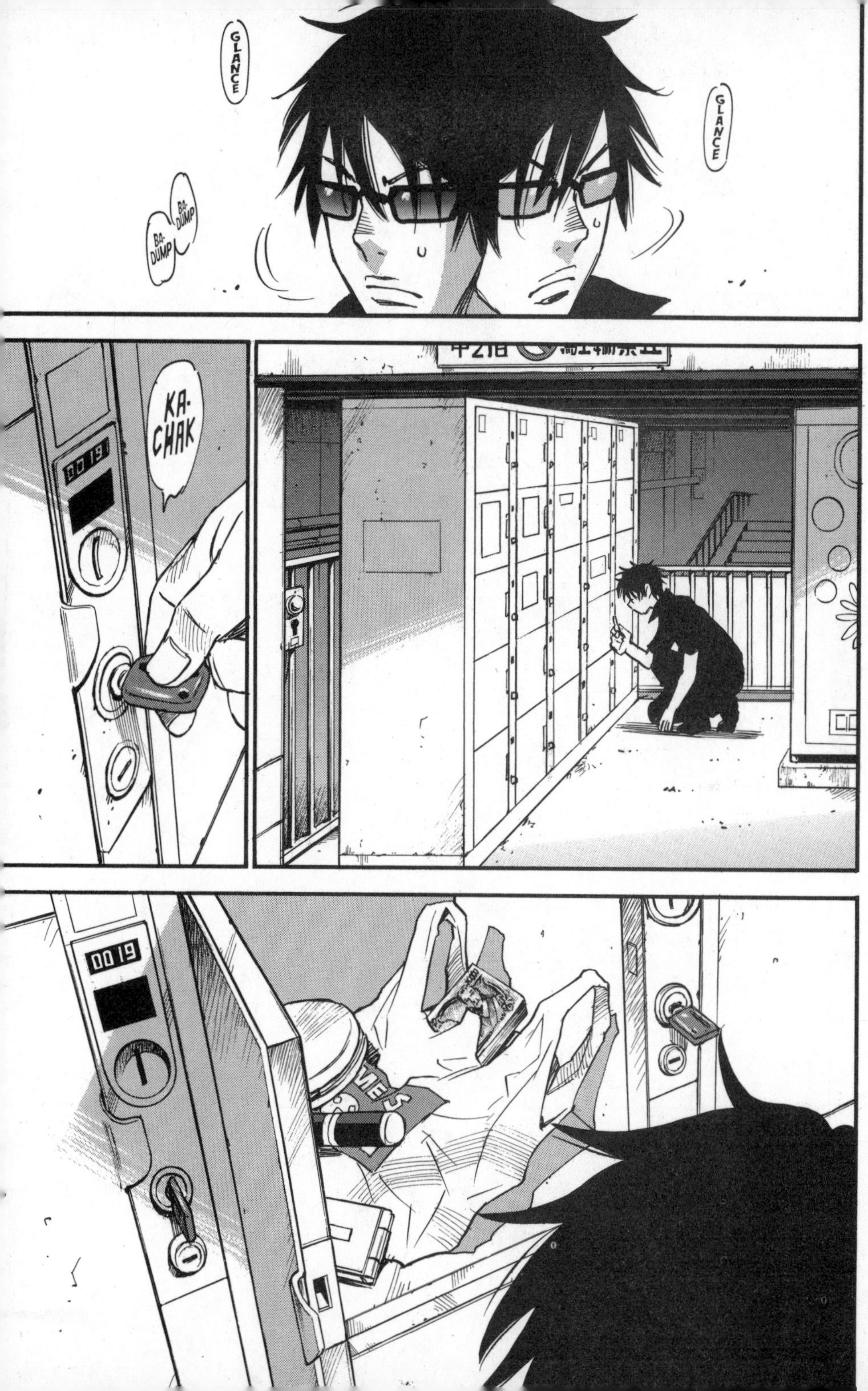
GLANCE
GLANCE
BA-DUMP
BA-DUMP
KA-CHAK
0019

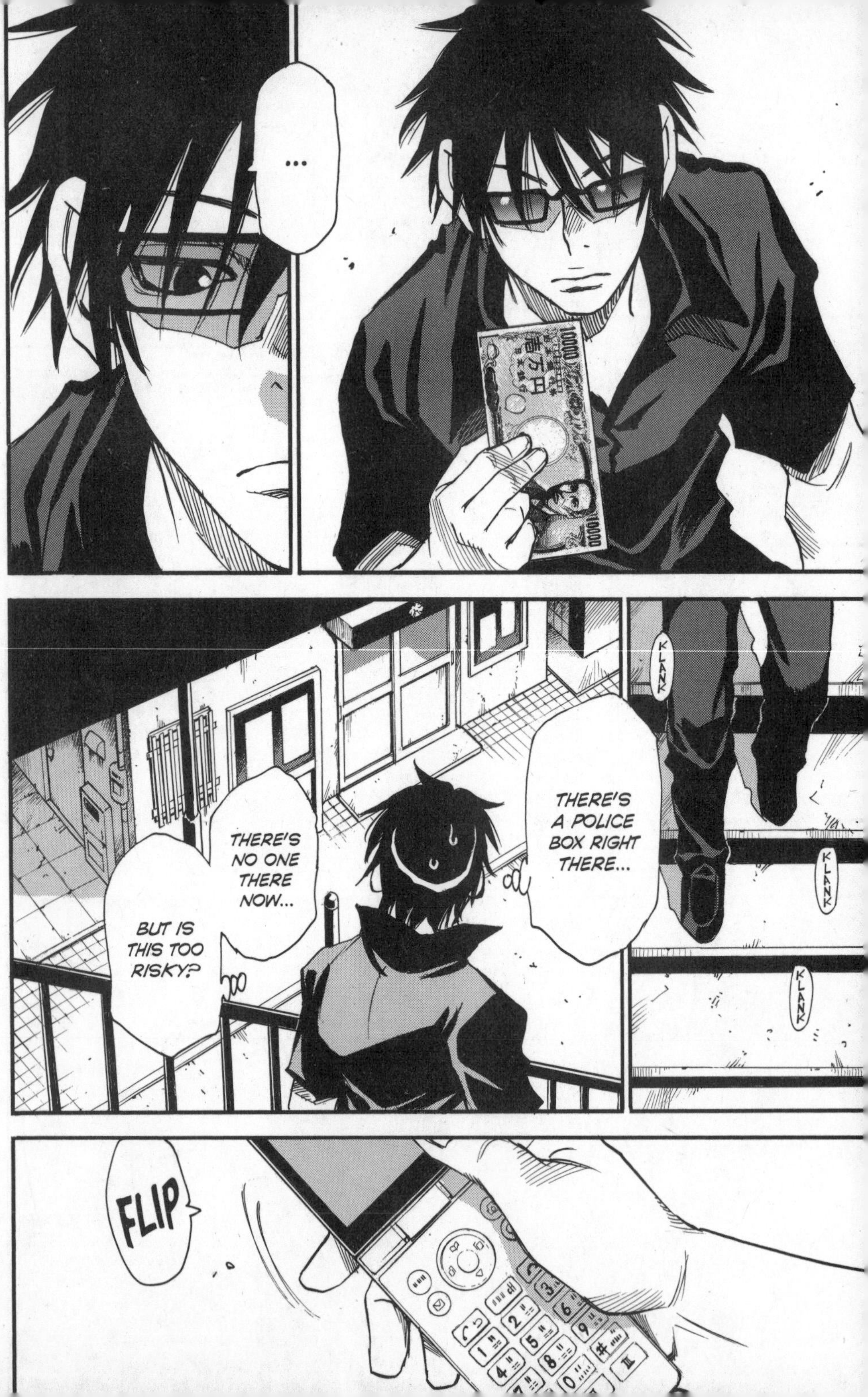
...
KLANK
KLANK
KLANK
THERE'S A POLICE BOX RIGHT THERE...
THERE'S NO ONE THERE NOW...
BUT IS THIS TOO RISKY?
FLIP

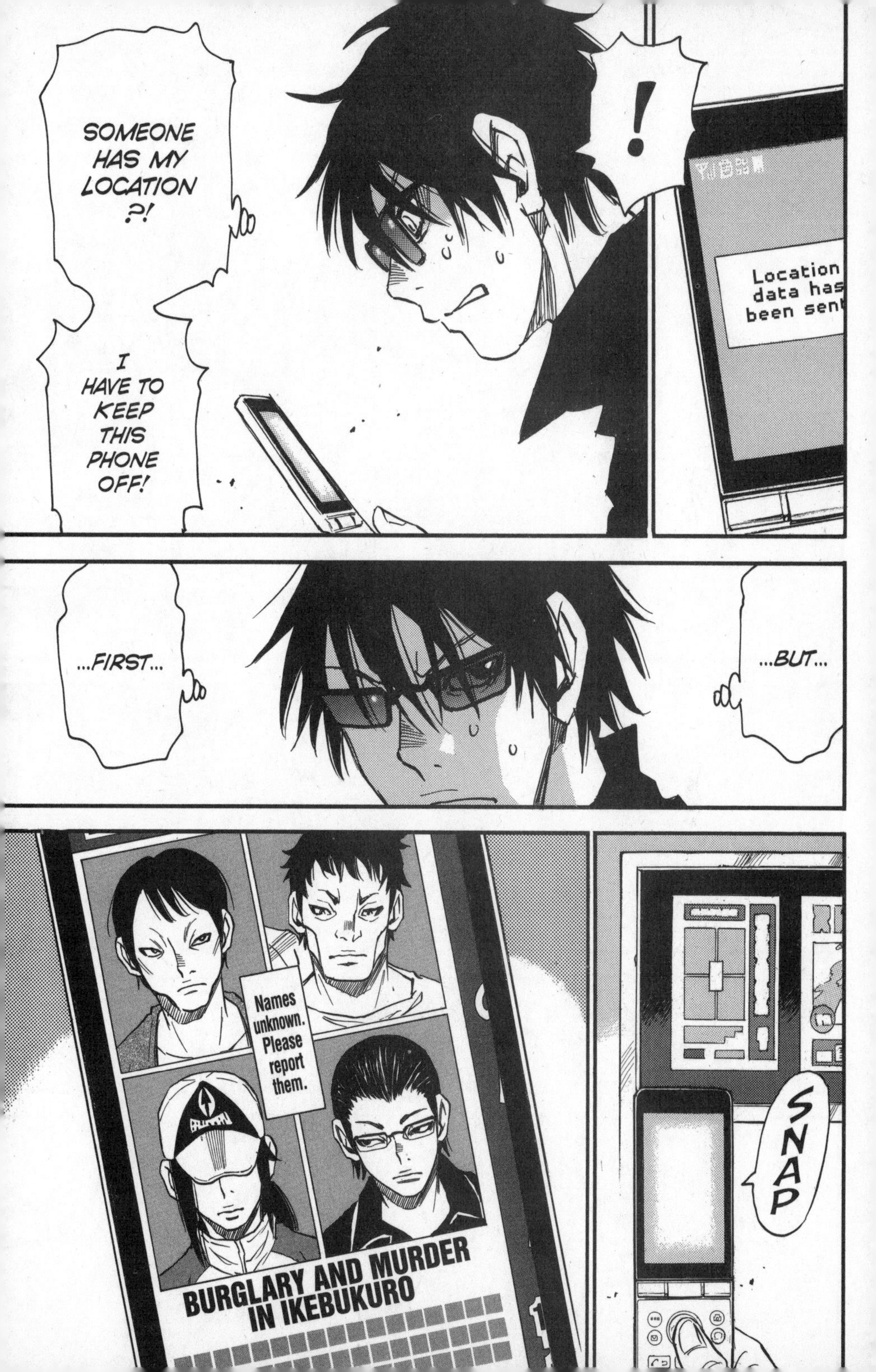
Location data has been sent
!
SOMEONE HAS MY LOCATION ?!
I HAVE TO KEEP THIS PHONE OFF!
...BUT...
...FIRST...
SNAP
Names unknown. Please report them.
BURGLARY AND MURDER IN IKEBUKURO

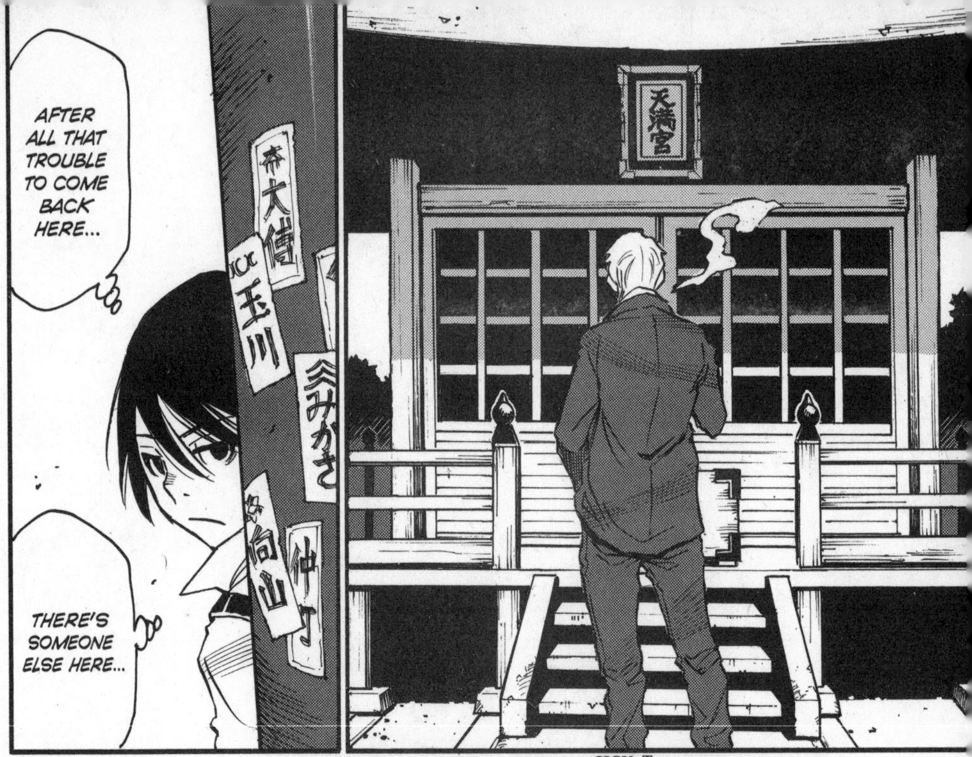
天満宮
AFTER ALL THAT TROUBLE TO COME BACK HERE...
THERE'S SOMEONE ELSE HERE...
SIGN: Tenmangu

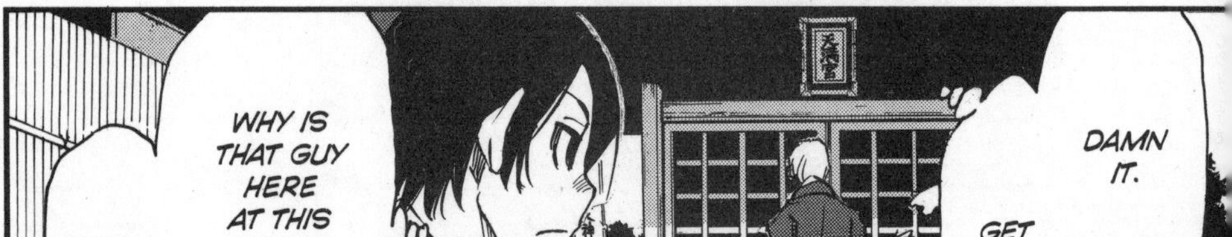
DAMN IT.
GET LOST.
WHY IS THAT GUY HERE AT THIS HOUR?
GET A JOB!

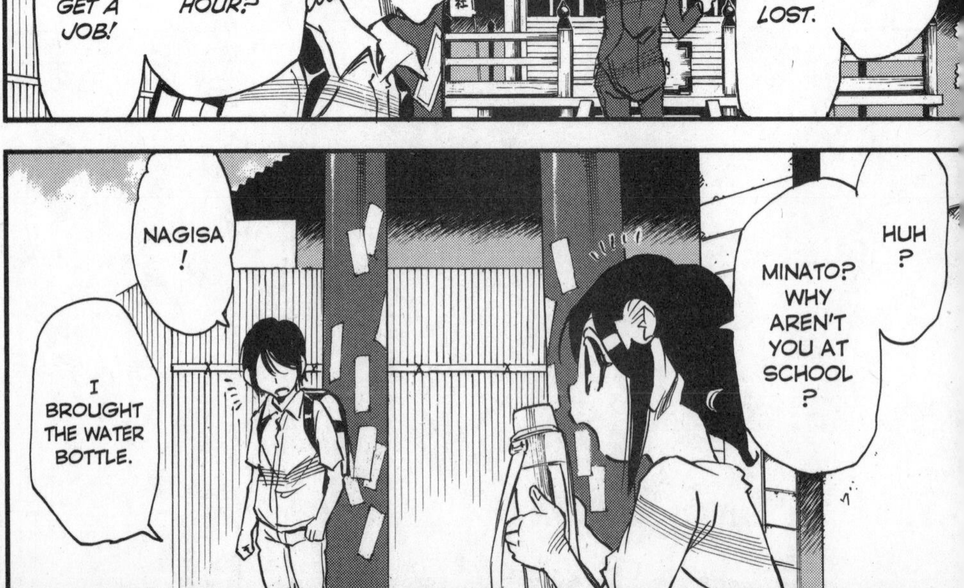
HUH?
MINATO? WHY AREN'T YOU AT SCHOOL?
NAGISA!
I BROUGHT THE WATER BOTTLE.

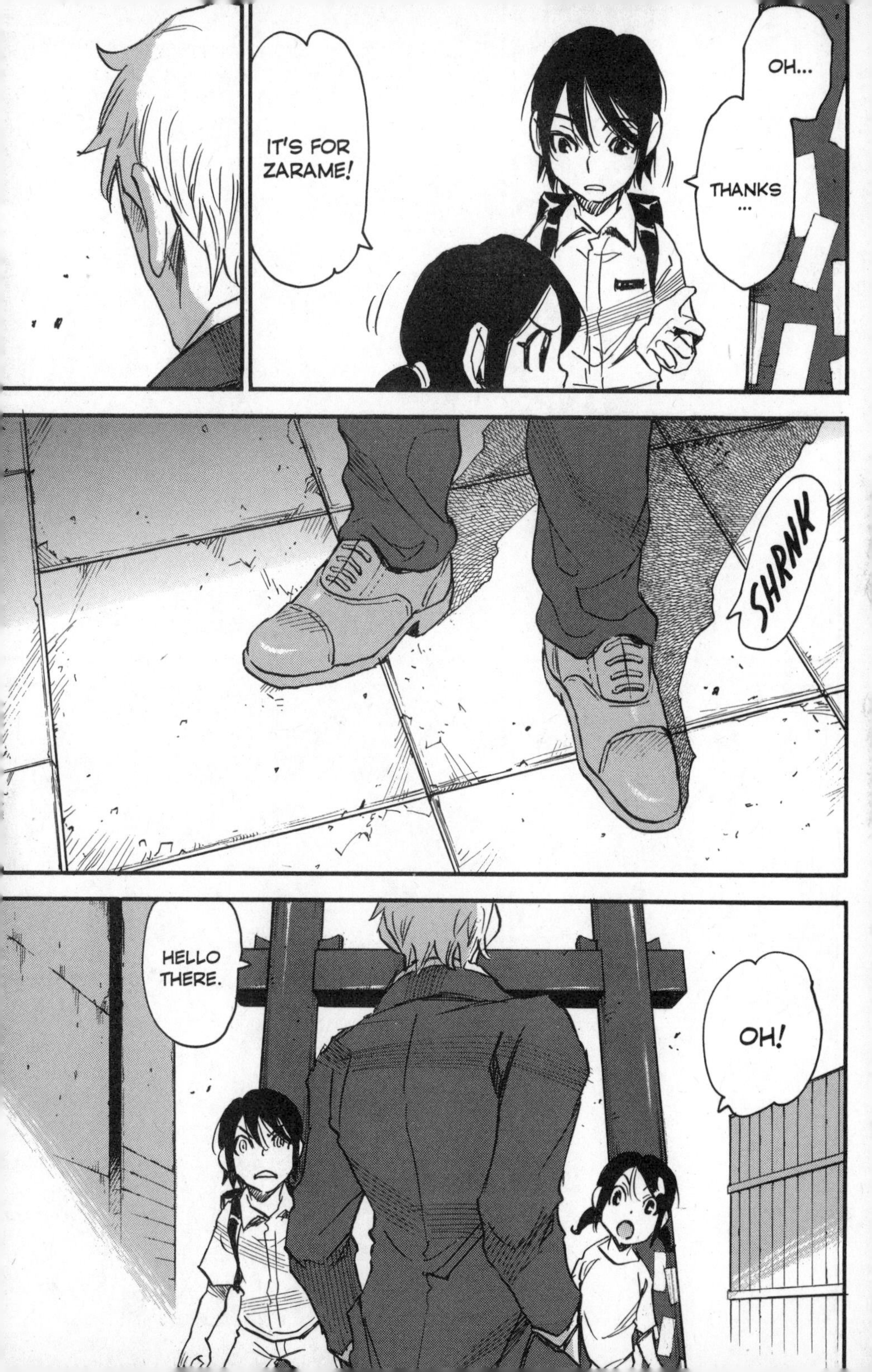
OH...
THANKS...
IT'S FOR ZARAME!
SHRNK
OH!
HELLO THERE.

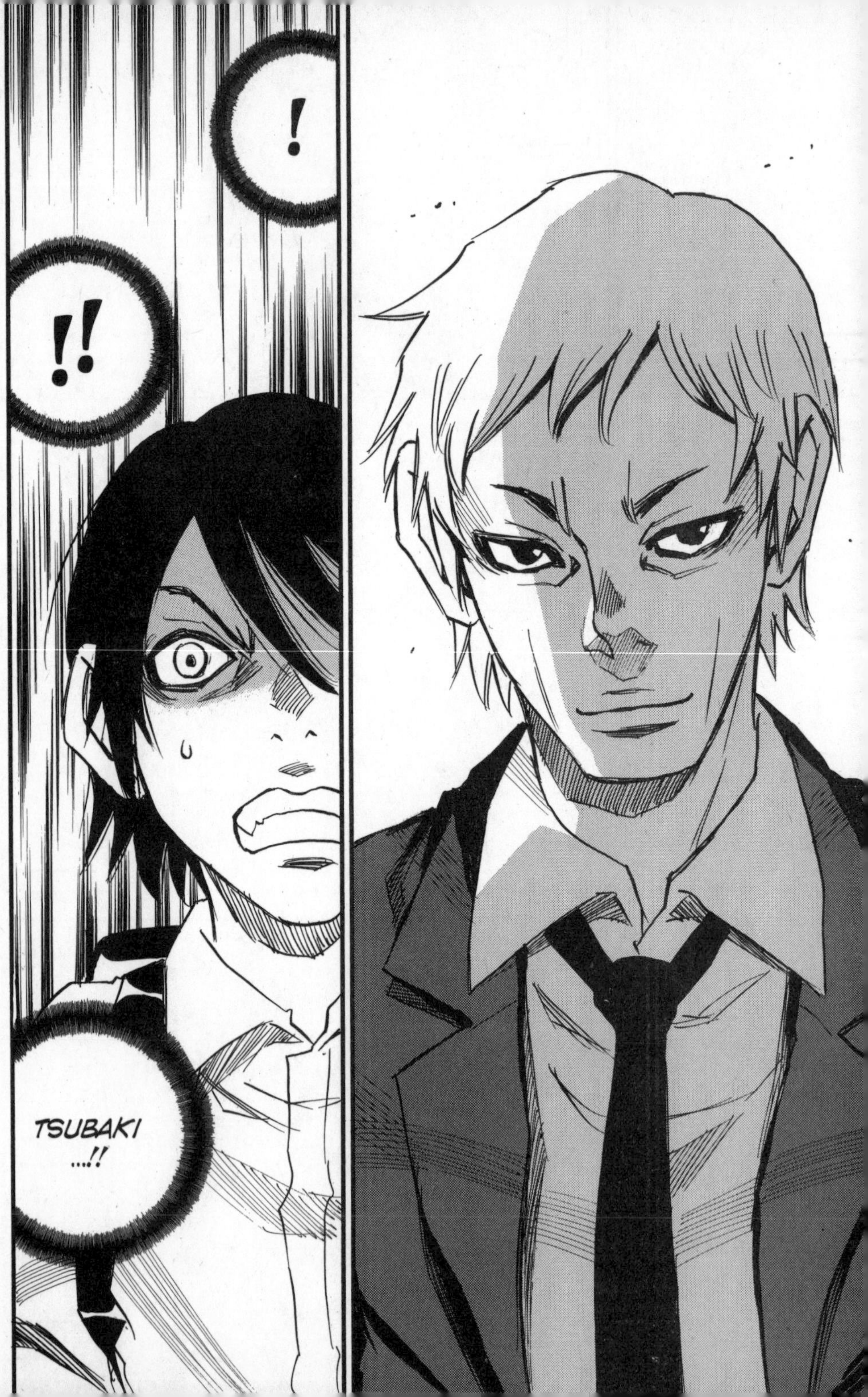
!
!!
TSUBAKI ...!!

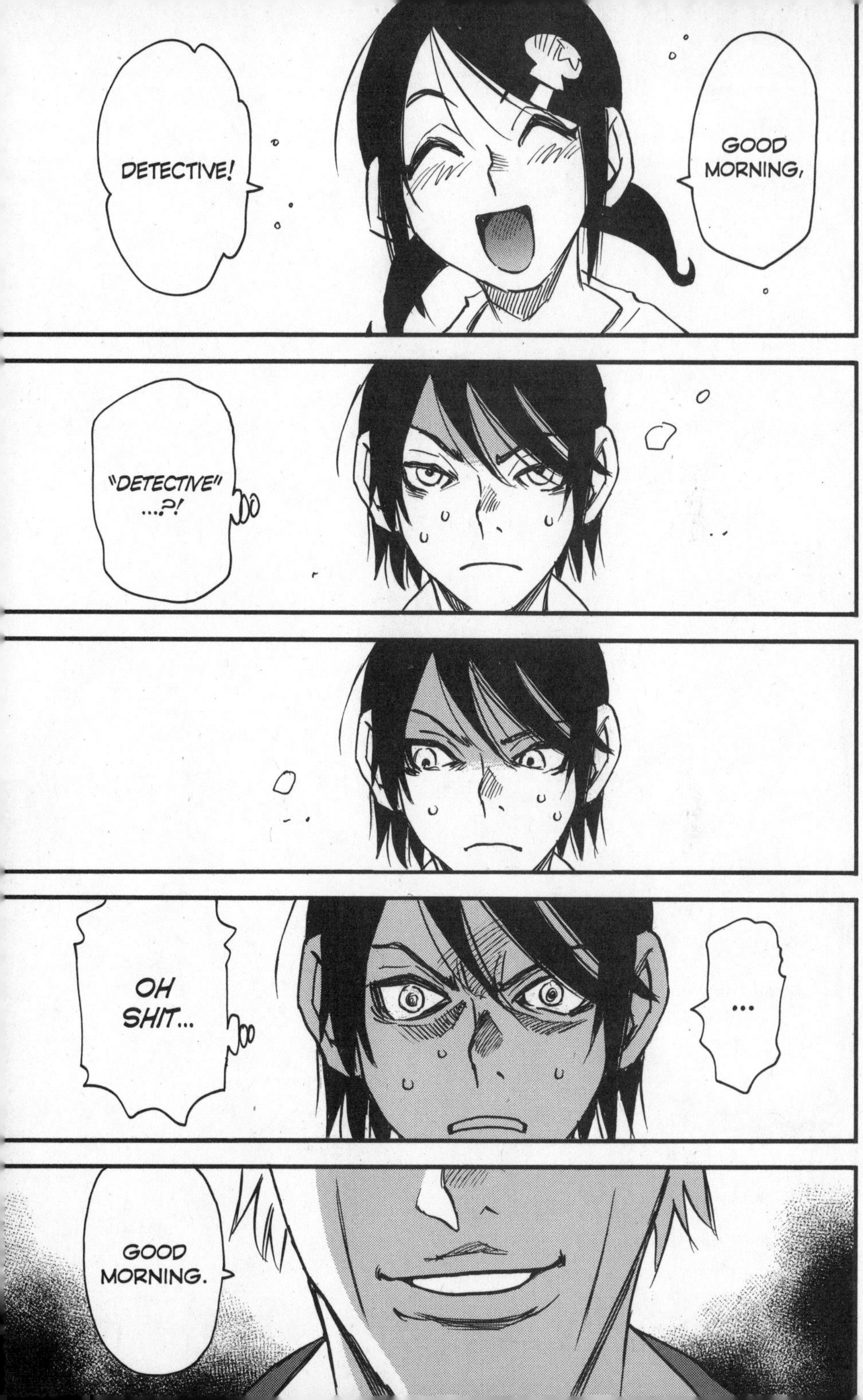
GOOD MORNING,
DETECTIVE!
"DETECTIVE" ...?!
...
OH SHIT...
GOOD MORNING.

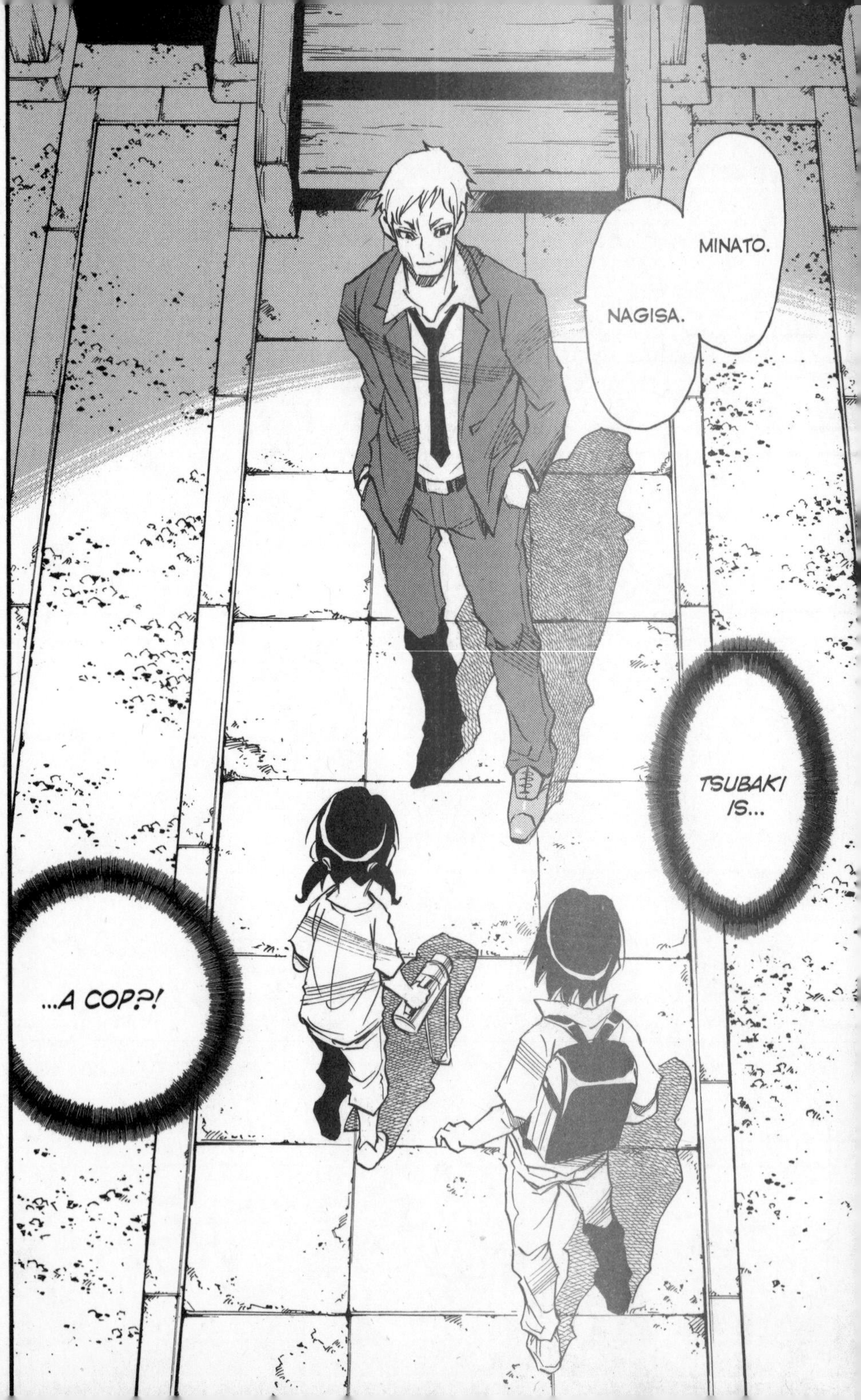
MINATO.
NAGISA.
TSUBAKI IS...
...A COP?!

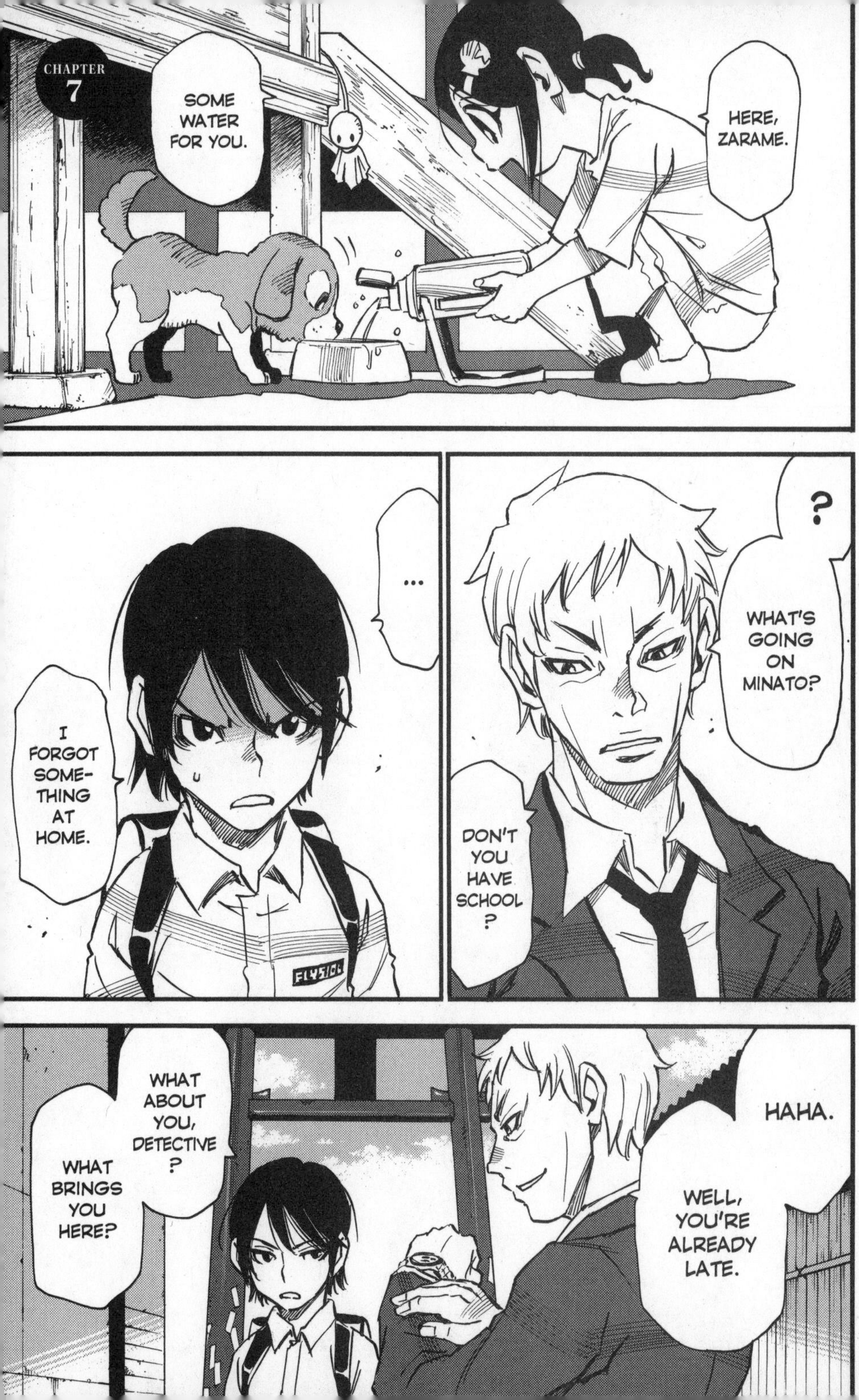
CHAPTER 7
HERE, ZARAME.
SOME WATER FOR YOU.
?
WHAT'S GOING ON MINATO?
DON'T YOU HAVE SCHOOL?
...
I FORGOT SOMETHING AT HOME.
HAHA.
WELL, YOU'RE ALREADY LATE.
WHAT ABOUT YOU, DETECTIVE?
WHAT BRINGS YOU HERE?

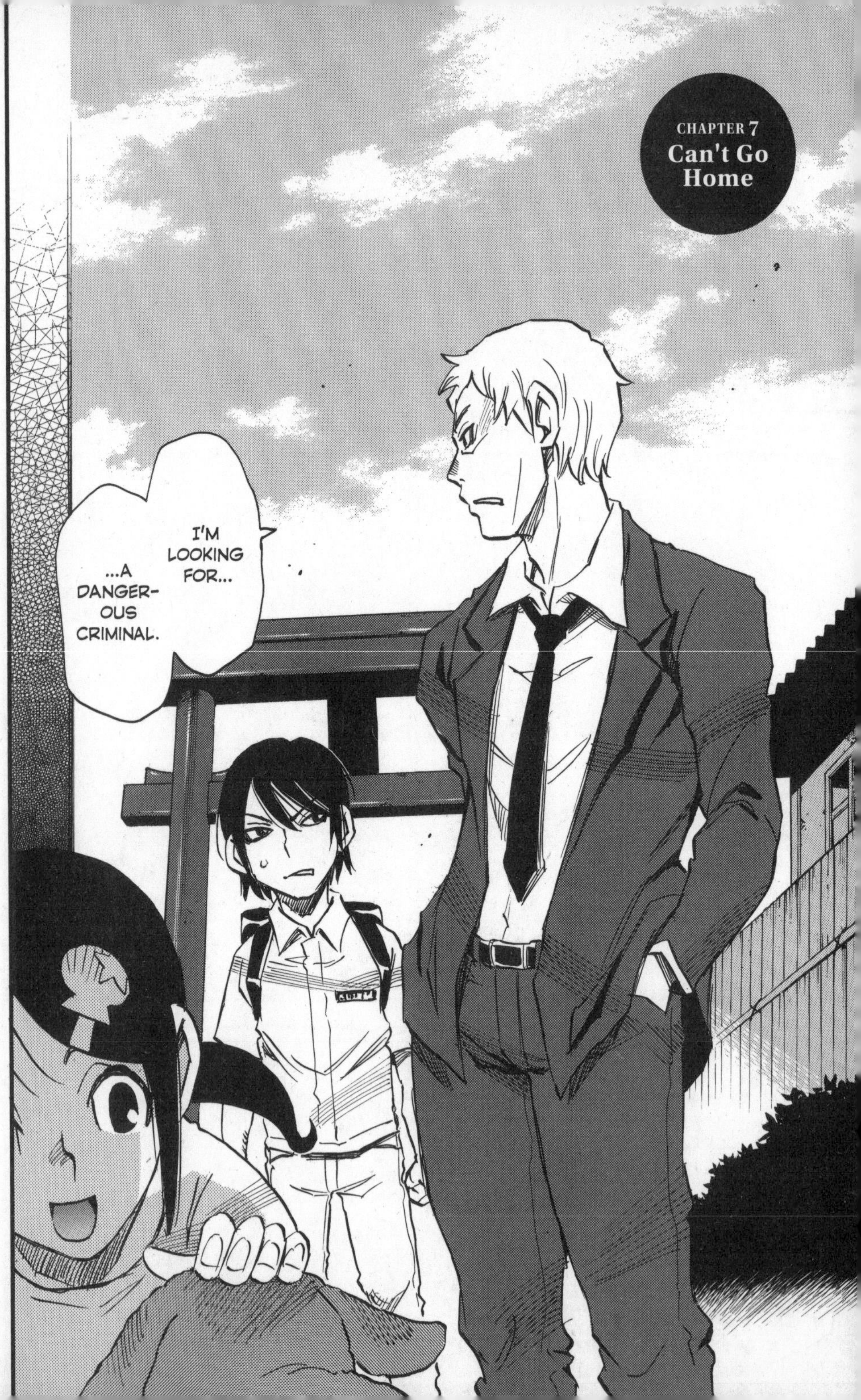
CHAPTER 7
Can't Go Home
I'M LOOKING FOR...
...A DANGER-OUS CRIMINAL.

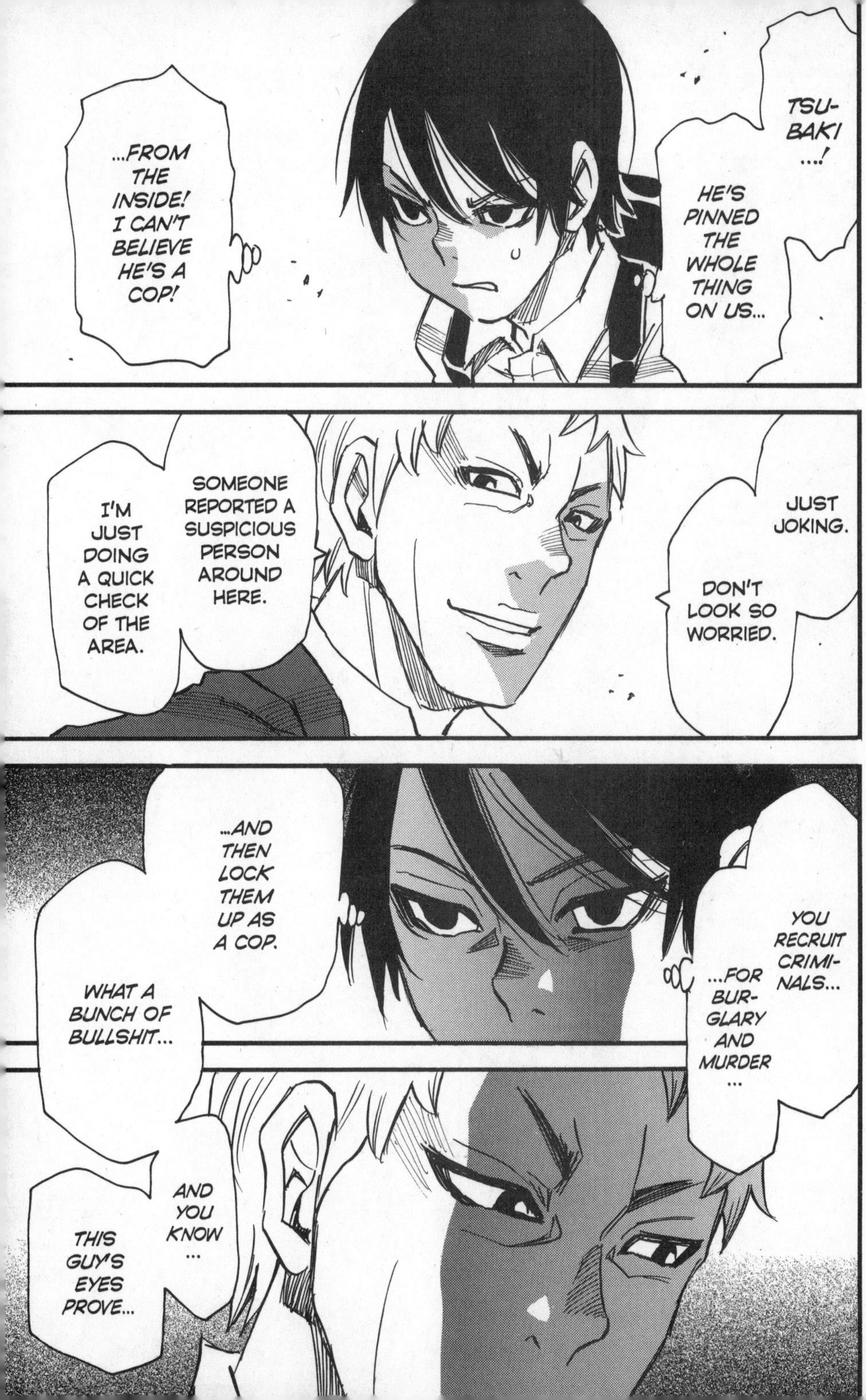
TSUBAKI ...!
HE'S PINNED THE WHOLE THING ON US...
...FROM THE INSIDE! I CAN'T BELIEVE HE'S A COP!
JUST JOKING.
DON'T LOOK SO WORRIED.
SOMEONE REPORTED A SUSPICIOUS PERSON AROUND HERE.
I'M JUST DOING A QUICK CHECK OF THE AREA.
YOU RECRUIT CRIMINALS...
...FOR BURGLARY AND MURDER...
...AND THEN LOCK THEM UP AS A COP.
WHAT A BUNCH OF BULLSHIT...
AND YOU KNOW...
THIS GUY'S EYES PROVE...

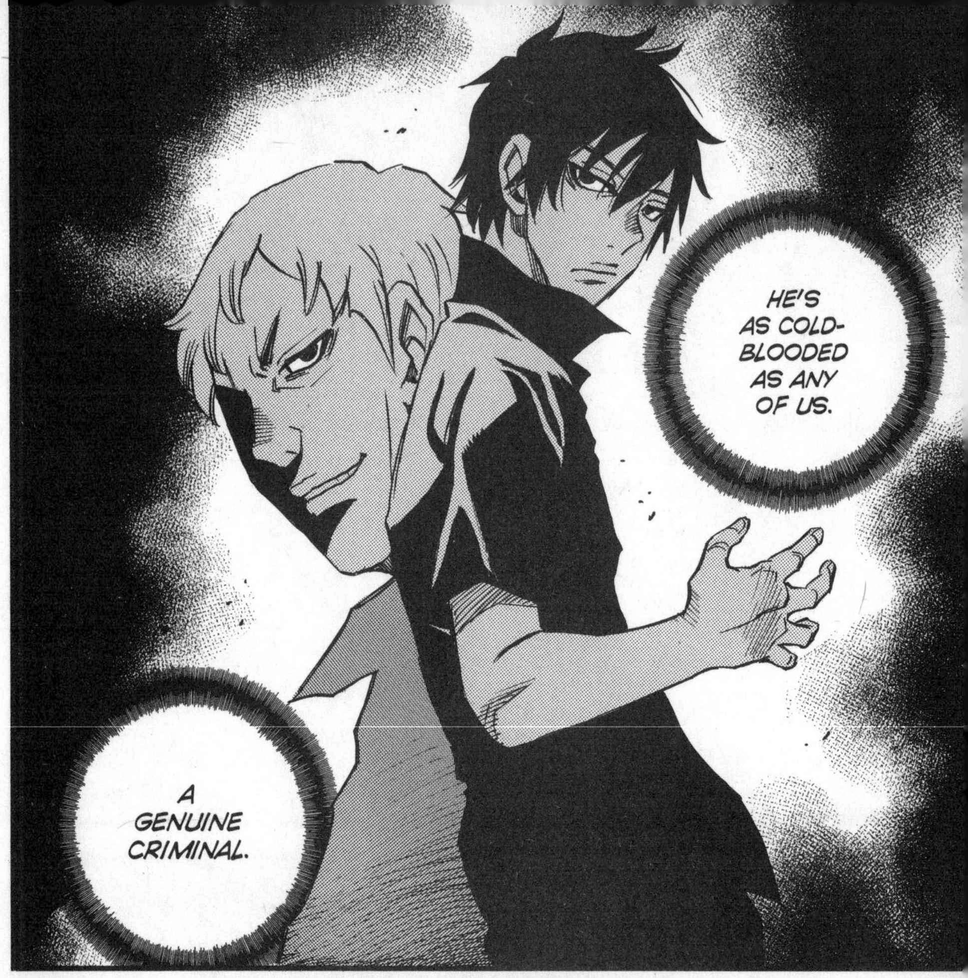
HE'S AS COLD-BLOODED AS ANY OF US.
A GENUINE CRIMINAL.
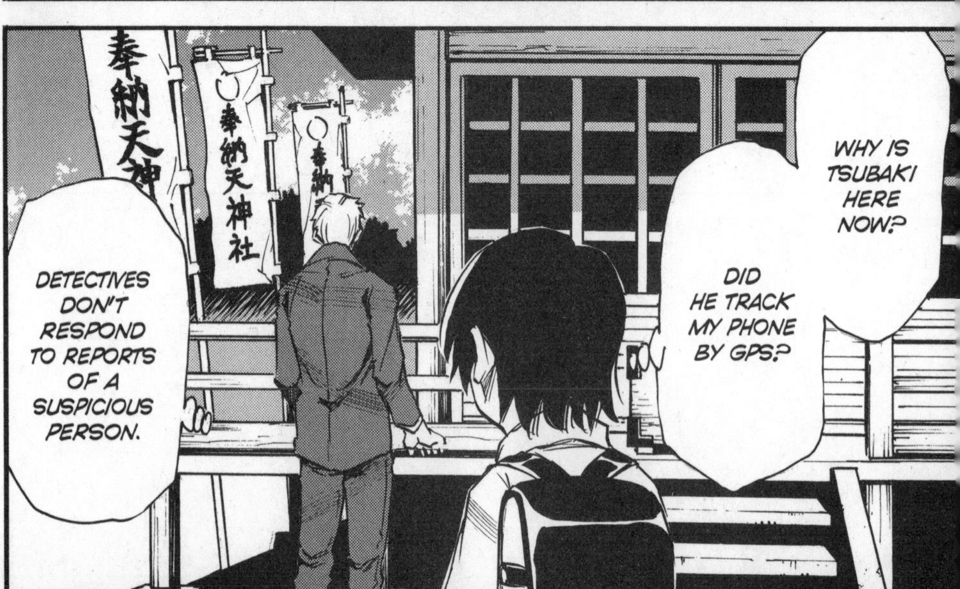
WHY IS TSUBAKI HERE NOW?
DID HE TRACK MY PHONE BY GPS?
奉納
奉納天神社
奉納天神
DETECTIVES DON'T RESPOND TO REPORTS OF A SUSPICIOUS PERSON.

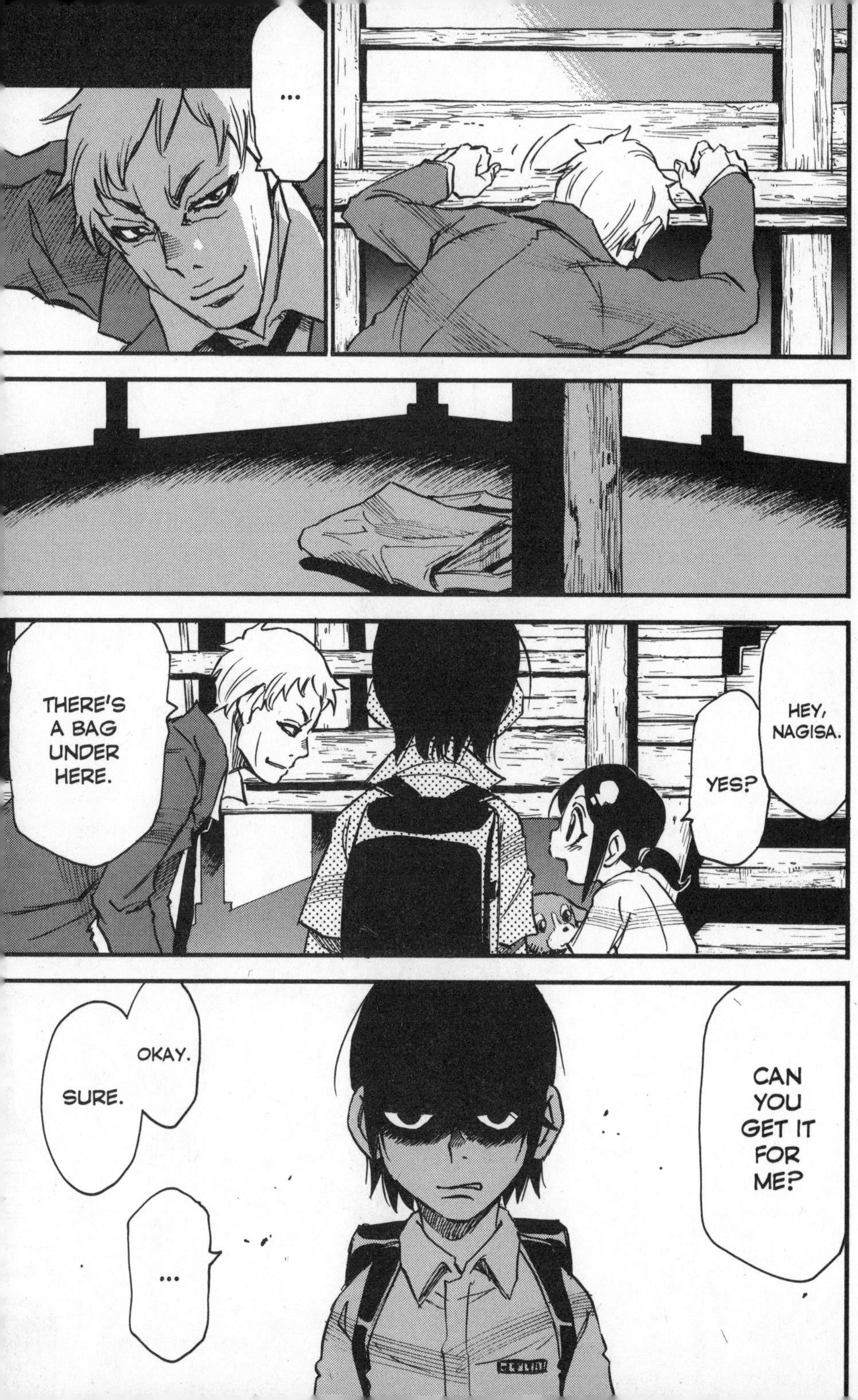
...
HEY, NAGISA.
YES?
THERE'S A BAG UNDER HERE.
CAN YOU GET IT FOR ME?
OKAY. SURE.
...

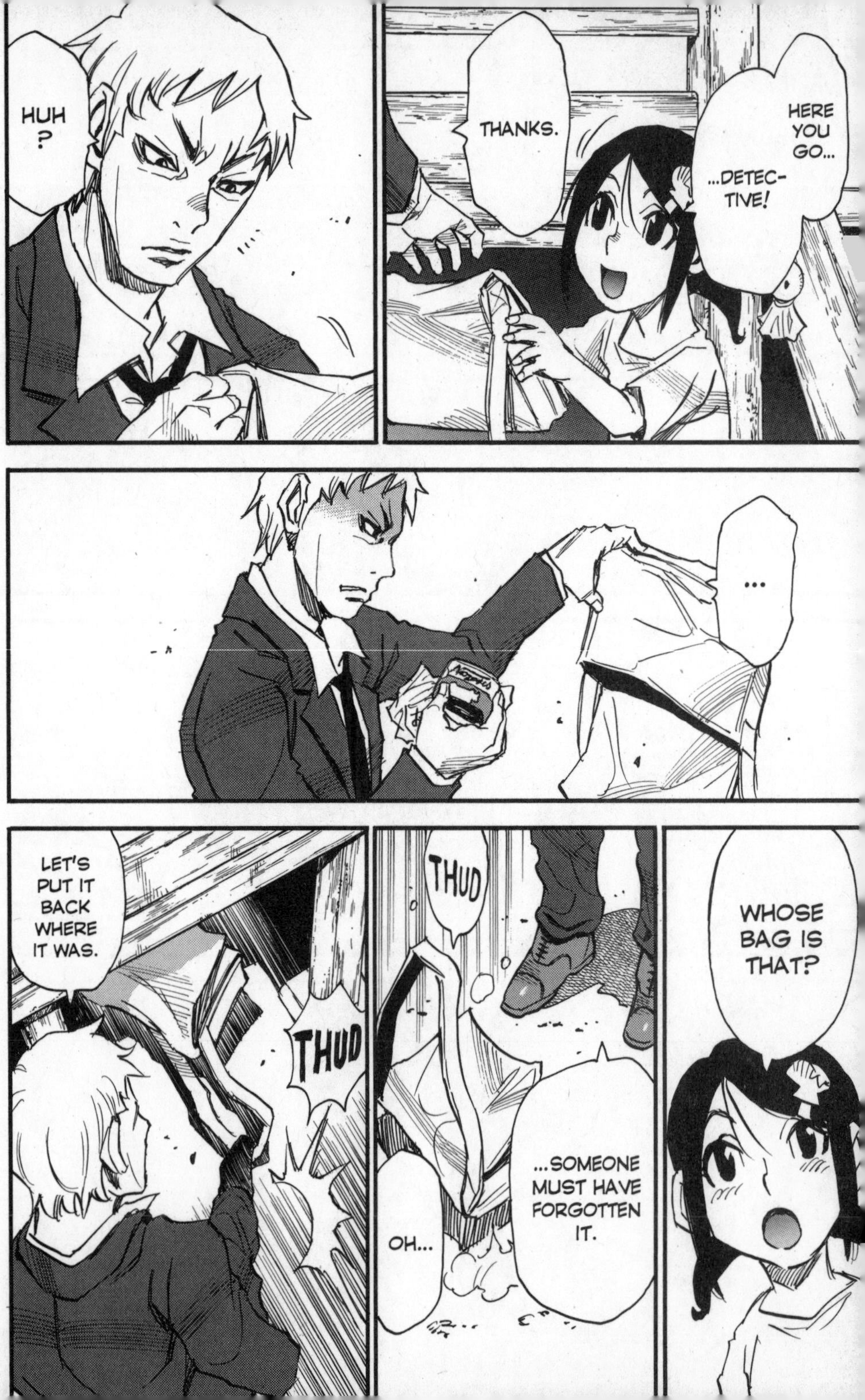
HERE YOU GO...
...DETECTIVE!
THANKS.
HUH?
...
WHOSE BAG IS THAT?
THUD
...SOMEONE MUST HAVE FORGOTTEN IT.
OH...
LET'S PUT IT BACK WHERE IT WAS.
THUD

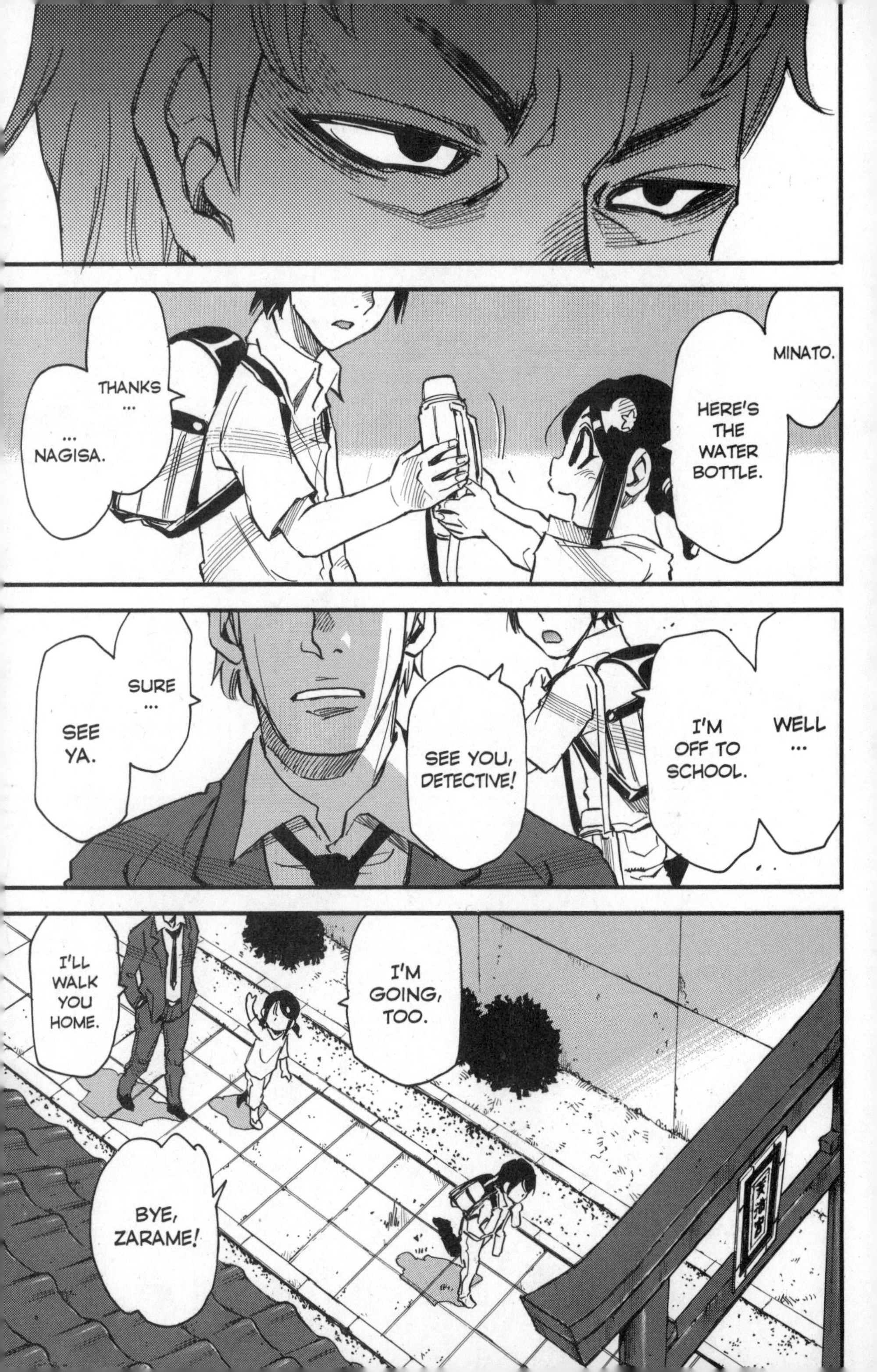

MINATO.
HERE'S THE WATER BOTTLE.
THANKS ...
... NAGISA.
WELL ...
I'M OFF TO SCHOOL.
SEE YOU, DETECTIVE!
SURE ...
SEE YA.
I'M GOING, TOO.
I'LL WALK YOU HOME.
BYE, ZARAME!

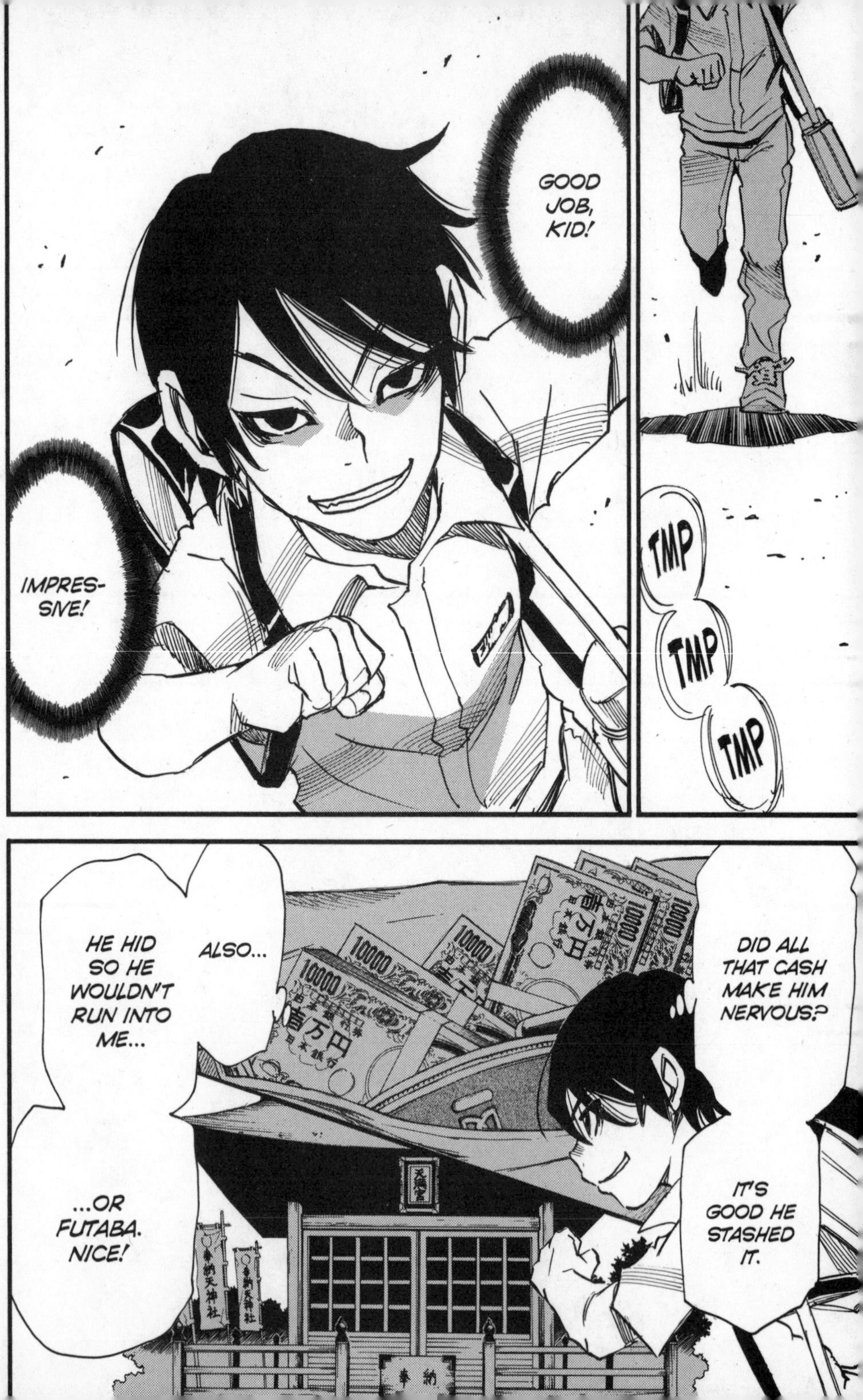
TMP
TMP
TMP
GOOD JOB, KID!
IMPRESSIVE!
DID ALL THAT CASH MAKE HIM NERVOUS?
IT'S GOOD HE STASHED IT.
ALSO...
HE HID SO HE WOULDN'T RUN INTO ME...
...OR FUTABA. NICE!

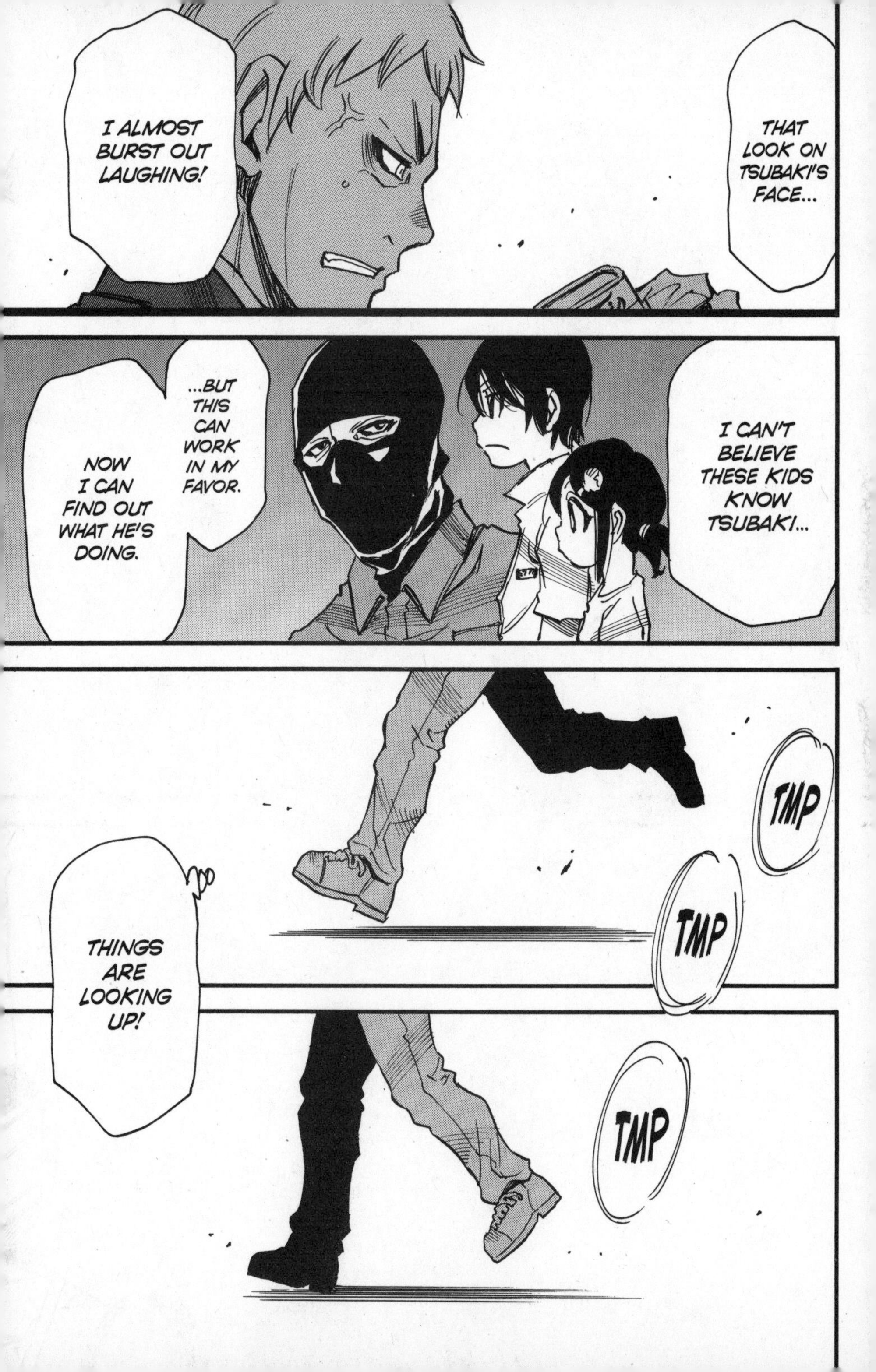
THAT LOOK ON TSUBAKI'S FACE...
I ALMOST BURST OUT LAUGHING!
I CAN'T BELIEVE THESE KIDS KNOW TSUBAKI...
...BUT THIS CAN WORK IN MY FAVOR.
NOW I CAN FIND OUT WHAT HE'S DOING.
TMP
TMP
THINGS ARE LOOKING UP!
TMP

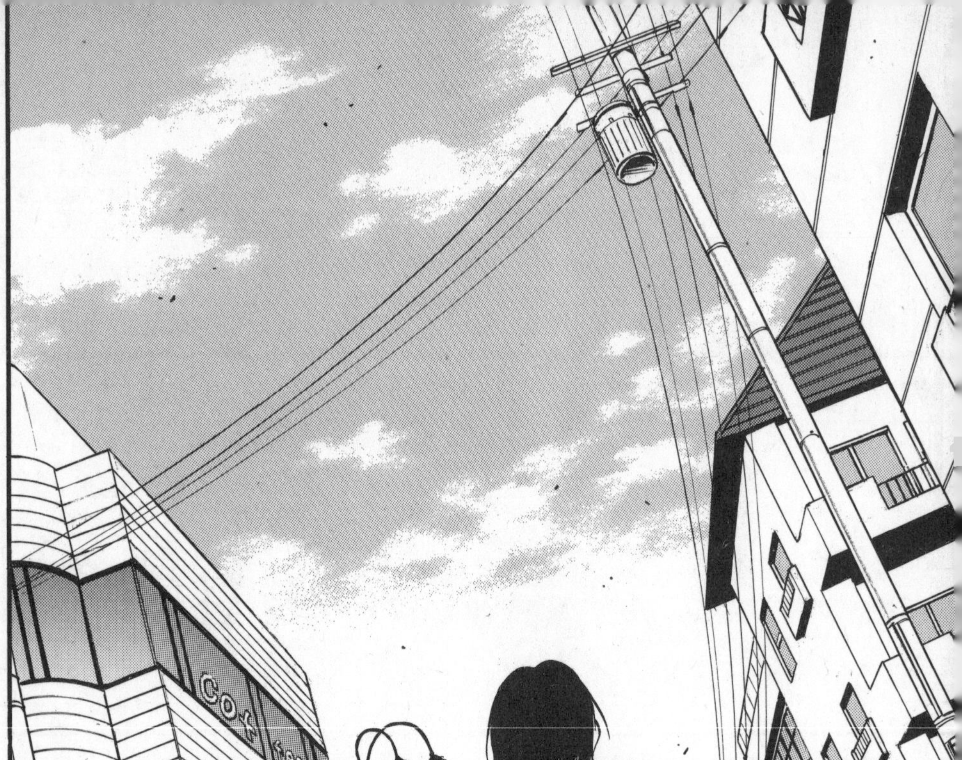
焼肉門
炭火焼

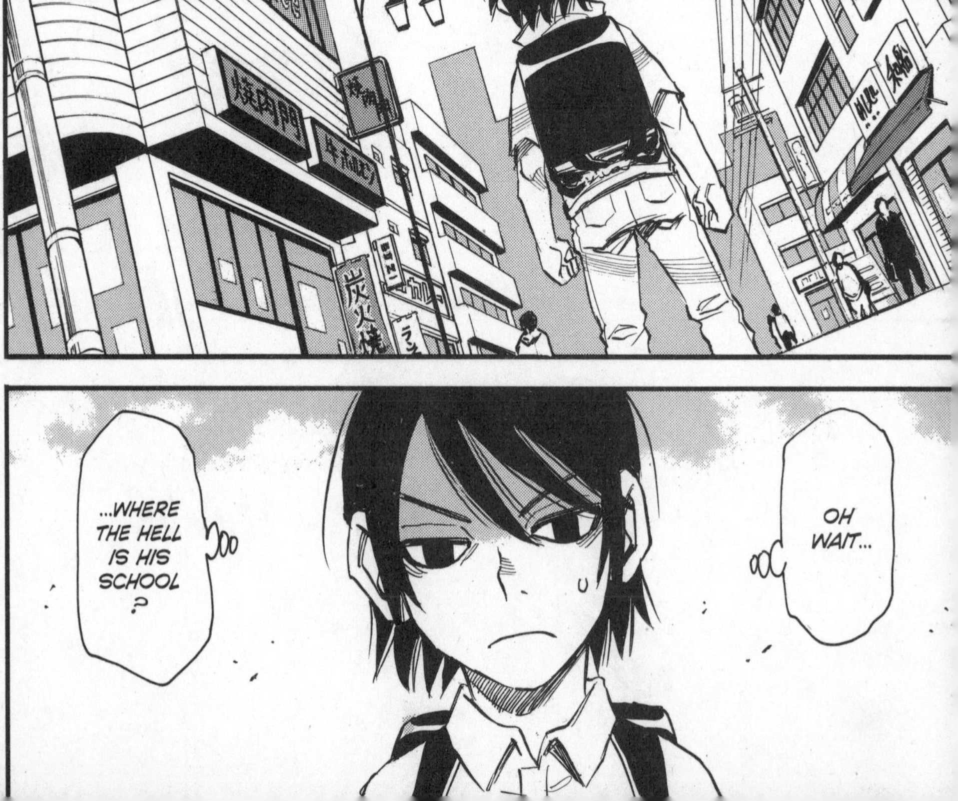
OH WAIT...
...WHERE THE HELL IS HIS SCHOOL?

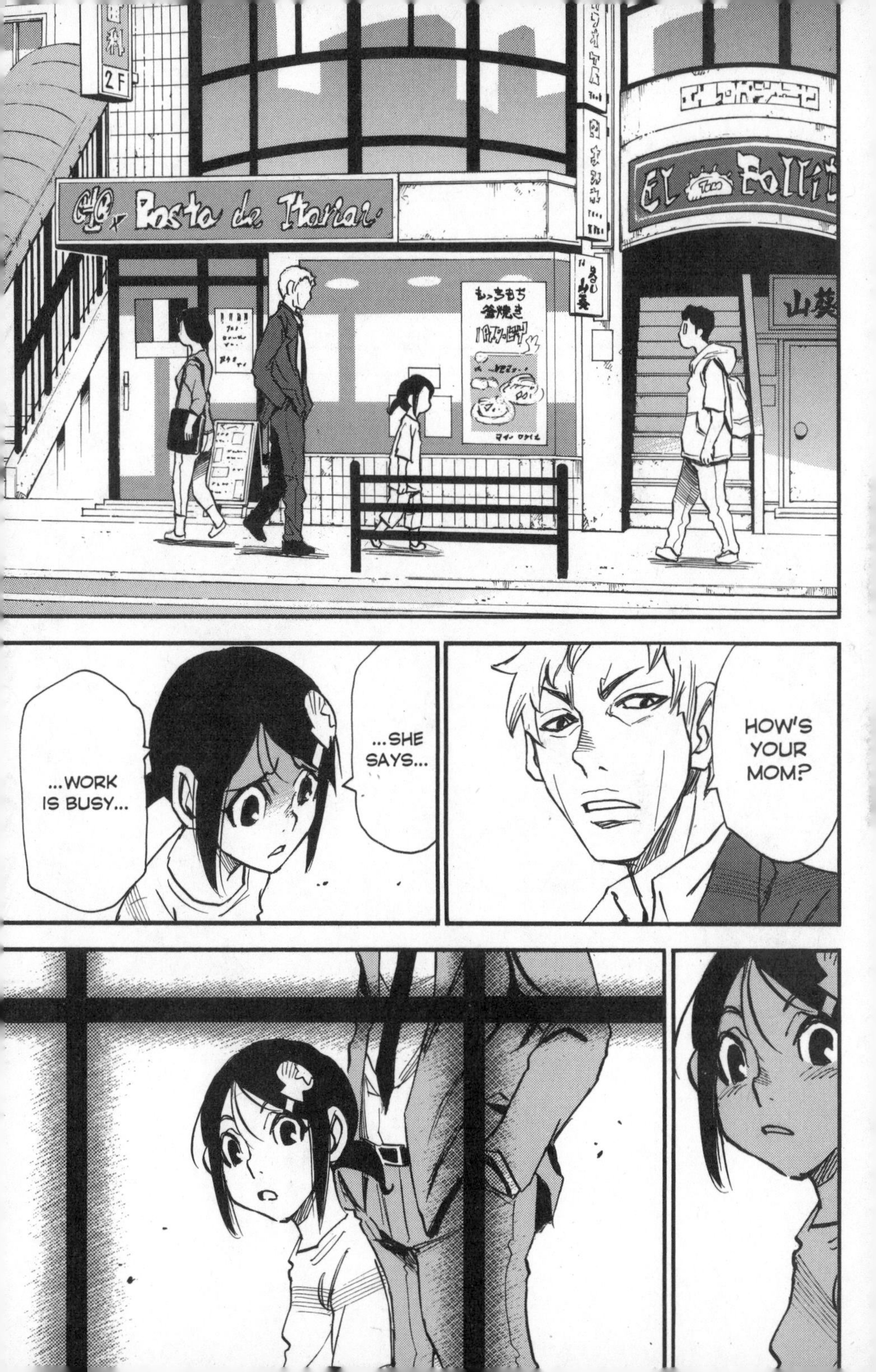
HOW'S YOUR MOM?
...SHE SAYS...
...WORK IS BUSY...

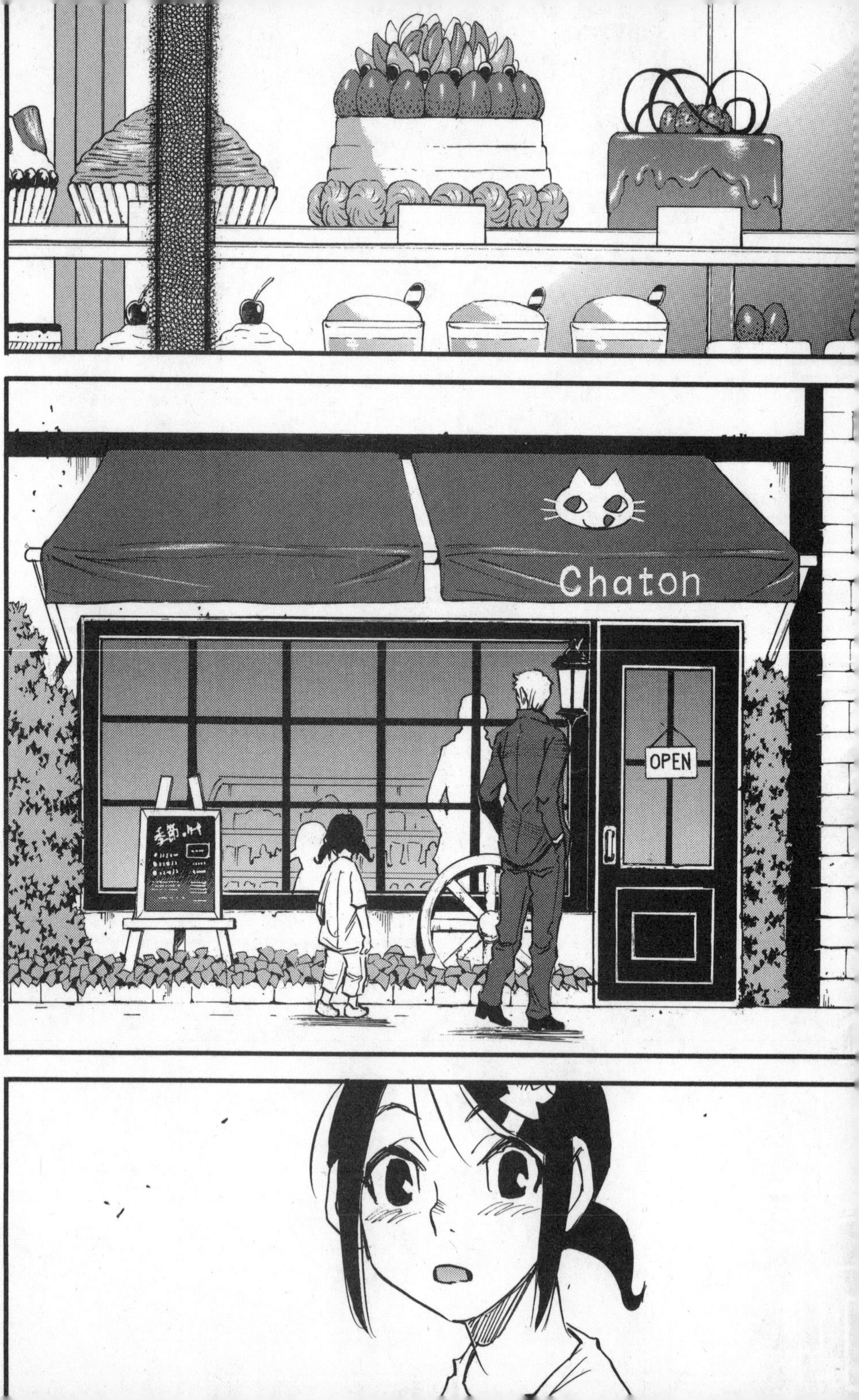
Chaton
OPEN

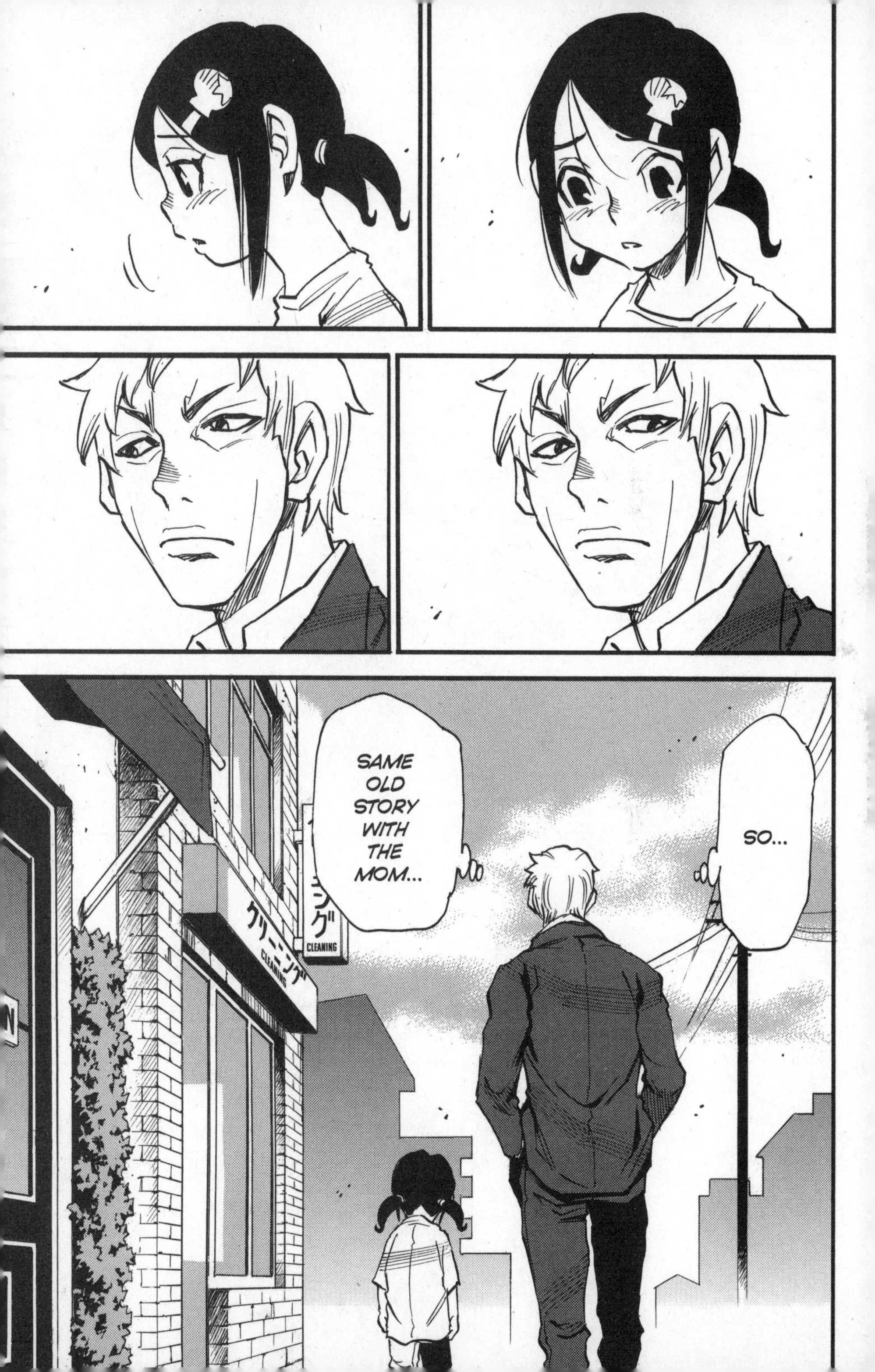
SO...
SAME OLD STORY WITH THE MOM...
ング
CLEANING
クリーニング
CLEANING

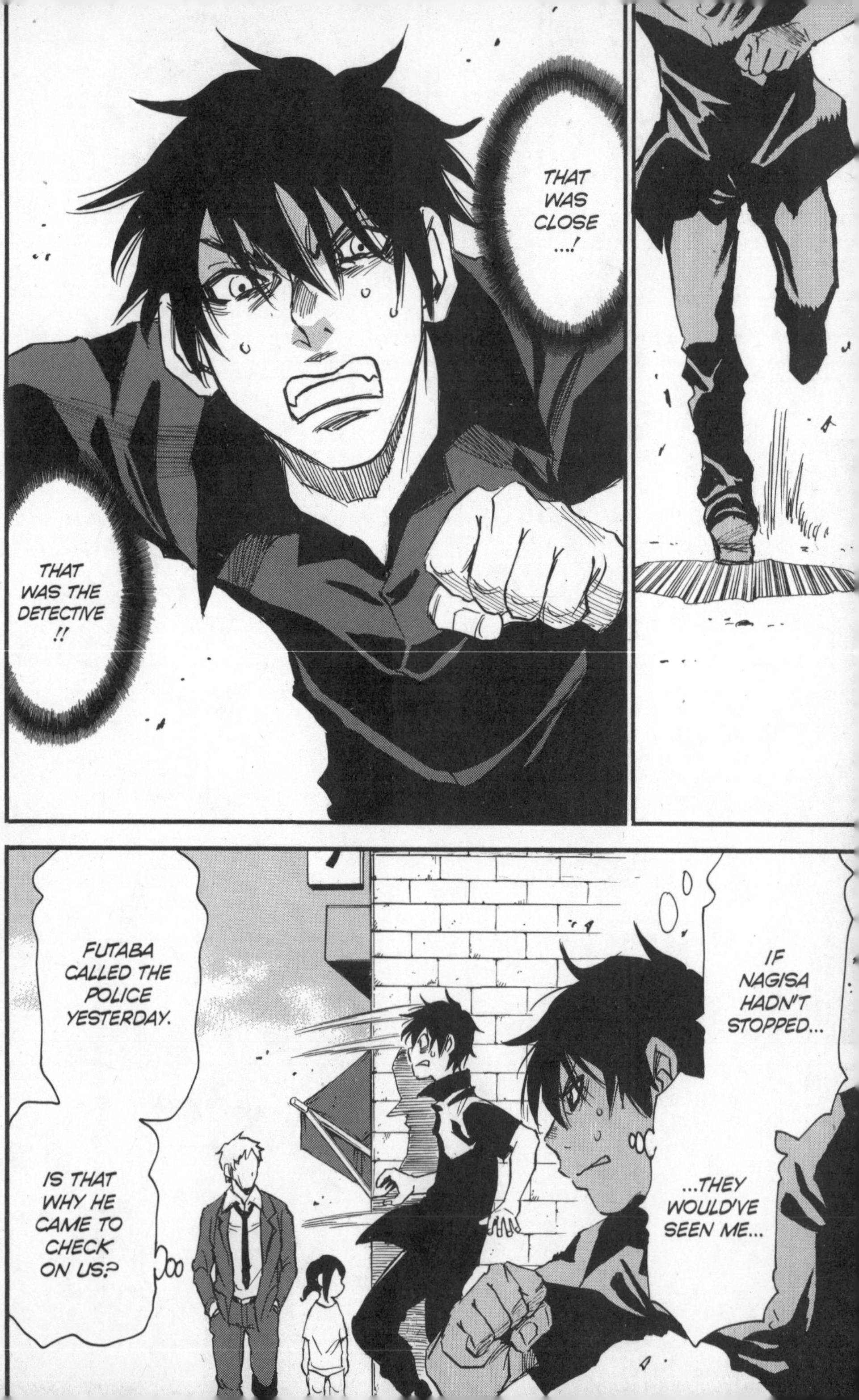
THAT WAS CLOSE ...!
THAT WAS THE DETECTIVE !!
IF NAGISA HADN'T STOPPED...
...THEY WOULD'VE SEEN ME...
FUTABA CALLED THE POLICE YESTERDAY.
IS THAT WHY HE CAME TO CHECK ON US?

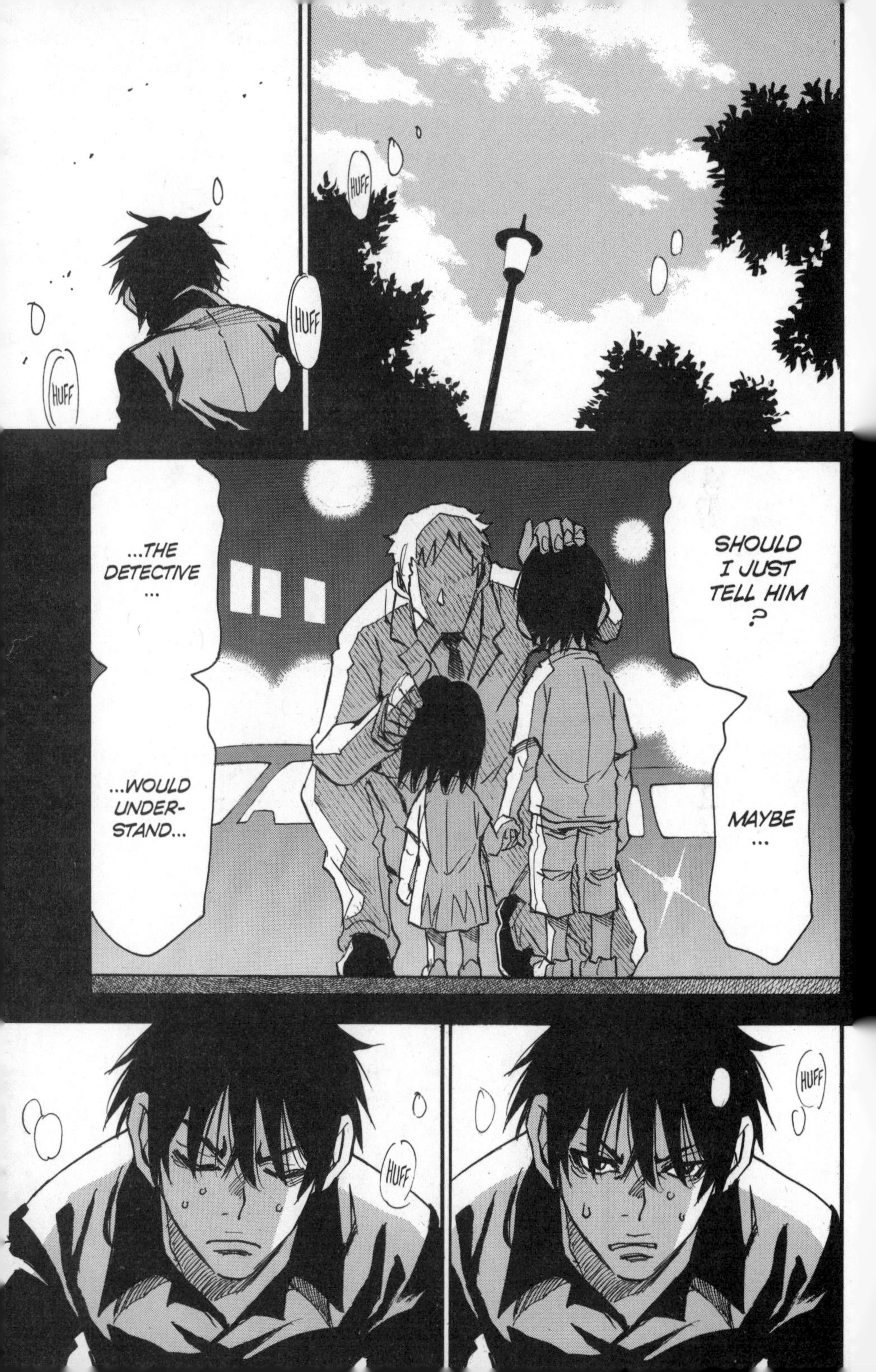
HUFF
HUFF
HUFF
SHOULD I JUST TELL HIM ?
MAYBE ...
...THE DETECTIVE ...
...WOULD UNDER-STAND...
HUFF
HUFF

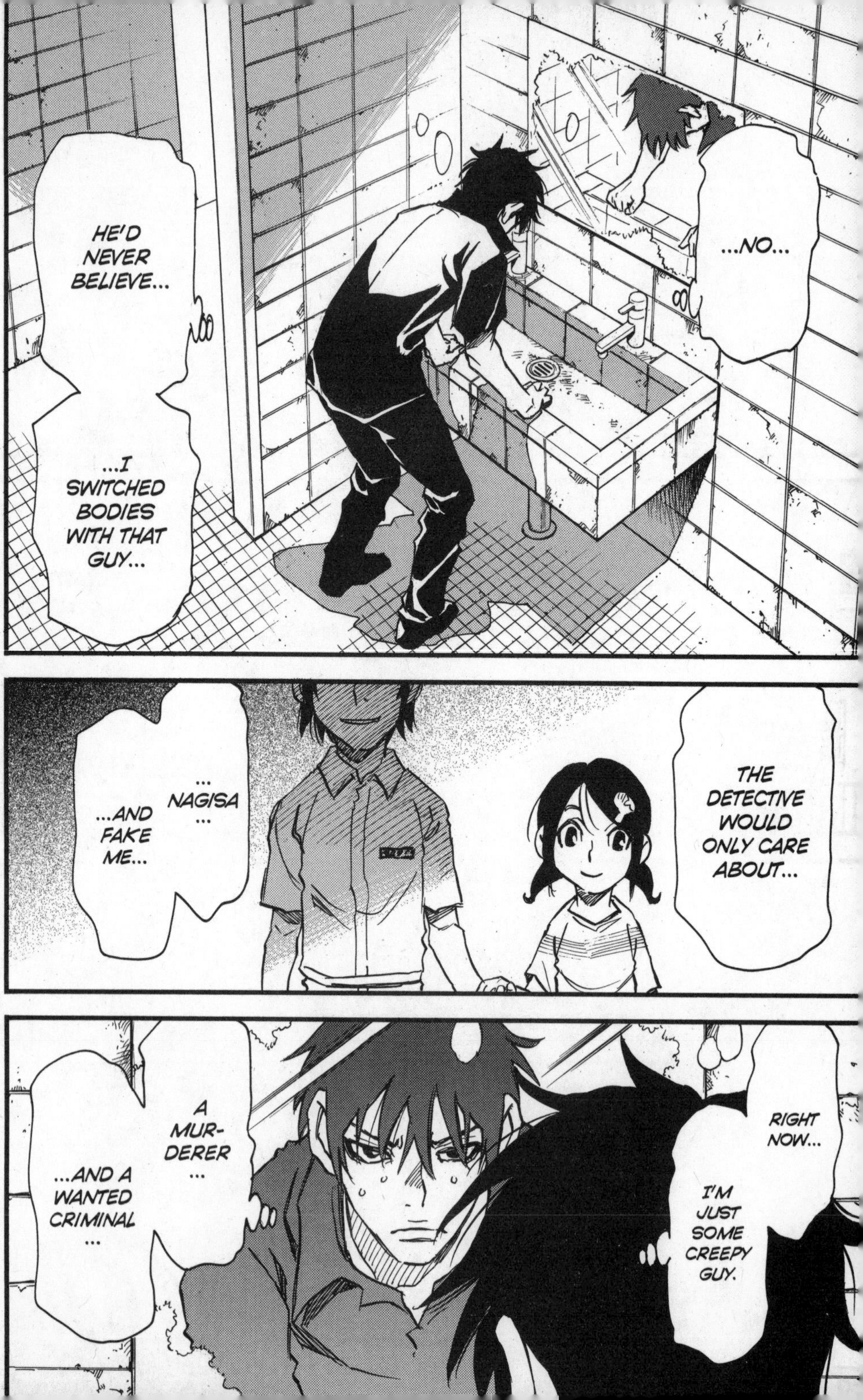
...NO...
HE'D NEVER BELIEVE...
...I SWITCHED BODIES WITH THAT GUY...
THE DETECTIVE WOULD ONLY CARE ABOUT...
...NAGISA...
...AND FAKE ME...
RIGHT NOW...
I'M JUST SOME CREEPY GUY.
A MURDERER...
...AND A WANTED CRIMINAL...

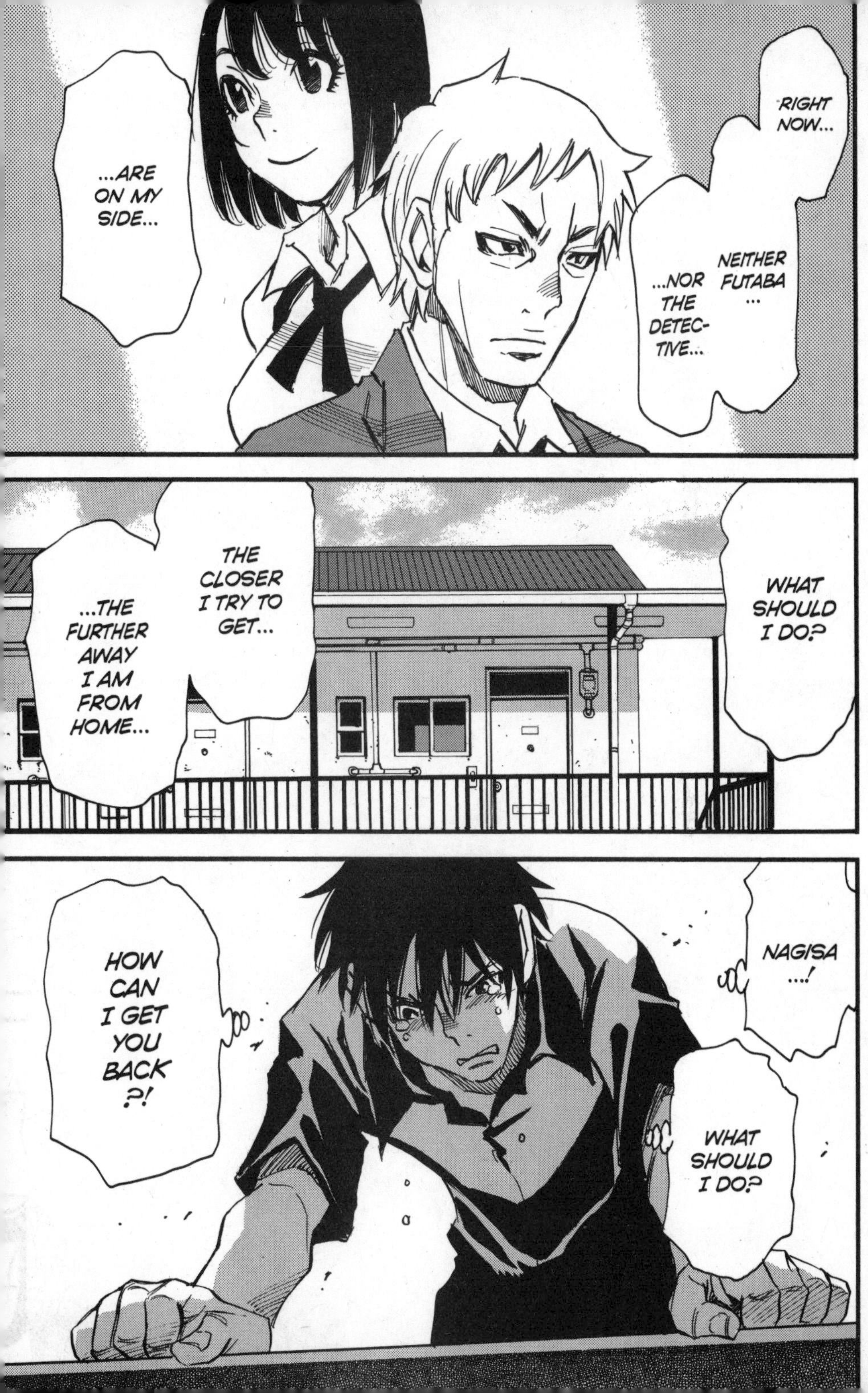
RIGHT NOW...
NEITHER FUTABA ...
...NOR THE DETECTIVE...
...ARE ON MY SIDE...
WHAT SHOULD I DO?
THE CLOSER I TRY TO GET...
...THE FURTHER AWAY I AM FROM HOME...
NAGISA ...!
WHAT SHOULD I DO?
HOW CAN I GET YOU BACK ?!

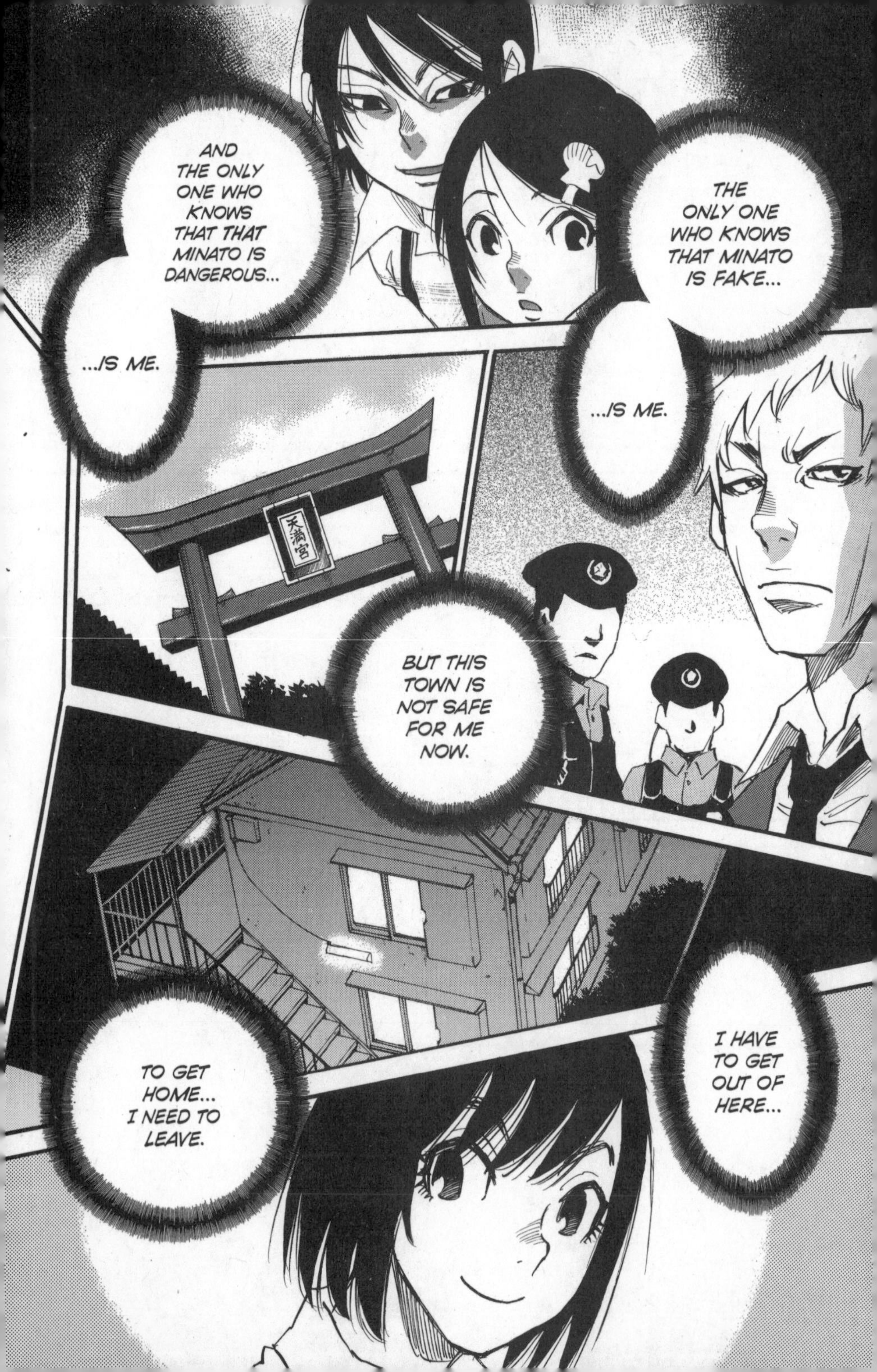

THE ONLY ONE WHO KNOWS THAT MINATO IS FAKE...
...IS ME.
AND THE ONLY ONE WHO KNOWS THAT THAT MINATO IS DANGEROUS...
...IS ME.
BUT THIS TOWN IS NOT SAFE FOR ME NOW.
I HAVE TO GET OUT OF HERE...
TO GET HOME... I NEED TO LEAVE.

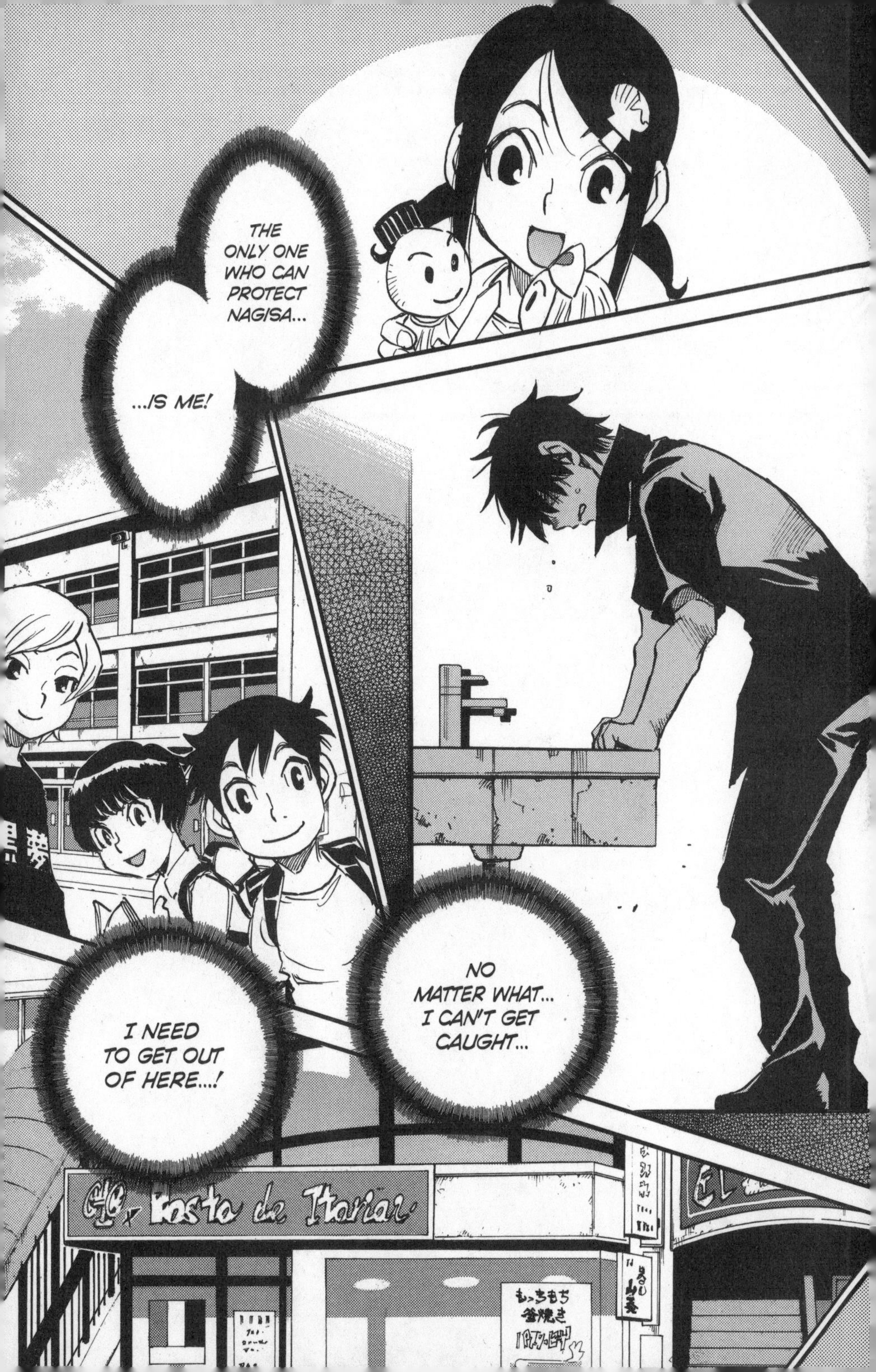
THE ONLY ONE WHO CAN PROTECT NAGISA...
...IS ME!
NO MATTER WHAT... I CAN'T GET CAUGHT...
I NEED TO GET OUT OF HERE...!

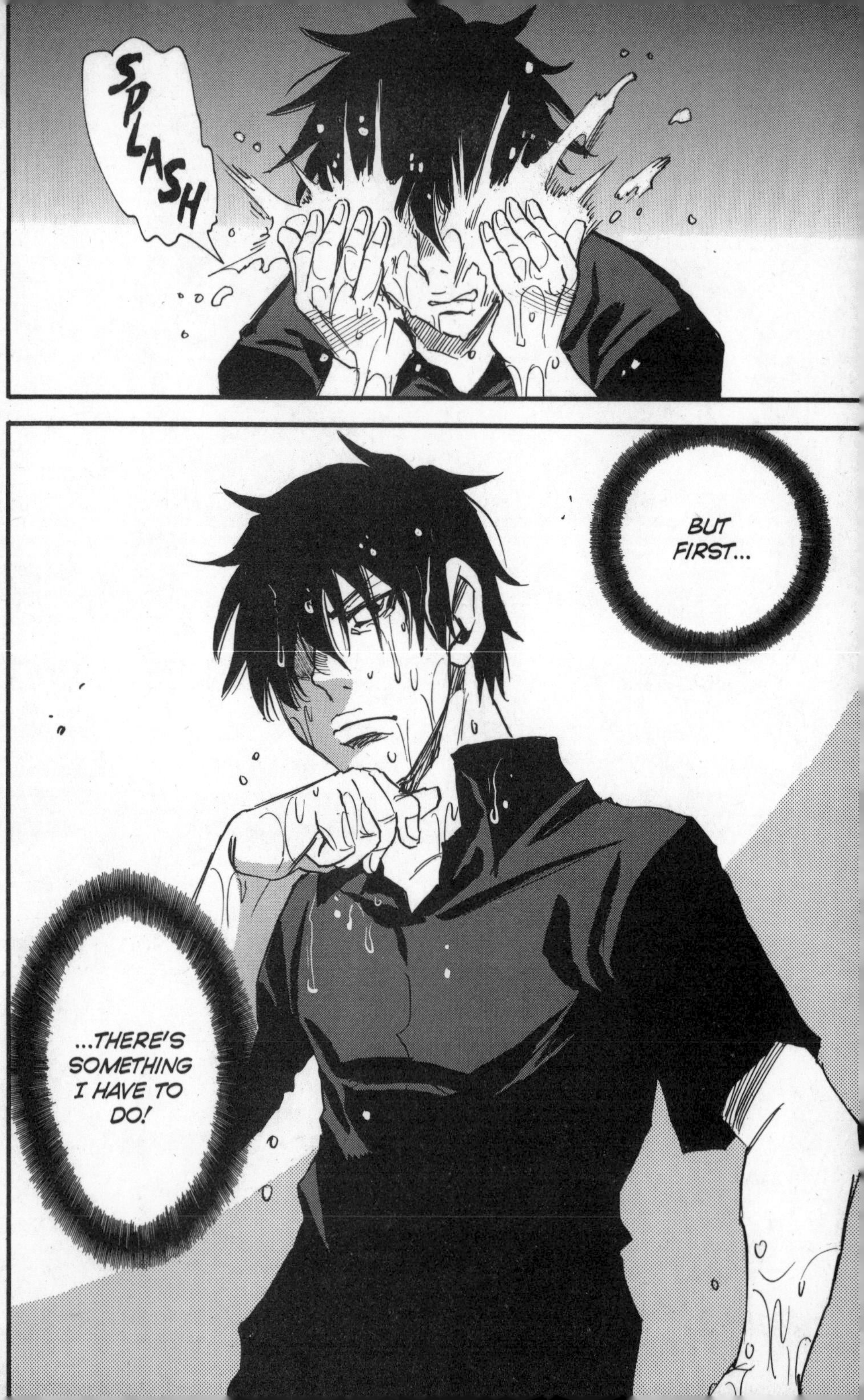
SPLASH
BUT FIRST...
...THERE'S SOMETHING I HAVE TO DO!

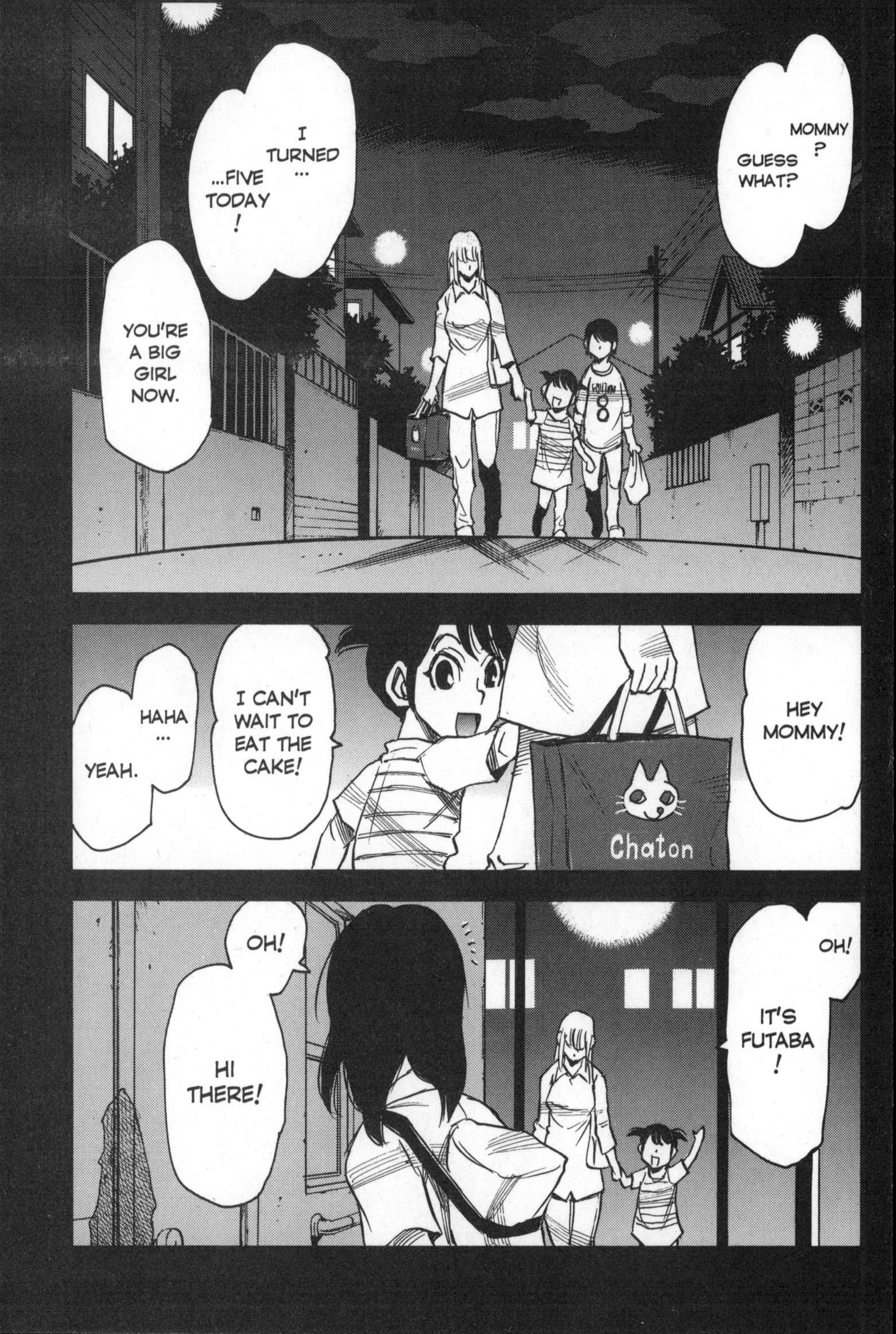
MOMMY? GUESS WHAT?
I TURNED... ...FIVE TODAY!
YOU'RE A BIG GIRL NOW.
HEY MOMMY!
Chaton
I CAN'T WAIT TO EAT THE CAKE!
HAHA... YEAH.
OH! IT'S FUTABA!
OH! HI THERE!

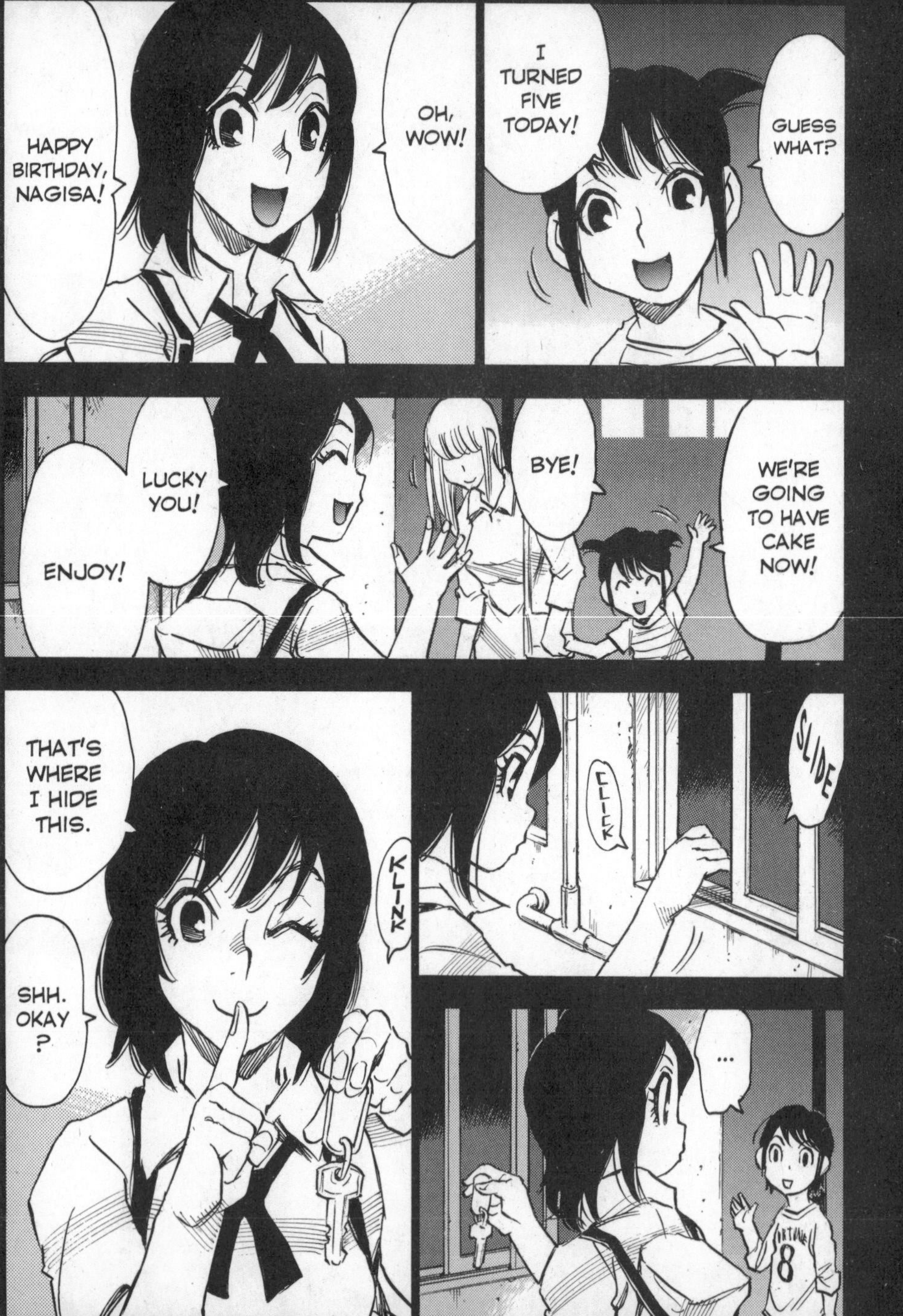
GUESS WHAT?
I TURNED FIVE TODAY!
OH, WOW!
HAPPY BIRTHDAY, NAGISA!
WE'RE GOING TO HAVE CAKE NOW!
BYE!
LUCKY YOU!
ENJOY!
SLIDE
CLICK
...
THAT'S WHERE I HIDE THIS.
KLINK
SHH. OKAY?

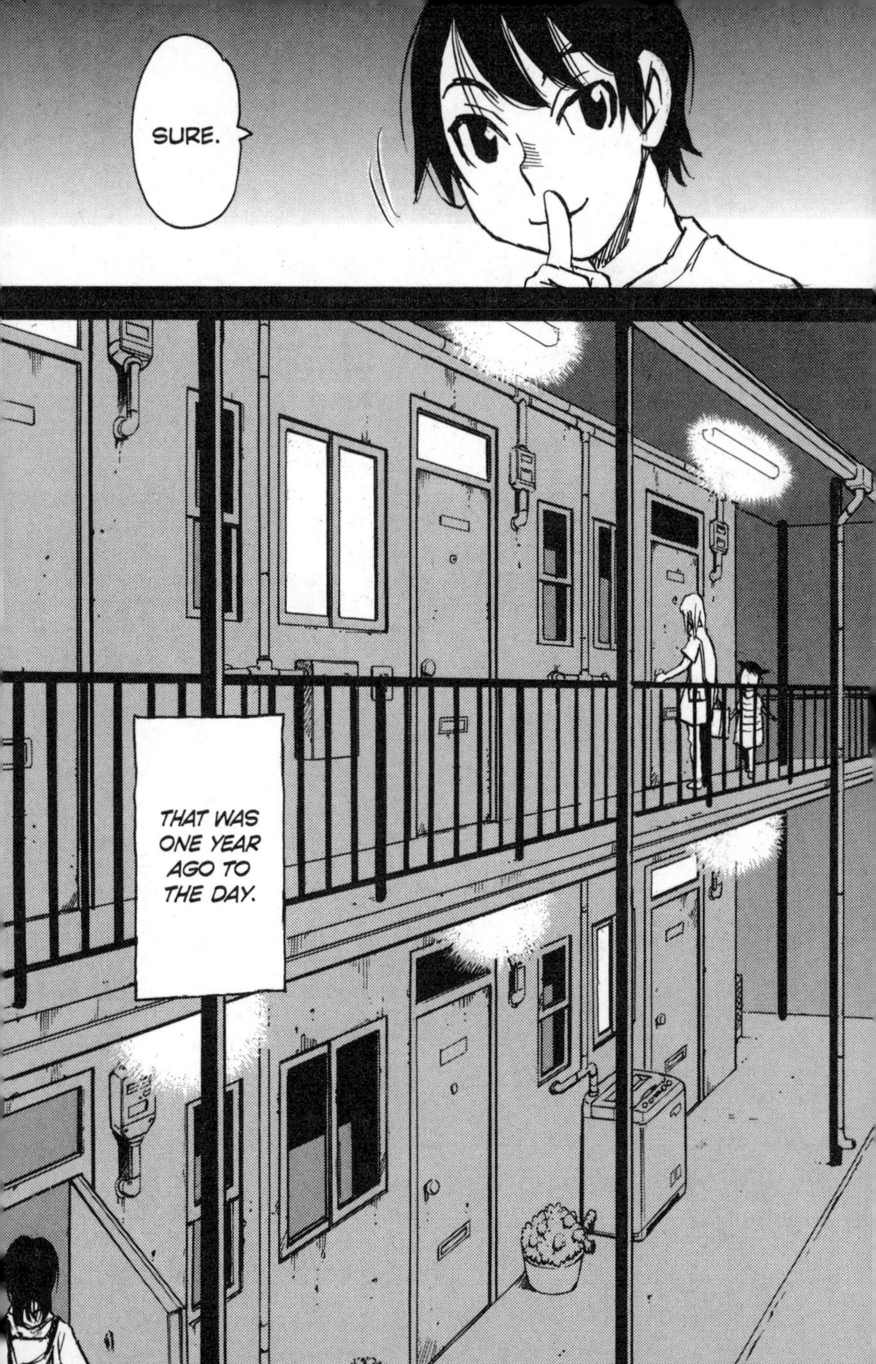
SURE.
THAT WAS ONE YEAR AGO TO THE DAY.

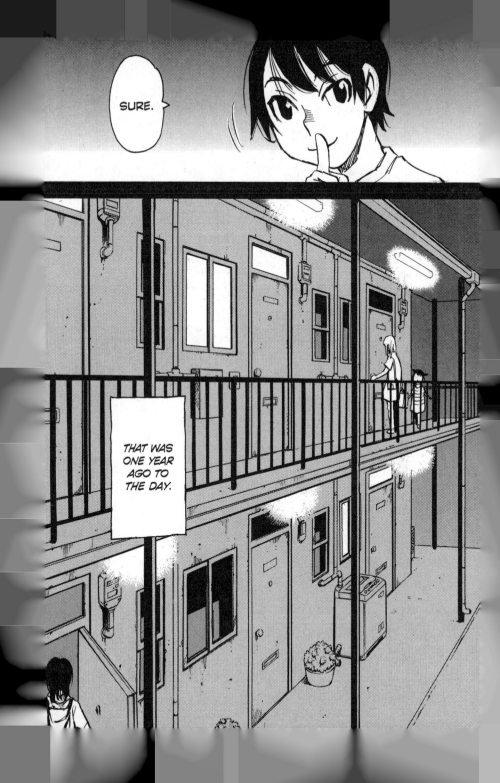

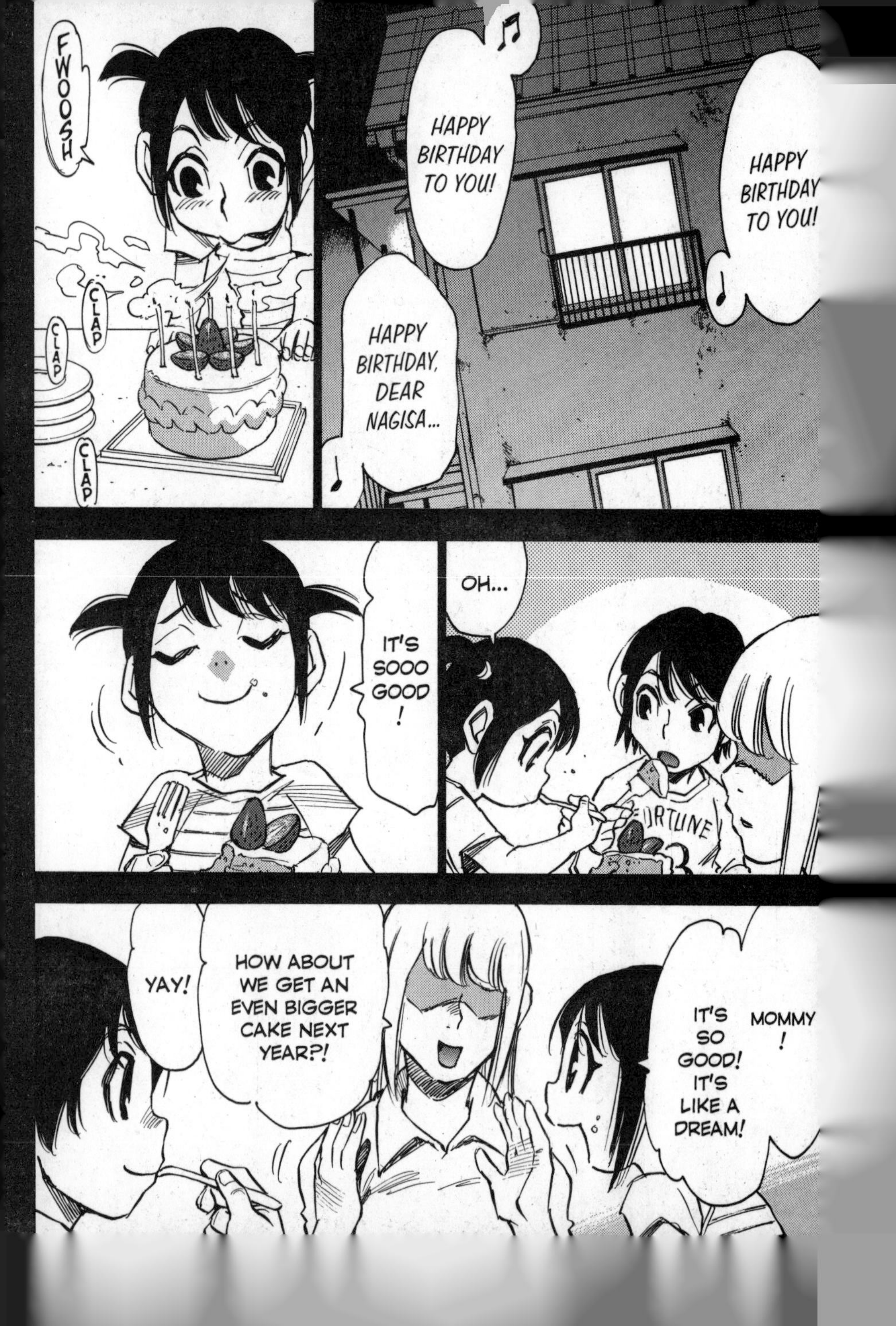
HAPPY BIRTHDAY TO YOU!
HAPPY BIRTHDAY TO YOU!
HAPPY BIRTHDAY, DEAR NAGISA...
FWOOSH
CLAP
CLAP
CLAP
OH...
IT'S SOOO GOOD!
MOMMY!
IT'S SO GOOD! IT'S LIKE A DREAM!
HOW ABOUT WE GET AN EVEN BIGGER CAKE NEXT YEAR?!
YAY!

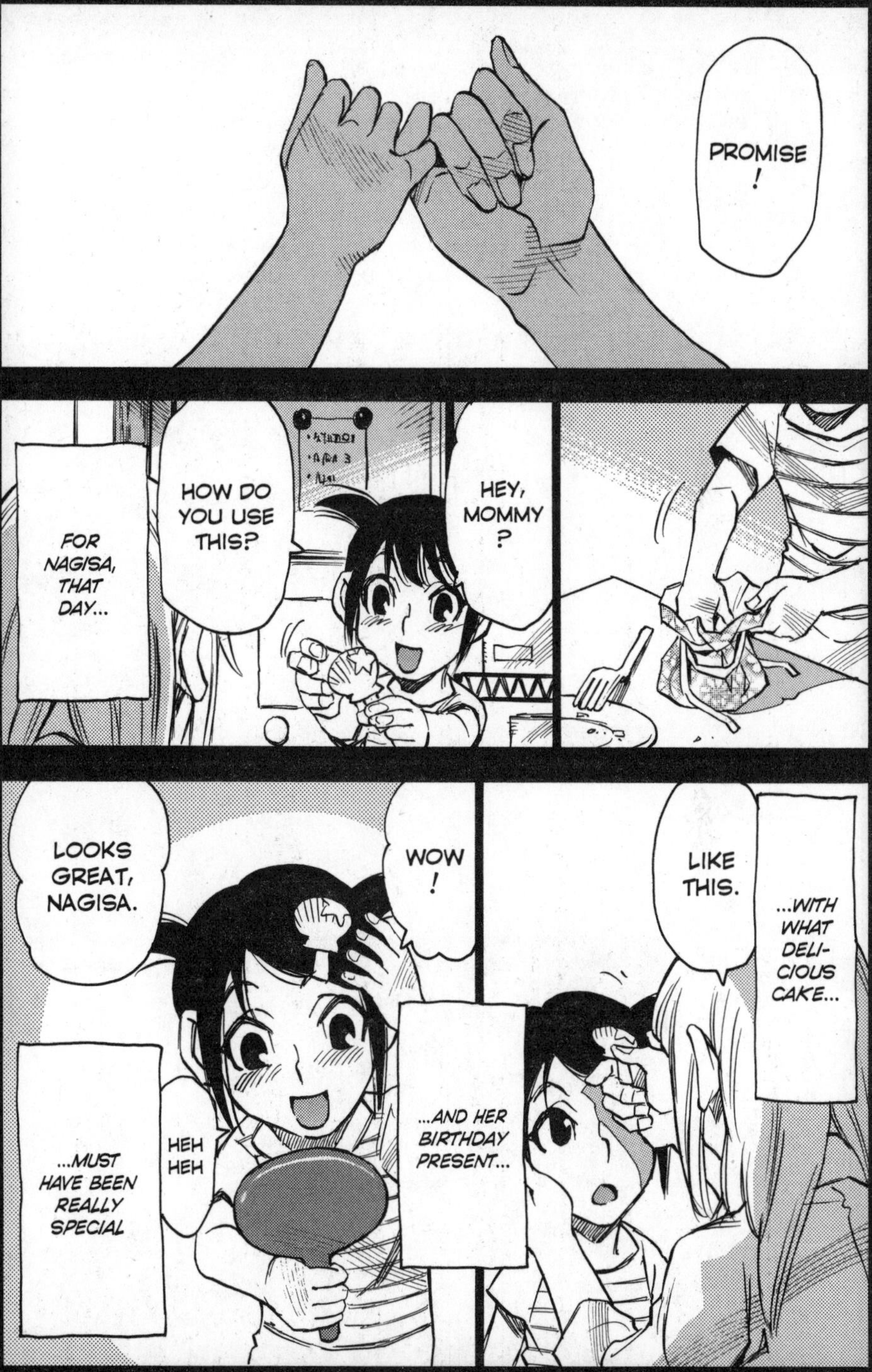
PROMISE!
HEY, MOMMY?
HOW DO YOU USE THIS?
FOR NAGISA, THAT DAY...
...WITH WHAT DELICIOUS CAKE...
LIKE THIS.
...AND HER BIRTHDAY PRESENT...
WOW!
LOOKS GREAT, NAGISA.
HEH HEH
...MUST HAVE BEEN REALLY SPECIAL

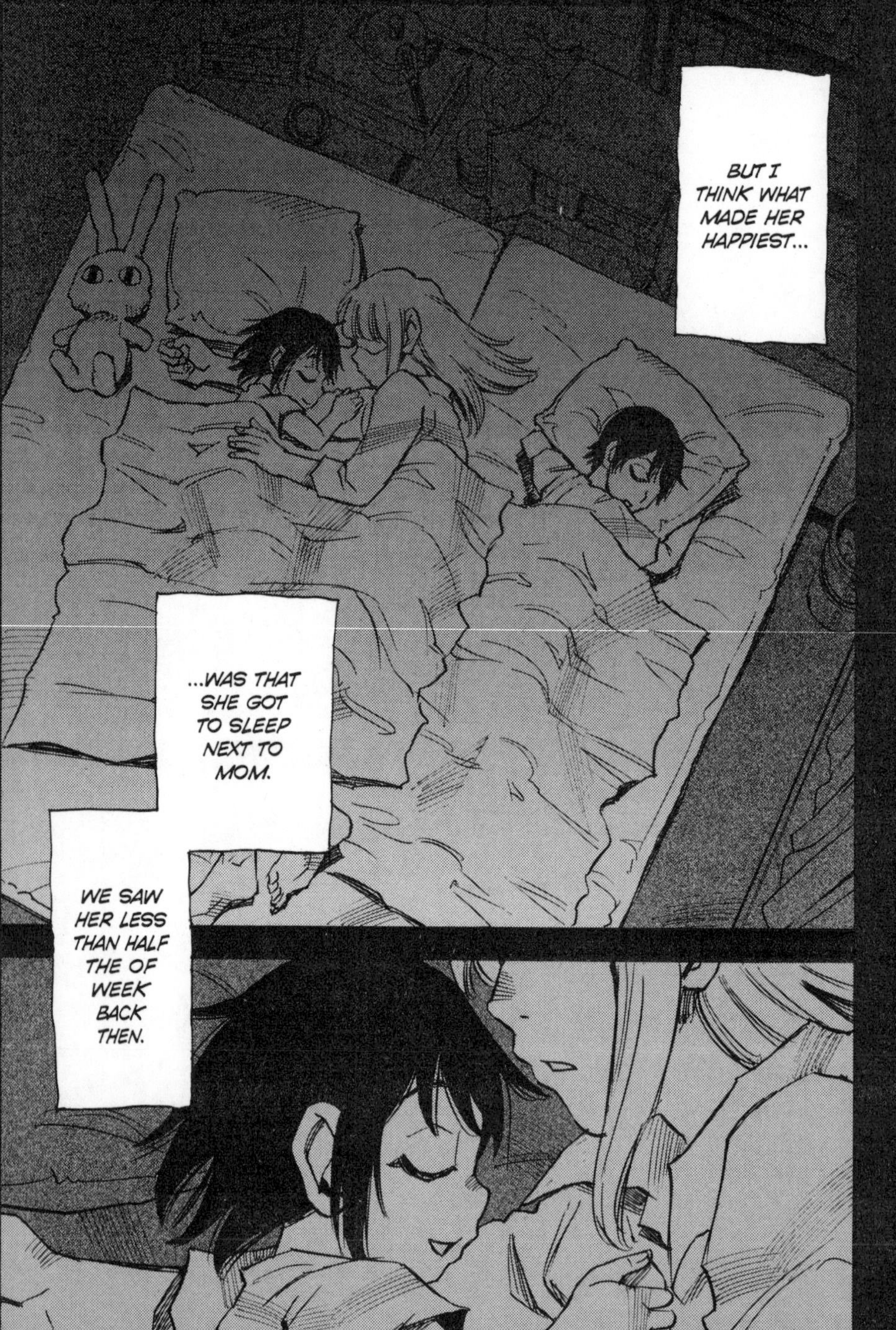
BUT I THINK WHAT MADE HER HAPPIEST...
...WAS THAT SHE GOT TO SLEEP NEXT TO MOM.
WE SAW HER LESS THAN HALF THE OF WEEK BACK THEN.

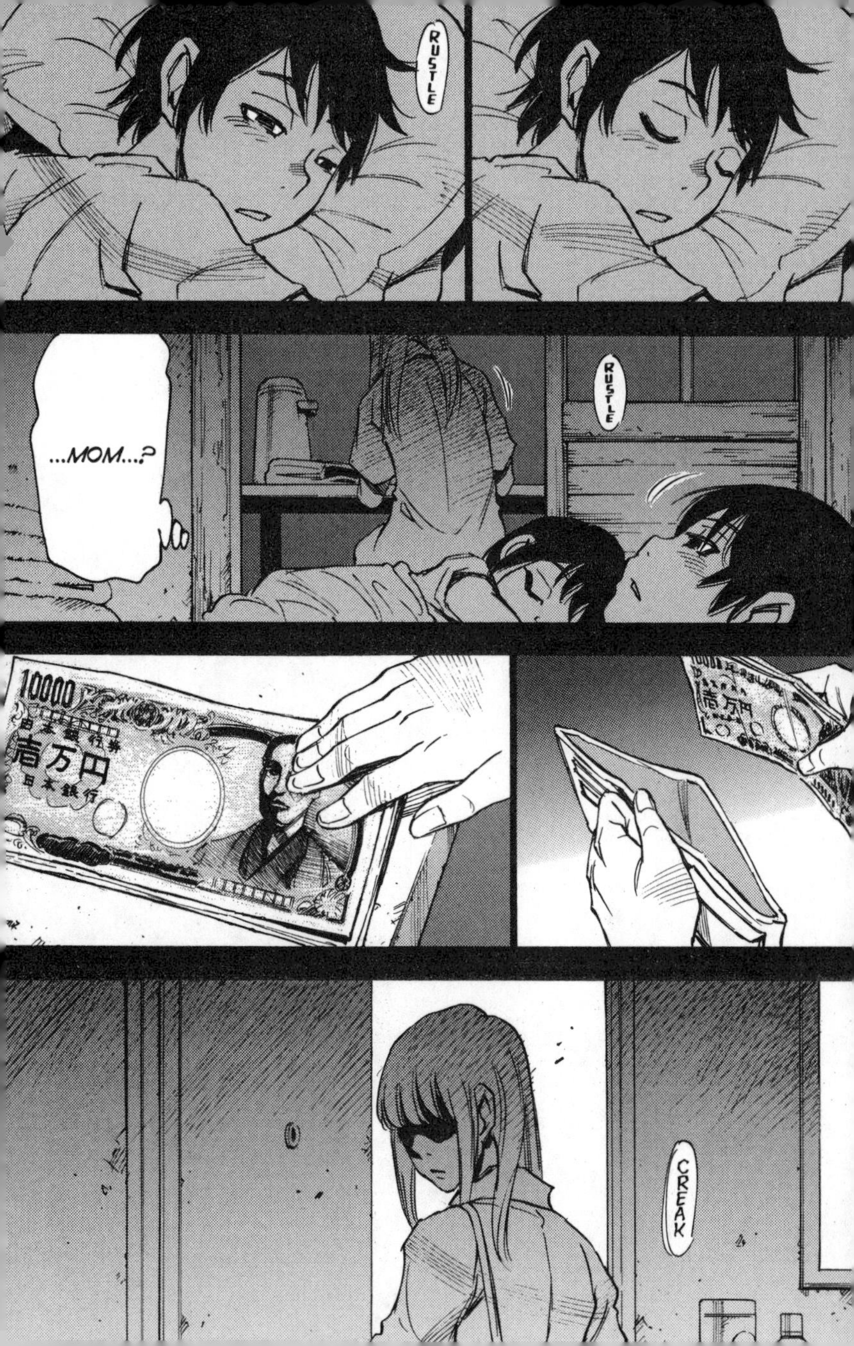
RUSTLE
RUSTLE
...MOM...?
CREAK

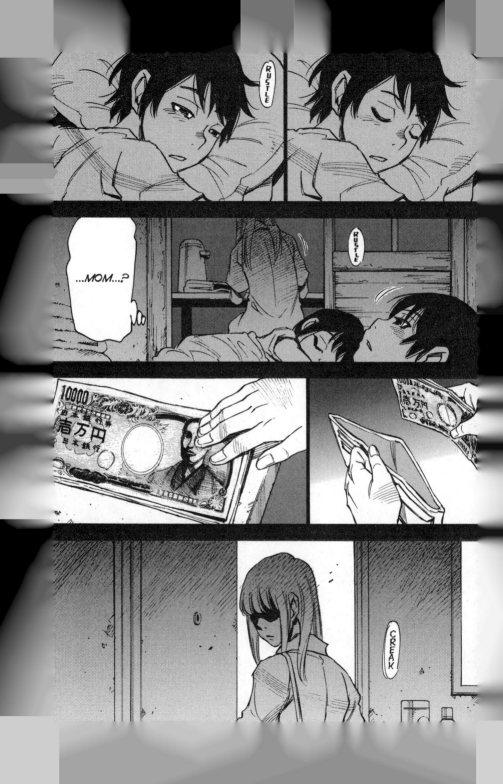

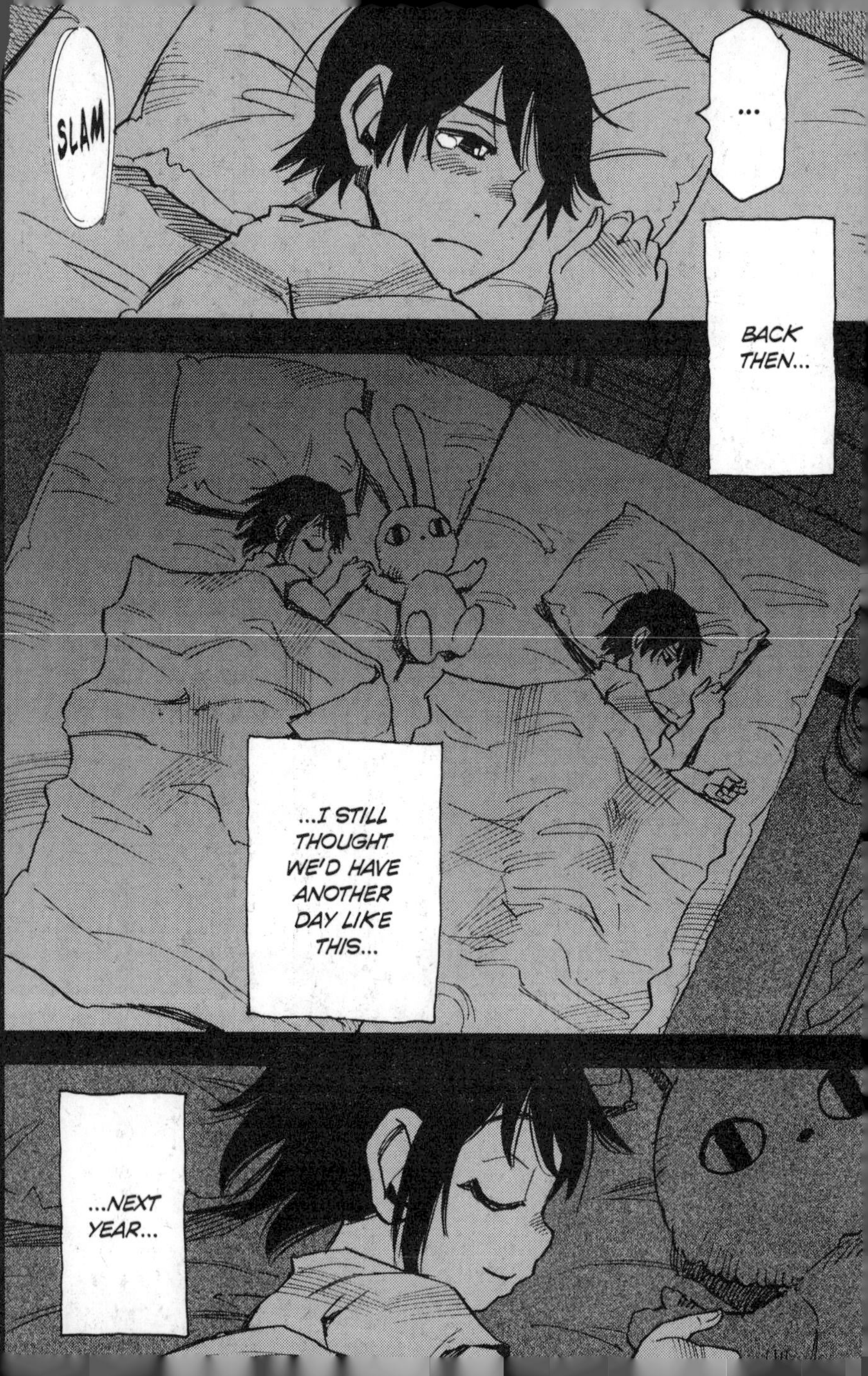
...
SLAM
BACK THEN...
...I STILL THOUGHT WE'D HAVE ANOTHER DAY LIKE THIS...
...NEXT YEAR...

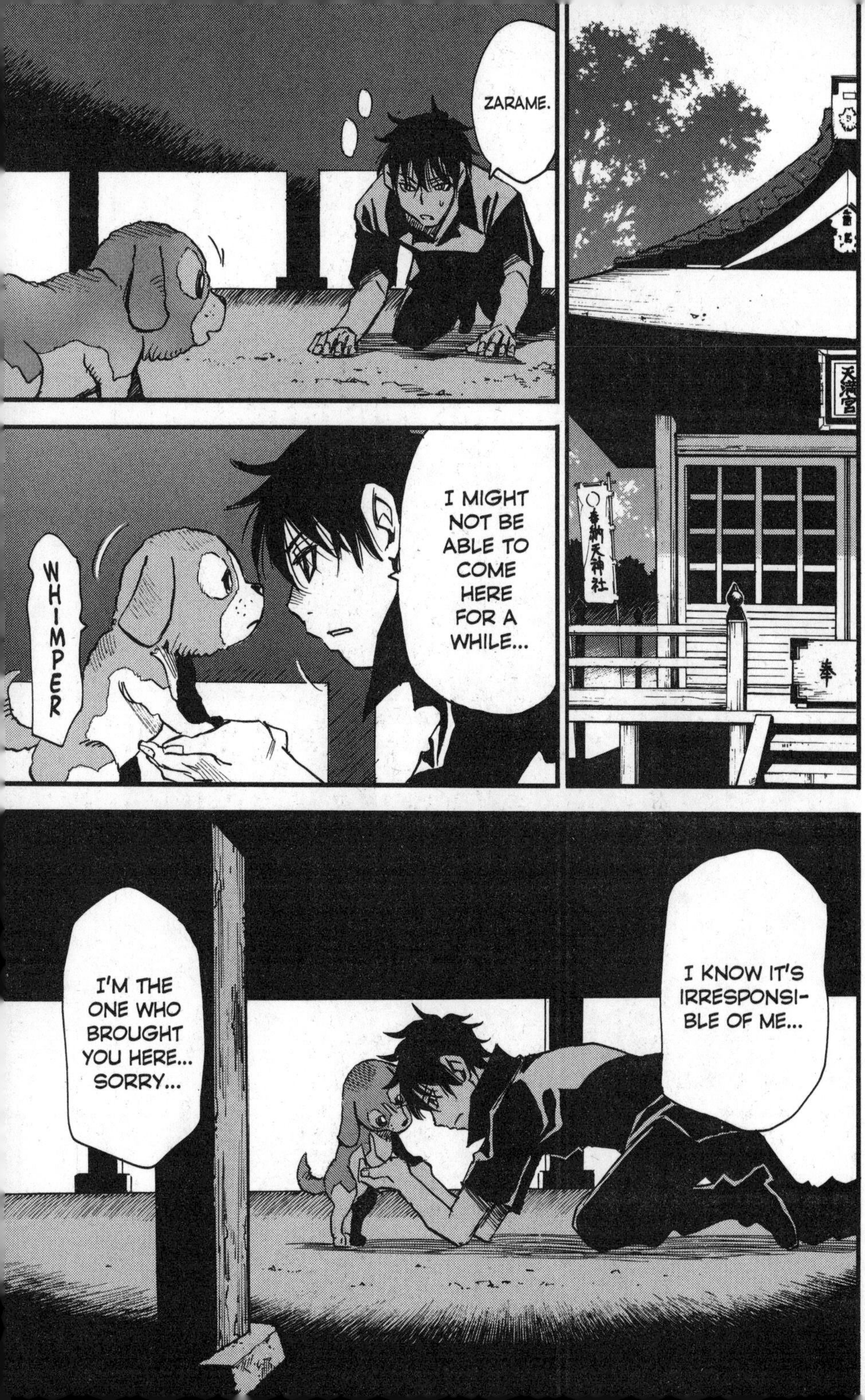
ZARAME.
I MIGHT NOT BE ABLE TO COME HERE FOR A WHILE...
WHIMPER
I KNOW IT'S IRRESPONSI-BLE OF ME...
I'M THE ONE WHO BROUGHT YOU HERE... SORRY...

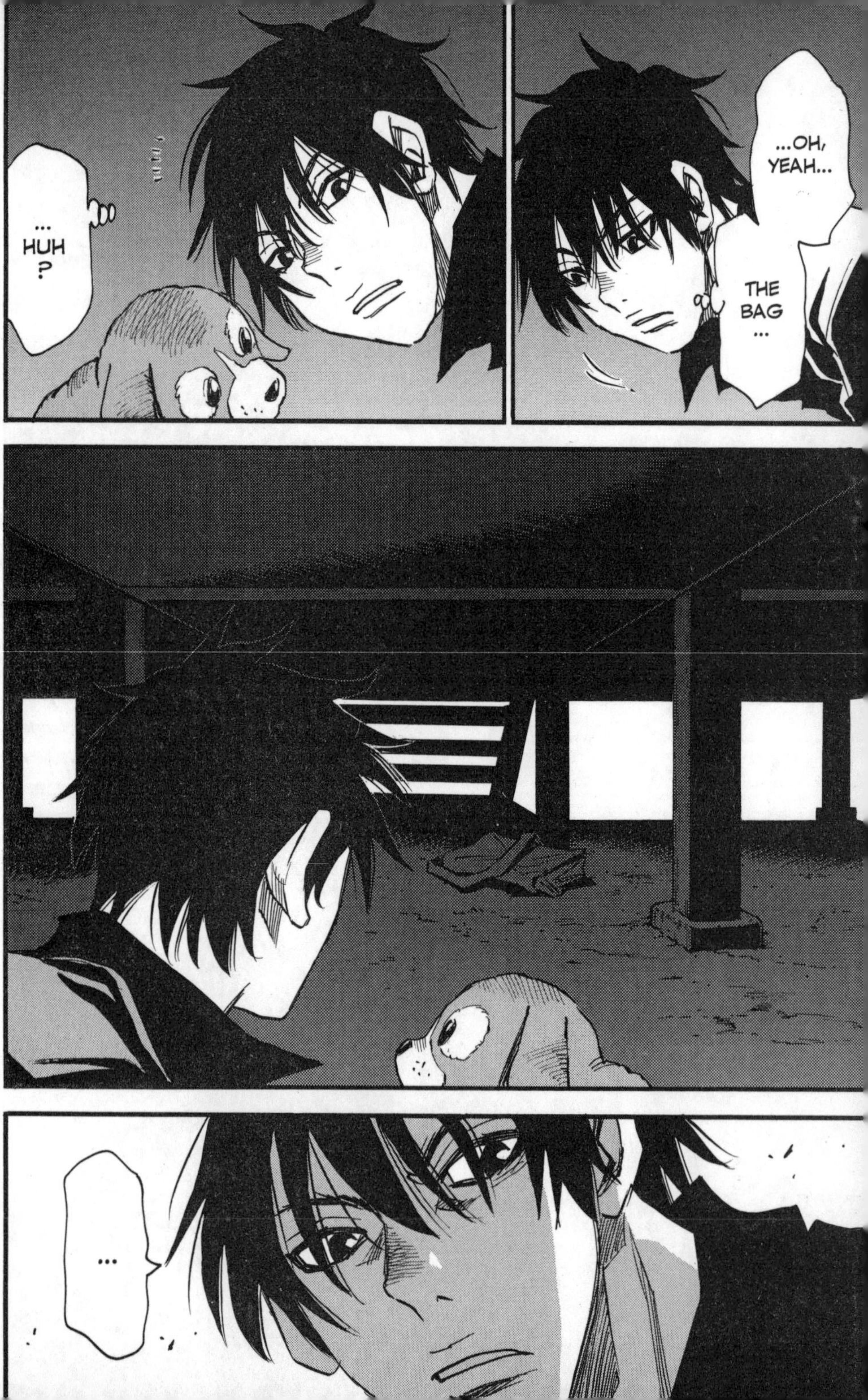
...OH, YEAH...
THE BAG ...
... HUH ?
...

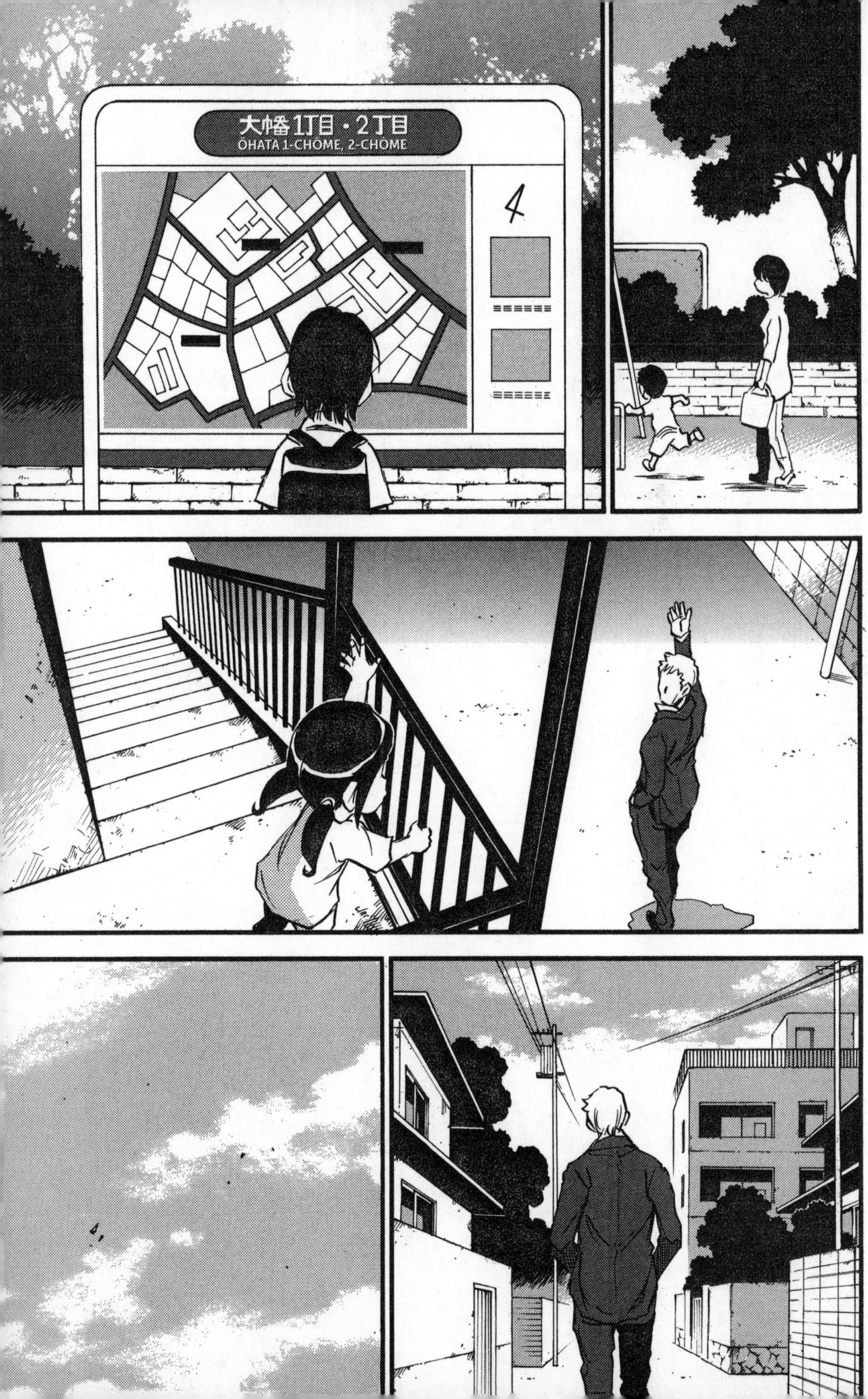
大幡1丁目・2丁目
OHATA 1-CHOME, 2-CHOME
4

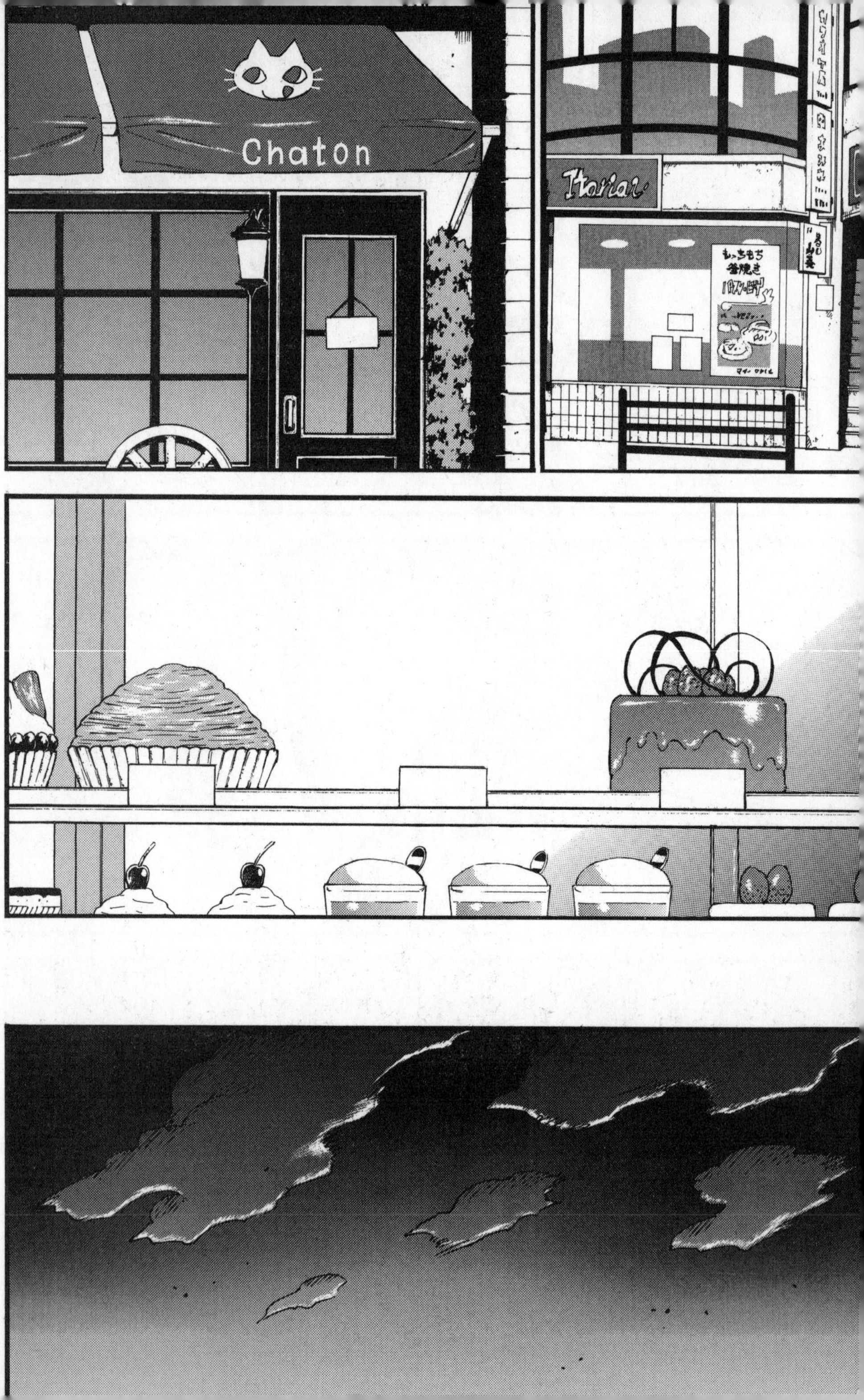
Itarian
もっちもち
釜焼き
パスタ・ピザ
Chaton

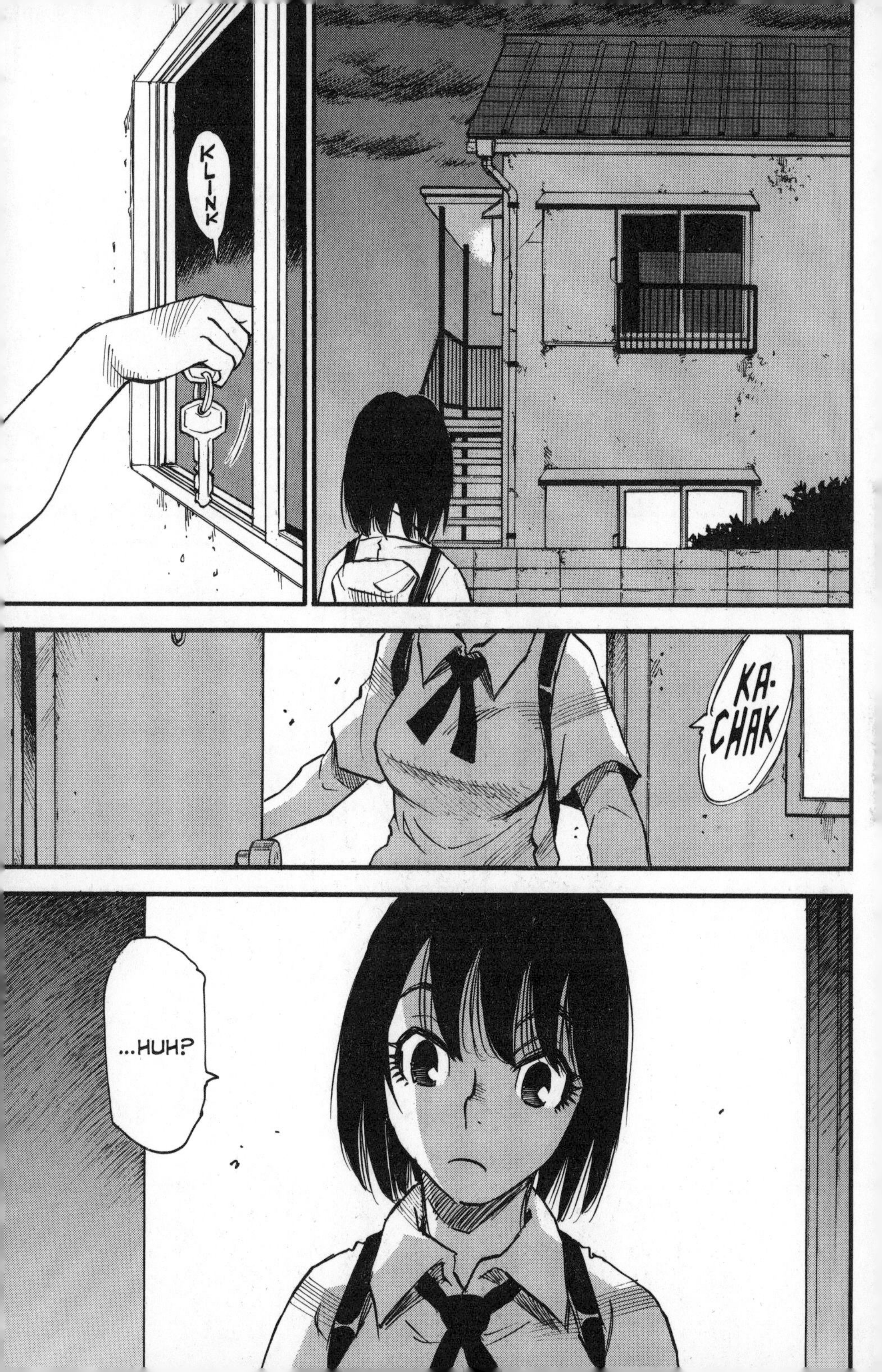
KLINK
KA-CHAK
...HUH?

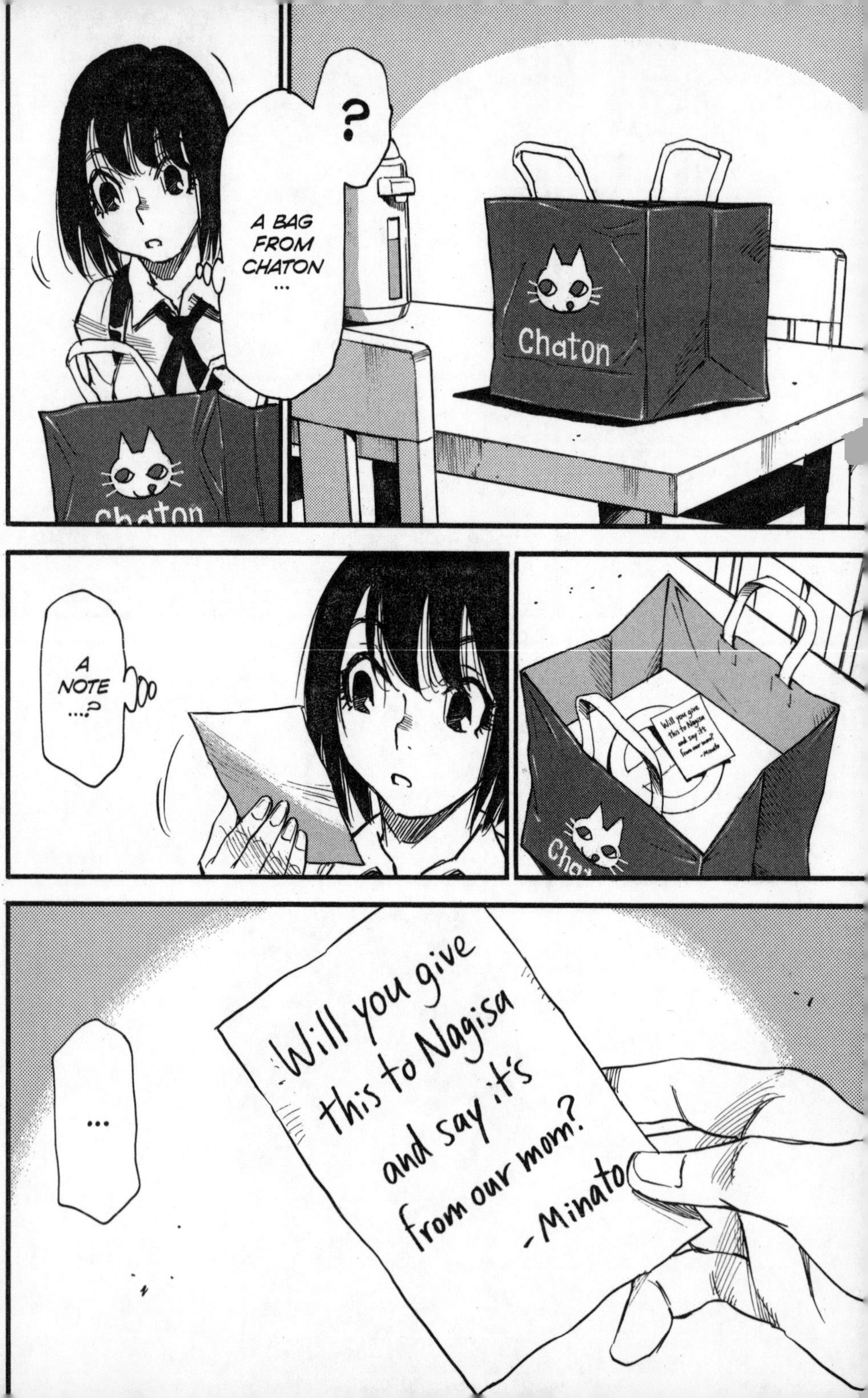
?
A BAG FROM CHATON ...
Chaton
A NOTE ...?
...
Will you give this to Nagisa and say it's from our mom?
-Minato

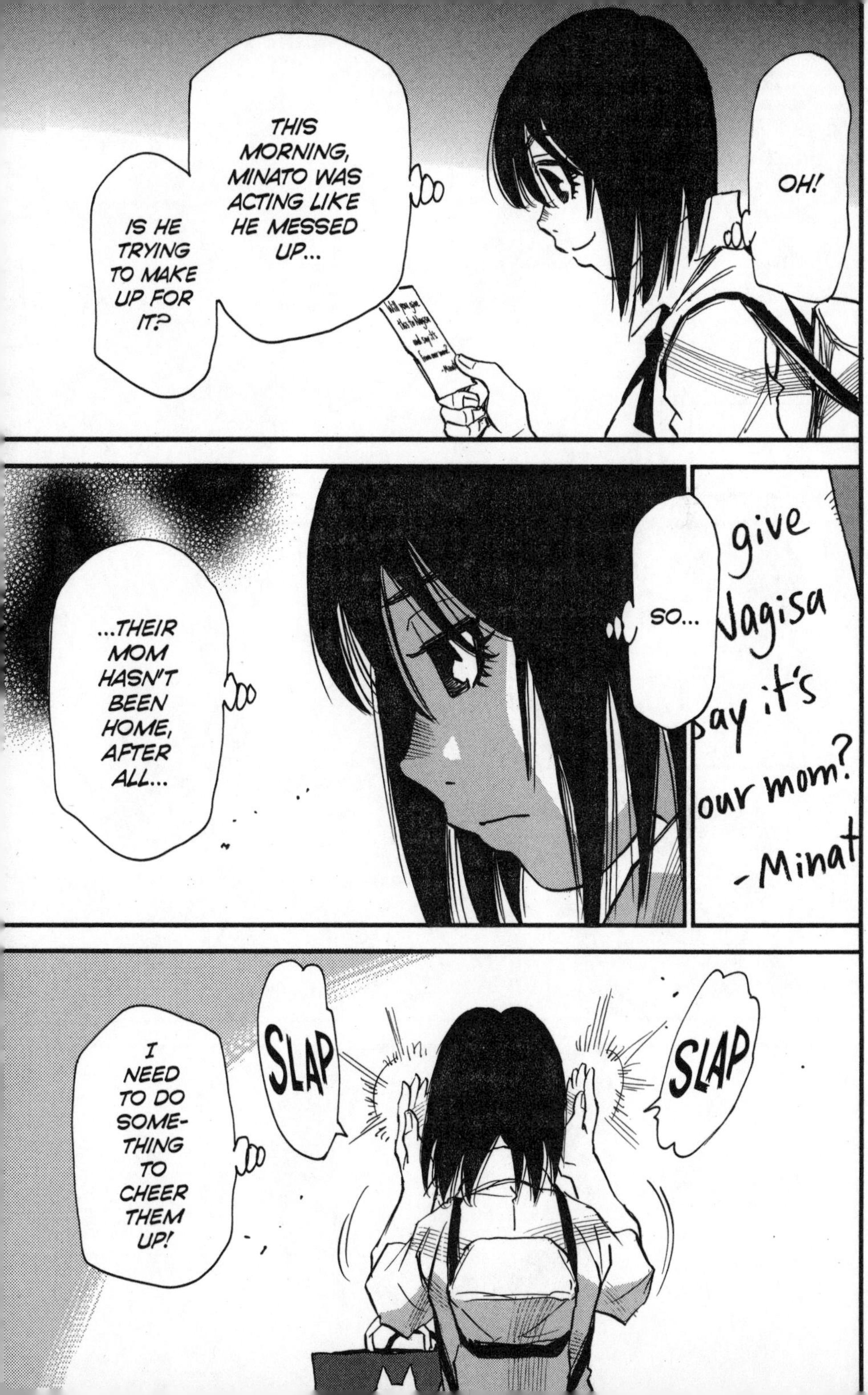
OH!
THIS MORNING, MINATO WAS ACTING LIKE HE MESSED UP...
IS HE TRYING TO MAKE UP FOR IT?
SO...
give Nagisa say it's our mom? -Minat
...THEIR MOM HASN'T BEEN HOME, AFTER ALL...
SLAP
SLAP
I NEED TO DO SOME-THING TO CHEER THEM UP!

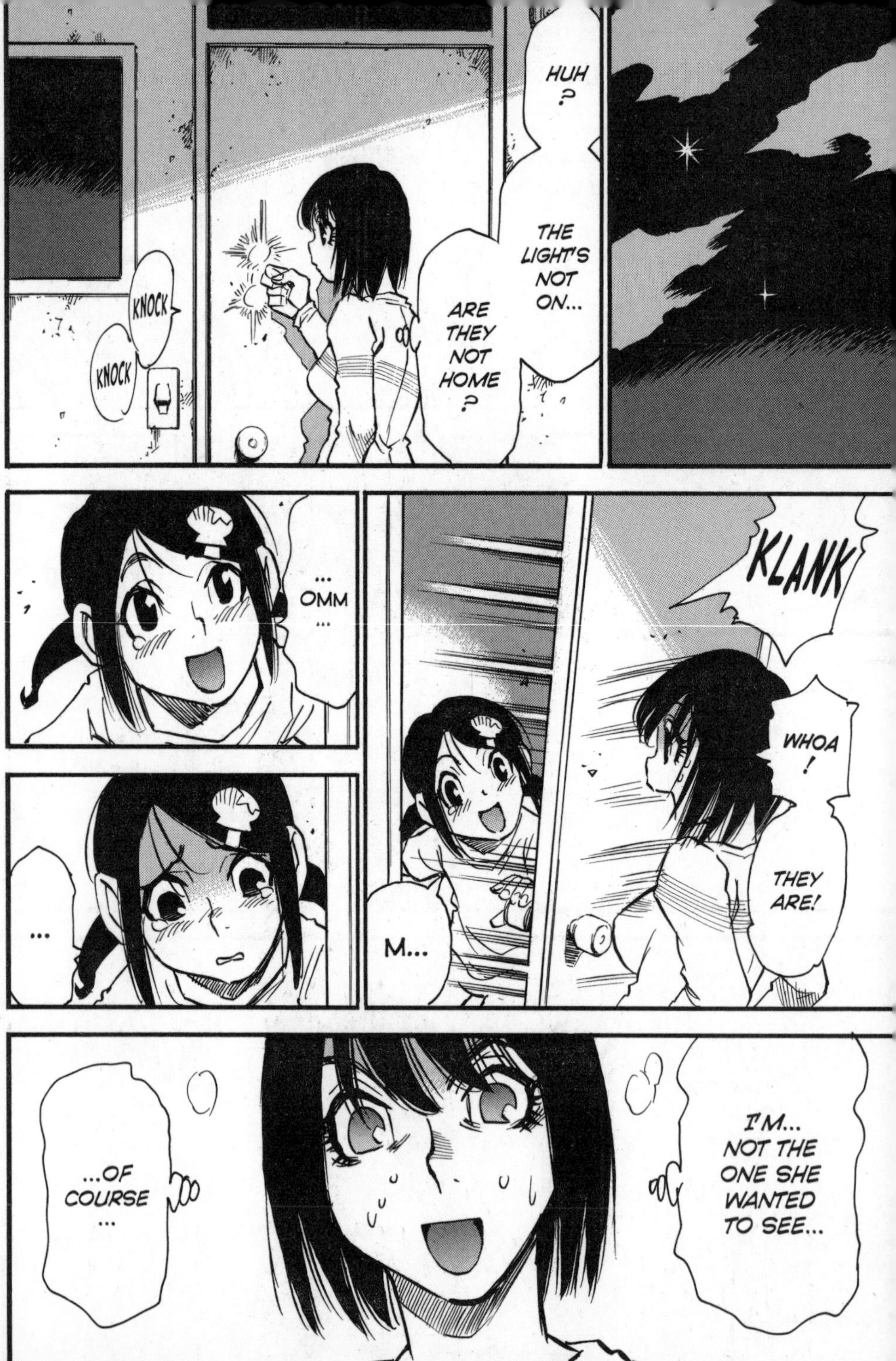
HUH?
THE LIGHT'S NOT ON...
ARE THEY NOT HOME?
KNOCK
KNOCK
KLANK
WHOA!
THEY ARE!
M...
...OMM...
...
I'M... NOT THE ONE SHE WANTED TO SEE...
...OF COURSE...

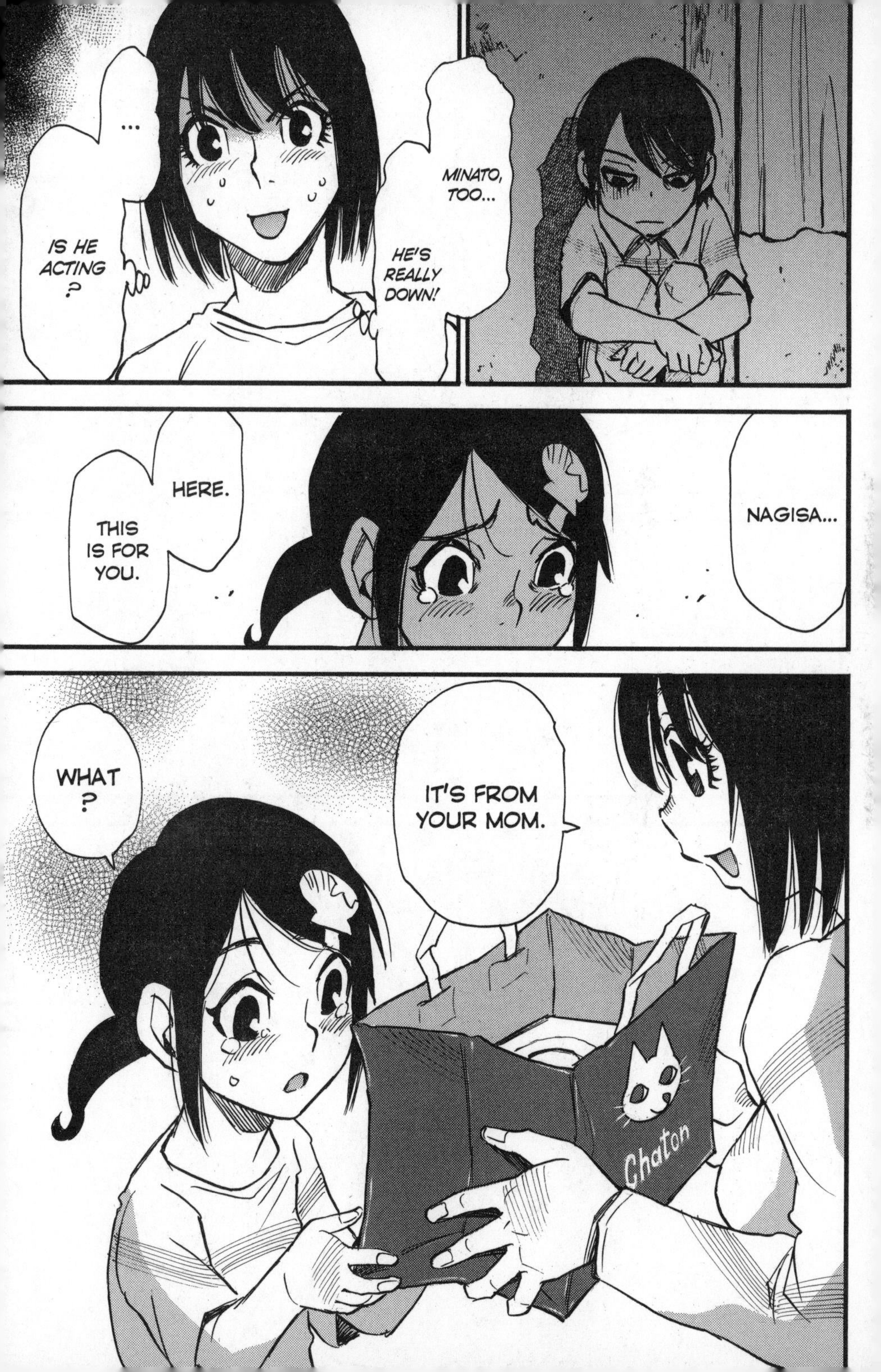
MINATO, TOO...
HE'S REALLY DOWN!
...
IS HE ACTING?
NAGISA...
HERE.
THIS IS FOR YOU.
IT'S FROM YOUR MOM.
WHAT?
Chaton

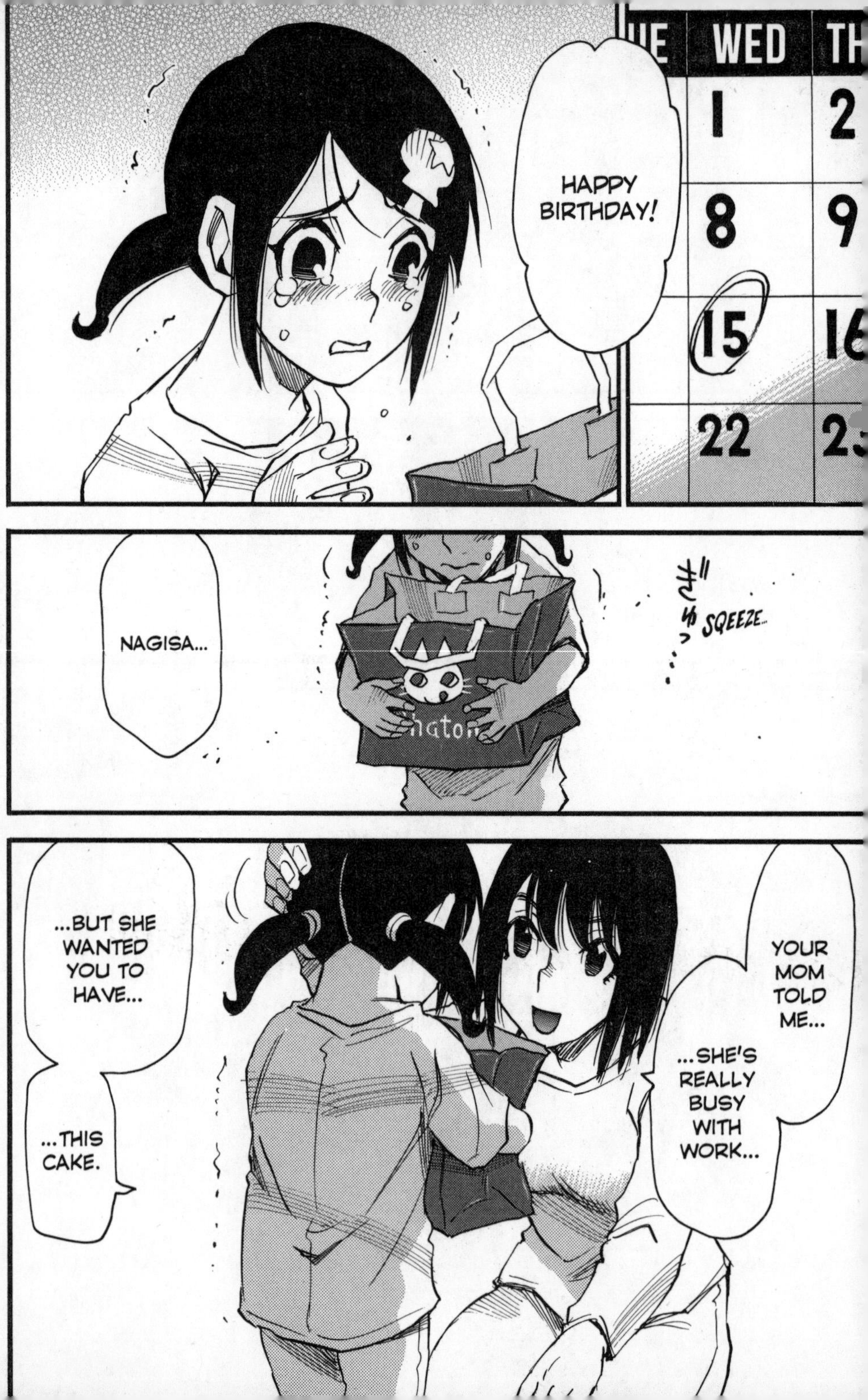
WED
1
2
8
9
15
22
HAPPY BIRTHDAY!
ぎゅっ SQEEZE...
NAGISA...
YOUR MOM TOLD ME...
...SHE'S REALLY BUSY WITH WORK...
...BUT SHE WANTED YOU TO HAVE...
...THIS CAKE.

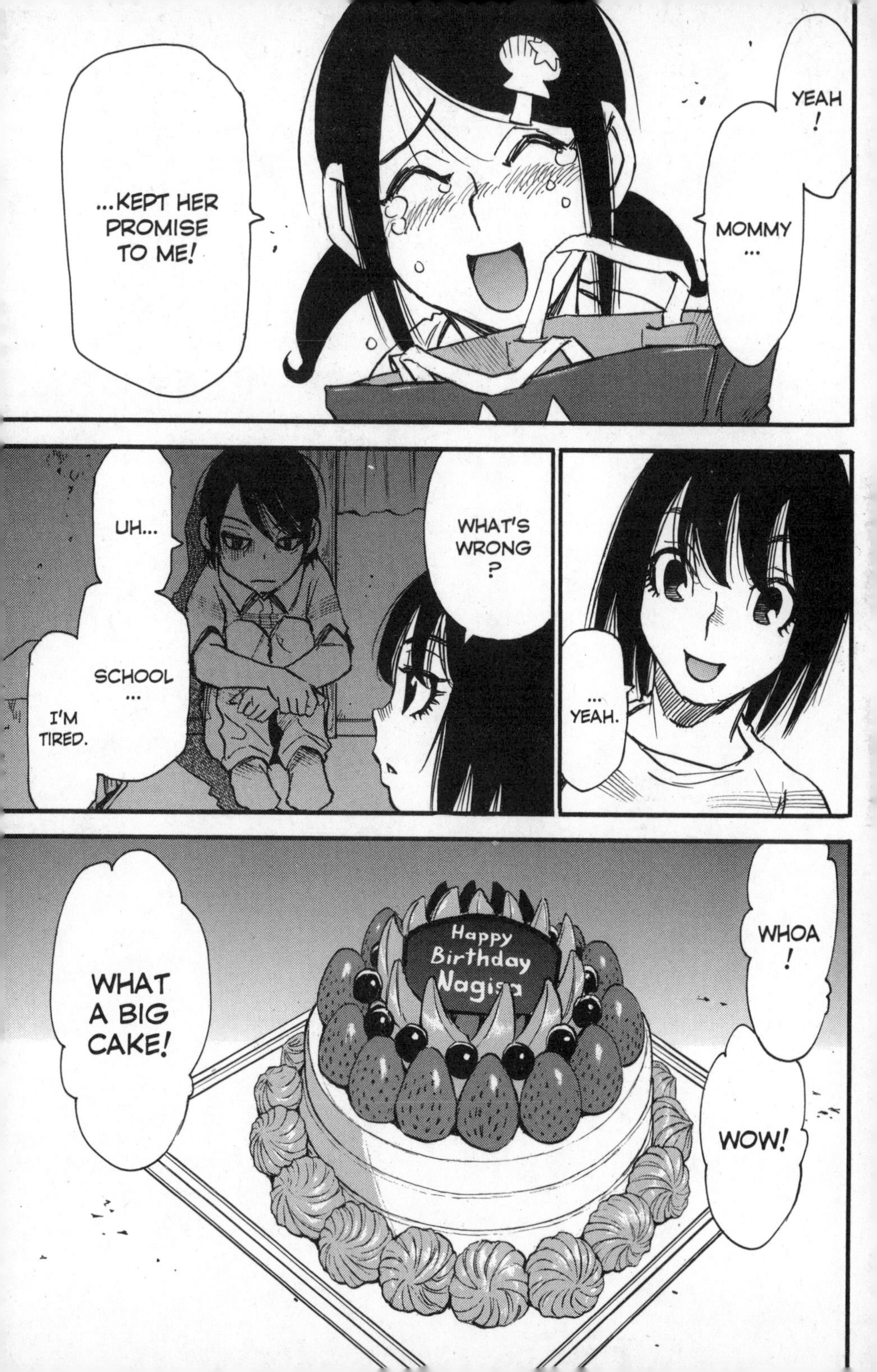
YEAH!
MOMMY...
...KEPT HER PROMISE TO ME!
...YEAH.
WHAT'S WRONG?
UH...
SCHOOL... I'M TIRED.
WHOA!
WOW!
Happy Birthday
WHAT A BIG CAKE!

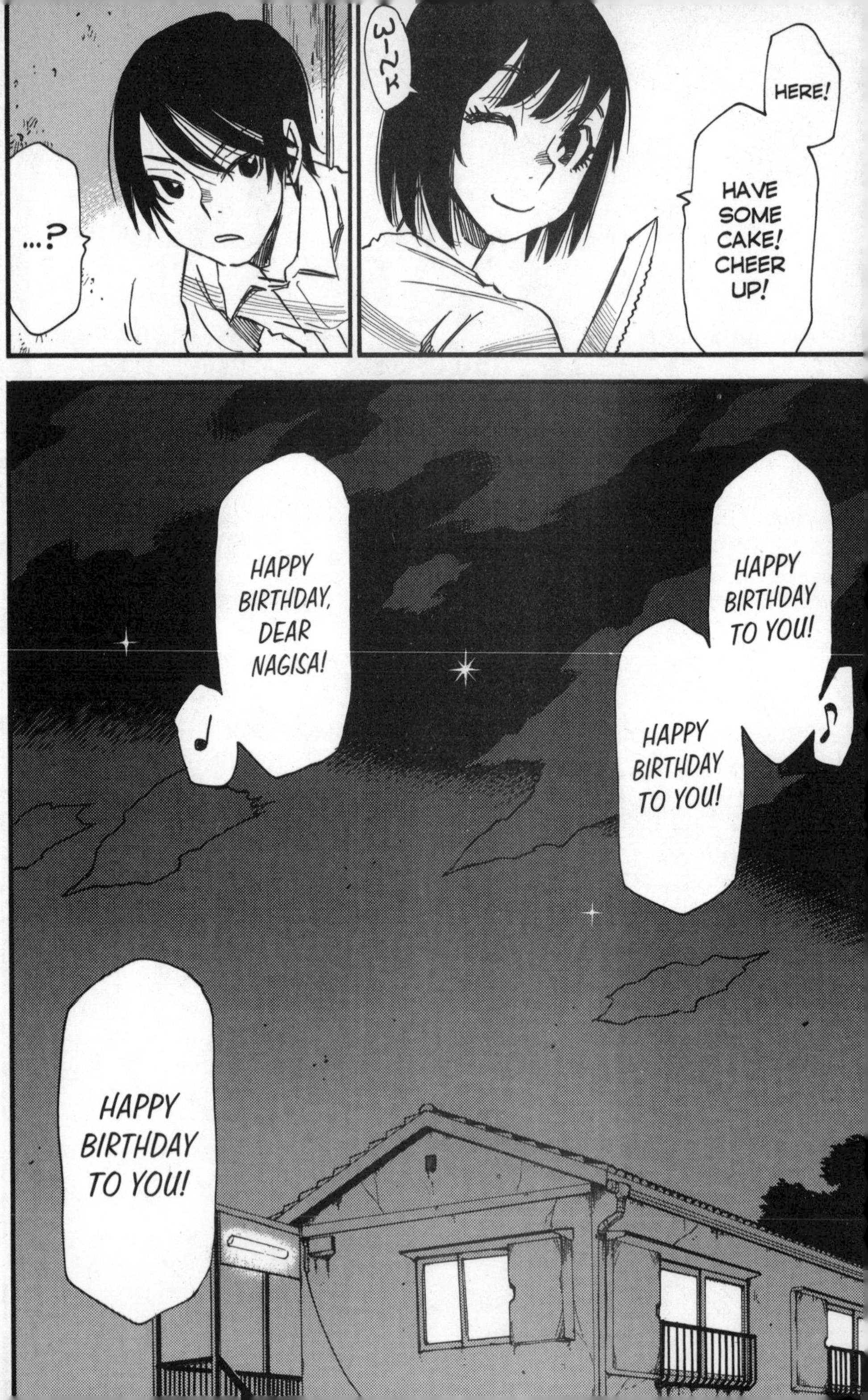
HERE!
HAVE SOME CAKE! CHEER UP!
...?
HAPPY BIRTHDAY TO YOU!
HAPPY BIRTHDAY TO YOU!
HAPPY BIRTHDAY, DEAR NAGISA!
HAPPY BIRTHDAY TO YOU!

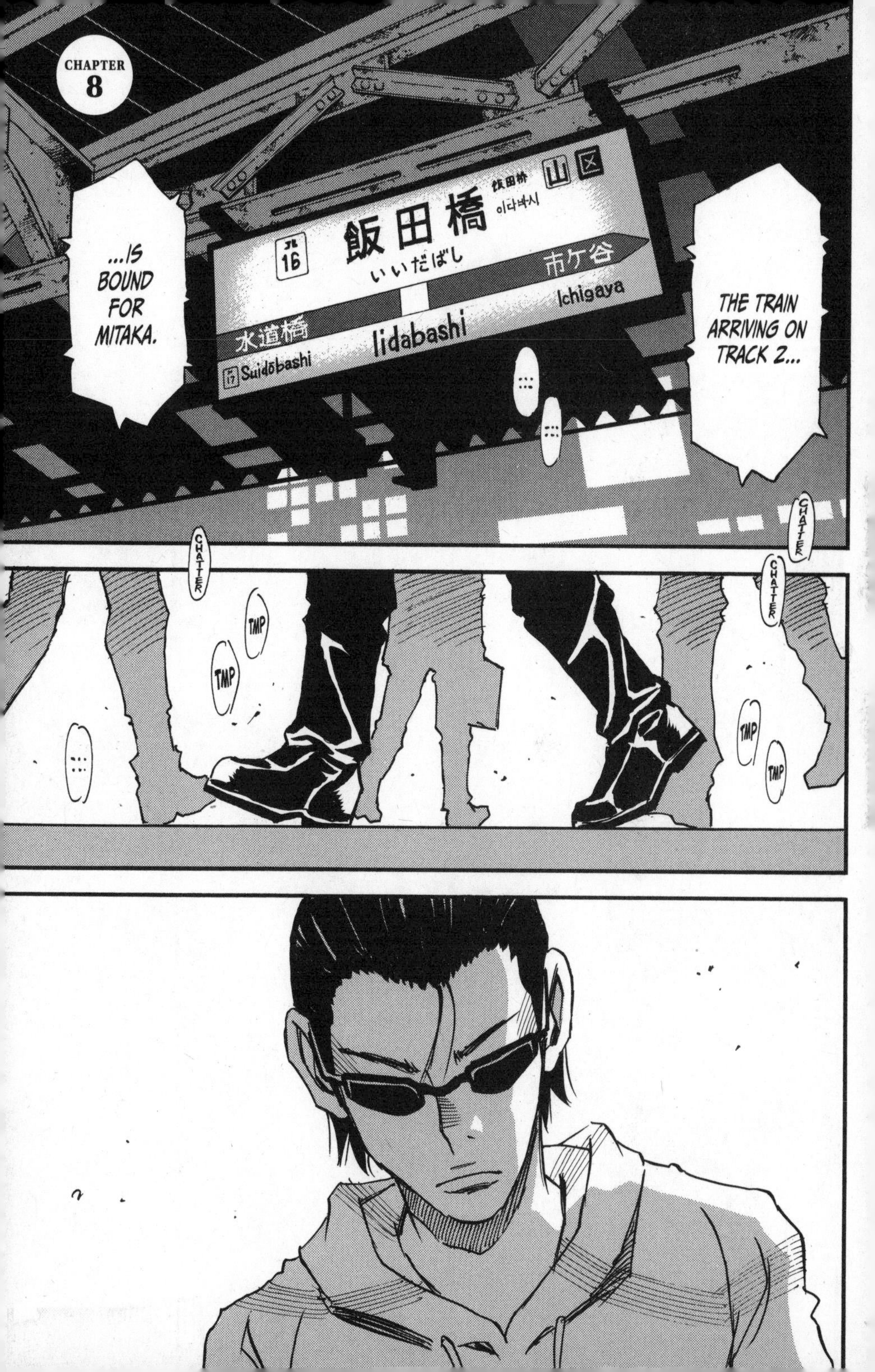
CHAPTER 8
THE TRAIN ARRIVING ON TRACK 2...
...IS BOUND FOR MITAKA.
飯田橋
いいだばし
JB 16
市ケ谷
Ichigaya
水道橋
Iidabashi
Suidōbashi
......
......
CHATTER
CHATTER
TMP
TMP
CHATTER
TMP
TMP
......

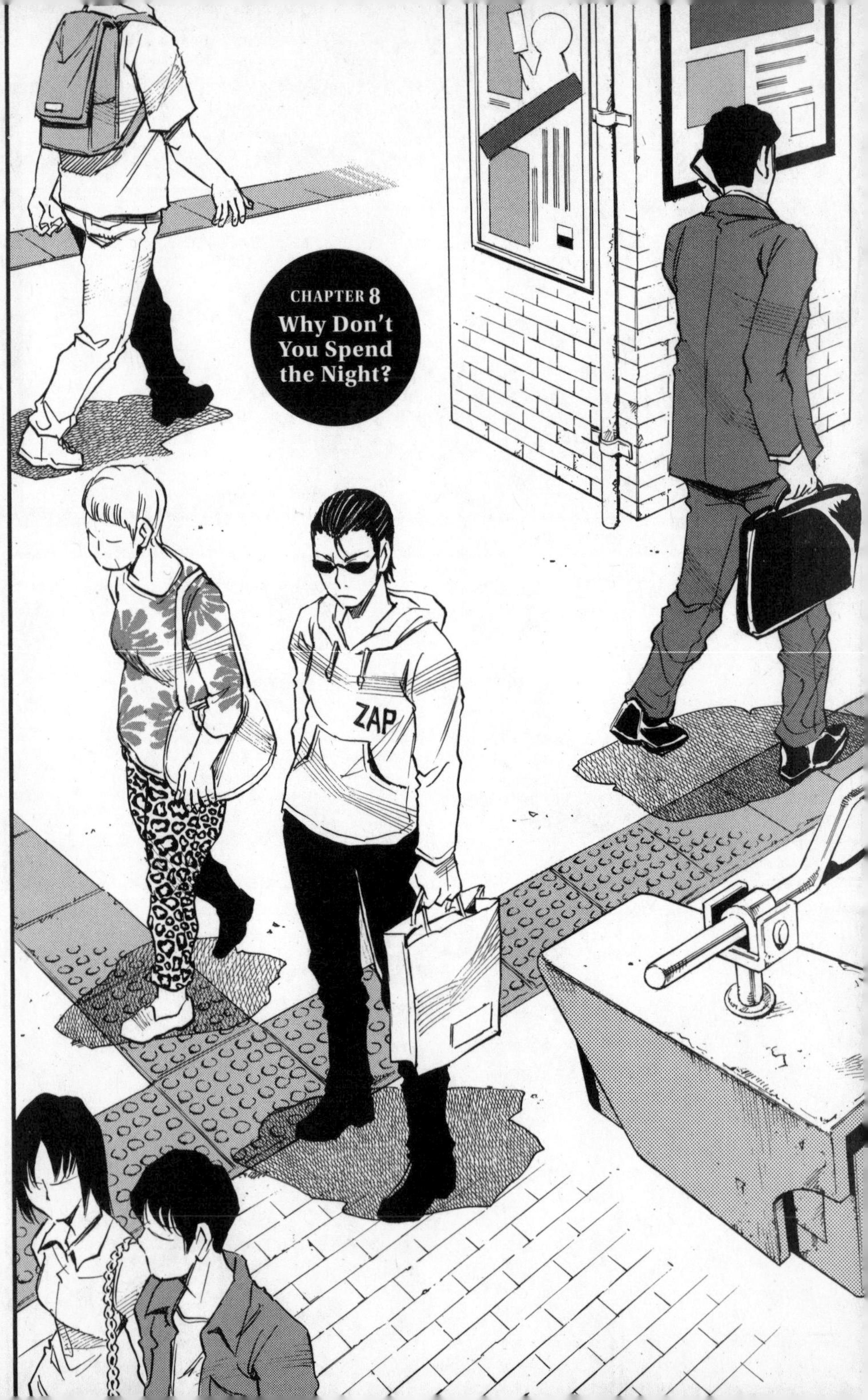
CHAPTER 8
Why Don't You Spend the Night?
ZAP

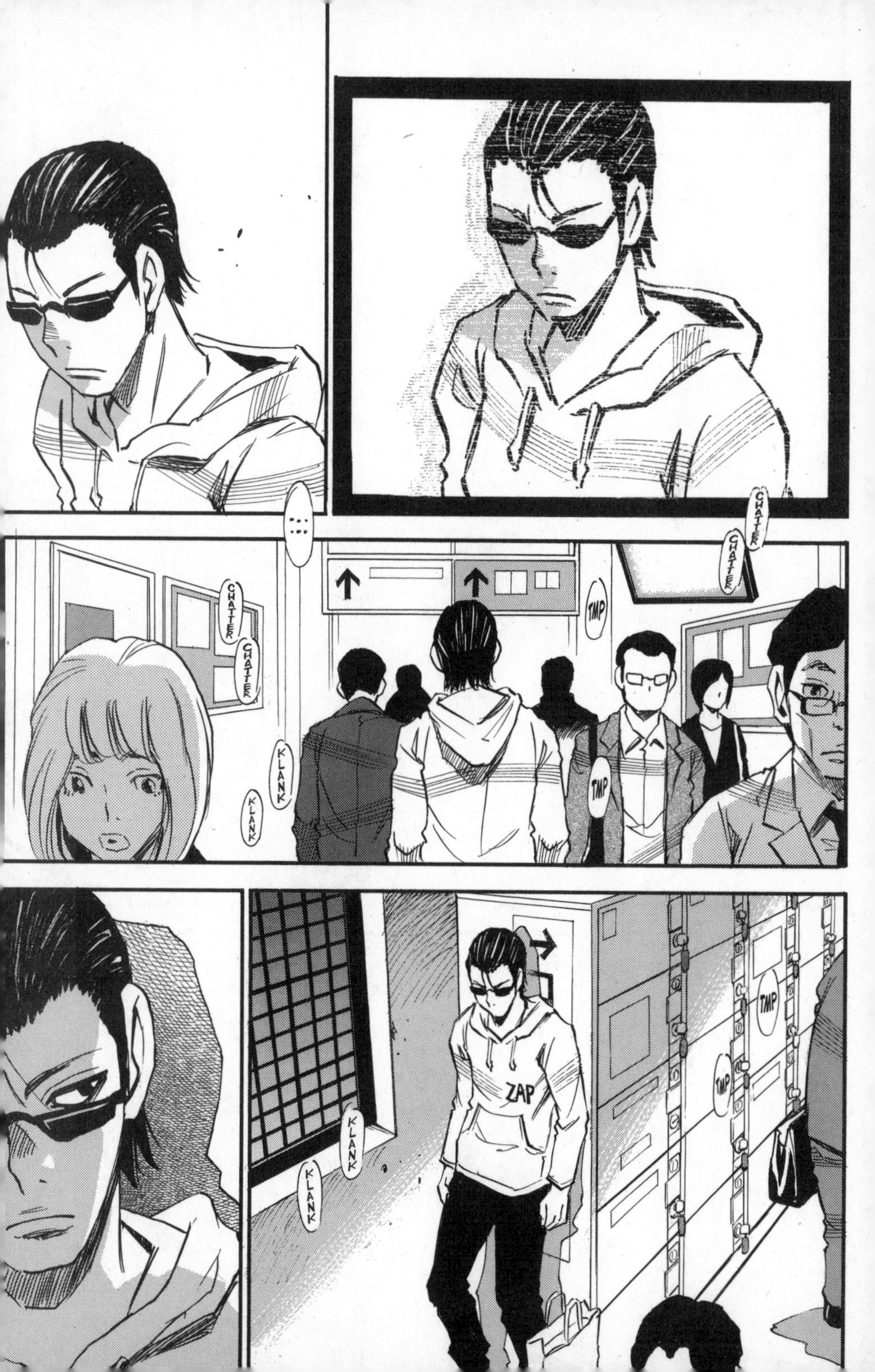
...
CHATTER
CHATTER
TMP
TMP
CHATTER
CHATTER
KLANK
KLANK
TMP
TMP
ZAP
KLANK
KLANK

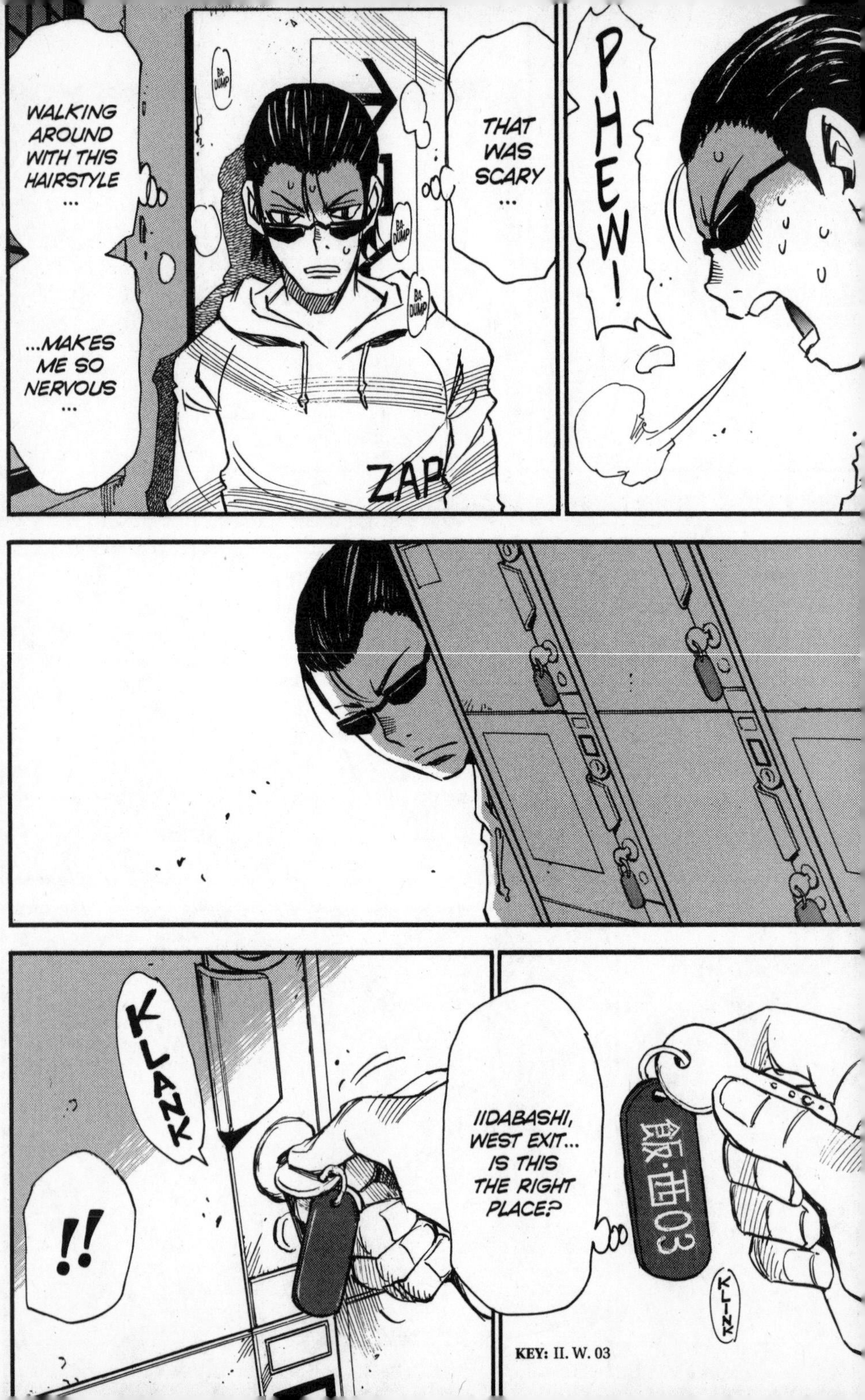
PHEW!
THAT WAS SCARY ...
BA-DUMP
BA-DUMP
BA-DUMP
WALKING AROUND WITH THIS HAIRSTYLE ...
...MAKES ME SO NERVOUS ...
ZAP
IIDABASHI, WEST EXIT... IS THIS THE RIGHT PLACE?
飯·西03
KLINK
KEY: II. W. 03
KLANK
!!

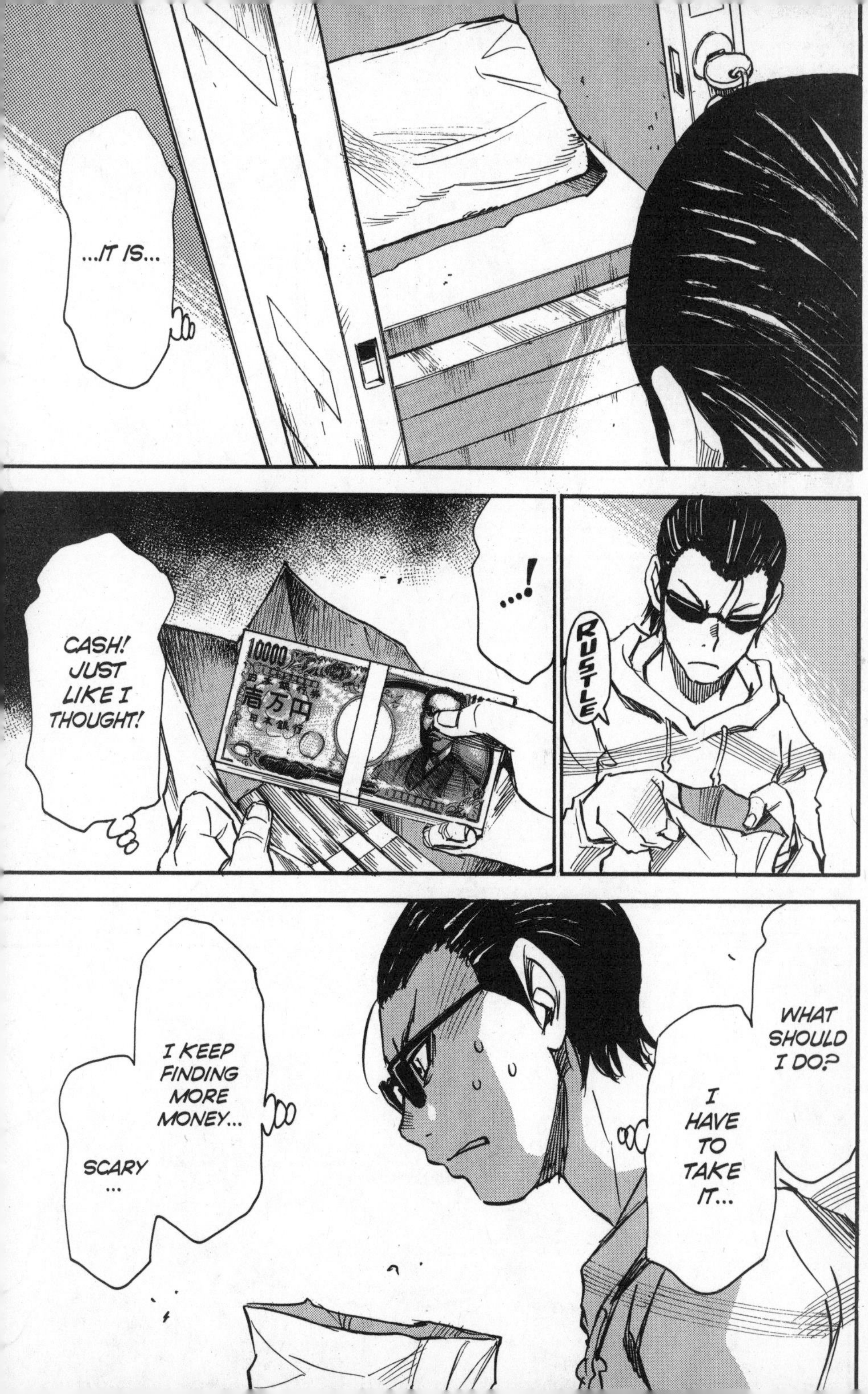
...IT IS...
RUSTLE
...!
10000
壱万円
CASH! JUST LIKE I THOUGHT!
WHAT SHOULD I DO?
I HAVE TO TAKE IT...
I KEEP FINDING MORE MONEY...
SCARY ...

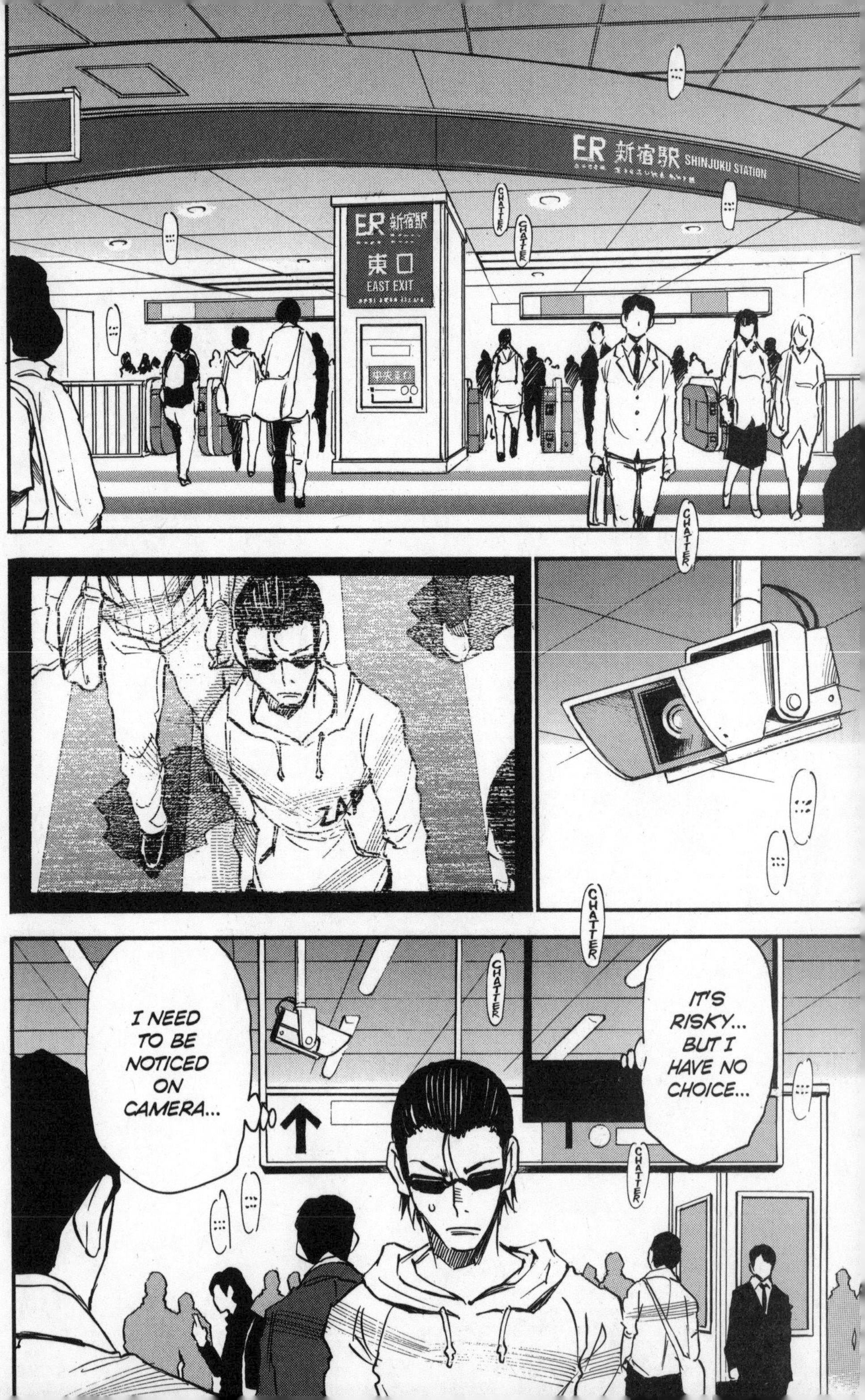
ER 新宿駅 SHINJUKU STATION
ER 新宿駅
東口
EAST EXIT
CHATTER
CHATTER
CHATTER
CHATTER
CHATTER
IT'S RISKY... BUT I HAVE NO CHOICE...
CHATTER
I NEED TO BE NOTICED ON CAMERA...

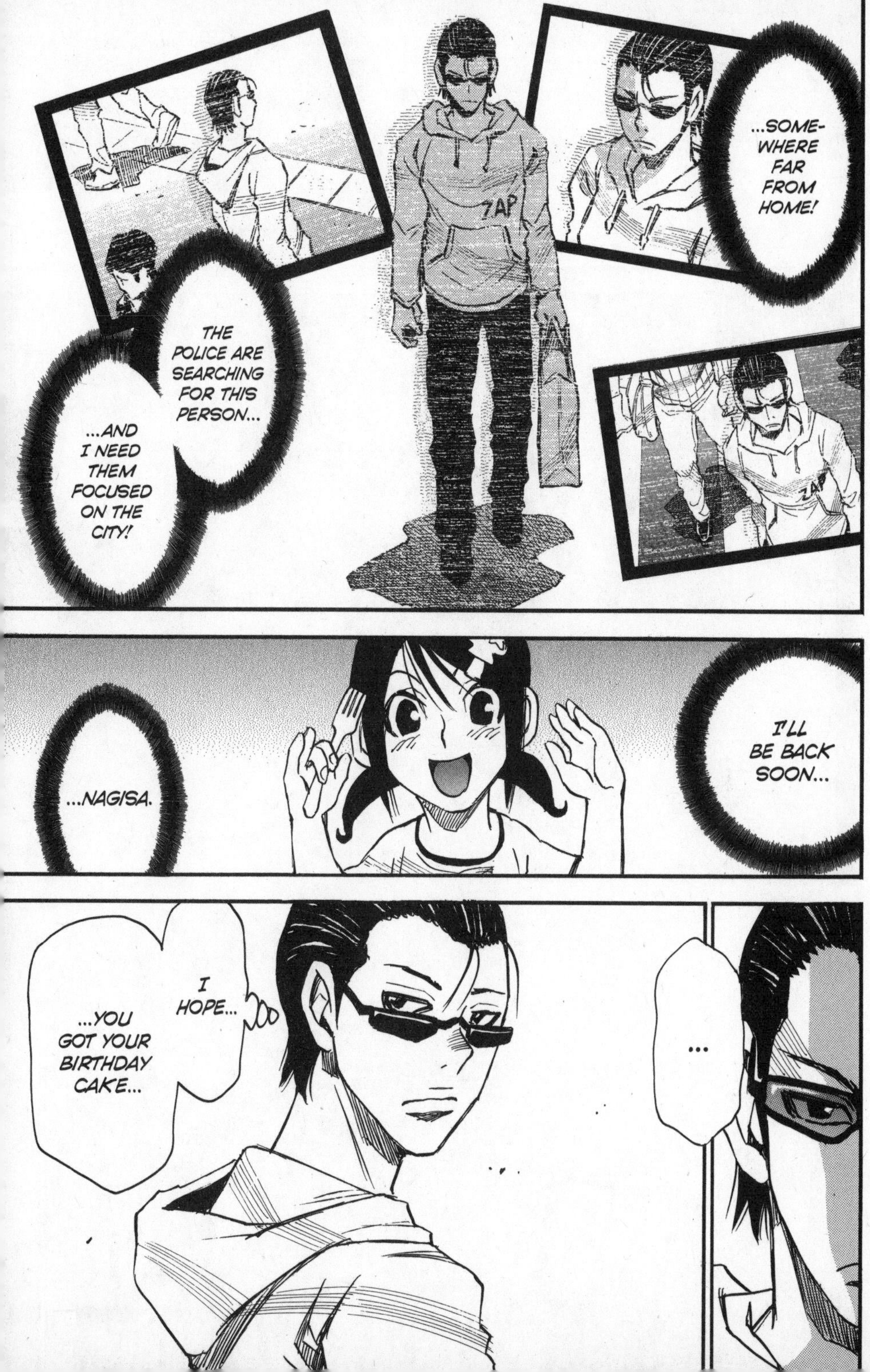
...SOME-WHERE FAR FROM HOME!
THE POLICE ARE SEARCHING FOR THIS PERSON...
...AND I NEED THEM FOCUSED ON THE CITY!
ZAP
I'LL BE BACK SOON...
...NAGISA.
...
I HOPE...
...YOU GOT YOUR BIRTHDAY CAKE...

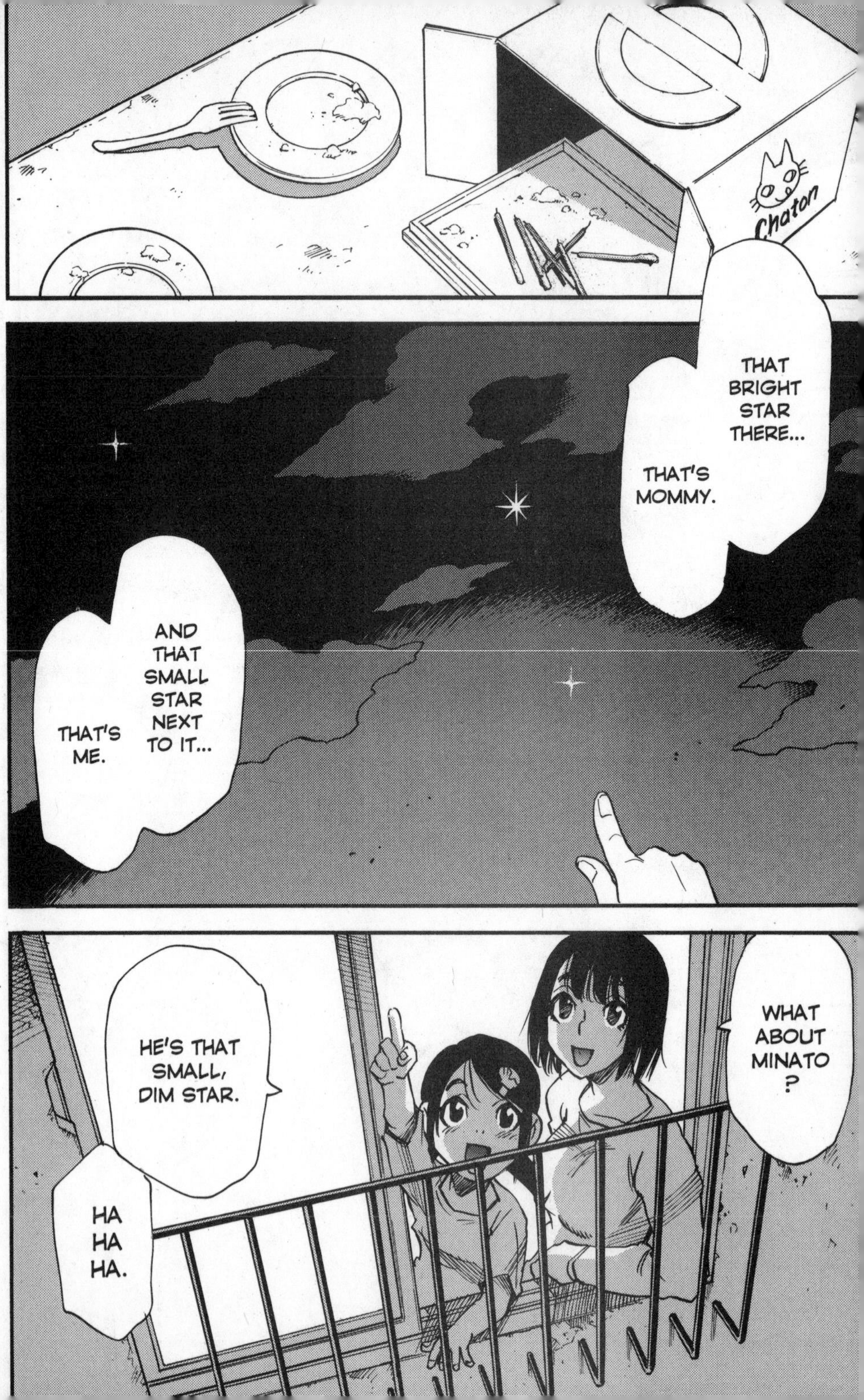
Chaton
THAT BRIGHT STAR THERE...
THAT'S MOMMY.
AND THAT SMALL STAR NEXT TO IT...
THAT'S ME.
WHAT ABOUT MINATO ?
HE'S THAT SMALL, DIM STAR.
HA HA HA.

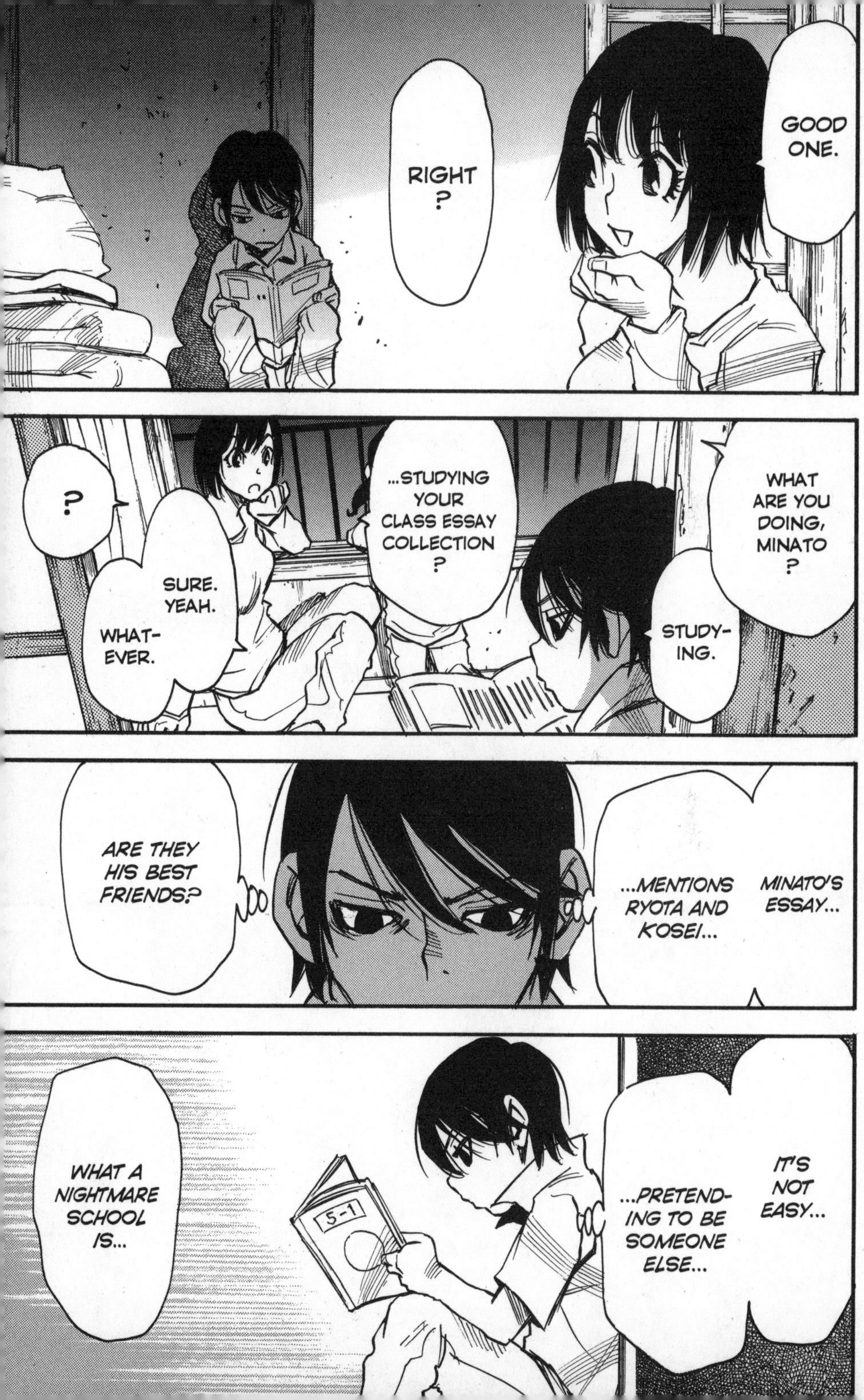
GOOD ONE.
RIGHT?
WHAT ARE YOU DOING, MINATO?
STUDYING.
...STUDYING YOUR CLASS ESSAY COLLECTION?
?
SURE. YEAH. WHATEVER.
MINATO'S ESSAY...
...MENTIONS RYOTA AND KOSEI...
ARE THEY HIS BEST FRIENDS?
IT'S NOT EASY...
...PRETENDING TO BE SOMEONE ELSE...
5-1
WHAT A NIGHTMARE SCHOOL IS...

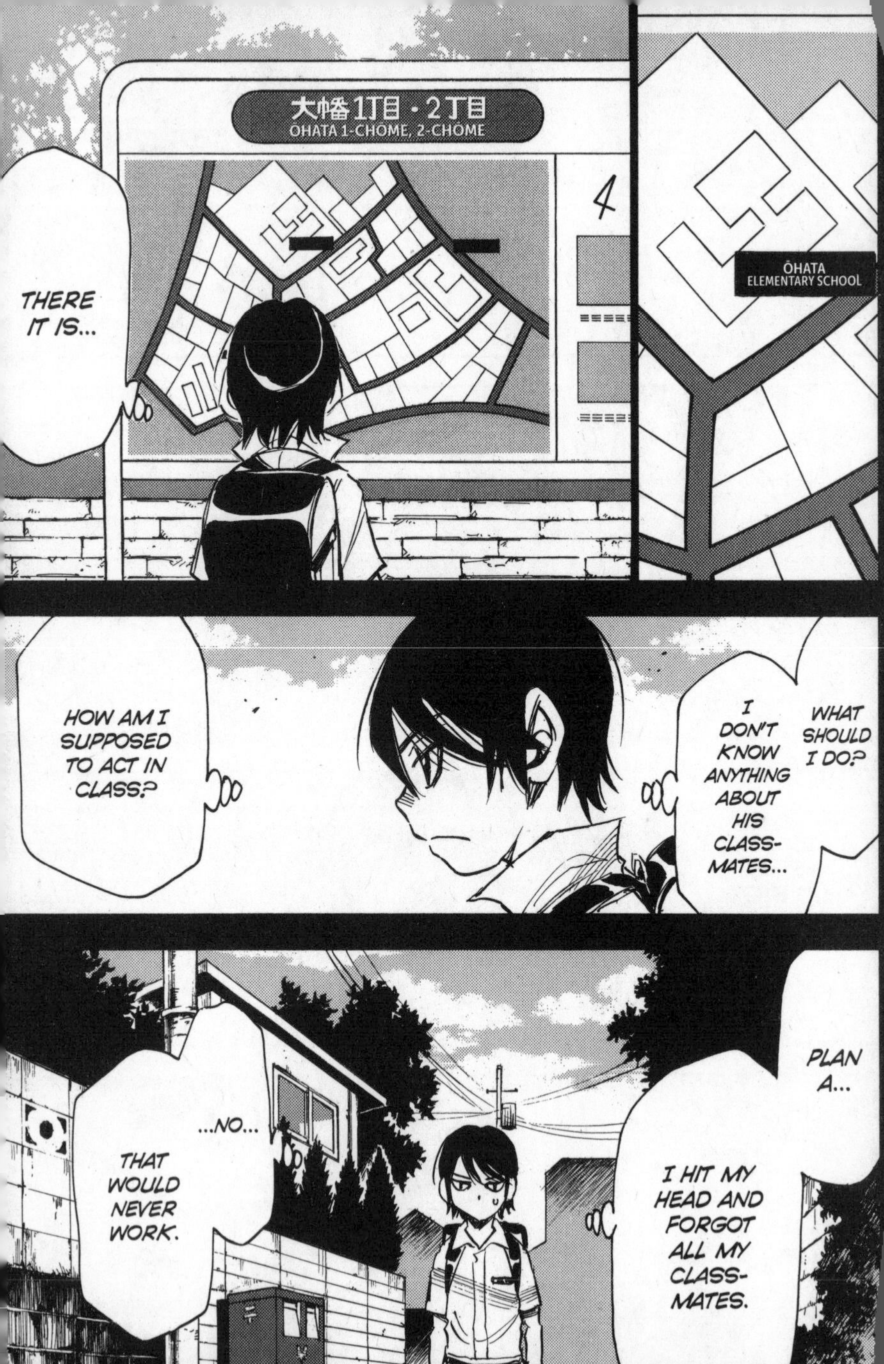
ŌHATA ELEMENTARY SCHOOL
大幡1丁目・2丁目
ŌHATA 1-CHŌME, 2-CHŌME
4
THERE IT IS...
WHAT SHOULD I DO?
I DON'T KNOW ANYTHING ABOUT HIS CLASS-MATES...
HOW AM I SUPPOSED TO ACT IN CLASS?
PLAN A...
I HIT MY HEAD AND FORGOT ALL MY CLASS-MATES.
...NO...
THAT WOULD NEVER WORK.

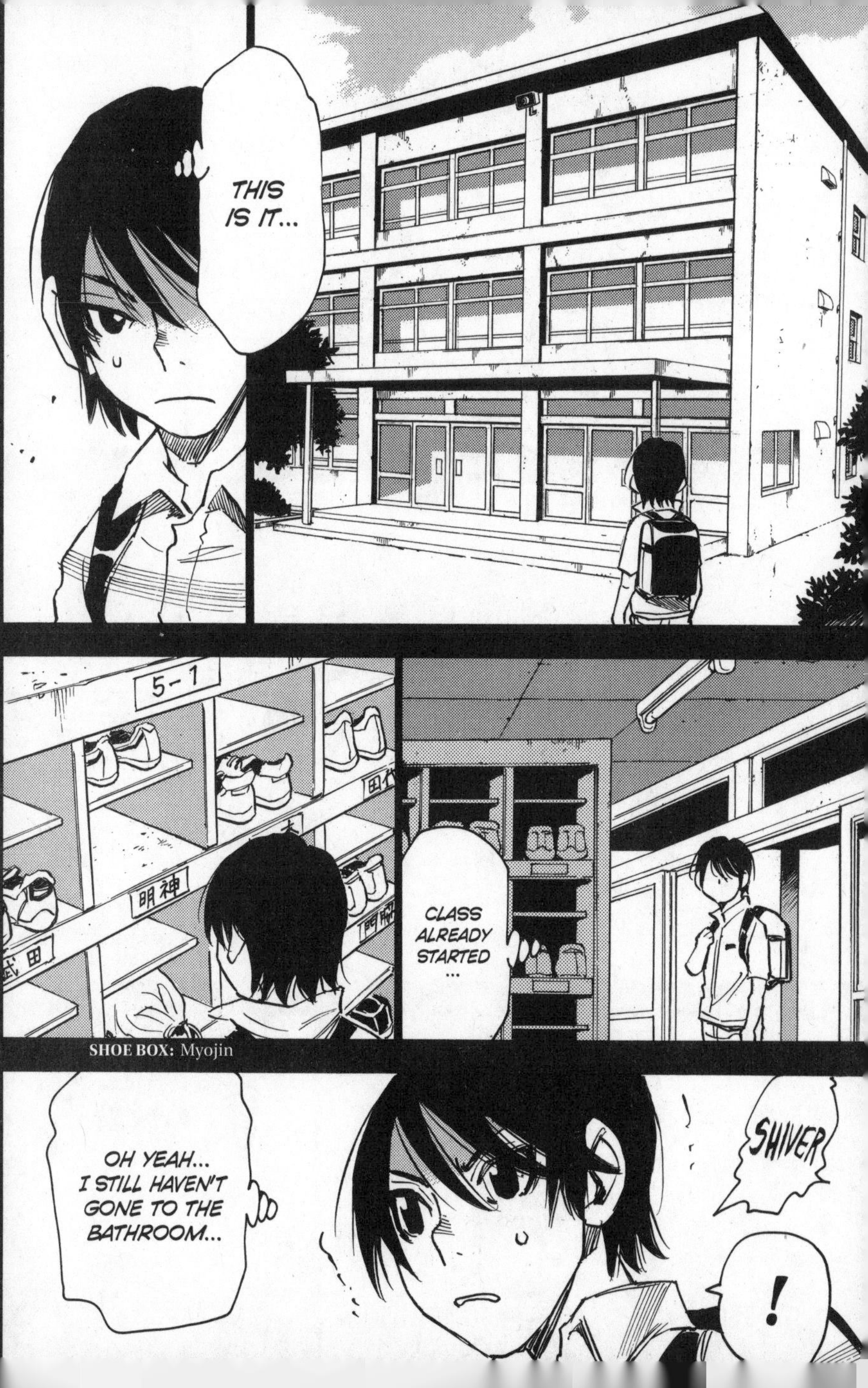
THIS IS IT...
CLASS ALREADY STARTED ...
5-1
明神
SHOE BOX: Myojin
SHIVER
!
OH YEAH... I STILL HAVEN'T GONE TO THE BATHROOM...

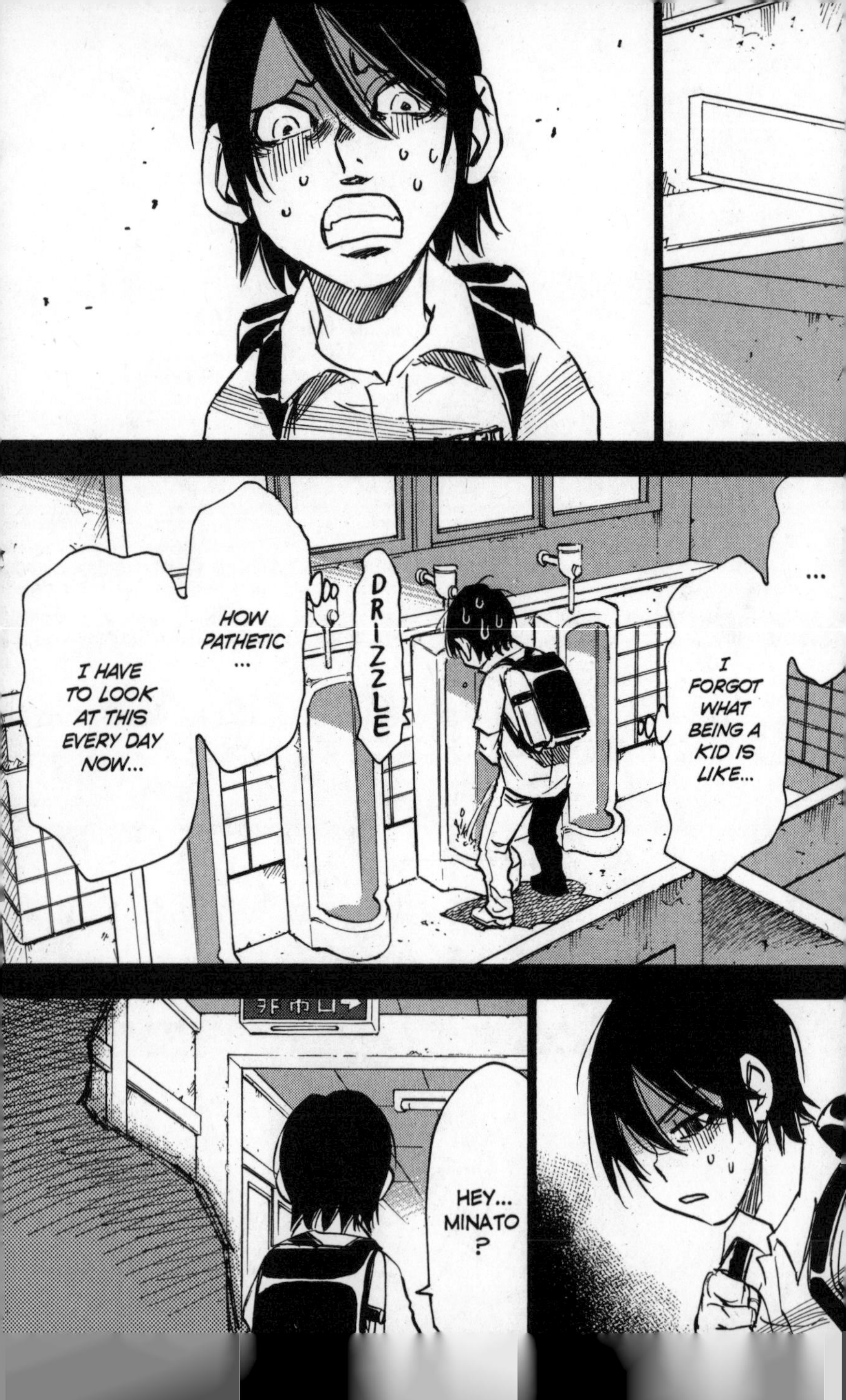
...
I FORGOT WHAT BEING A KID IS LIKE...
DRIZZLE
HOW PATHETIC ...
I HAVE TO LOOK AT THIS EVERY DAY NOW...
HEY... MINATO ?

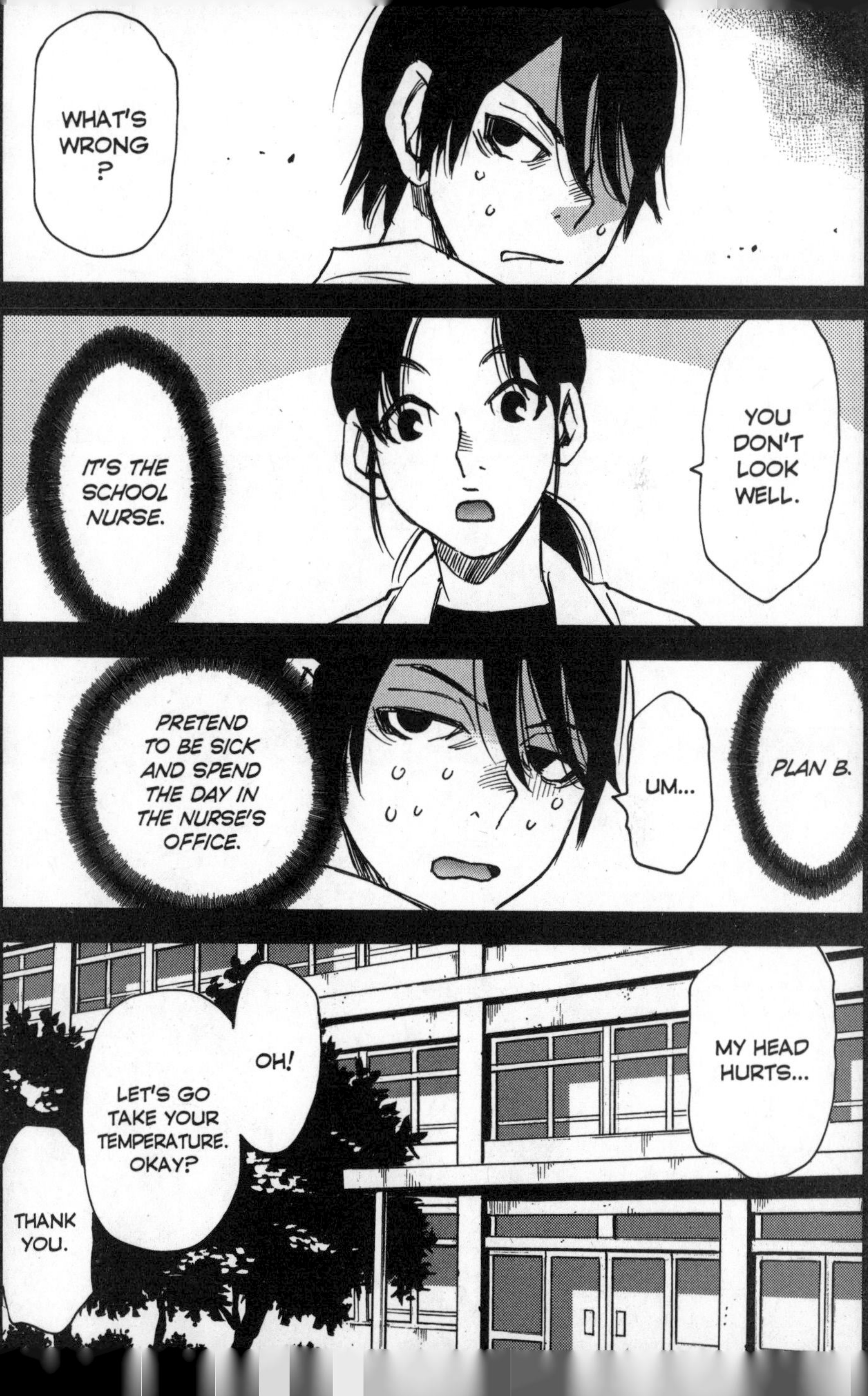
WHAT'S WRONG?
YOU DON'T LOOK WELL.
IT'S THE SCHOOL NURSE.
PLAN B.
UM...
PRETEND TO BE SICK AND SPEND THE DAY IN THE NURSE'S OFFICE.
MY HEAD HURTS...
OH!
LET'S GO TAKE YOUR TEMPERATURE. OKAY?
THANK YOU.

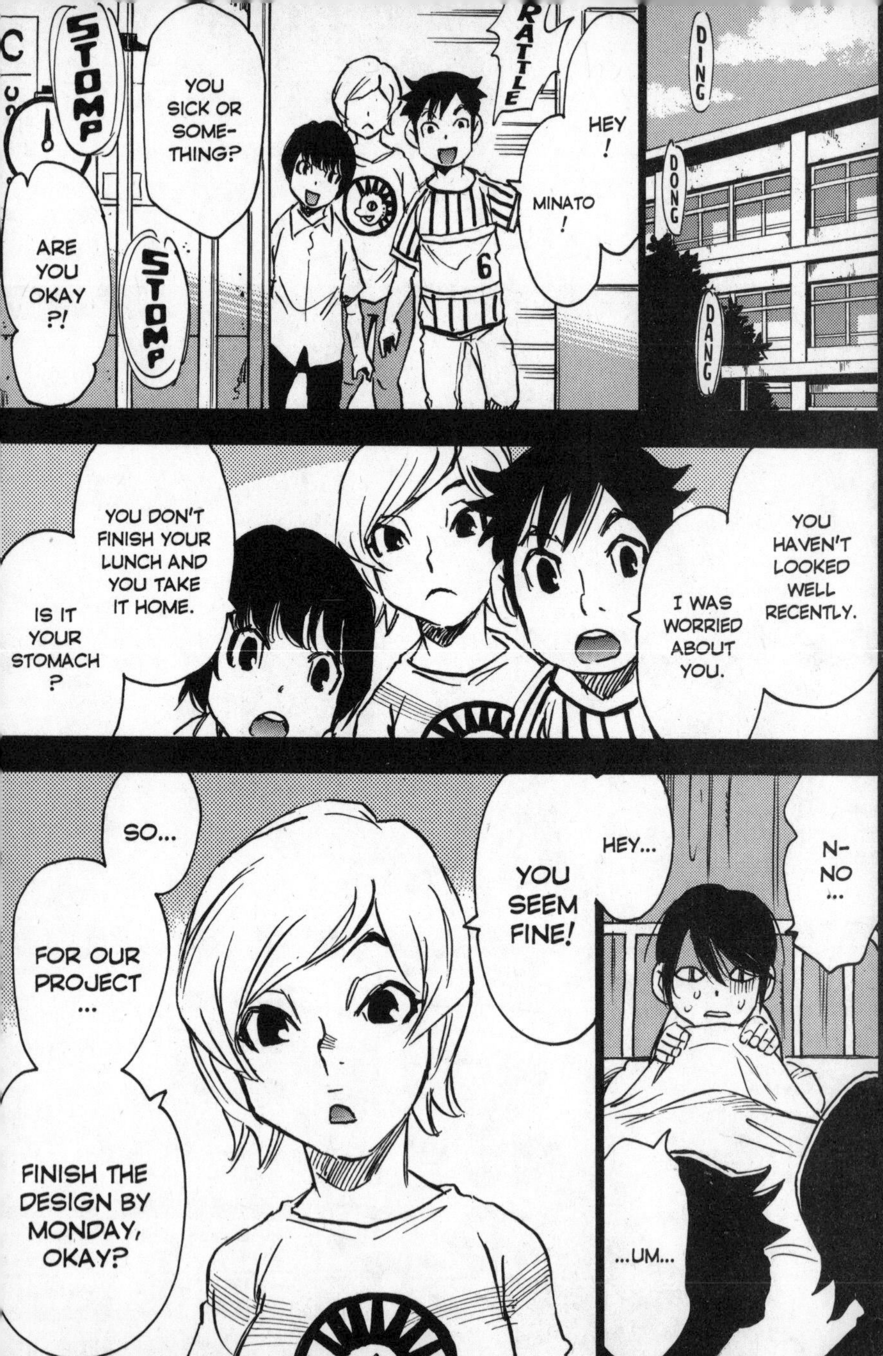
DING
DONG
DANG
RATTLE
HEY! MINATO!
STOMP
YOU SICK OR SOME-THING?
ARE YOU OKAY?!
STOMP
YOU HAVEN'T LOOKED WELL RECENTLY.
I WAS WORRIED ABOUT YOU.
YOU DON'T FINISH YOUR LUNCH AND YOU TAKE IT HOME.
IS IT YOUR STOMACH?
N-NO...
...UM...
HEY...
YOU SEEM FINE!
SO...
FOR OUR PROJECT...
FINISH THE DESIGN BY MONDAY, OKAY?

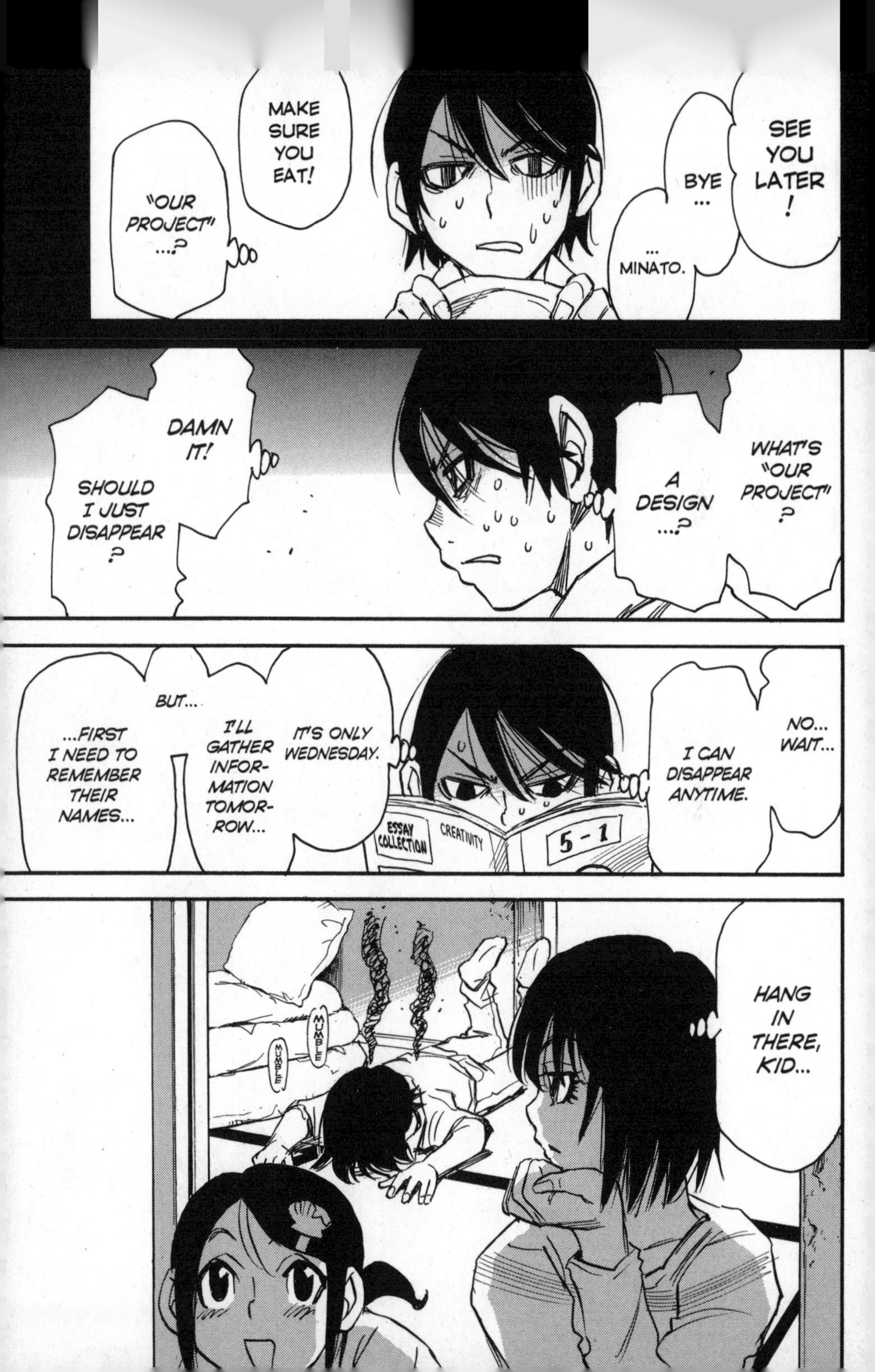
SEE YOU LATER!
BYE ...
... MINATO.
MAKE SURE YOU EAT!
"OUR PROJECT" ...?
WHAT'S "OUR PROJECT"?
A DESIGN ...?
DAMN IT!
SHOULD I JUST DISAPPEAR?
NO... WAIT...
I CAN DISAPPEAR ANYTIME.
IT'S ONLY WEDNESDAY.
I'LL GATHER INFORMATION TOMORROW...
ESSAY COLLECTION
CREATIVITY
5-1
BUT...
...FIRST I NEED TO REMEMBER THEIR NAMES...
HANG IN THERE, KID...
MUMBLE
MUMBLE

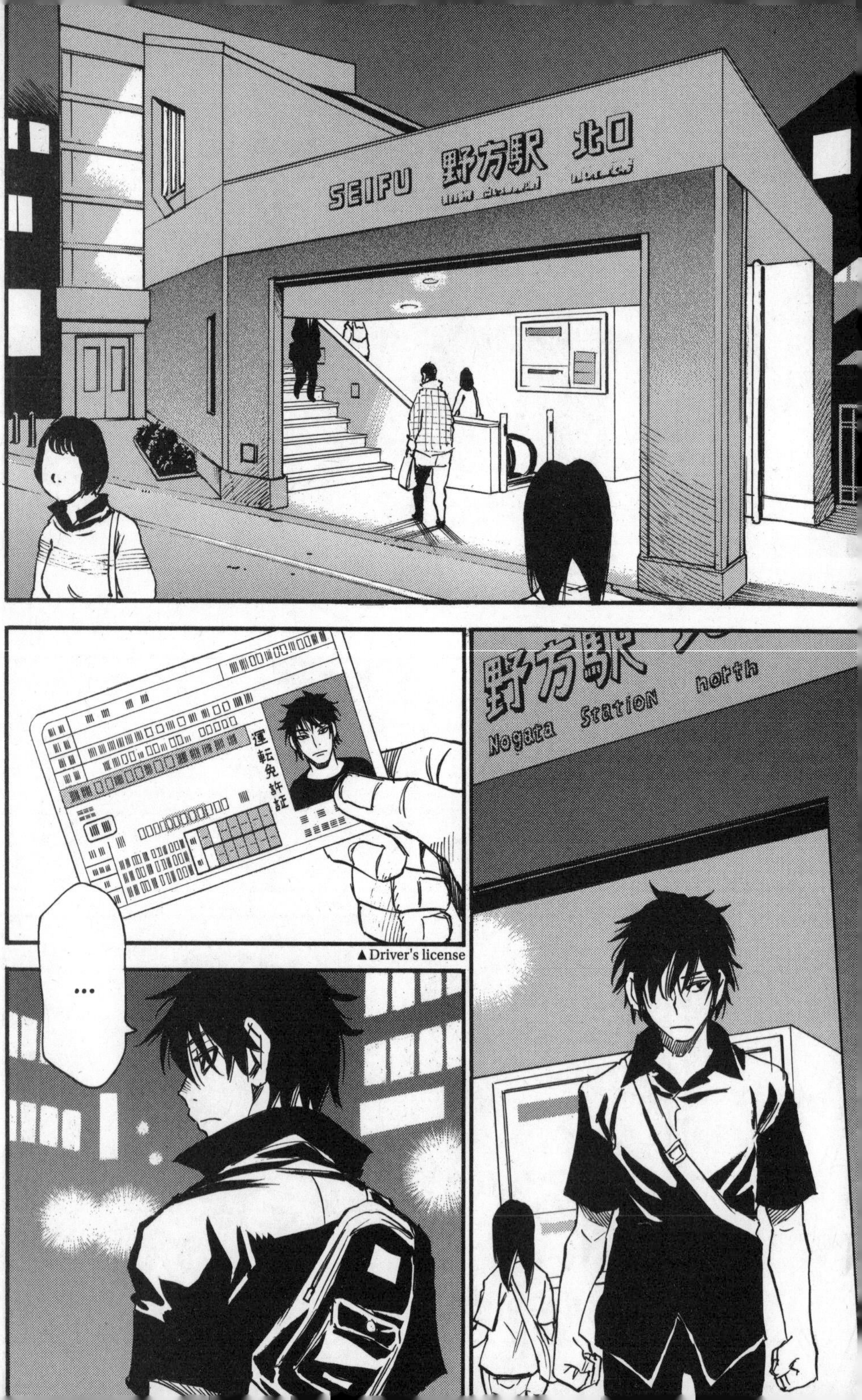
SEIFU 野方駅 北口
野方駅
Nogata Station north
運転免許証
▲Driver's license
...

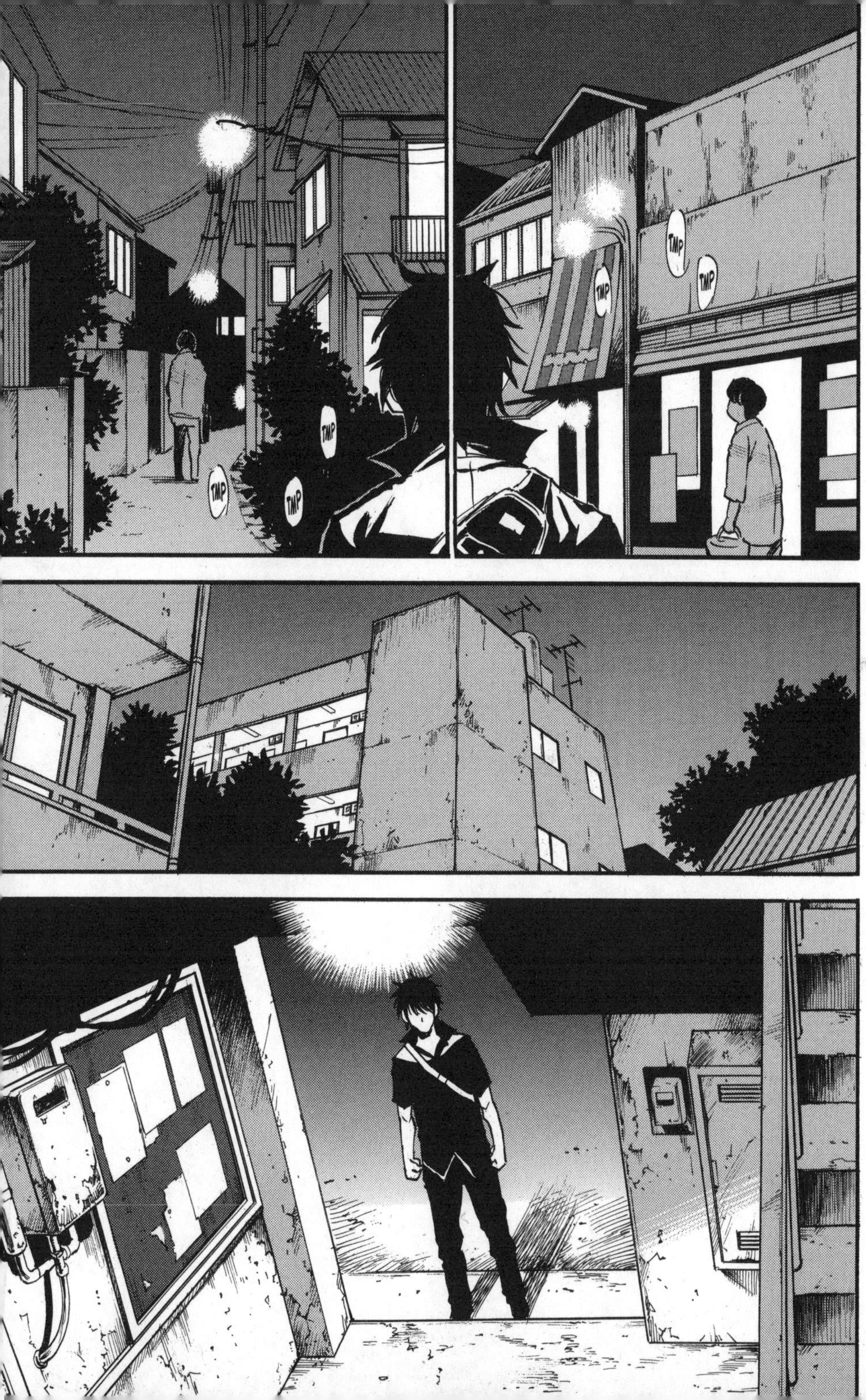
TMP
TMP
TMP
TMP
TMP
TMP

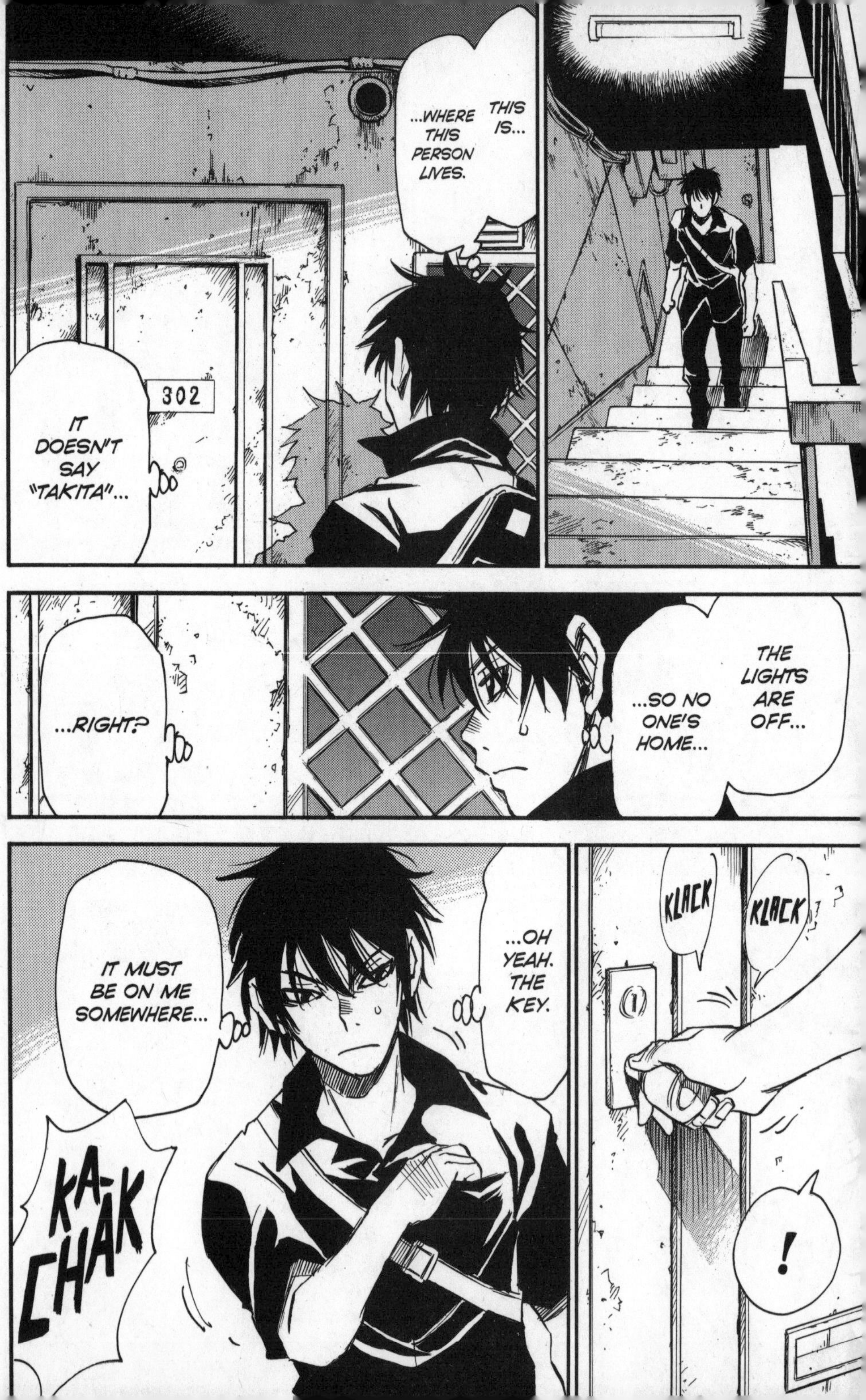
THIS IS... ...WHERE THIS PERSON LIVES.
302
IT DOESN'T SAY "TAKITA"...
THE LIGHTS ARE OFF... ...SO NO ONE'S HOME...
...RIGHT?
KLACK
KLACK
!
...OH YEAH. THE KEY.
IT MUST BE ON ME SOMEWHERE...
KA-CHAK

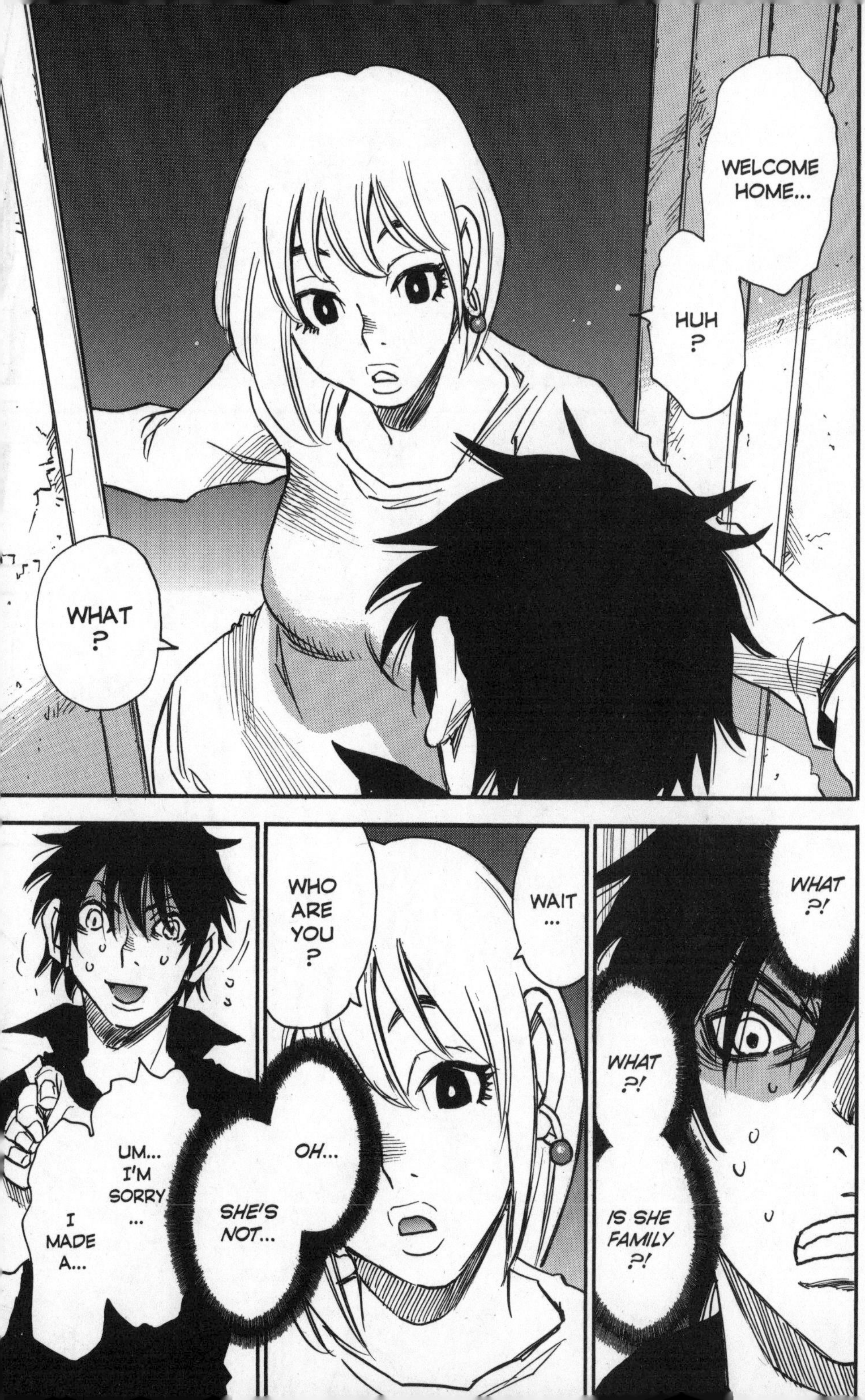
WELCOME HOME...
HUH ?
WHAT ?
WHAT ?!
WHAT ?!
IS SHE FAMILY ?!
WAIT ...
WHO ARE YOU ?
OH...
SHE'S NOT...
UM... I'M SORRY ...
I MADE A...

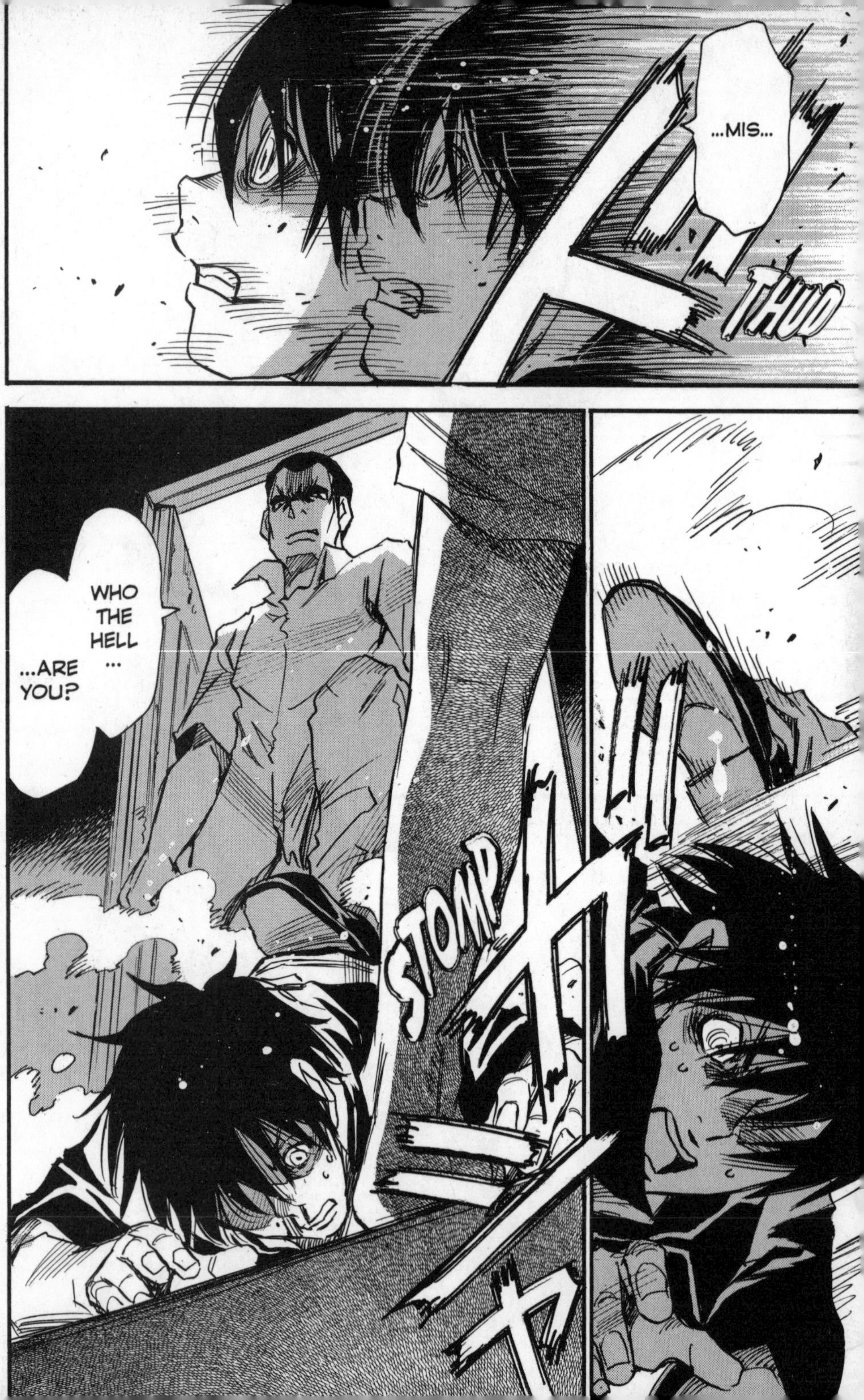
...MIS...
THUD
WHO THE HELL ...
...ARE YOU?
STOMP

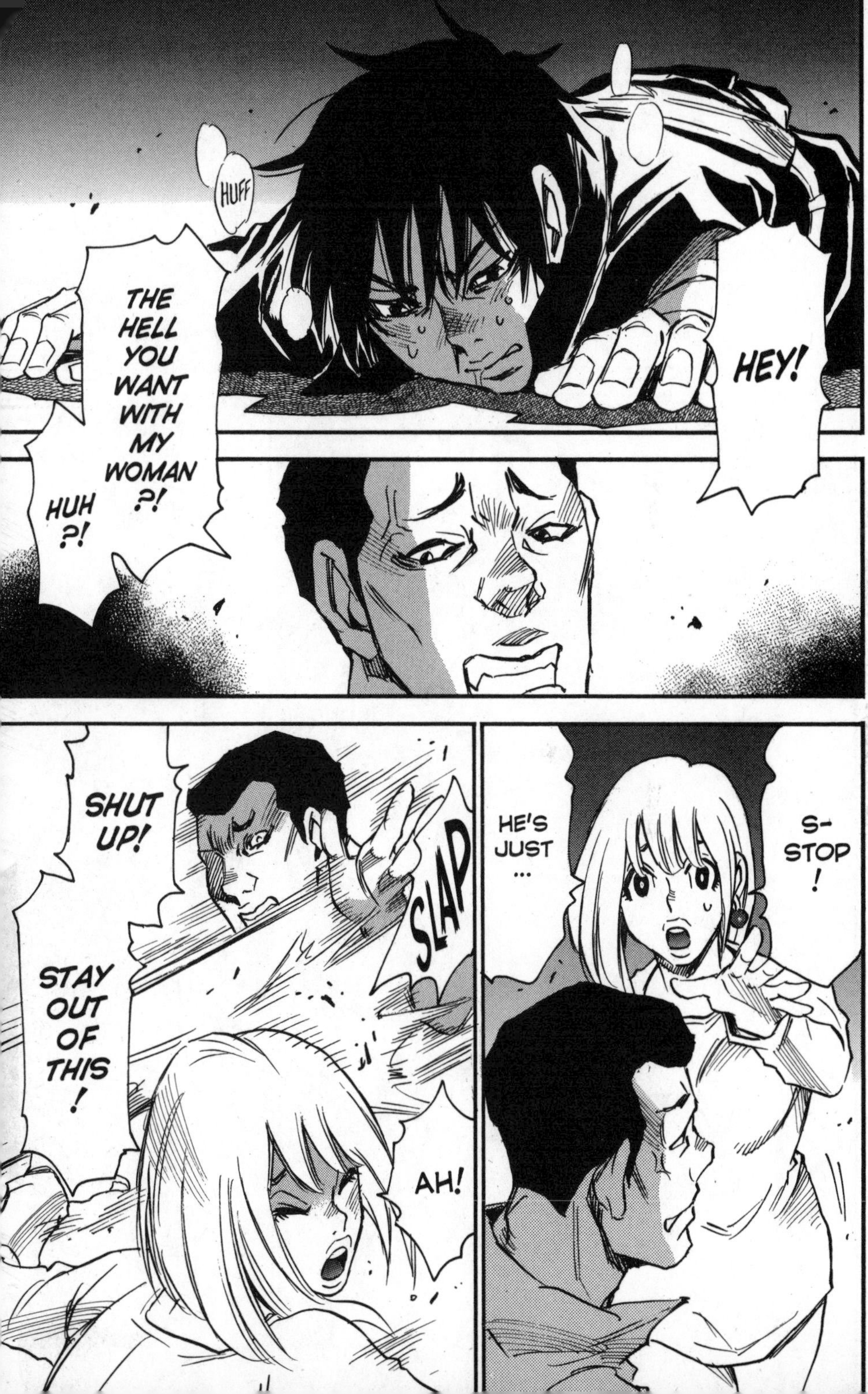
HUFF
HEY!
THE HELL YOU WANT WITH MY WOMAN ?!
HUH ?!
S-STOP !
HE'S JUST ...
SHUT UP!
SLAP
STAY OUT OF THIS !
AH!

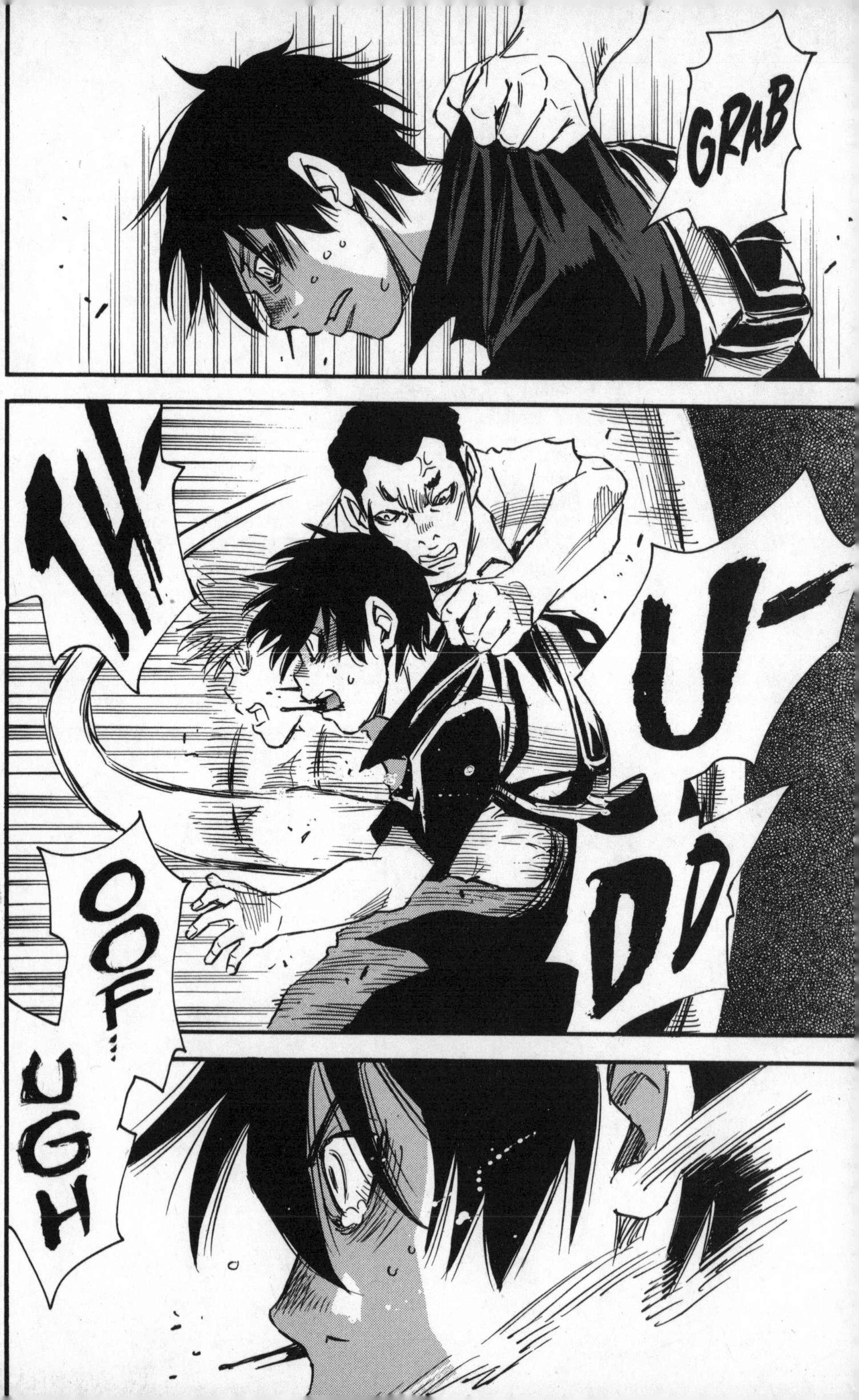
GRAB
THU-UDD
OOF...
UGH

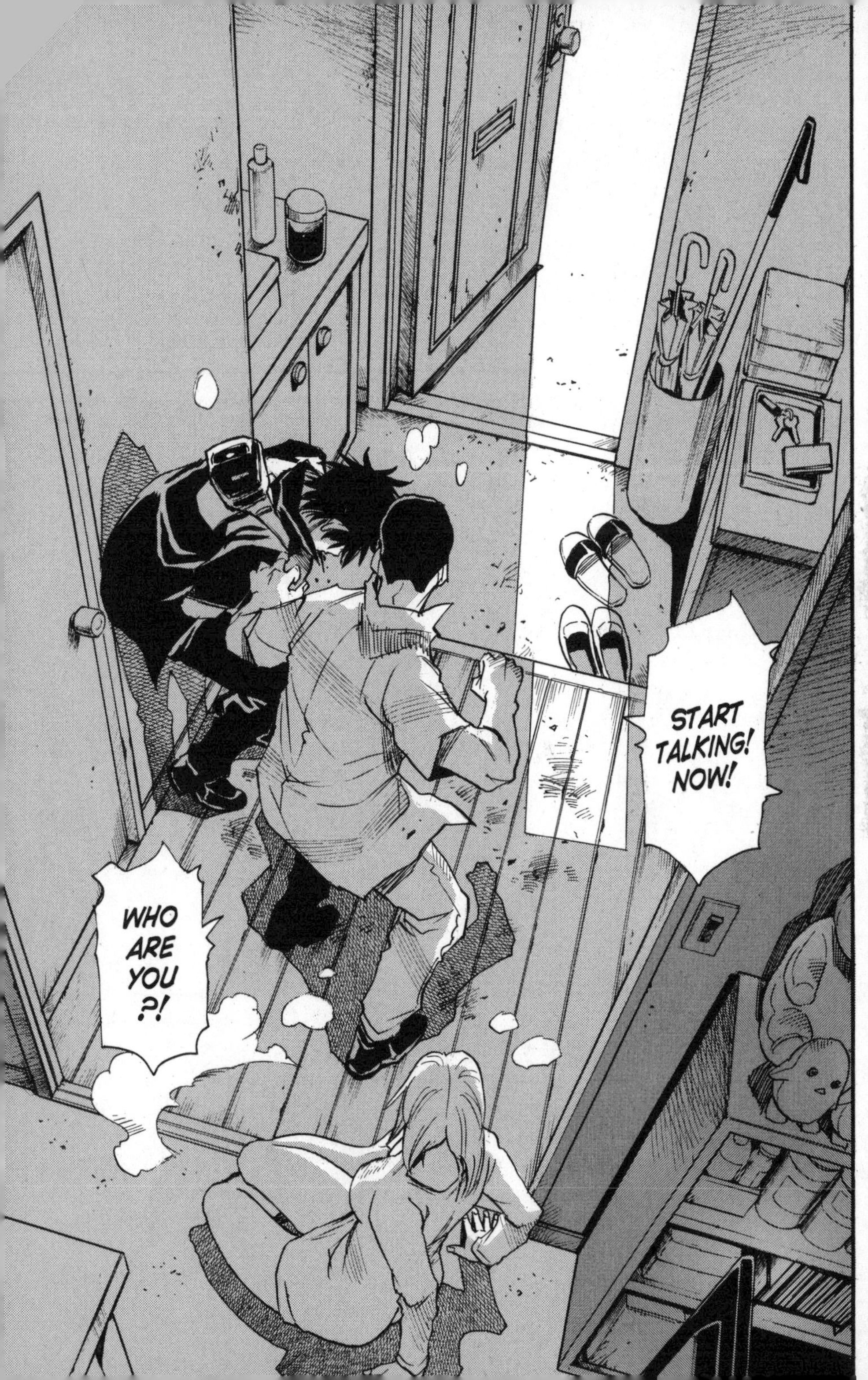
START TALKING! NOW!
WHO ARE YOU ?!

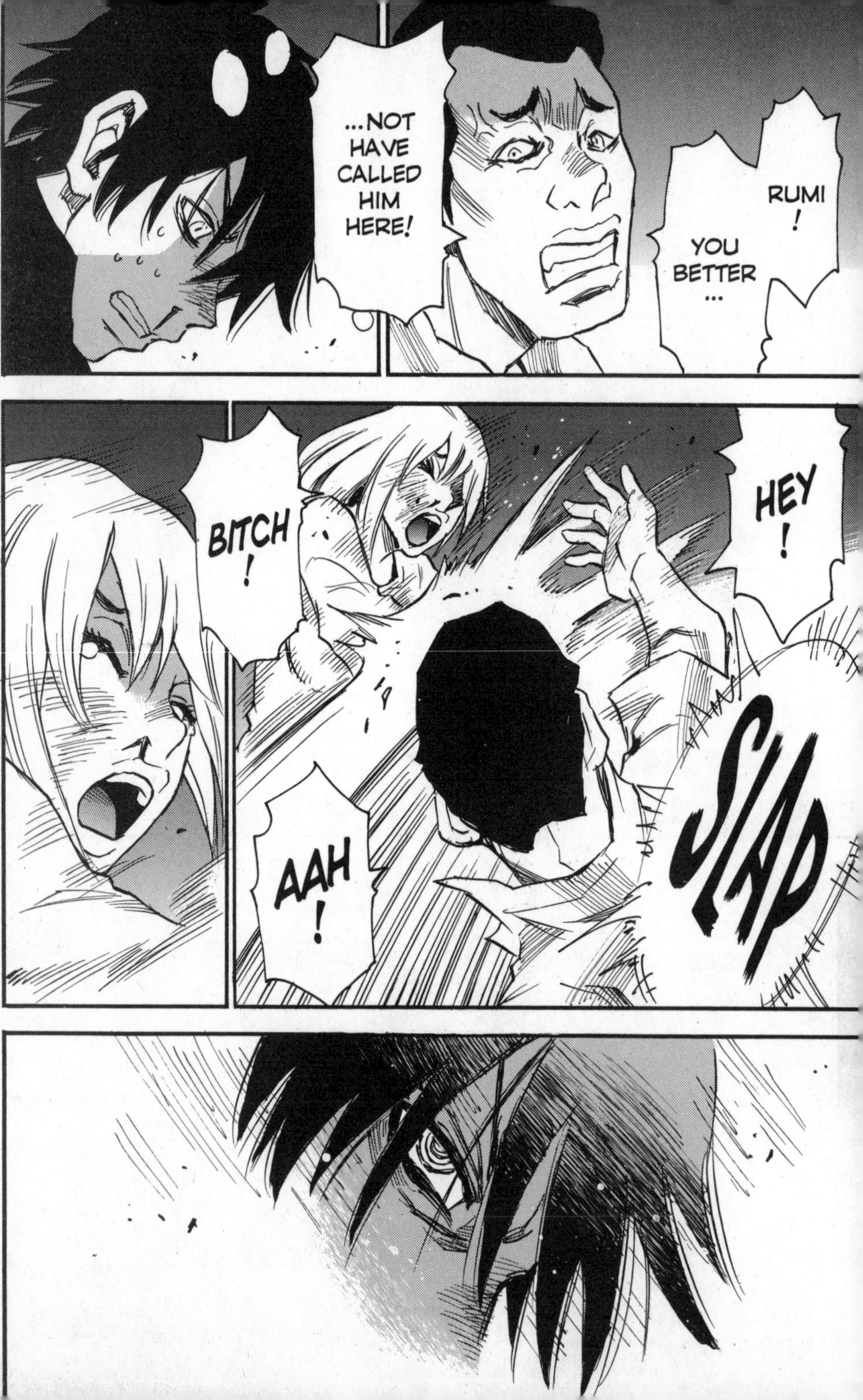
RUMI! YOU BETTER...
...NOT HAVE CALLED HIM HERE!
HEY!
BITCH!
SLAP
AAH!

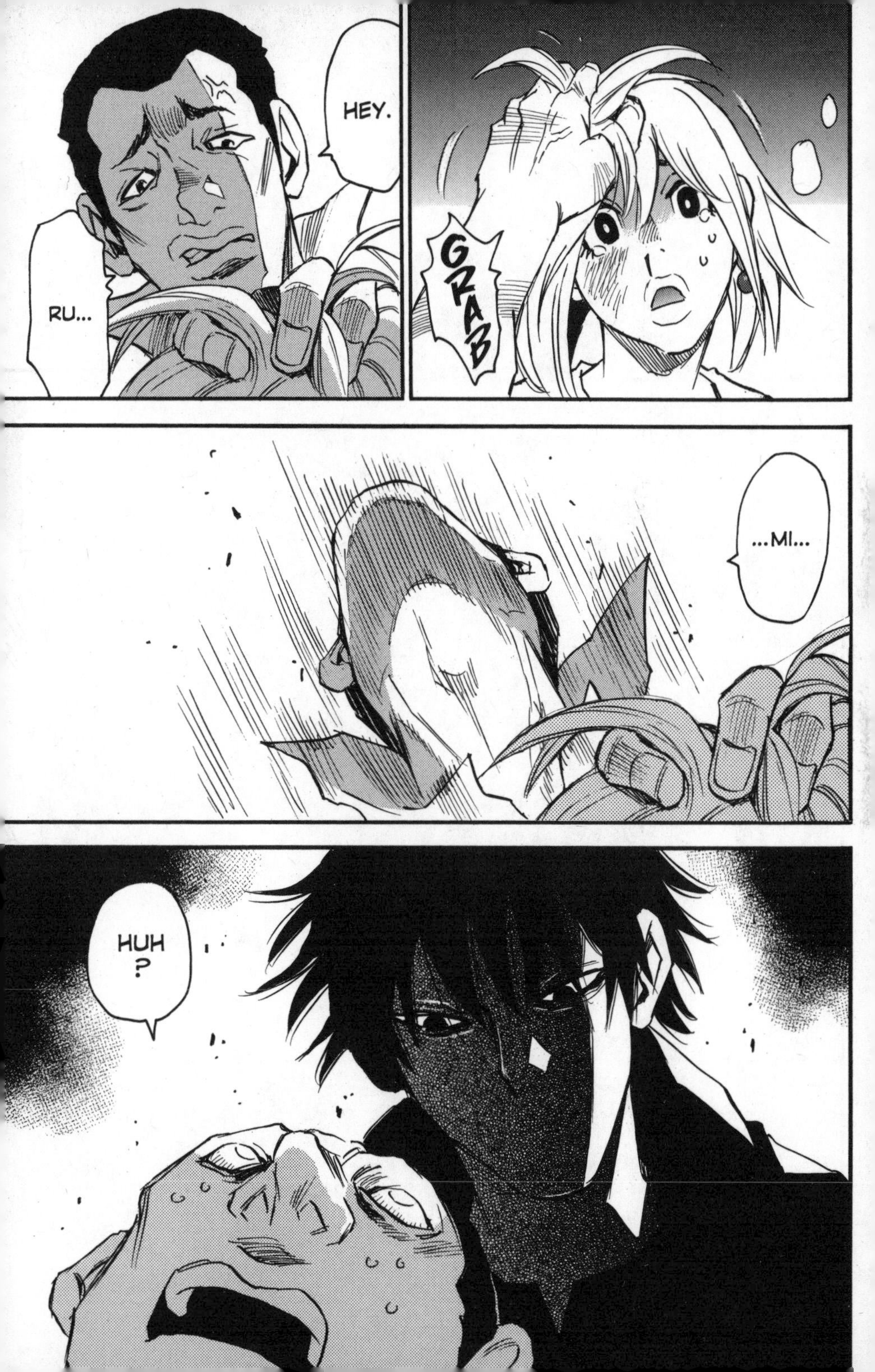
GRAB
HEY.
RU...
...MI...
HUH?

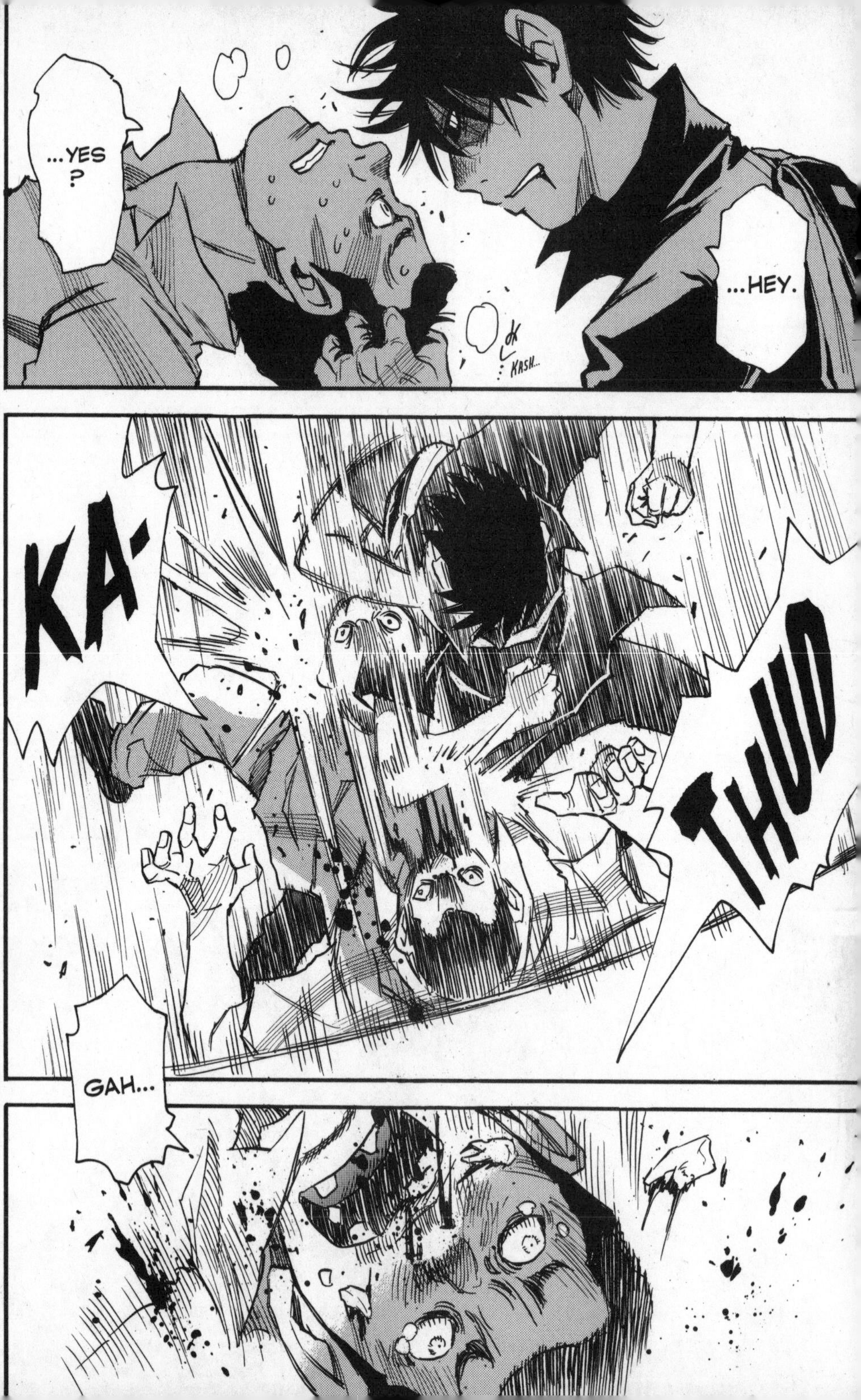
...HEY.
KASH...
...YES?
KA-
THUD
GAH...

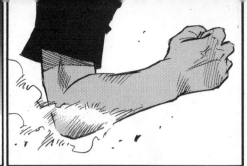

NEVER
...

...HIT HER
AGAIN.

THUD

IF YOU
DO IT
AGAIN...

I'LL
...

...KILL
YOU.

F...

FINE
...

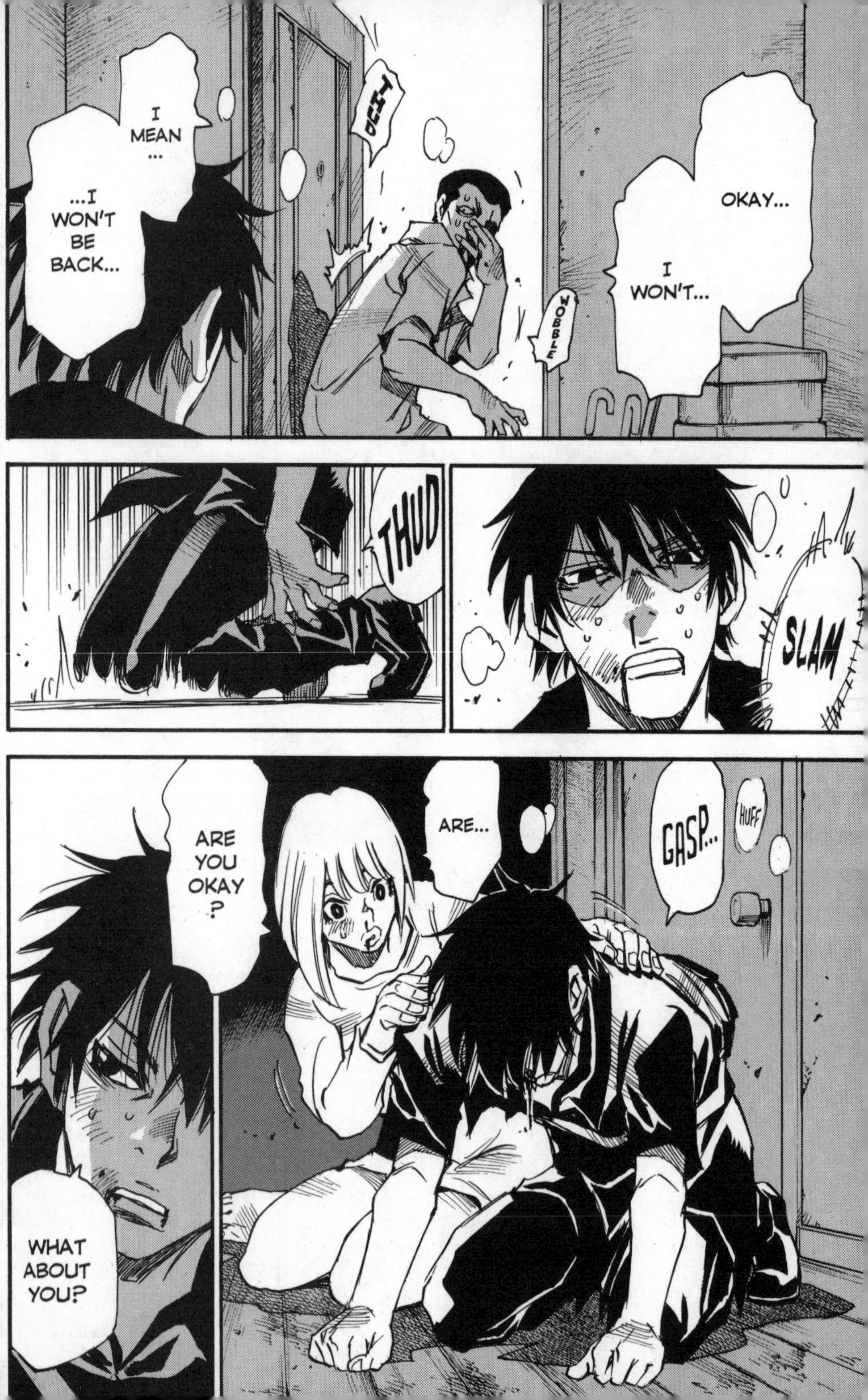
OKAY...
I WON'T...
THUD
WOBBLE
I MEAN...
...I WON'T BE BACK...
SLAM
THUD
GASP...
HUFF
ARE...
ARE YOU OKAY?
WHAT ABOUT YOU?

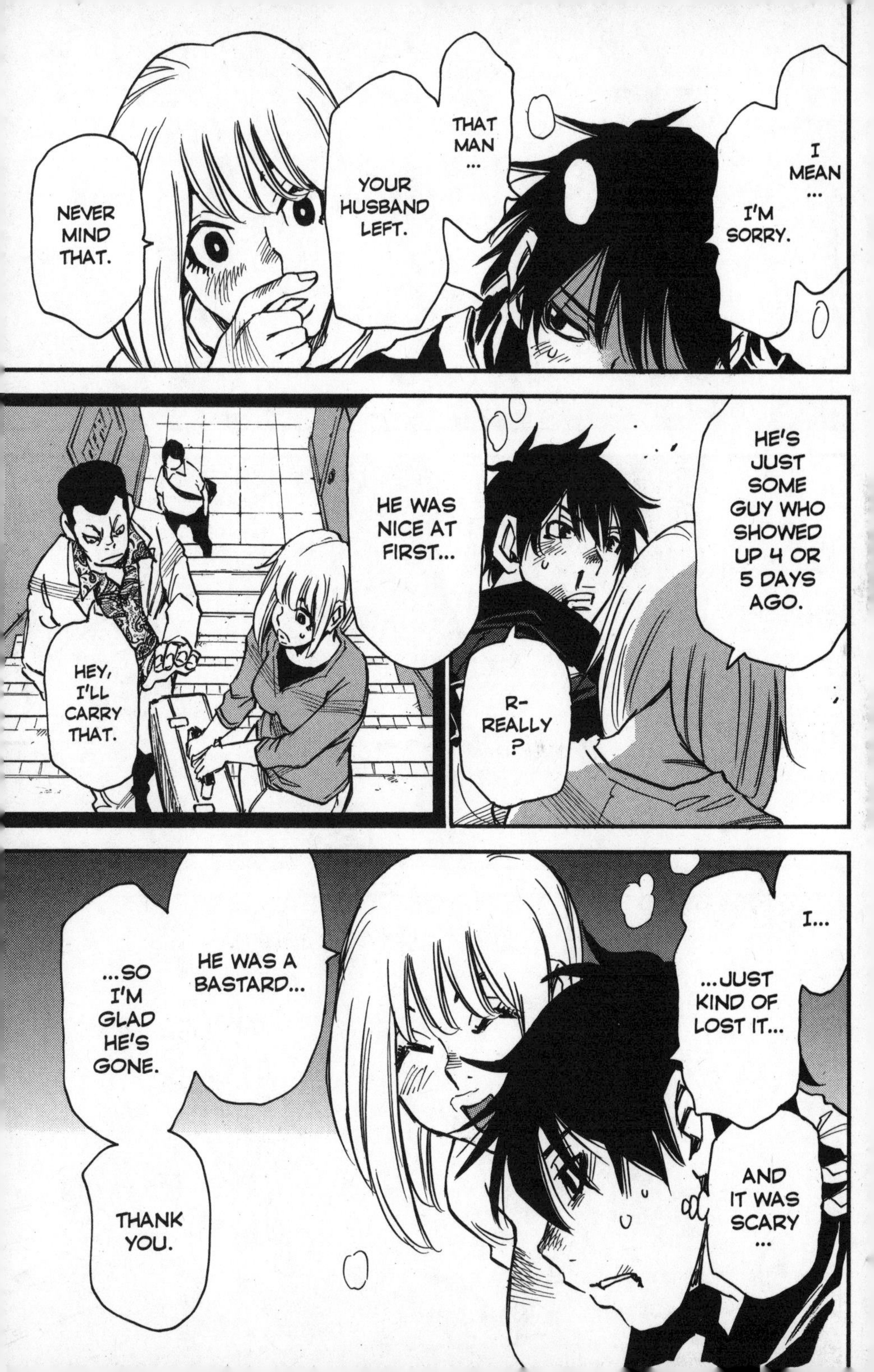
I MEAN ...
I'M SORRY.
THAT MAN ...
YOUR HUSBAND LEFT.
NEVER MIND THAT.
HE'S JUST SOME GUY WHO SHOWED UP 4 OR 5 DAYS AGO.
R-REALLY ?
HE WAS NICE AT FIRST...
HEY, I'LL CARRY THAT.
I...
...JUST KIND OF LOST IT...
AND IT WAS SCARY ...
HE WAS A BASTARD...
...SO I'M GLAD HE'S GONE.
THANK YOU.

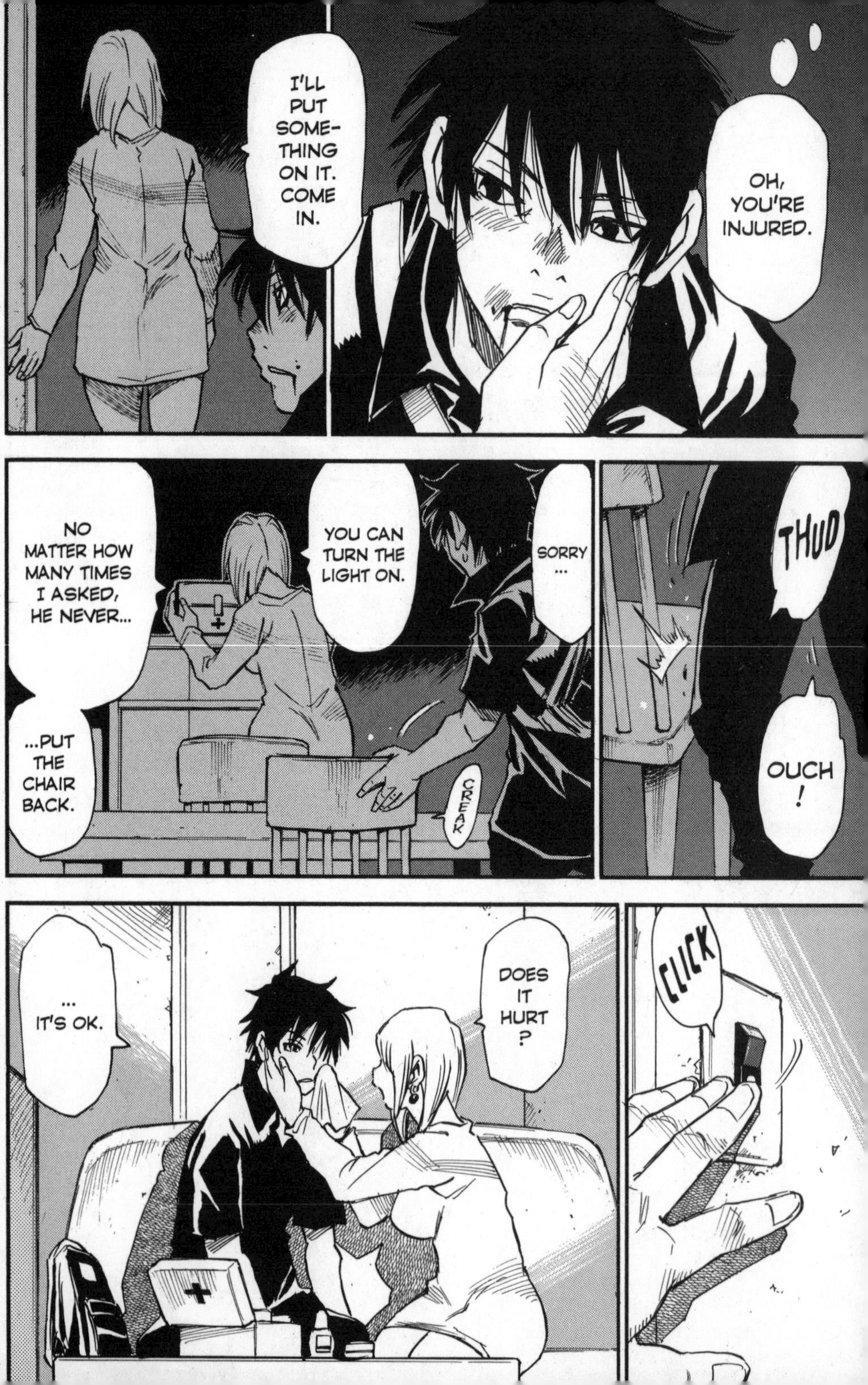
OH, YOU'RE INJURED.
I'LL PUT SOME-THING ON IT. COME IN.
THUD
OUCH!
SORRY...
YOU CAN TURN THE LIGHT ON.
CREAK
NO MATTER HOW MANY TIMES I ASKED, HE NEVER...
...PUT THE CHAIR BACK.
CLICK
DOES IT HURT?
... IT'S OK.

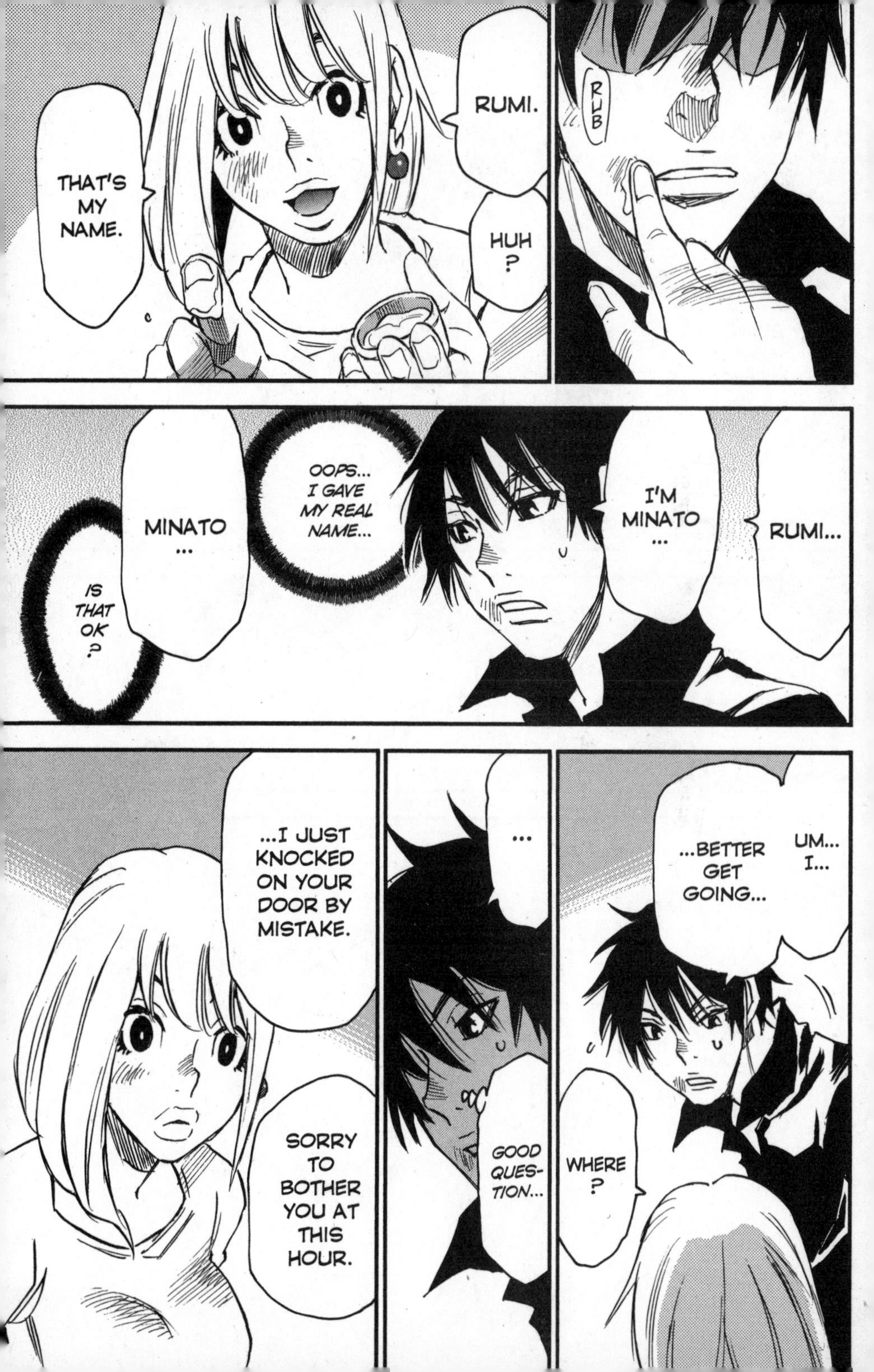
RUB
RUMI.
HUH?
THAT'S MY NAME.
RUMI...
I'M MINATO...
OOPS... I GAVE MY REAL NAME...
MINATO...
IS THAT OK?
UM... I...
...BETTER GET GOING...
WHERE?
...
GOOD QUESTION...
...I JUST KNOCKED ON YOUR DOOR BY MISTAKE.
SORRY TO BOTHER YOU AT THIS HOUR.

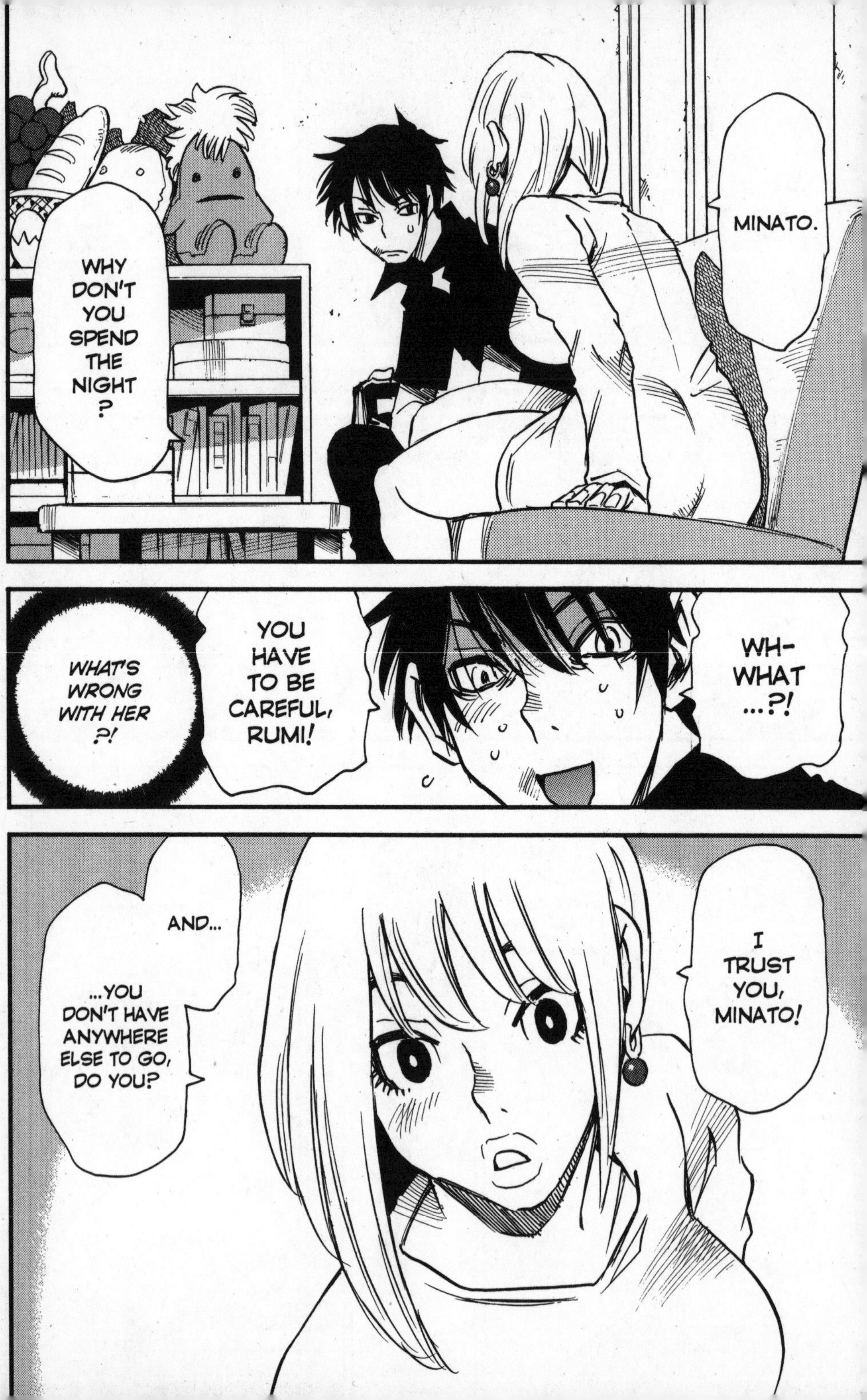
MINATO.
WHY DON'T YOU SPEND THE NIGHT?
WH-WHAT...?!
YOU HAVE TO BE CAREFUL, RUMI!
WHAT'S WRONG WITH HER?!
I TRUST YOU, MINATO!
AND...
...YOU DON'T HAVE ANYWHERE ELSE TO GO, DO YOU?

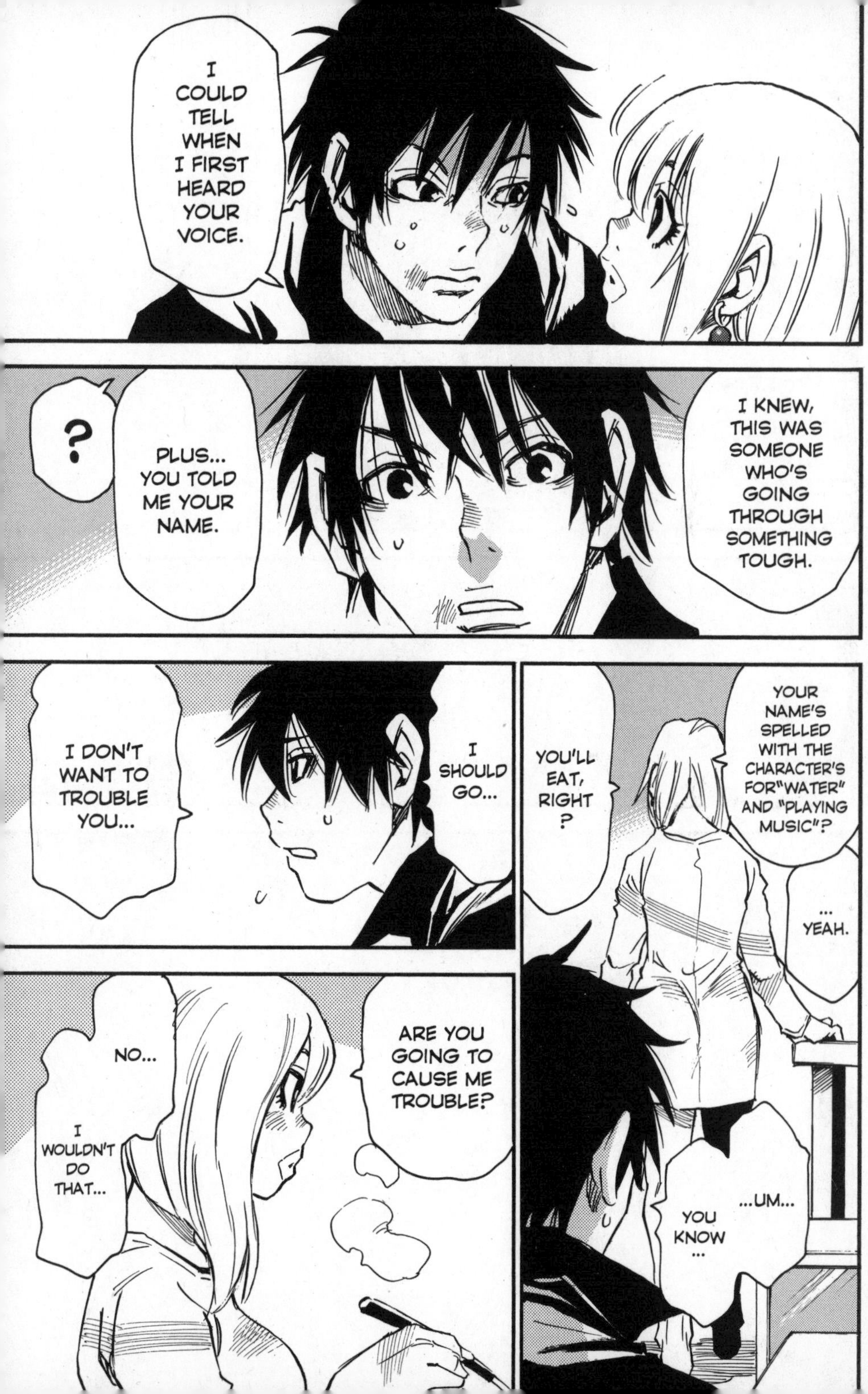
I COULD TELL WHEN I FIRST HEARD YOUR VOICE.
I KNEW, THIS WAS SOMEONE WHO'S GOING THROUGH SOMETHING TOUGH.
PLUS... YOU TOLD ME YOUR NAME.
?
YOUR NAME'S SPELLED WITH THE CHARACTER'S FOR "WATER" AND "PLAYING MUSIC"?
YOU'LL EAT, RIGHT?
... YEAH.
...UM...
YOU KNOW ...
I SHOULD GO...
I DON'T WANT TO TROUBLE YOU...
ARE YOU GOING TO CAUSE ME TROUBLE?
NO...
I WOULDN'T DO THAT...

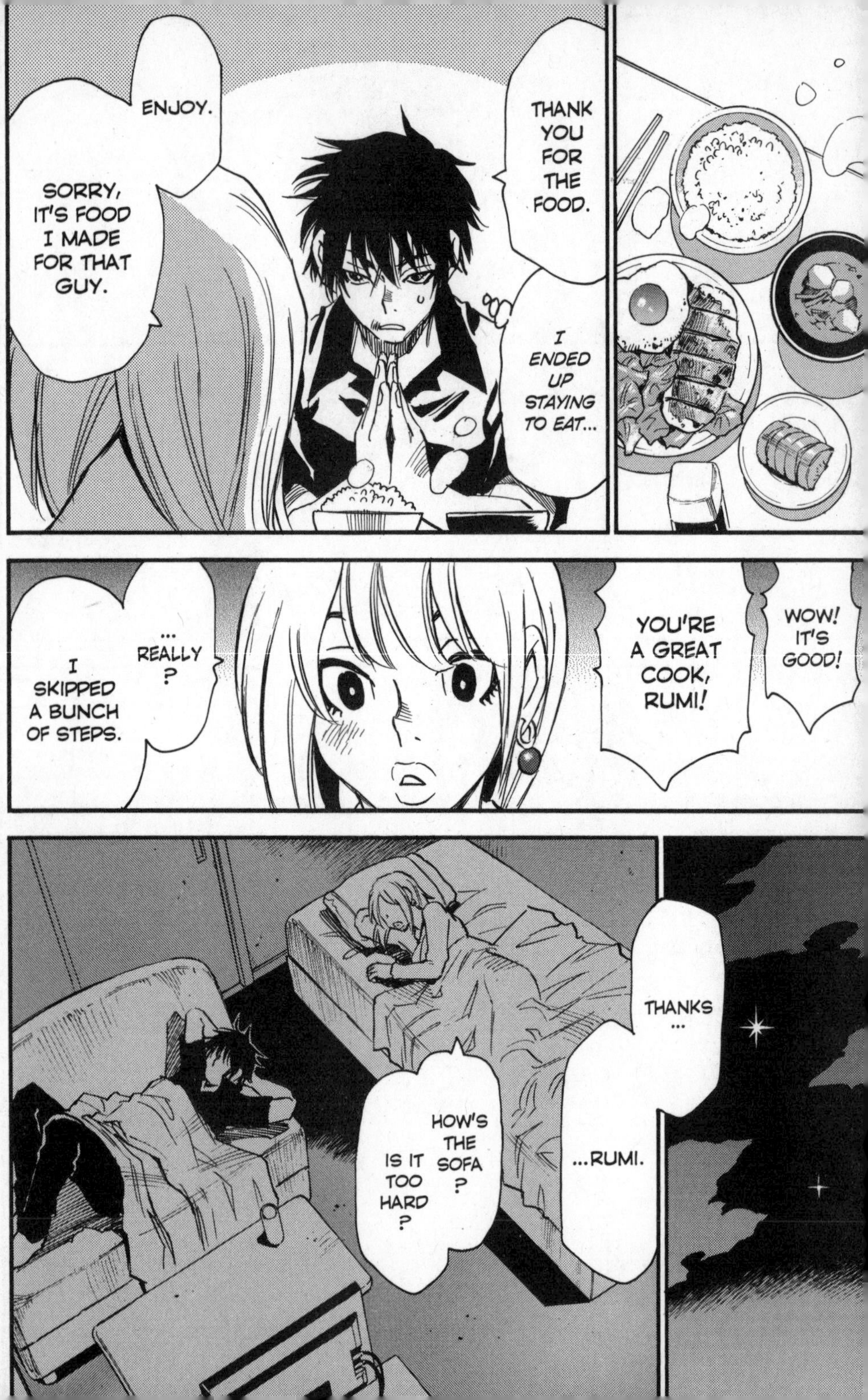
THANK YOU FOR THE FOOD.
I ENDED UP STAYING TO EAT...
ENJOY.
SORRY, IT'S FOOD I MADE FOR THAT GUY.
WOW! IT'S GOOD!
YOU'RE A GREAT COOK, RUMI!
...REALLY?
I SKIPPED A BUNCH OF STEPS.
THANKS...
...RUMI.
HOW'S THE SOFA?
IS IT TOO HARD?

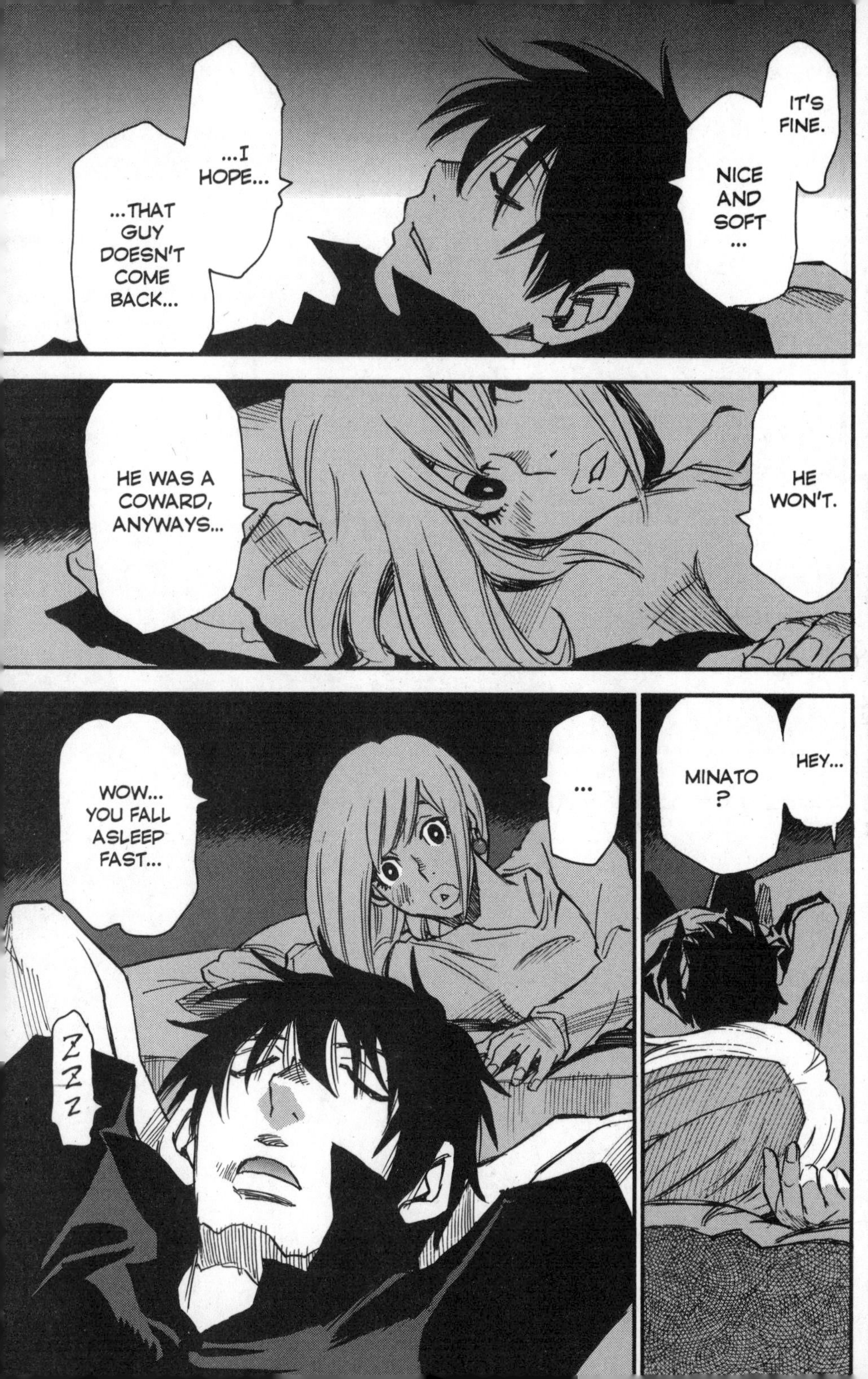
IT'S FINE.
NICE AND SOFT...
...I HOPE...
...THAT GUY DOESN'T COME BACK...
HE WON'T.
HE WAS A COWARD, ANYWAYS...
HEY...
MINATO?
...
WOW... YOU FALL ASLEEP FAST...
ZZZ

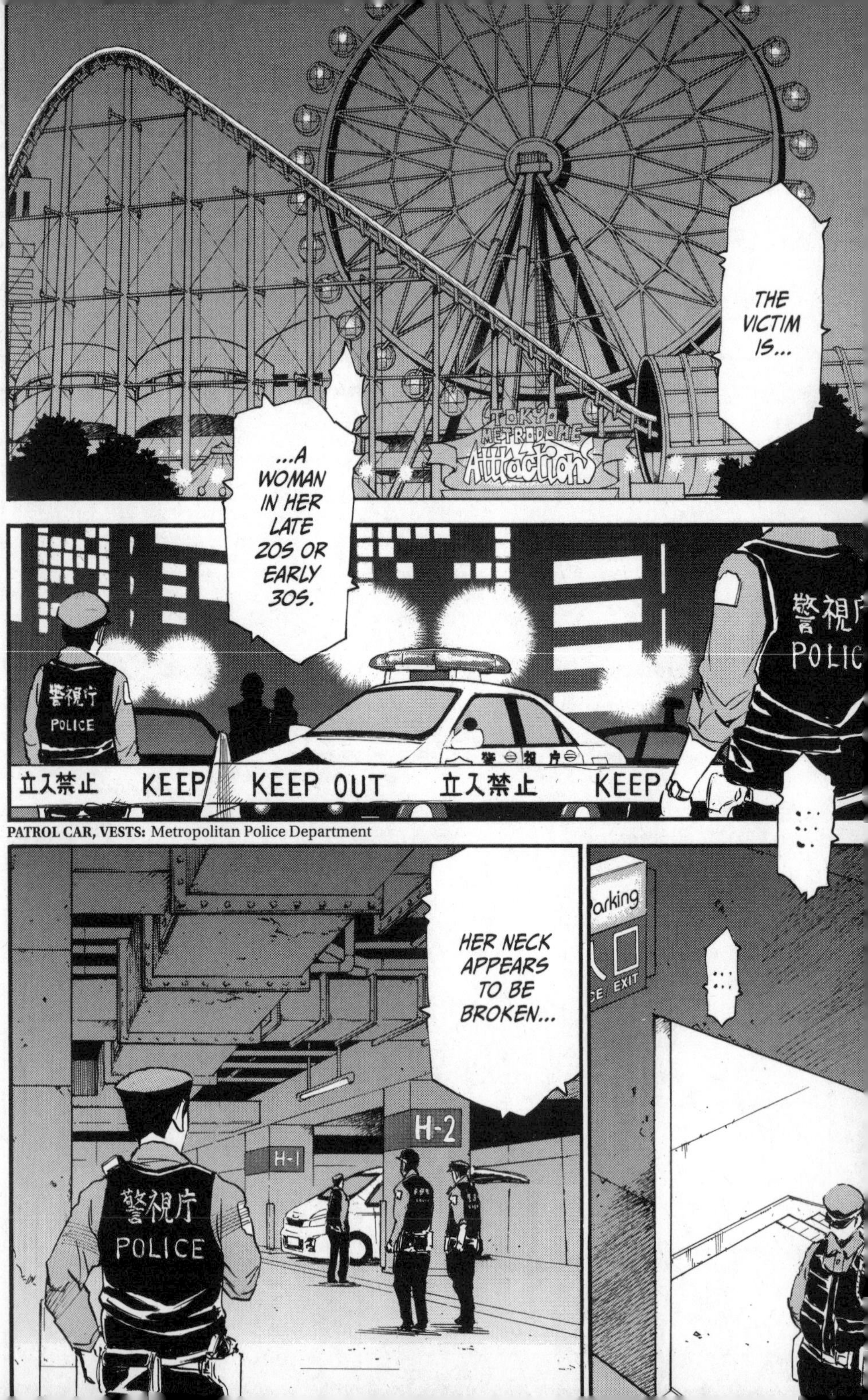
THE VICTIM IS...
...A WOMAN IN HER LATE 20S OR EARLY 30S.
TOKYO METRODOME Attractions
...
警視庁 POLICE
立入禁止 KEEP KEEP OUT 立入禁止 KEEP
...
HER NECK APPEARS TO BE BROKEN...
Parking
EXIT
H-2
H-1
警視庁 POLICE
PATROL CAR, VESTS: Metropolitan Police Department

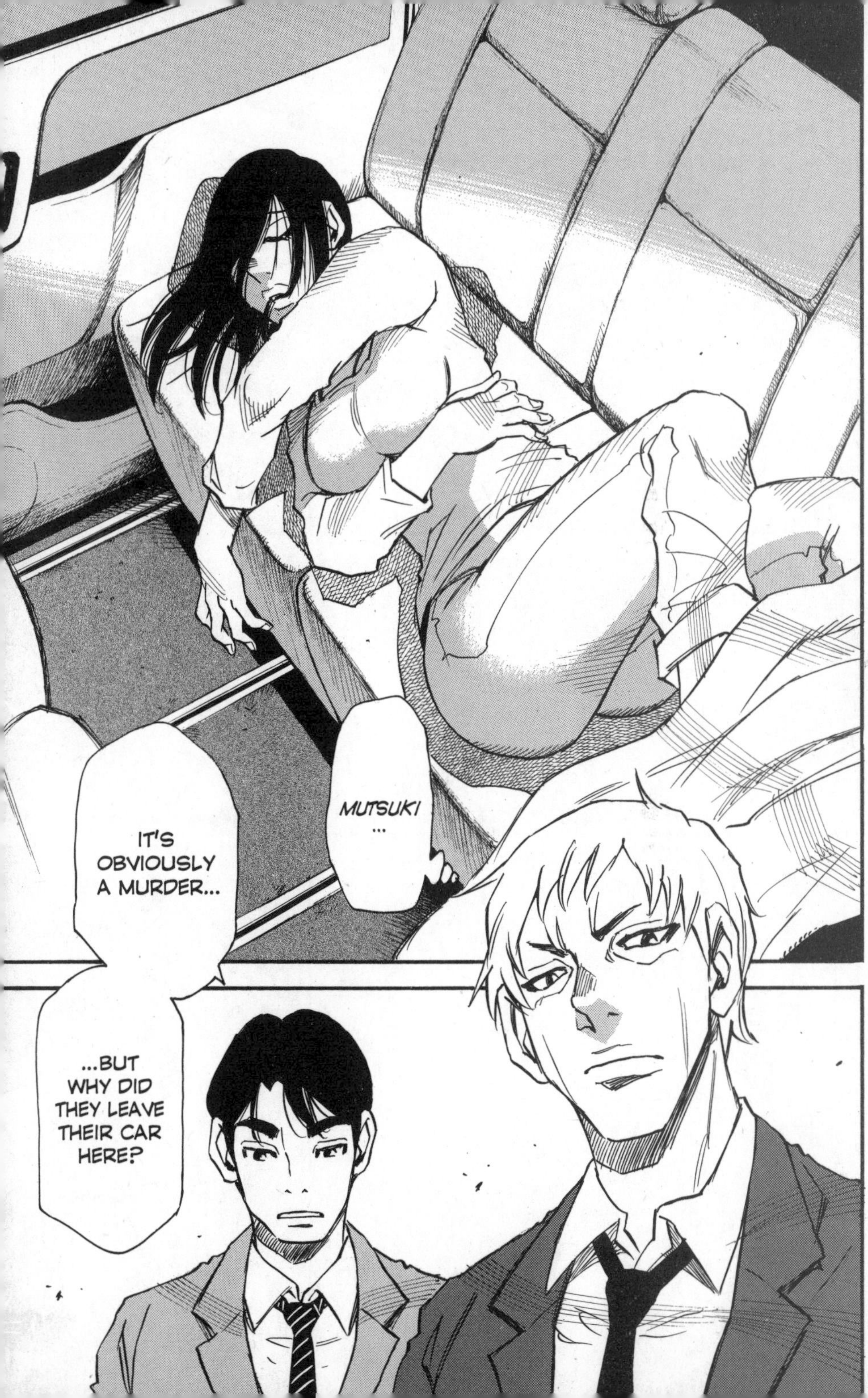
MUTSUKI ...
IT'S OBVIOUSLY A MURDER...
...BUT WHY DID THEY LEAVE THEIR CAR HERE?

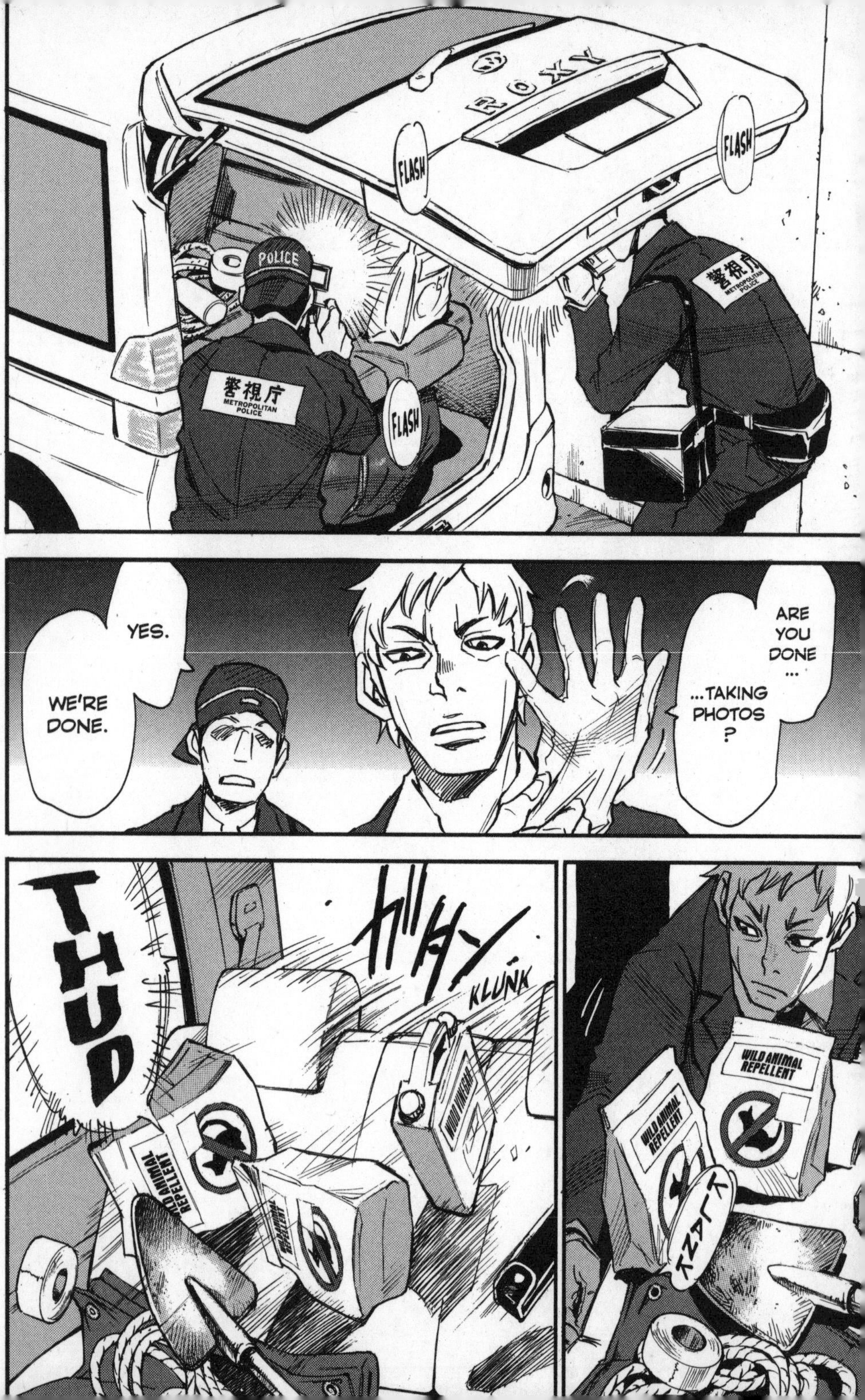ROXY
FLASH
FLASH
POLICE
警視庁 METROPOLITAN POLICE
FLASH
警視庁 METROPOLITAN POLICE
ARE YOU DONE ...
...TAKING PHOTOS ?
YES.
WE'RE DONE.
WILD ANIMAL REPELLENT
WILD ANIMAL REPELLENT
KLUNK
WOOD VINEGAR
WILD ANIMAL REPELLENT
THUD

OH...!

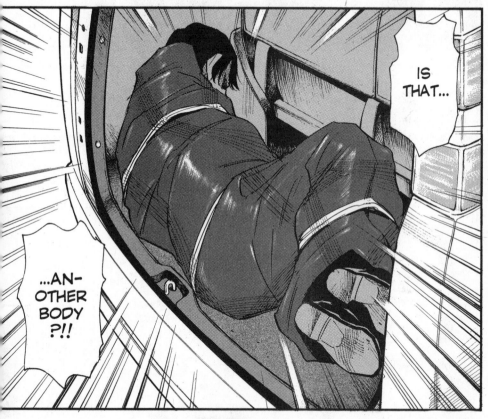

IS THAT...

...AN- OTHER BODY ?!!

CLICK

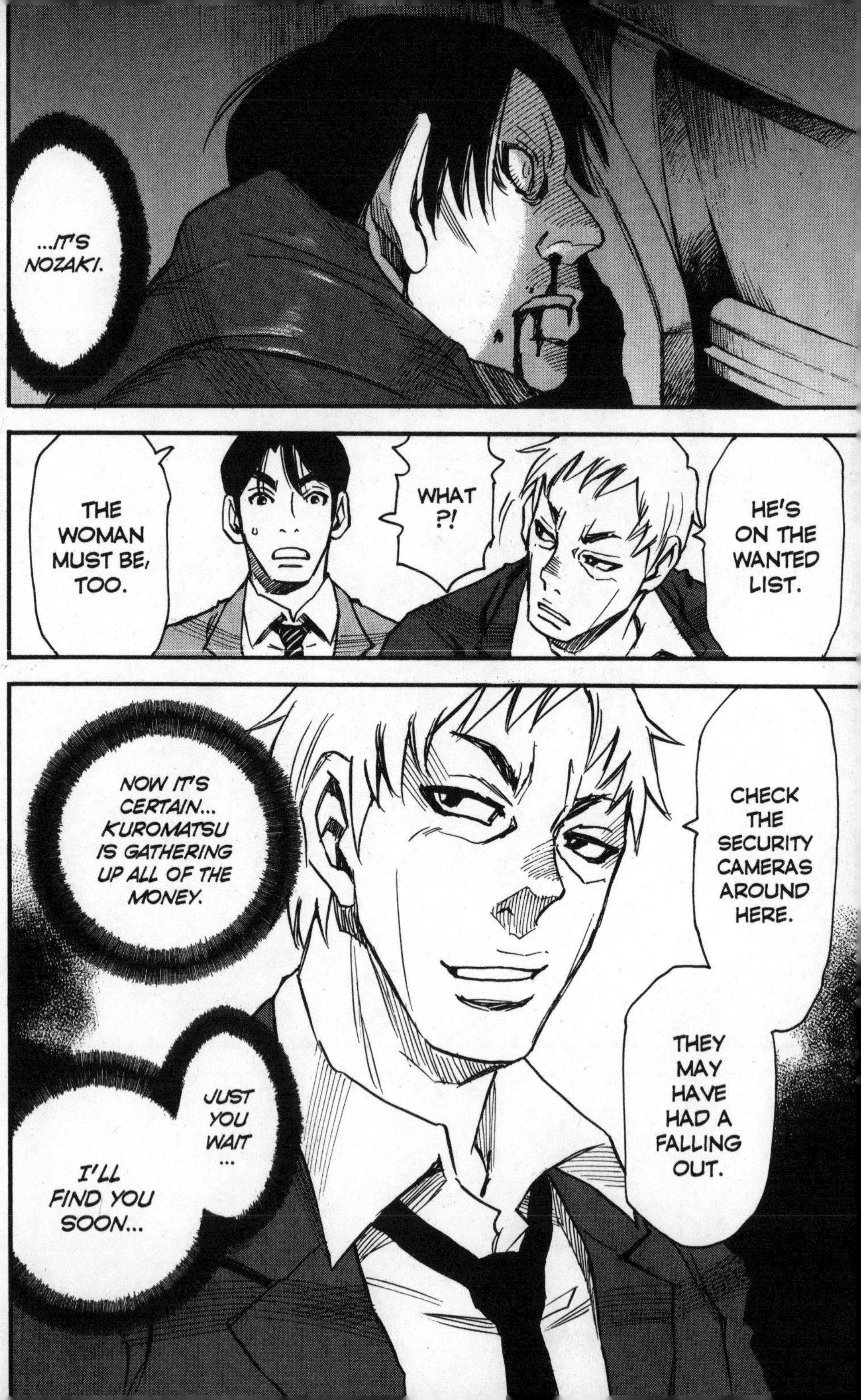
...IT'S NOZAKI.
HE'S ON THE WANTED LIST.
WHAT ?!
THE WOMAN MUST BE, TOO.
CHECK THE SECURITY CAMERAS AROUND HERE.
NOW IT'S CERTAIN... KUROMATSU IS GATHERING UP ALL OF THE MONEY.
THEY MAY HAVE HAD A FALLING OUT.
JUST YOU WAIT ...
I'LL FIND YOU SOON...

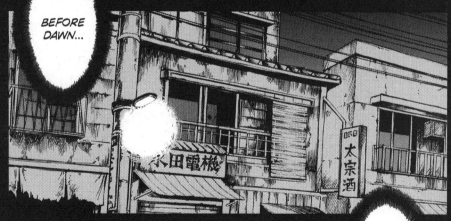

CHAPTER **9**
The Trackers
Are Coming

IT ALWAYS HAPPENED IN THE EARLY HOURS...

BEFORE DAWN...

CREAK

WHEN IT WAS STILL DARK...

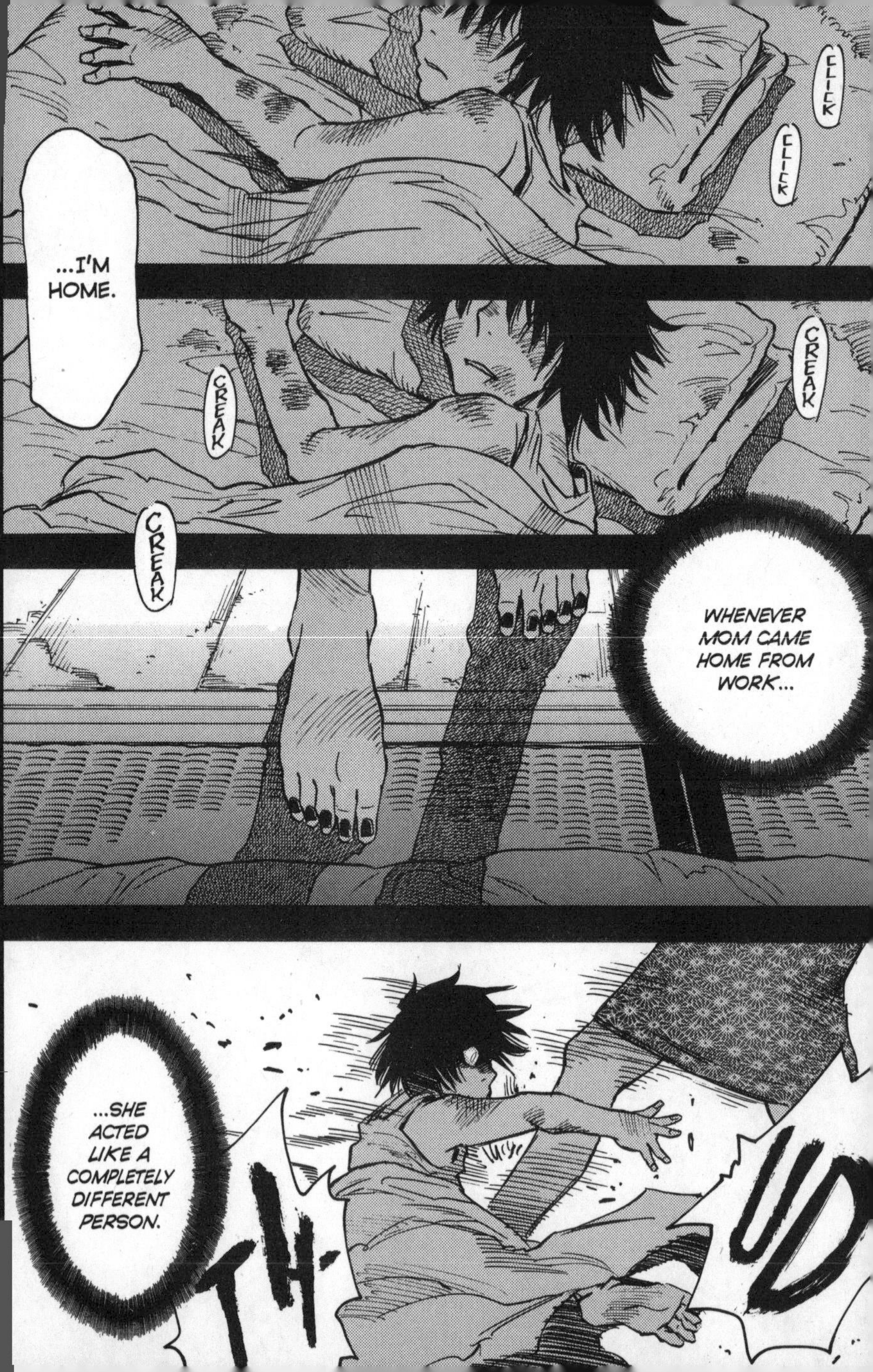
CLICK
CLICK
...I'M HOME.
CREAK
CREAK
WHENEVER MOM CAME HOME FROM WORK...
CREAK
...SHE ACTED LIKE A COMPLETELY DIFFERENT PERSON.
THUD

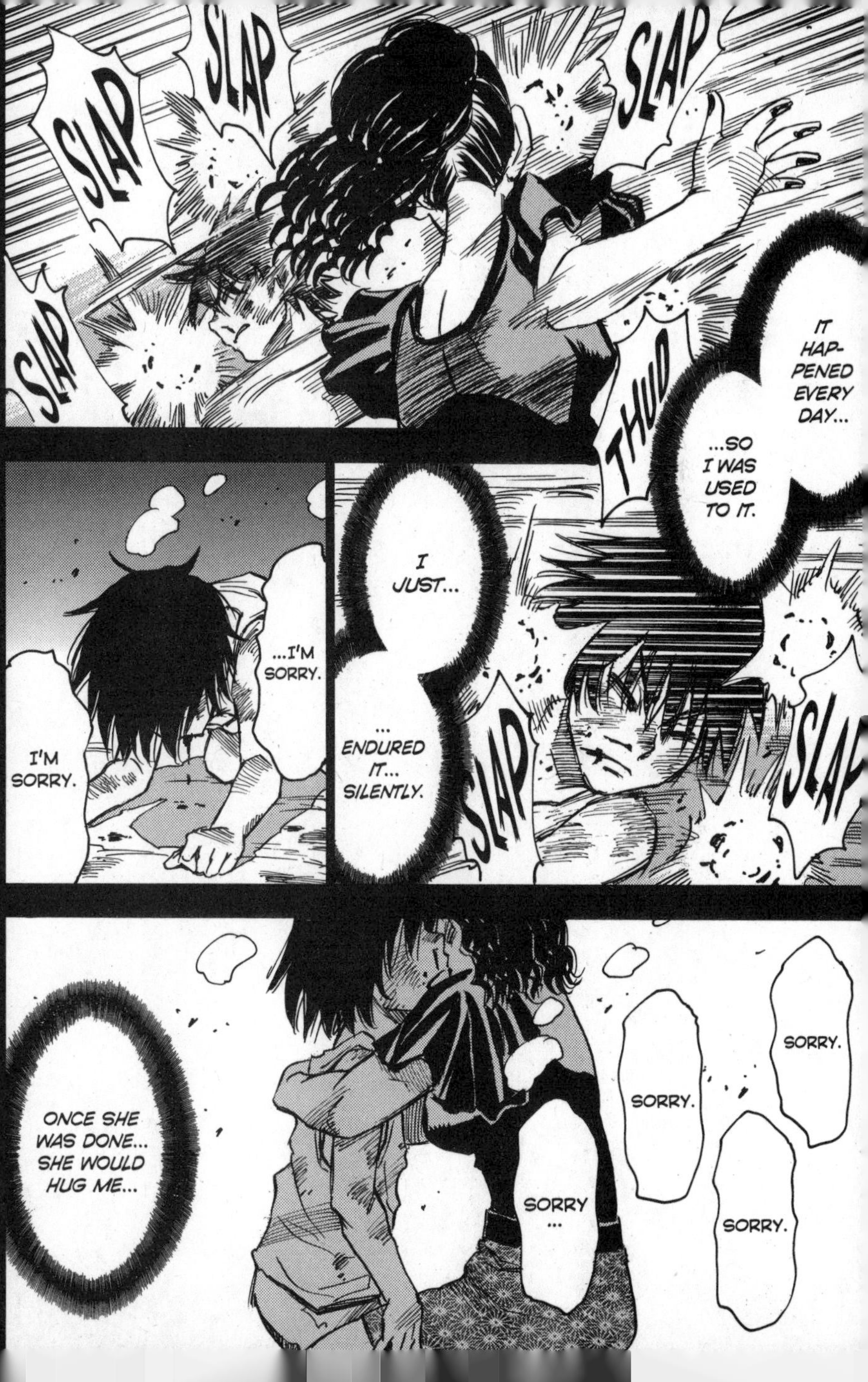
SLAP
SLAP
SLAP
SLAP
IT HAP-PENED EVERY DAY...
...SO I WAS USED TO IT.
THUD
SLAP
SLAP
I JUST...
...ENDURED IT... SILENTLY.
...I'M SORRY.
I'M SORRY.
SORRY.
SORRY.
SORRY.
SORRY...
ONCE SHE WAS DONE... SHE WOULD HUG ME...

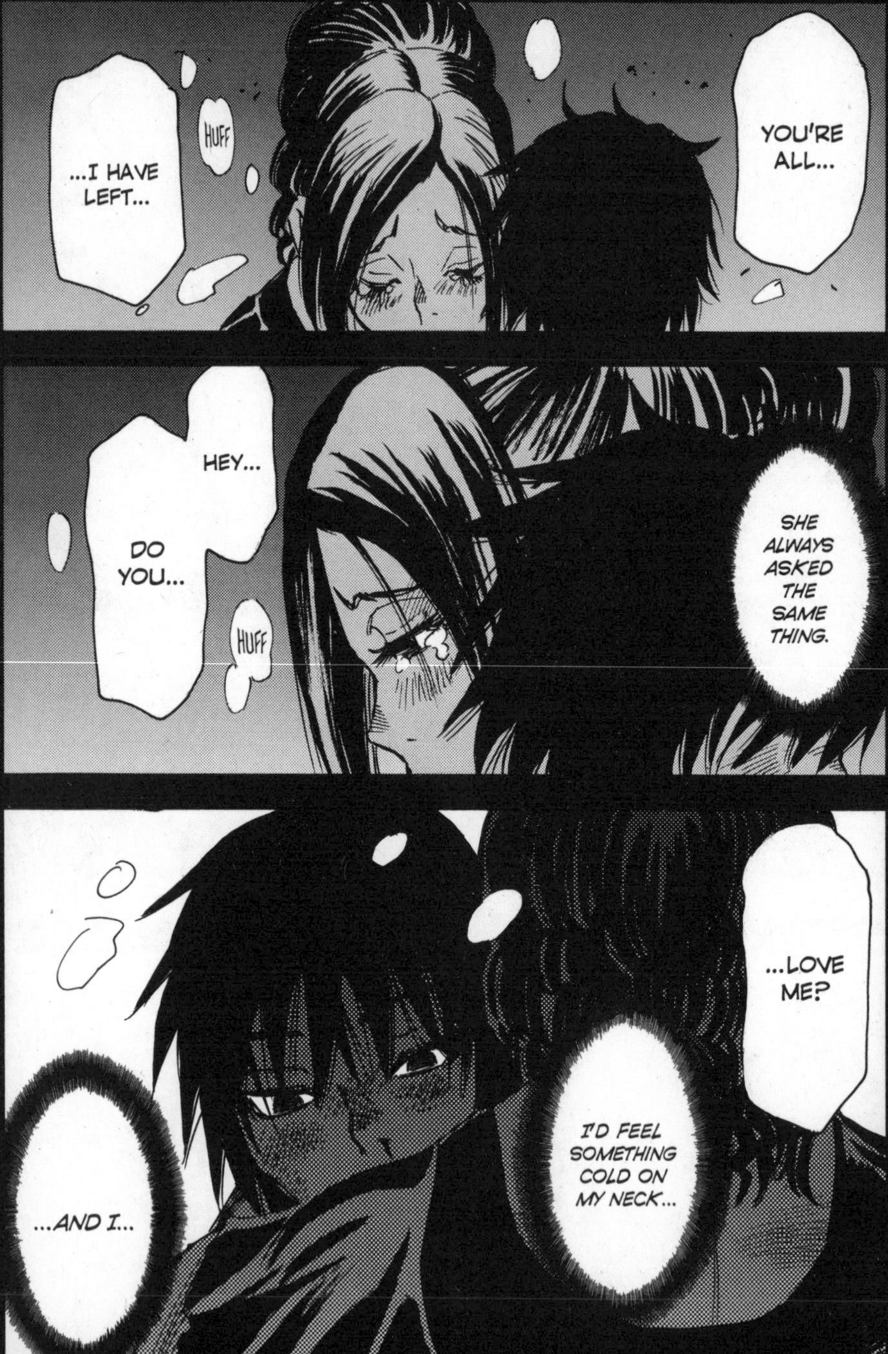
YOU'RE ALL...
HUFF
...I HAVE LEFT...
SHE ALWAYS ASKED THE SAME THING.
HEY...
DO YOU...
HUFF
...LOVE ME?
I'D FEEL SOMETHING COLD ON MY NECK...
...AND I...

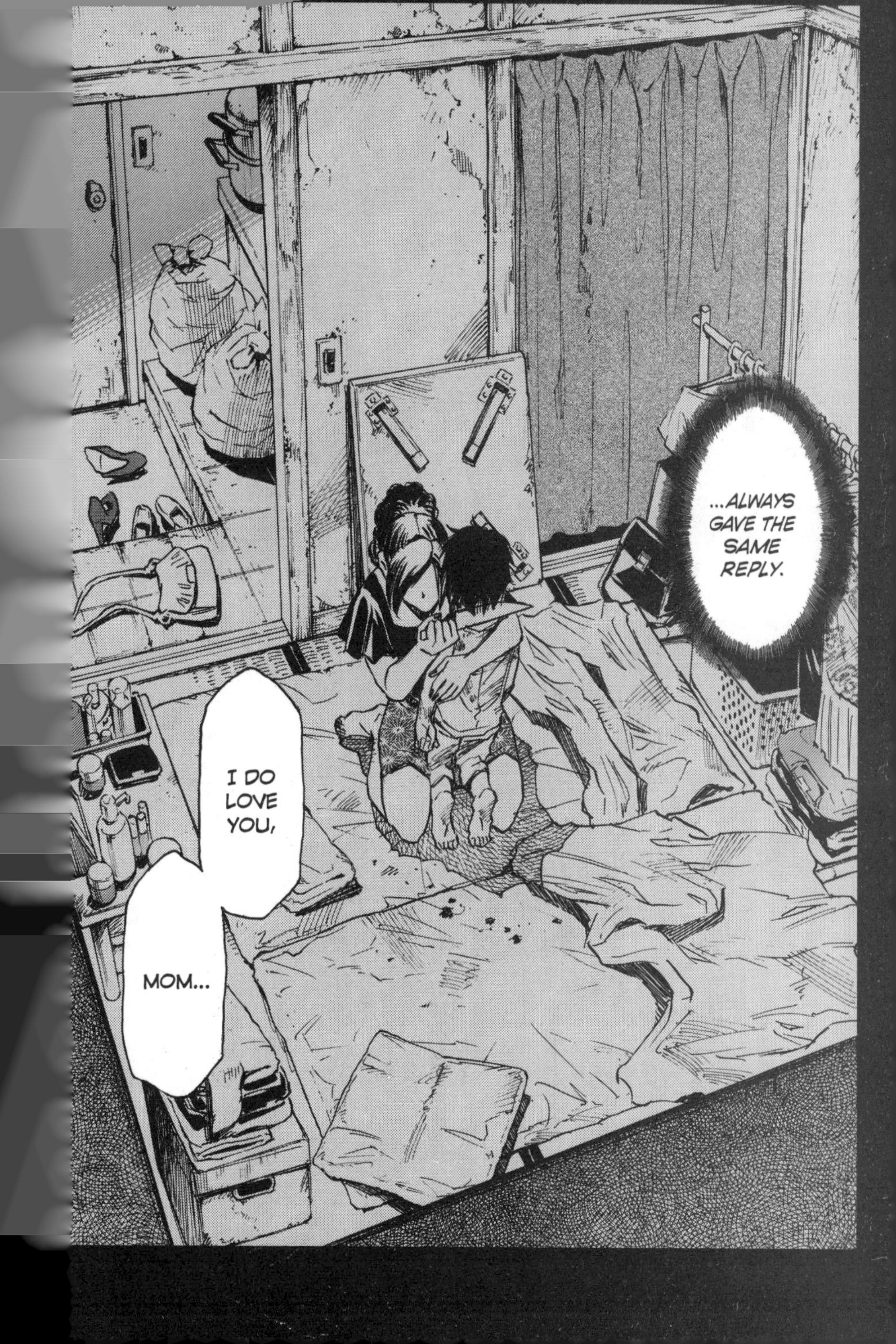
...ALWAYS GAVE THE SAME REPLY.
I DO LOVE YOU,
MOM...

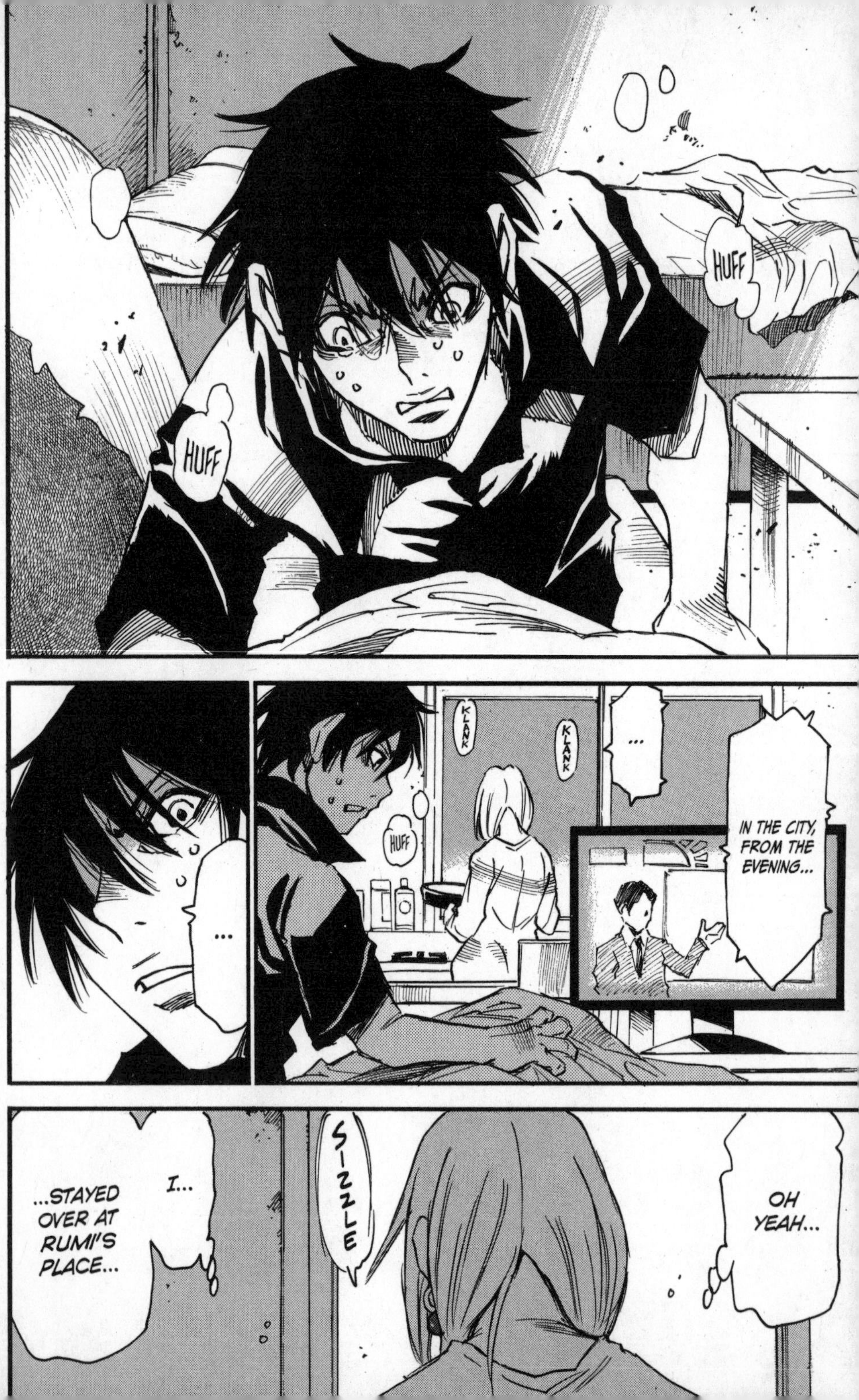
HUFF
HUFF
IN THE CITY, FROM THE EVENING...
...
KLANK
KLANK
HUFF
...
OH YEAH...
SIZZLE
I...
...STAYED OVER AT RUMI'S PLACE...

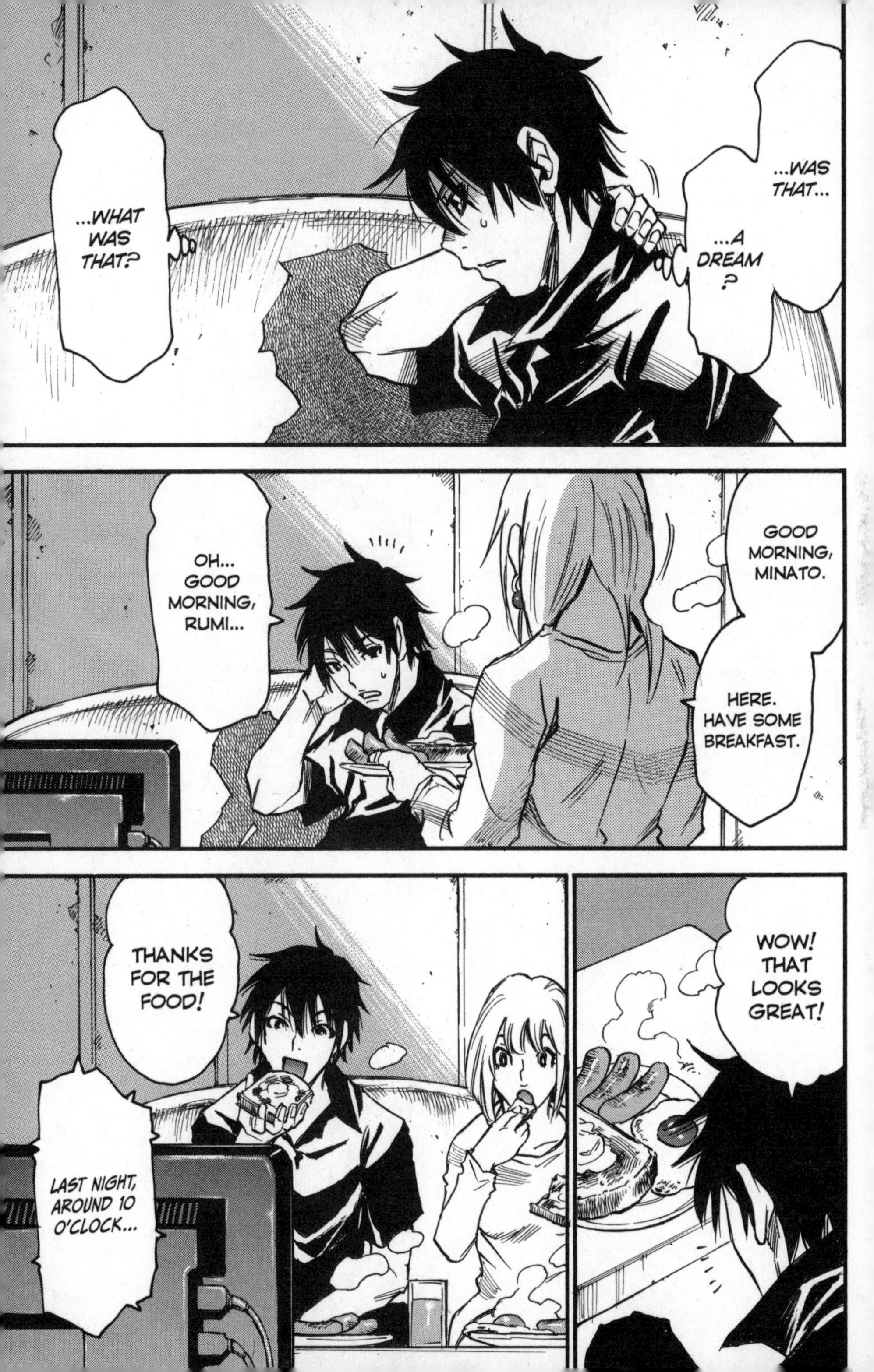
...WAS THAT...
...A DREAM?
...WHAT WAS THAT?
GOOD MORNING, MINATO.
HERE. HAVE SOME BREAKFAST.
OH... GOOD MORNING, RUMI...
WOW! THAT LOOKS GREAT!
THANKS FOR THE FOOD!
LAST NIGHT, AROUND 10 O'CLOCK...

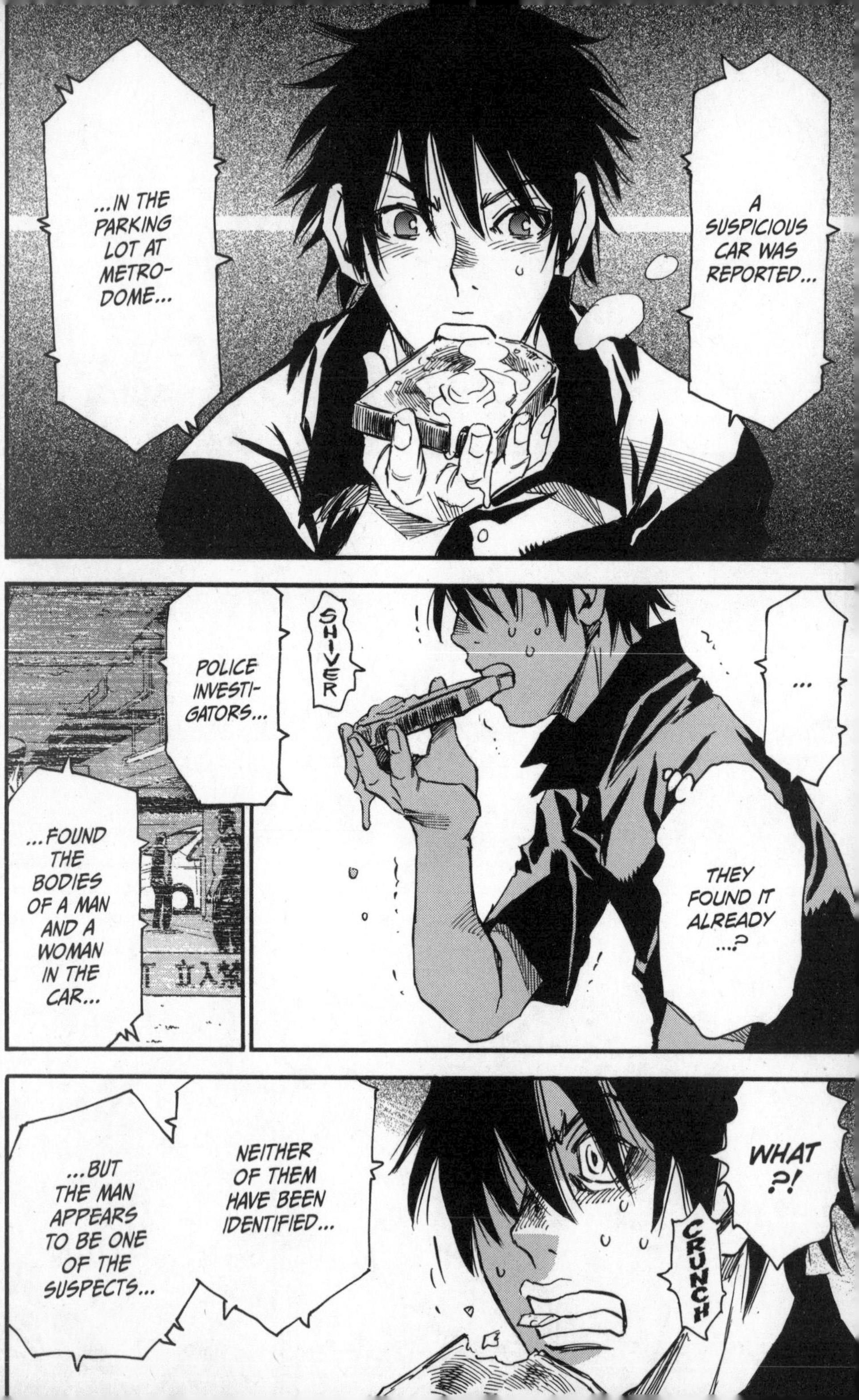
A SUSPICIOUS CAR WAS REPORTED...
...IN THE PARKING LOT AT METRO-DOME...
...
SHIVER
THEY FOUND IT ALREADY ...?
POLICE INVESTI-GATORS...
...FOUND THE BODIES OF A MAN AND A WOMAN IN THE CAR...
WHAT ?!
CRUNCH
NEITHER OF THEM HAVE BEEN IDENTIFIED...
...BUT THE MAN APPEARS TO BE ONE OF THE SUSPECTS...

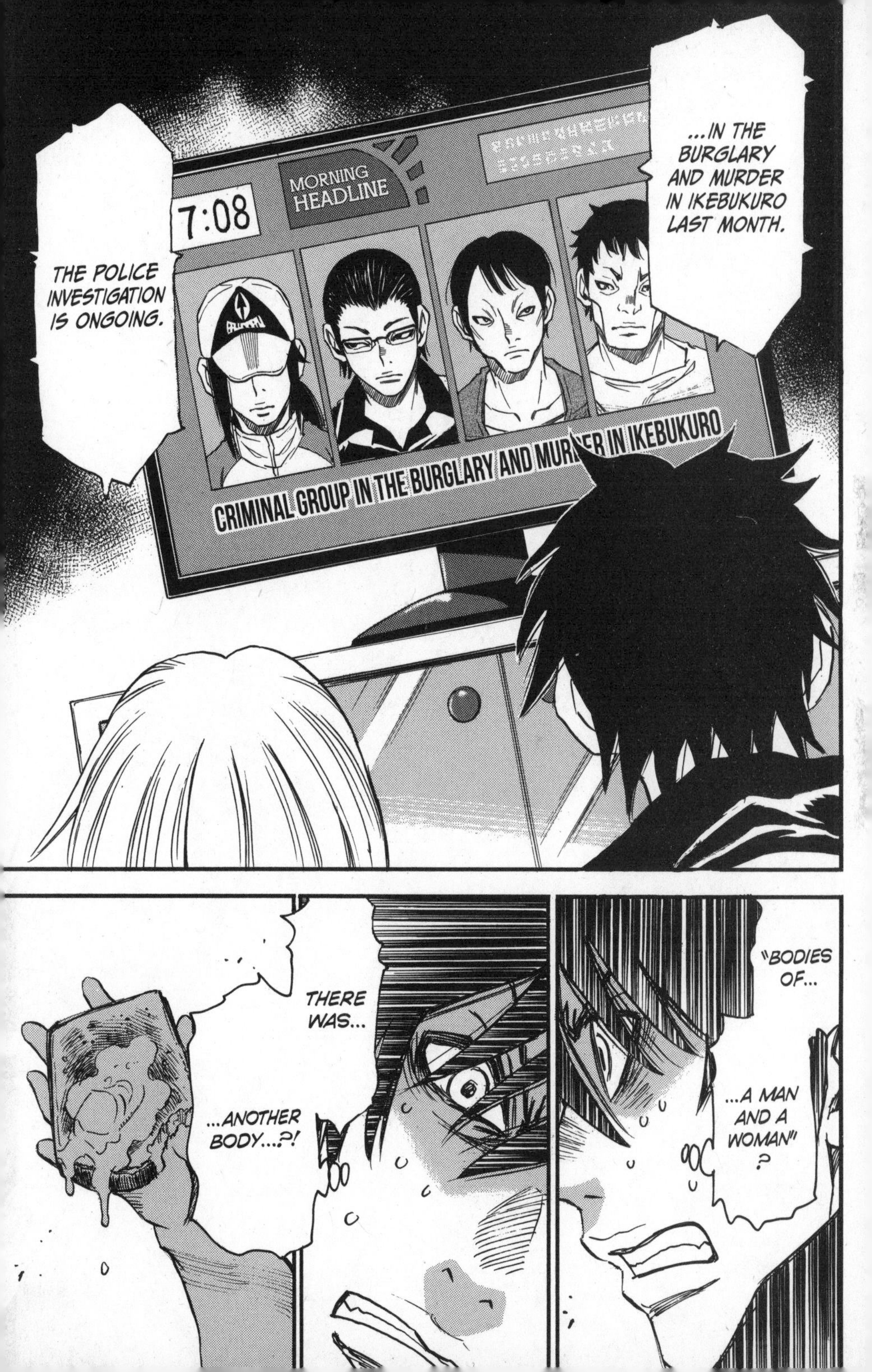
...IN THE BURGLARY AND MURDER IN IKEBUKURO LAST MONTH.
7:08
MORNING HEADLINE
THE POLICE INVESTIGATION IS ONGOING.
CRIMINAL GROUP IN THE BURGLARY AND MUR
ER IN IKEBUKURO
"BODIES OF...
...A MAN AND A WOMAN"?
THERE WAS...
...ANOTHER BODY...?!

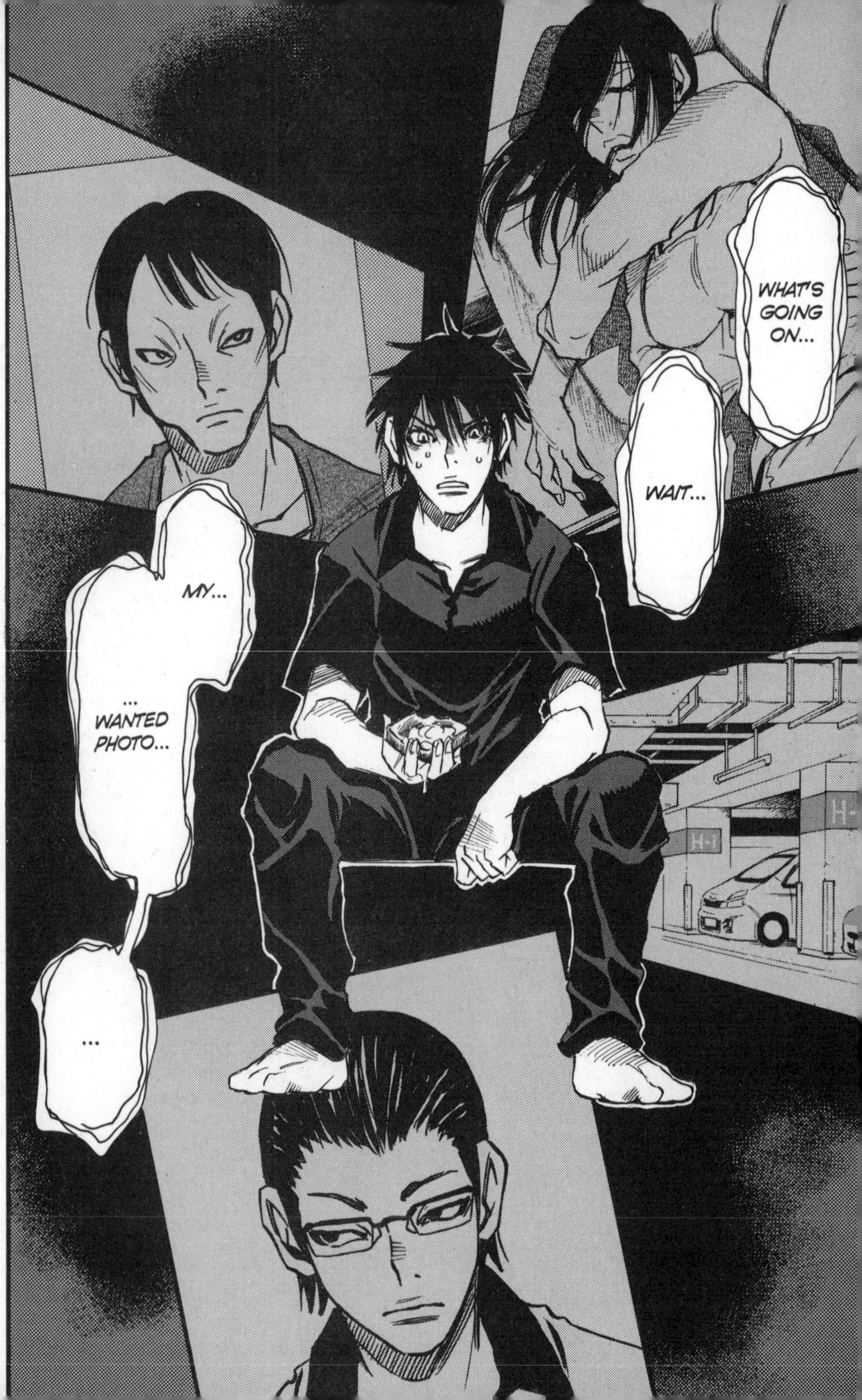
WHAT'S GOING ON...
WAIT...
MY...
... WANTED PHOTO...
...

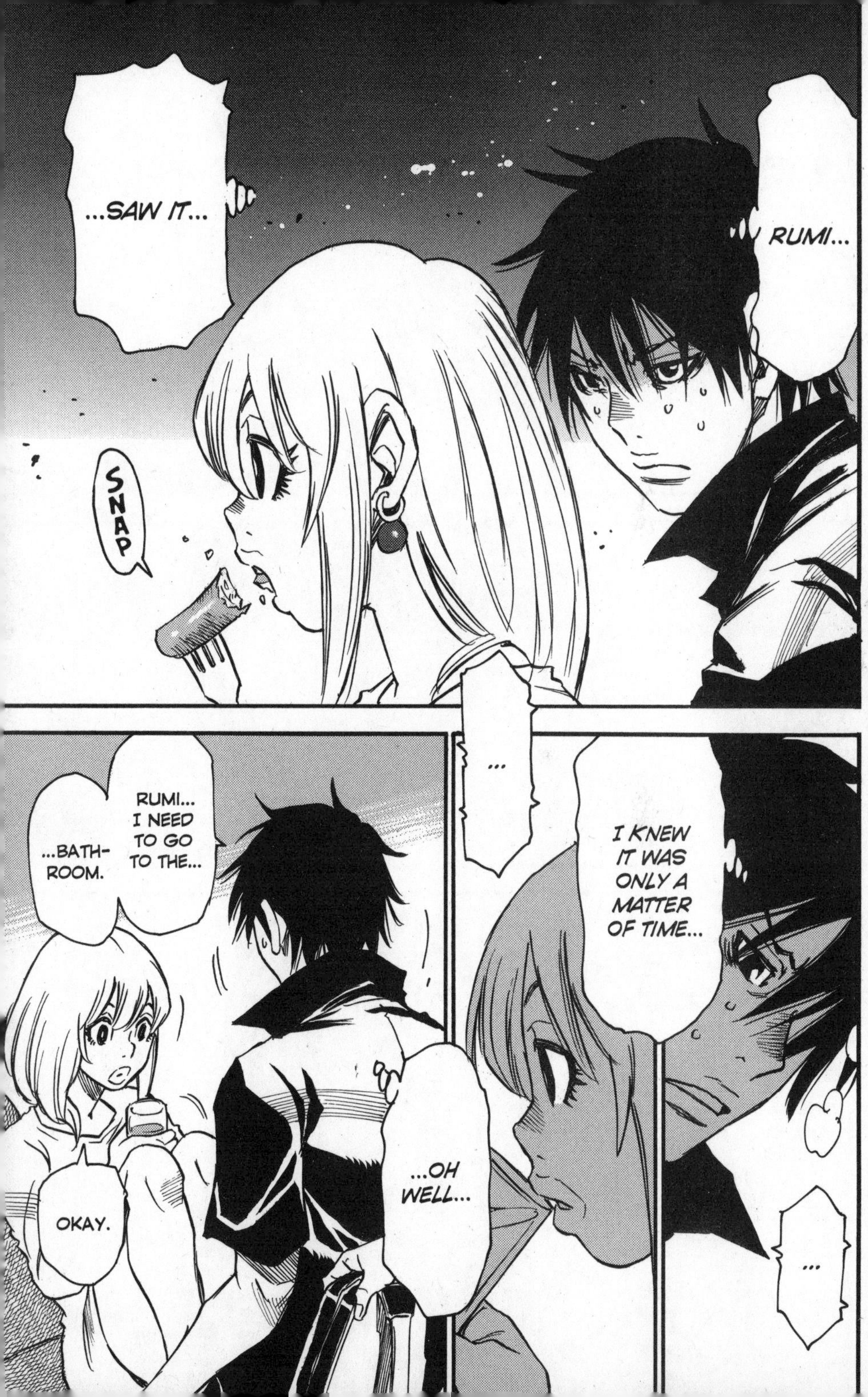
RUMI...
...SAW IT...
SNAP
...
I KNEW IT WAS ONLY A MATTER OF TIME...
...
RUMI... I NEED TO GO TO THE...
...BATH-ROOM.
...OH WELL...
OKAY.

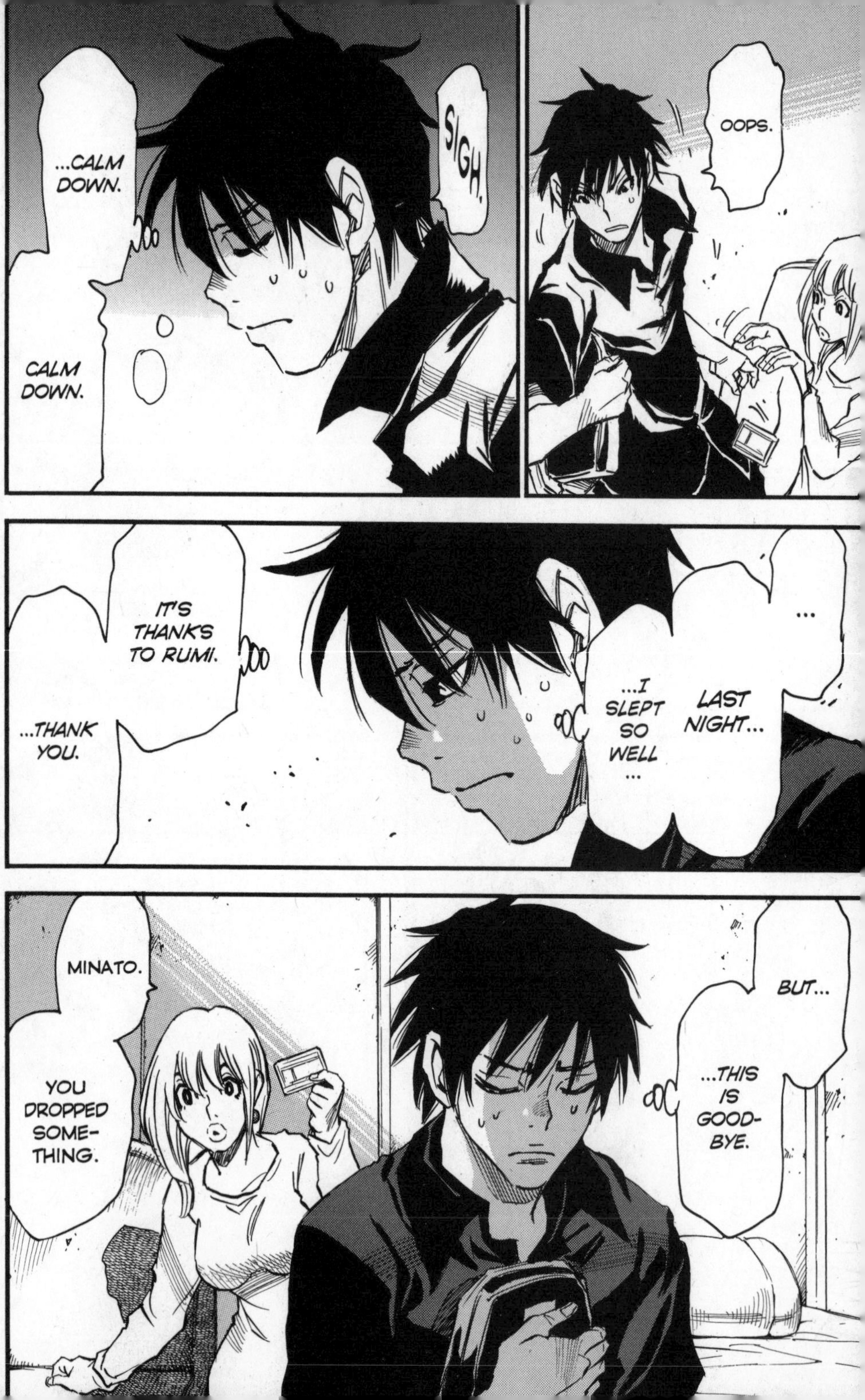
OOPS.
SIGH.
...CALM DOWN.
CALM DOWN.
...
LAST NIGHT...
...I SLEPT SO WELL ...
IT'S THANKS TO RUMI.
...THANK YOU.
BUT...
...THIS IS GOOD-BYE.
MINATO.
YOU DROPPED SOME-THING.

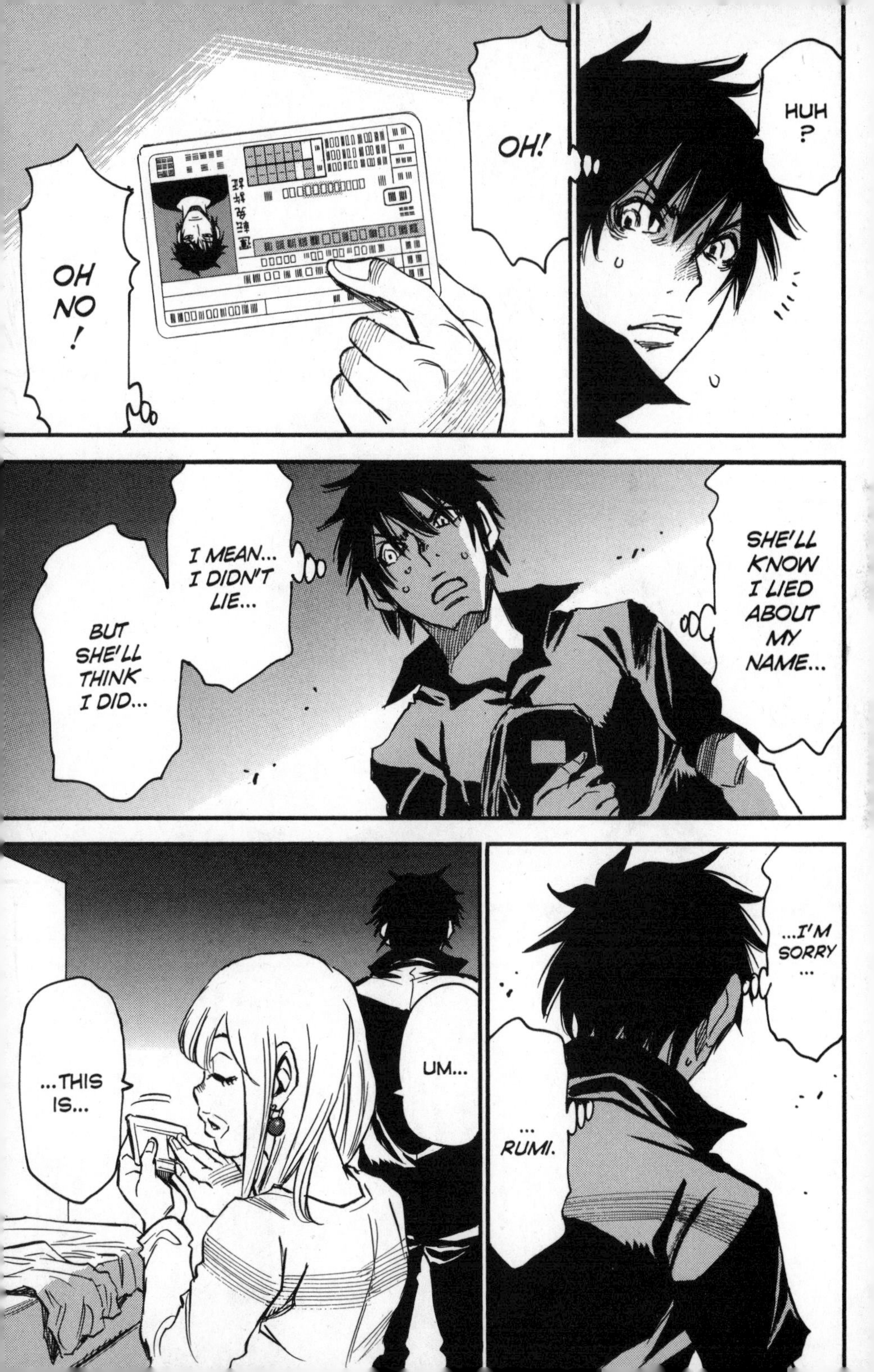
HUH?
OH!
OH NO!
SHE'LL KNOW I LIED ABOUT MY NAME...
I MEAN... I DIDN'T LIE...
BUT SHE'LL THINK I DID...
...I'M SORRY...
...RUMI.
UM...
...THIS IS...

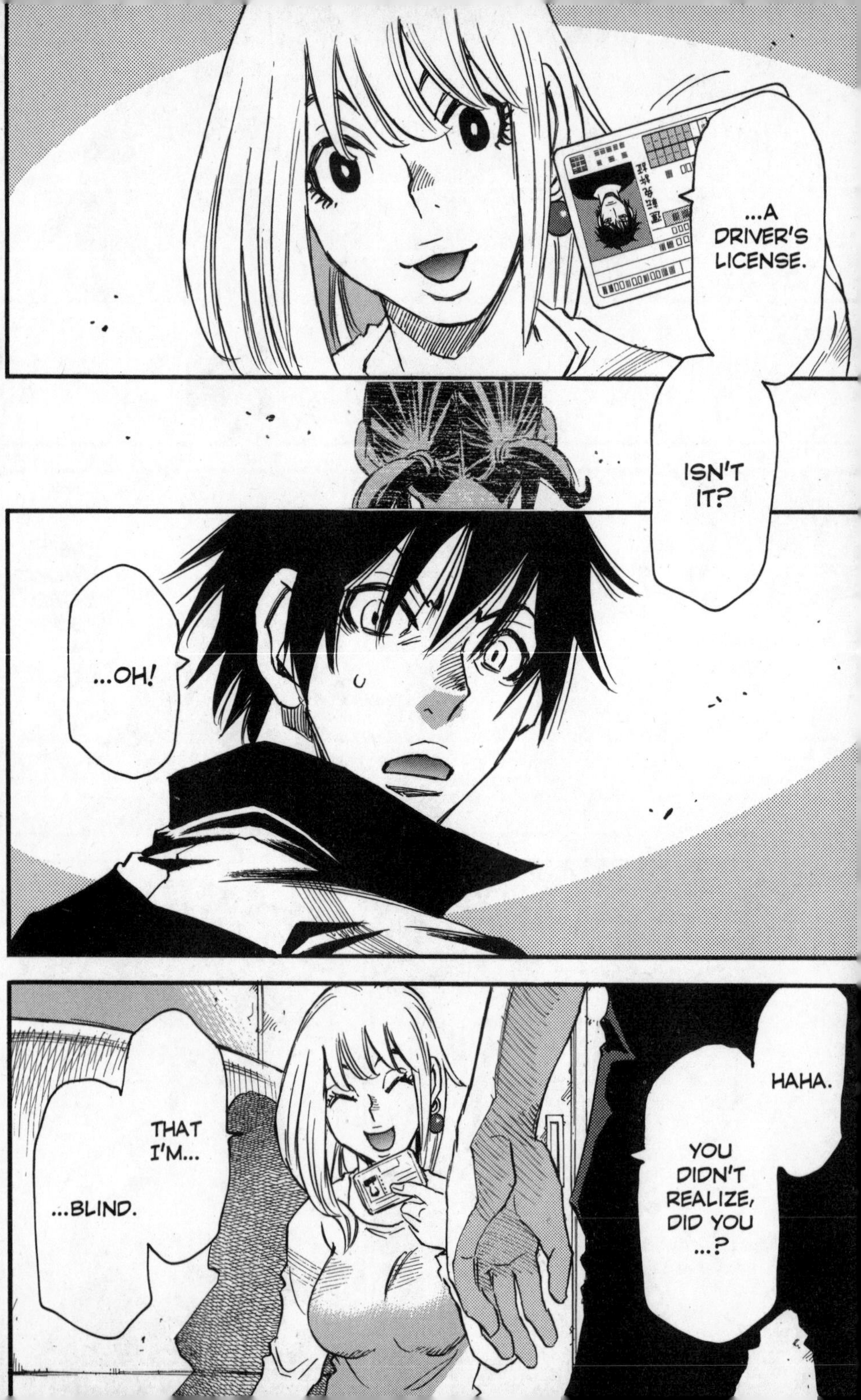
...A DRIVER'S LICENSE.
ISN'T IT?
...OH!
HAHA.
YOU DIDN'T REALIZE, DID YOU ...?
THAT I'M...
...BLIND.

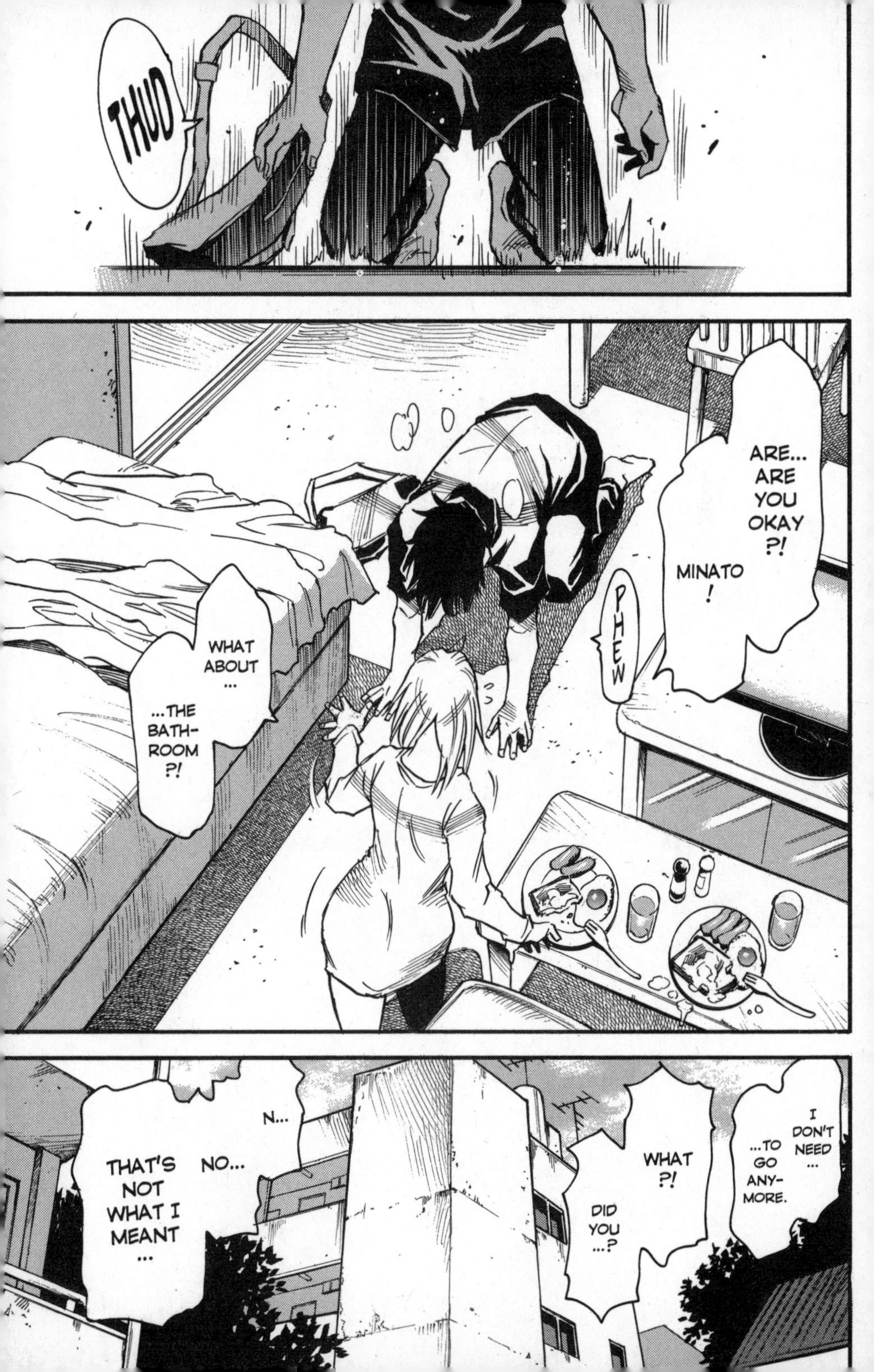
THUD
ARE... ARE YOU OKAY?! MINATO!
PHEW
WHAT ABOUT... ...THE BATHROOM?!
I DON'T NEED... ...TO GO ANYMORE.
WHAT?! DID YOU...?
N... NO... THAT'S NOT WHAT I MEANT...

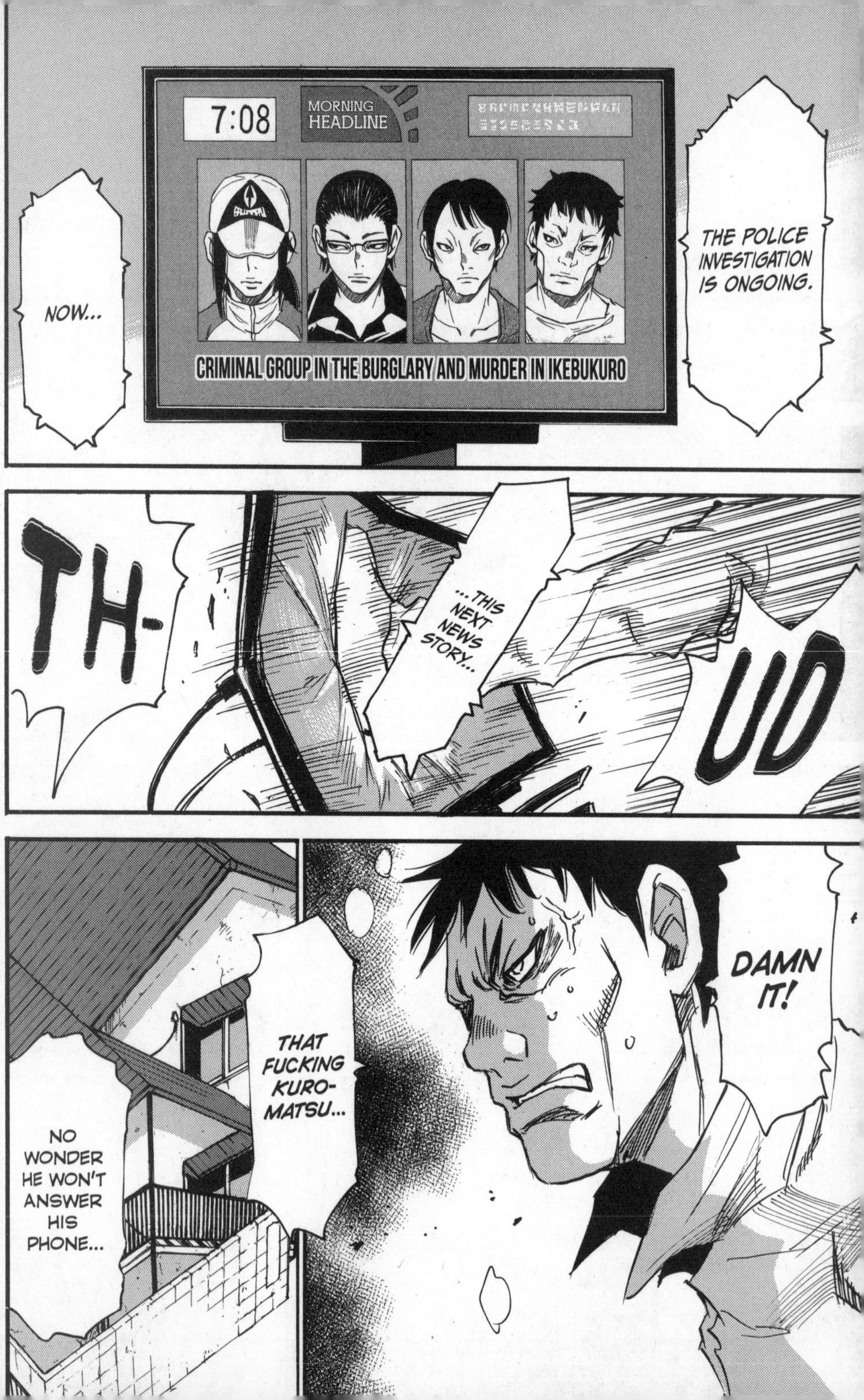
THE POLICE INVESTIGATION IS ONGOING.
7:08
MORNING HEADLINE
CRIMINAL GROUP IN THE BURGLARY AND MURDER IN IKEBUKURO
NOW...
...THIS NEXT NEWS STORY...
TH-
UD
DAMN IT!
THAT FUCKING KURO-MATSU...
NO WONDER HE WON'T ANSWER HIS PHONE...

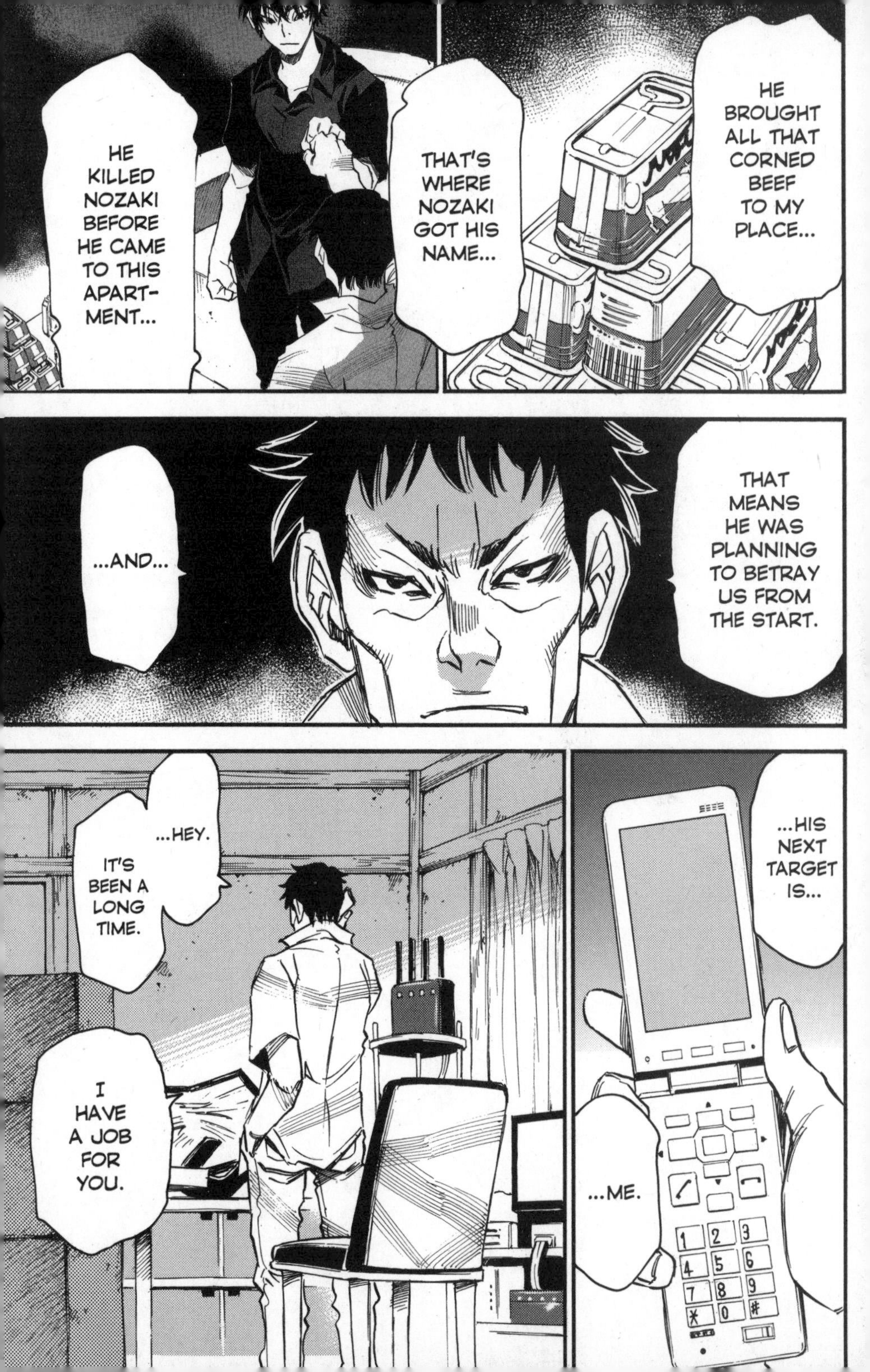
HE BROUGHT ALL THAT CORNED BEEF TO MY PLACE...
THAT'S WHERE NOZAKI GOT HIS NAME...
HE KILLED NOZAKI BEFORE HE CAME TO THIS APART-MENT...
THAT MEANS HE WAS PLANNING TO BETRAY US FROM THE START.
...AND...
...HIS NEXT TARGET IS...
...ME.
...HEY.
IT'S BEEN A LONG TIME.
I HAVE A JOB FOR YOU.

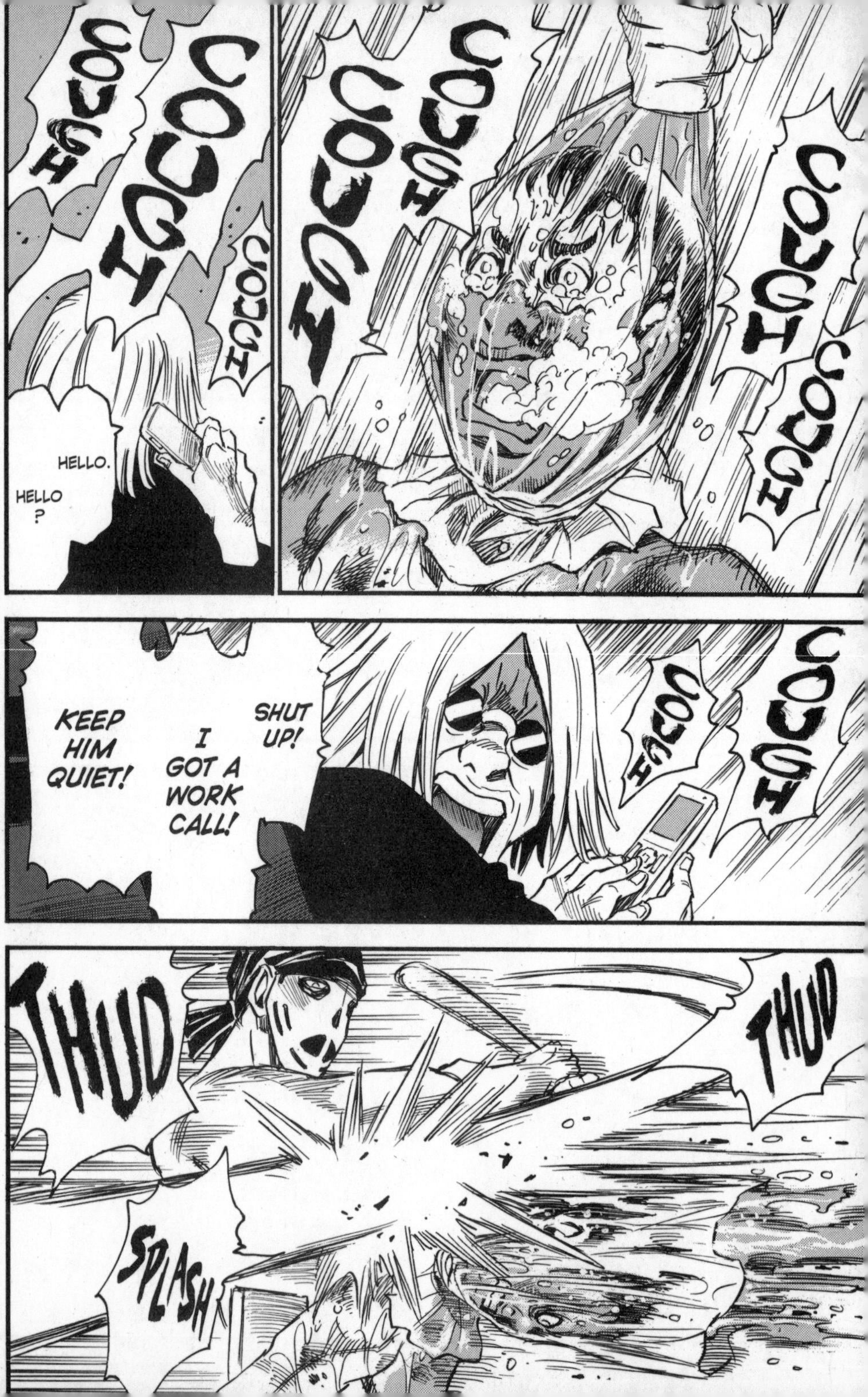
COUGH
COUGH
COUGH
COUGH
COUGH
COUGH
COUGH
HELLO.
HELLO ?
COUGH
COUGH
SHUT UP!
I GOT A WORK CALL!
KEEP HIM QUIET!
THUD
THUD
SPLASH

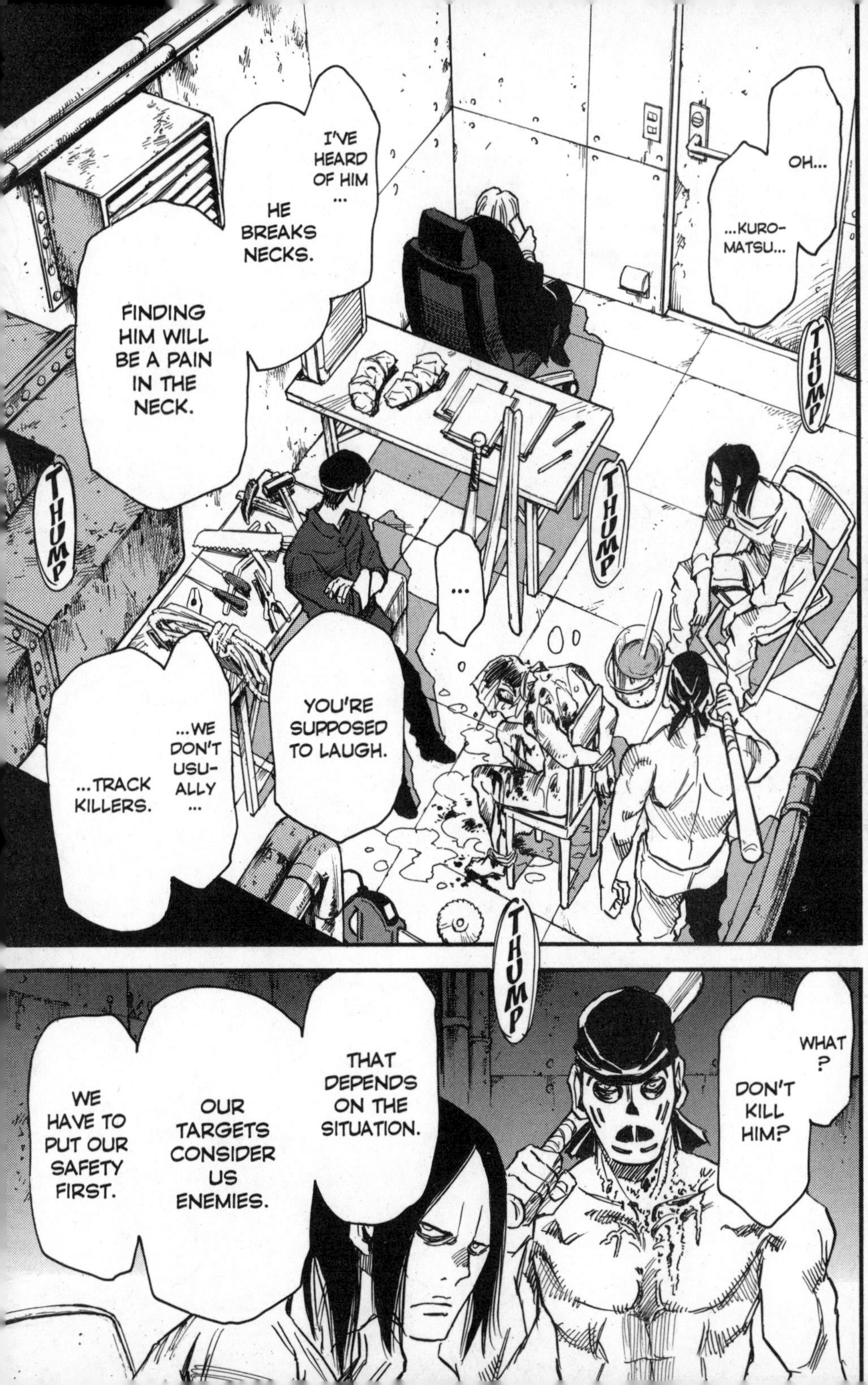
OH... ...KURO-MATSU...
THUMP
I'VE HEARD OF HIM...
HE BREAKS NECKS.
FINDING HIM WILL BE A PAIN IN THE NECK.
THUMP
...
THUMP
YOU'RE SUPPOSED TO LAUGH.
...WE DON'T USU-ALLY...
...TRACK KILLERS.
THUMP
WHAT? DON'T KILL HIM?
THAT DEPENDS ON THE SITUATION.
OUR TARGETS CONSIDER US ENEMIES.
WE HAVE TO PUT OUR SAFETY FIRST.

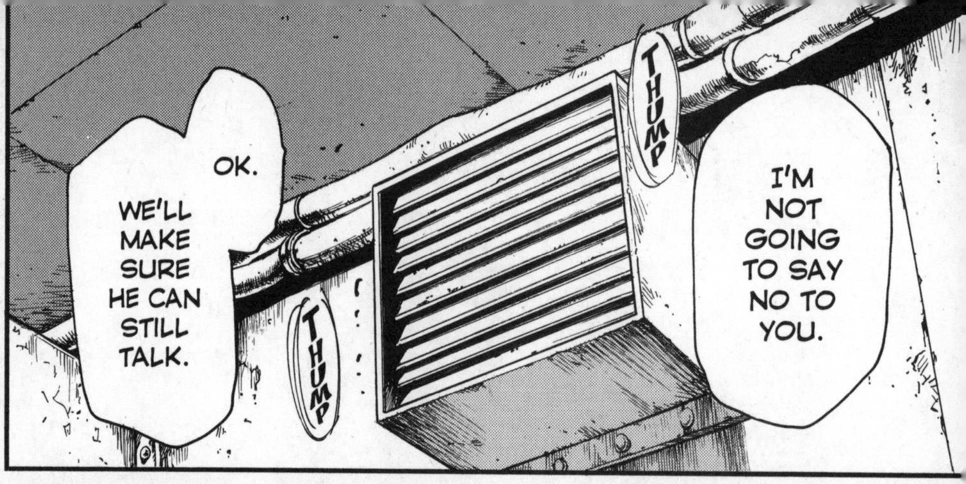
I'M NOT GOING TO SAY NO TO YOU.
THUMP
THUMP
OK.
WE'LL MAKE SURE HE CAN STILL TALK.
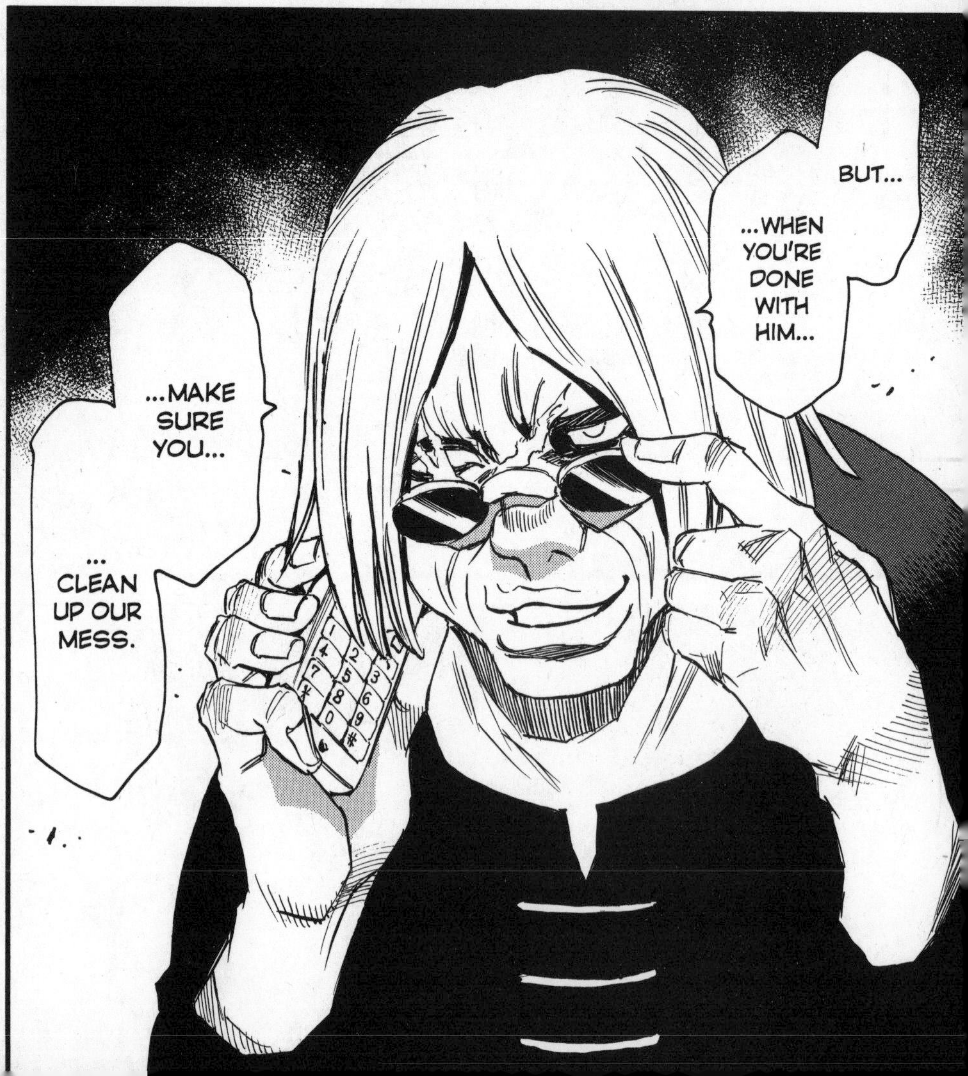
BUT...
...WHEN YOU'RE DONE WITH HIM...
...MAKE SURE YOU...
... CLEAN UP OUR MESS.

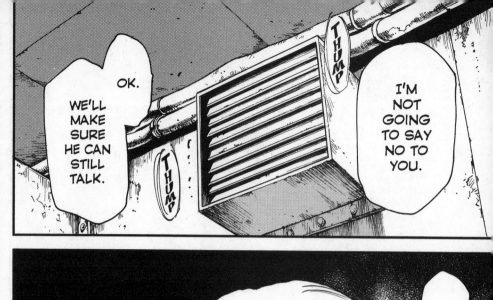

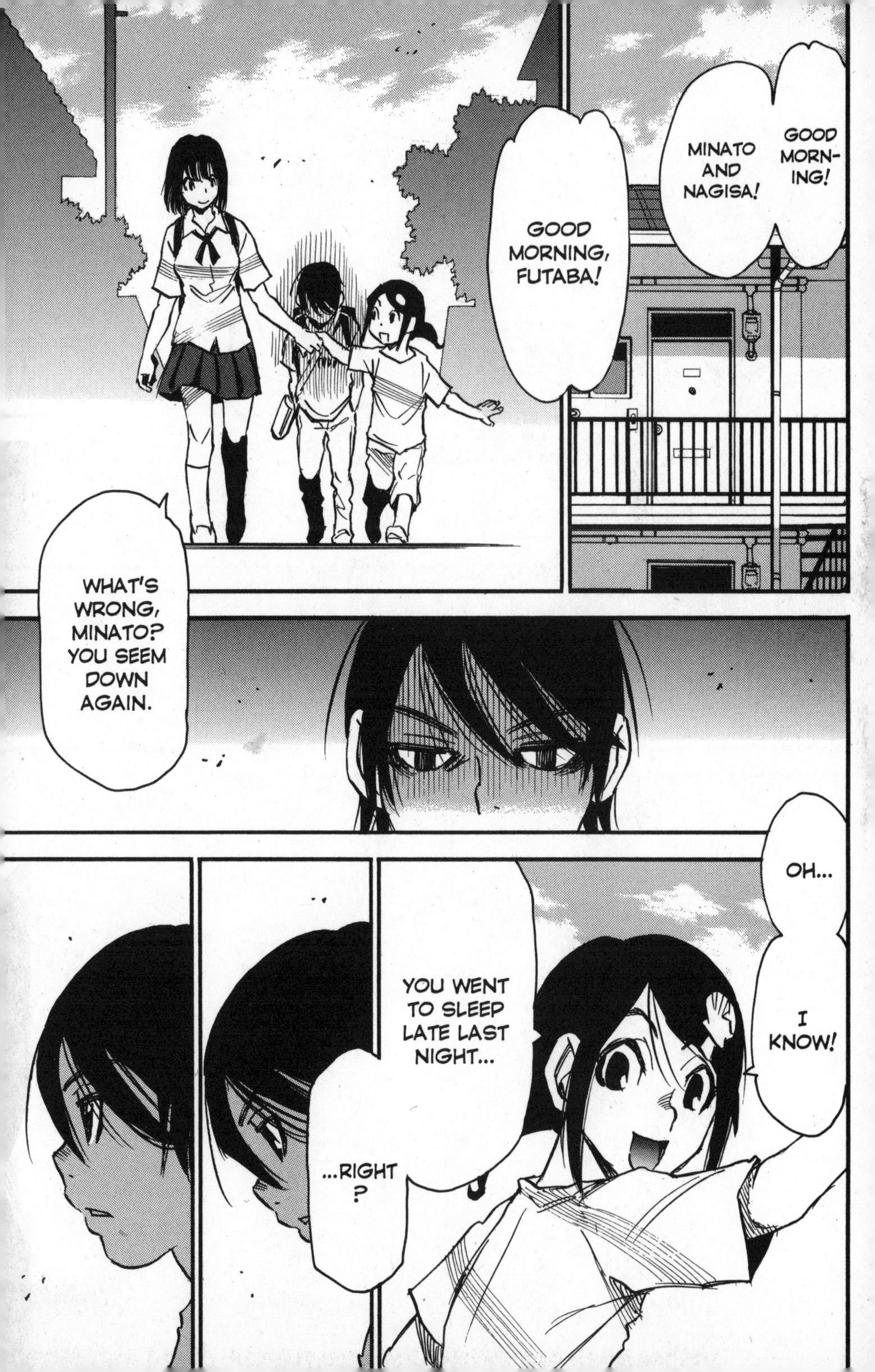
GOOD MORNING! MINATO AND NAGISA!
GOOD MORNING, FUTABA!
WHAT'S WRONG, MINATO? YOU SEEM DOWN AGAIN.
OH... I KNOW!
YOU WENT TO SLEEP LATE LAST NIGHT...
...RIGHT?

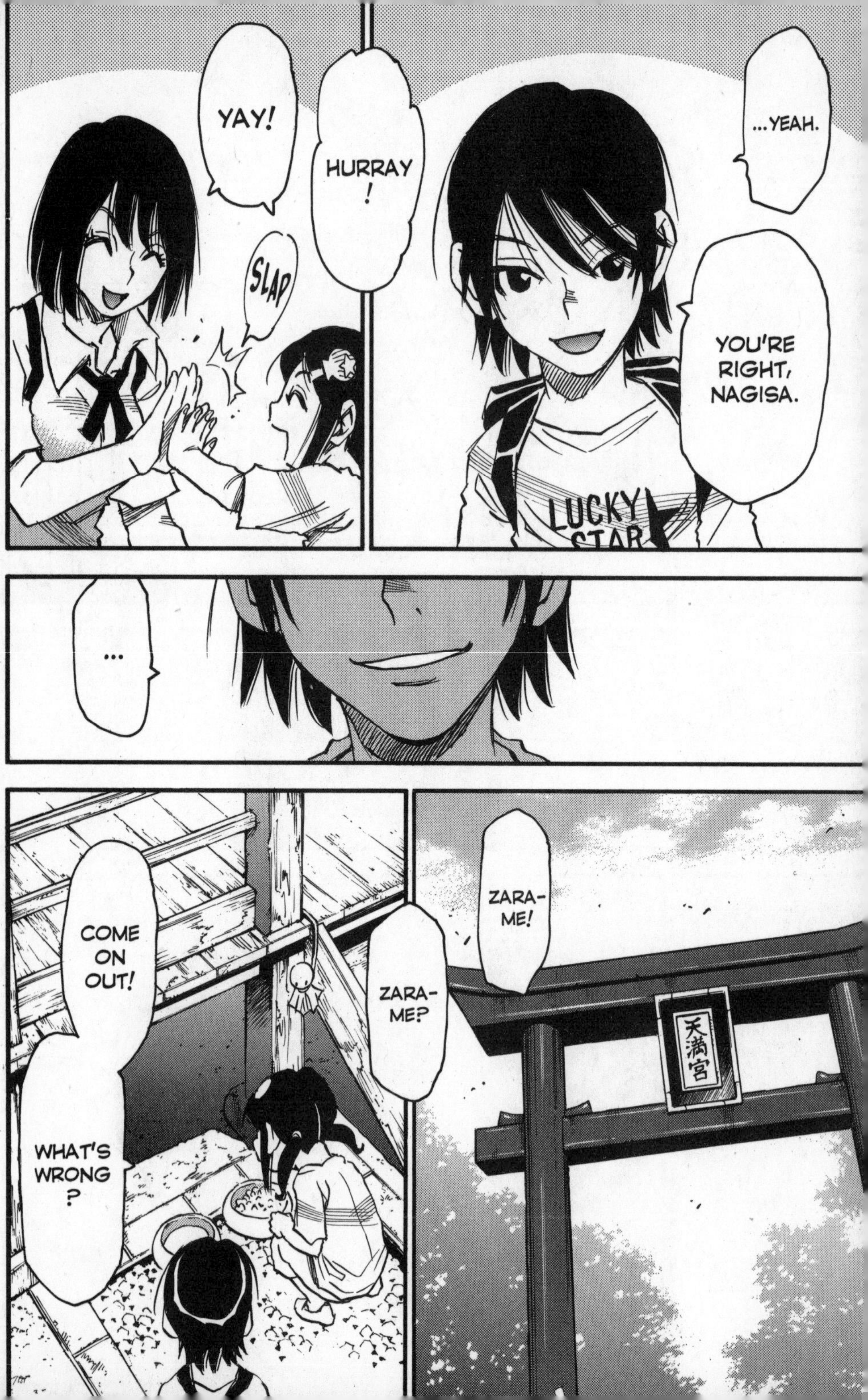
...YEAH.
YOU'RE RIGHT, NAGISA.
LUCKY
HURRAY!
YAY!
SLAP
...
ZARA-ME!
天満宮
ZARA-ME?
COME ON OUT!
WHAT'S WRONG?

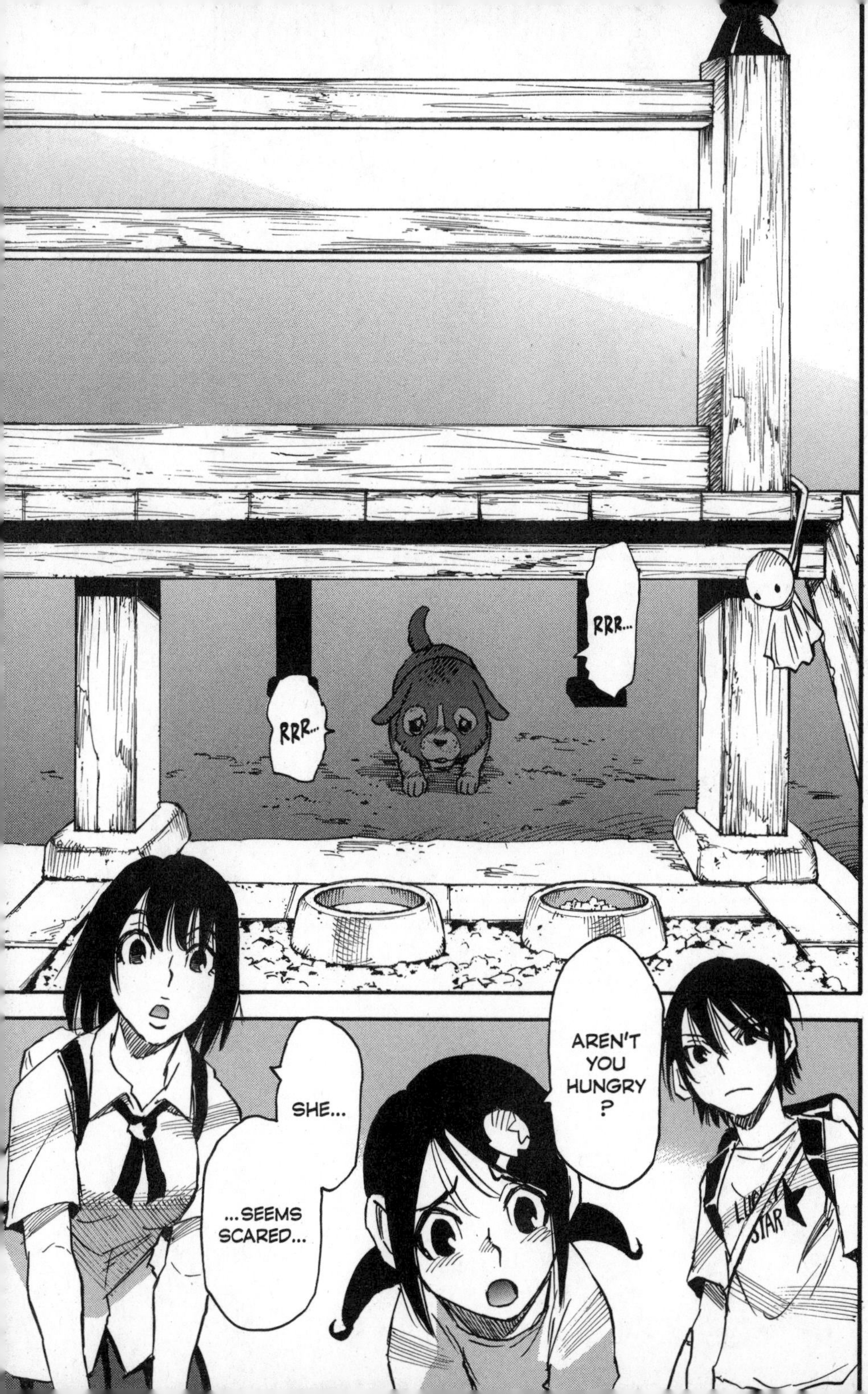
RRR...
RRR...
AREN'T YOU HUNGRY ?
SHE...
...SEEMS SCARED...

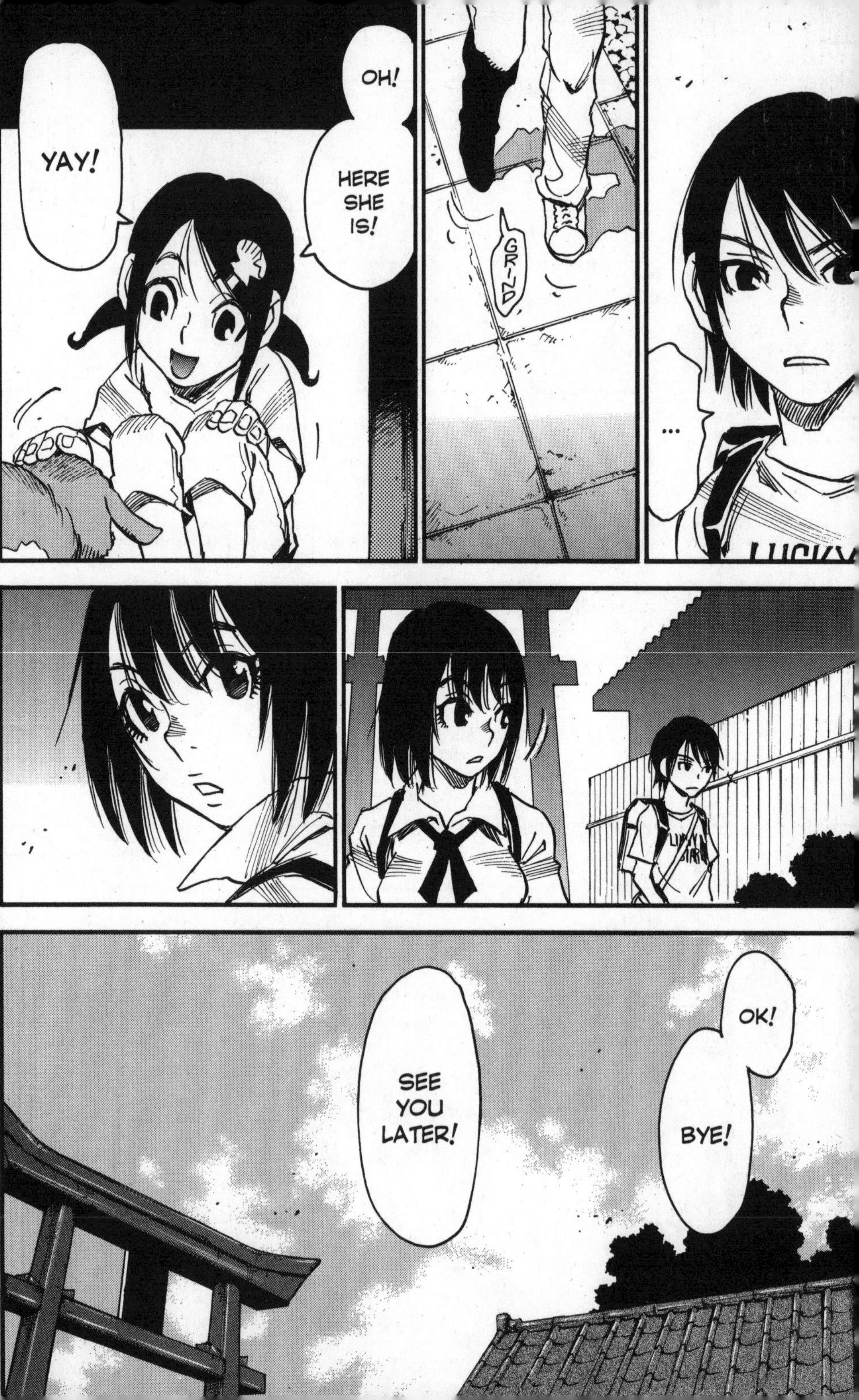
...
GRIND
OH!
HERE SHE IS!
YAY!
OK!
BYE!
SEE YOU LATER!

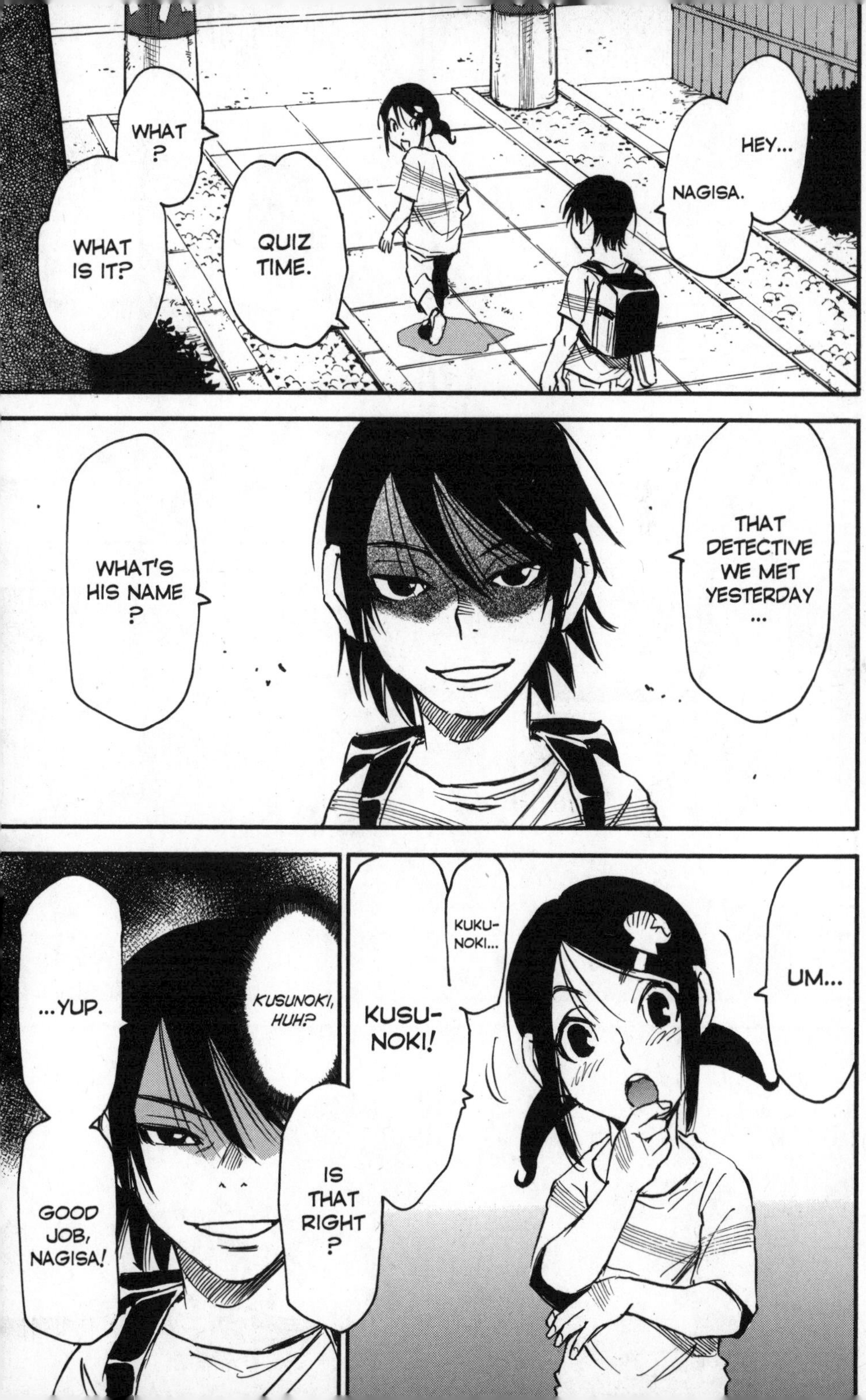
HEY...
NAGISA.
WHAT?
QUIZ TIME.
WHAT IS IT?
THAT DETECTIVE WE MET YESTERDAY...
WHAT'S HIS NAME?
UM...
KUKU-NOKI...
KUSU-NOKI!
IS THAT RIGHT?
KUSUNOKI, HUH?
...YUP.
GOOD JOB, NAGISA!

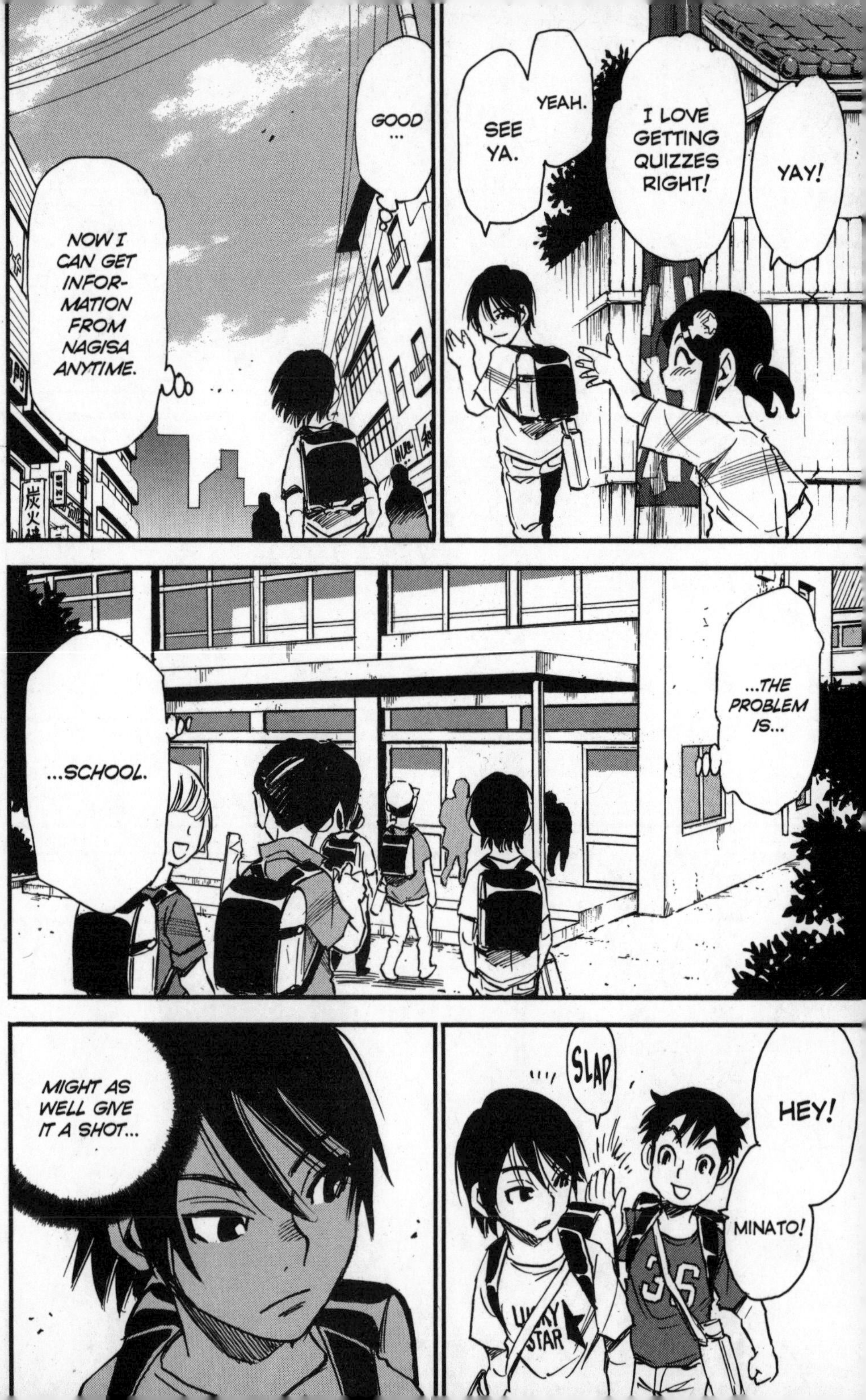
YAY!
I LOVE GETTING QUIZZES RIGHT!
YEAH. SEE YA.
GOOD ...
NOW I CAN GET INFORMATION FROM NAGISA ANYTIME.
...THE PROBLEM IS...
...SCHOOL.
HEY! MINATO!
SLAP
MIGHT AS WELL GIVE IT A SHOT...

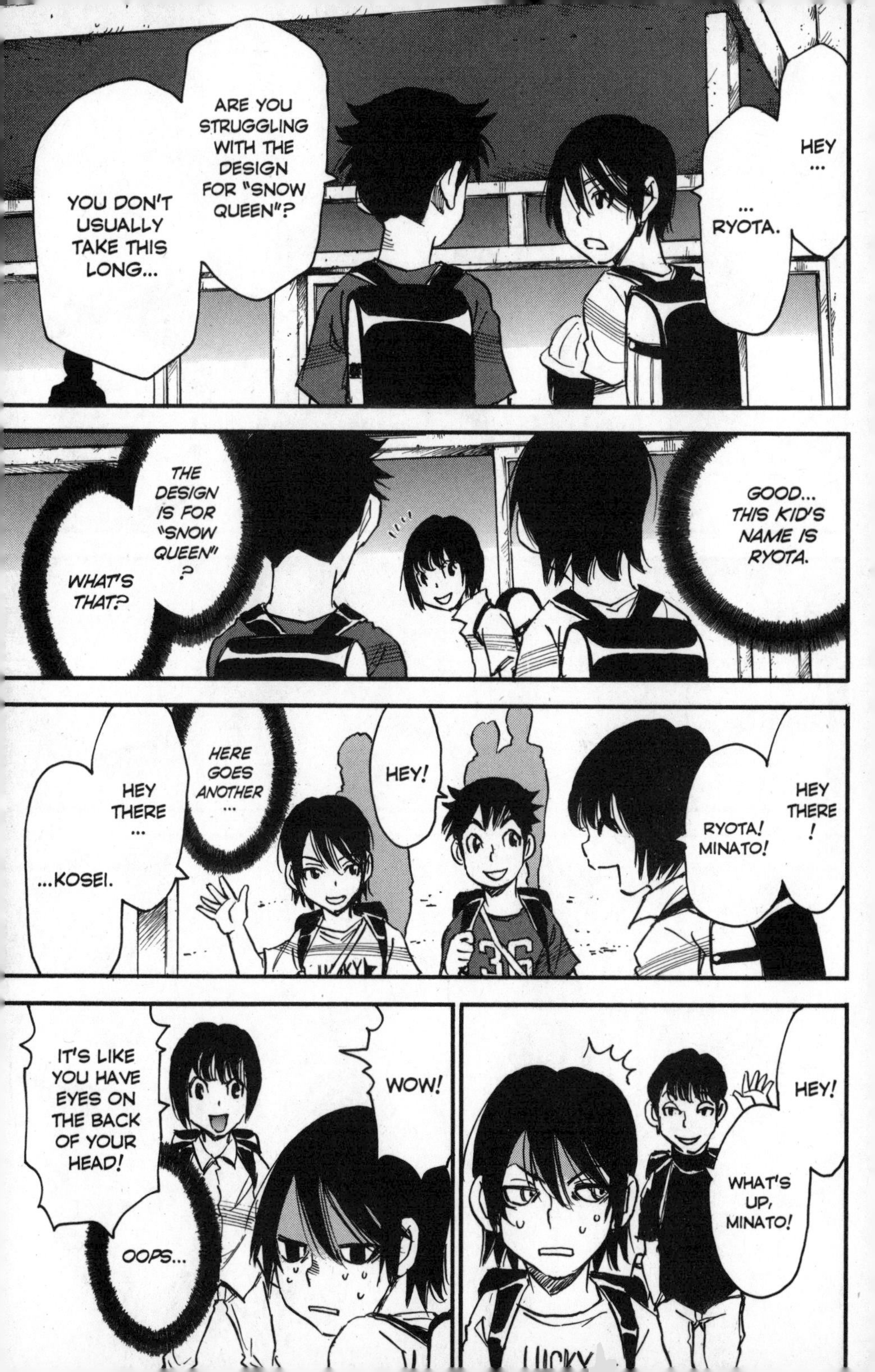
HEY ... ... RYOTA.
ARE YOU STRUGGLING WITH THE DESIGN FOR "SNOW QUEEN"?
YOU DON'T USUALLY TAKE THIS LONG...
GOOD... THIS KID'S NAME IS RYOTA.
THE DESIGN IS FOR "SNOW QUEEN"?
WHAT'S THAT?
HEY THERE!
RYOTA! MINATO!
HEY!
HERE GOES ANOTHER ...
HEY THERE ...
...KOSEI.
HEY!
WHAT'S UP, MINATO!
WOW!
IT'S LIKE YOU HAVE EYES ON THE BACK OF YOUR HEAD!
OOPS...

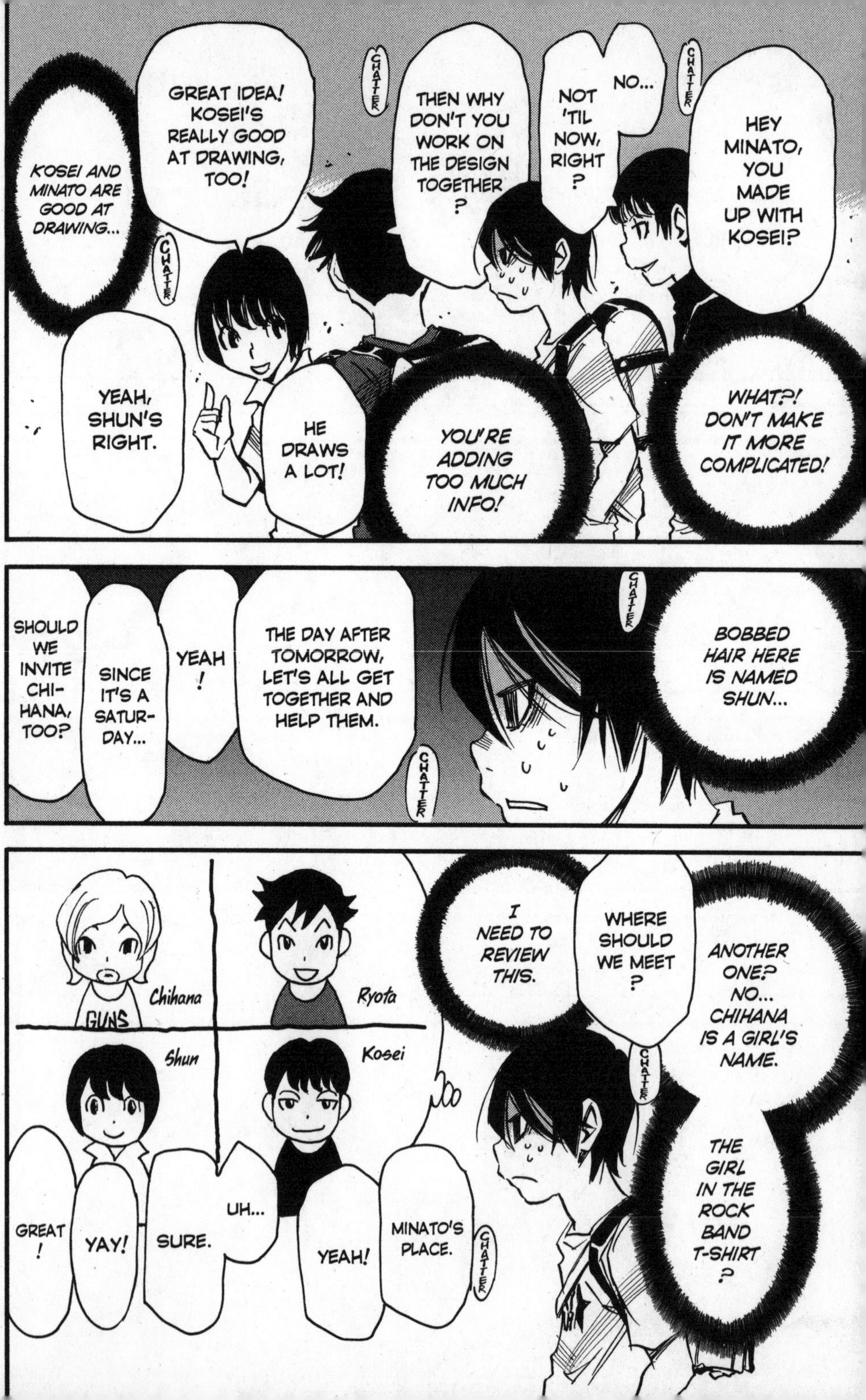
HEY MINATO, YOU MADE UP WITH KOSEI?
CHATTER
NO...
NOT 'TIL NOW, RIGHT?
THEN WHY DON'T YOU WORK ON THE DESIGN TOGETHER?
CHATTER
GREAT IDEA! KOSEI'S REALLY GOOD AT DRAWING, TOO!
KOSEI AND MINATO ARE GOOD AT DRAWING...
CHATTER
WHAT?! DON'T MAKE IT MORE COMPLICATED!
YOU'RE ADDING TOO MUCH INFO!
HE DRAWS A LOT!
YEAH, SHUN'S RIGHT.
BOBBED HAIR HERE IS NAMED SHUN...
CHATTER
THE DAY AFTER TOMORROW, LET'S ALL GET TOGETHER AND HELP THEM.
YEAH!
SINCE IT'S A SATURDAY...
SHOULD WE INVITE CHIHANA, TOO?
CHATTER
ANOTHER ONE? NO... CHIHANA IS A GIRL'S NAME.
WHERE SHOULD WE MEET?
I NEED TO REVIEW THIS.
Ryota
Chihana
GUNS
Kosei
Shun
CHATTER
THE GIRL IN THE ROCK BAND T-SHIRT?
CHATTER
MINATO'S PLACE.
YEAH!
UH...
SURE.
YAY!
GREAT!

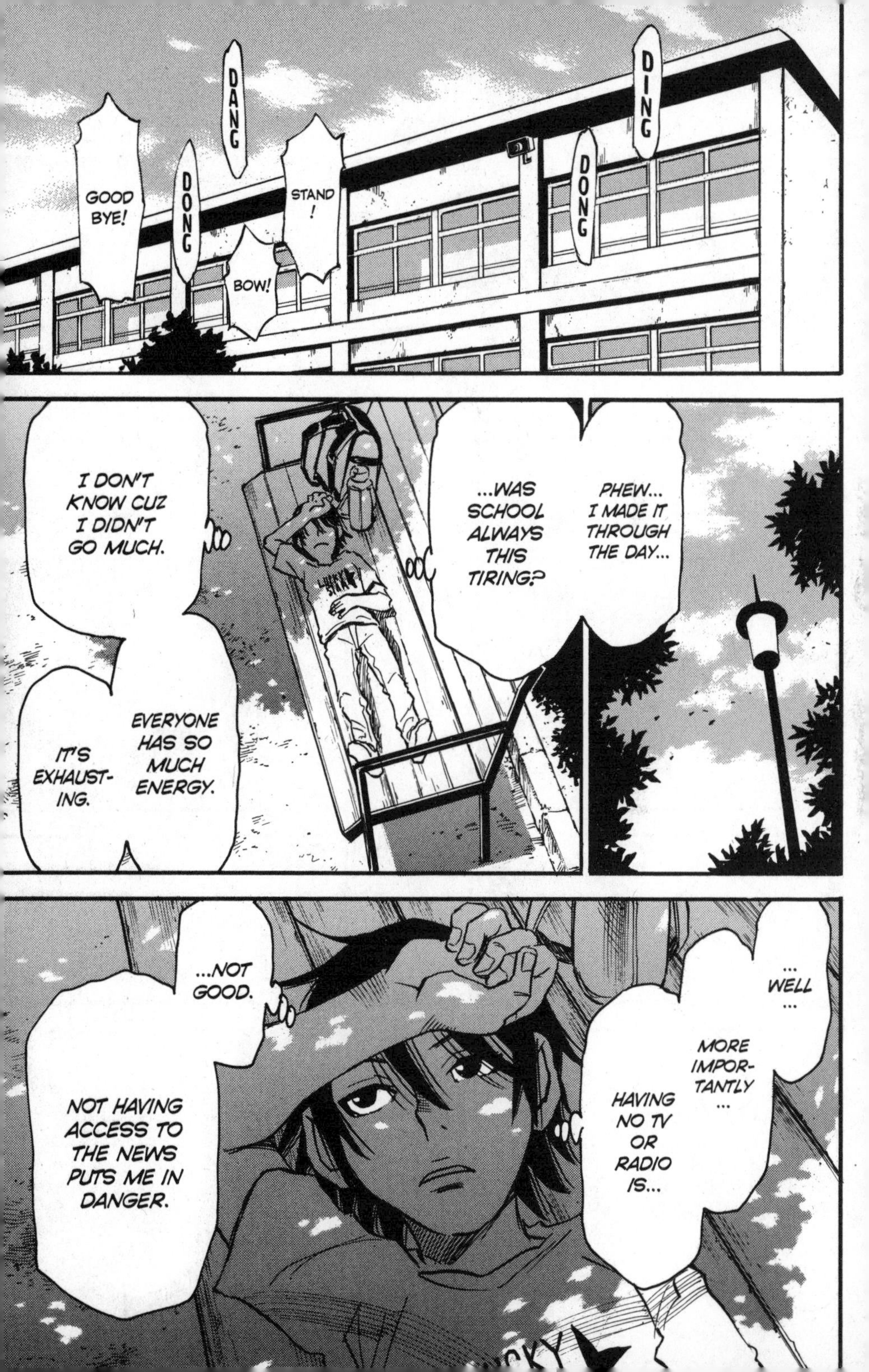
DING
DONG
DANG
STAND!
BOW!
DONG
GOOD BYE!
PHEW... I MADE IT THROUGH THE DAY...
...WAS SCHOOL ALWAYS THIS TIRING?
I DON'T KNOW CUZ I DIDN'T GO MUCH.
EVERYONE HAS SO MUCH ENERGY.
IT'S EXHAUST-ING.
...WELL...
MORE IMPOR-TANTLY...
HAVING NO TV OR RADIO IS...
...NOT GOOD.
NOT HAVING ACCESS TO THE NEWS PUTS ME IN DANGER.

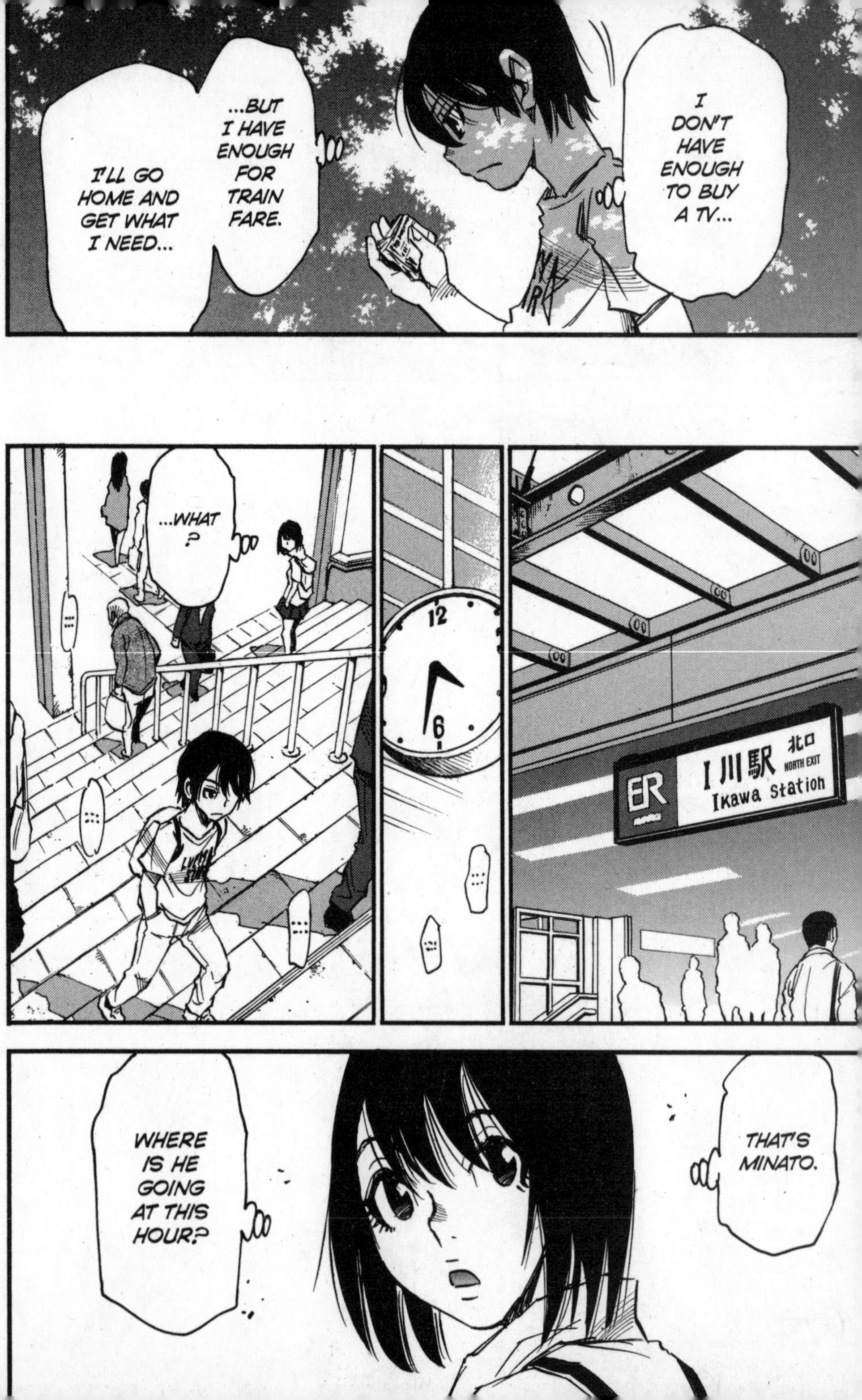
I DON'T HAVE ENOUGH TO BUY A TV...
...BUT I HAVE ENOUGH FOR TRAIN FARE.
I'LL GO HOME AND GET WHAT I NEED...
ER
I川駅 北口 NORTH EXIT
Ikawa Station
...WHAT?
THAT'S MINATO.
WHERE IS HE GOING AT THIS HOUR?

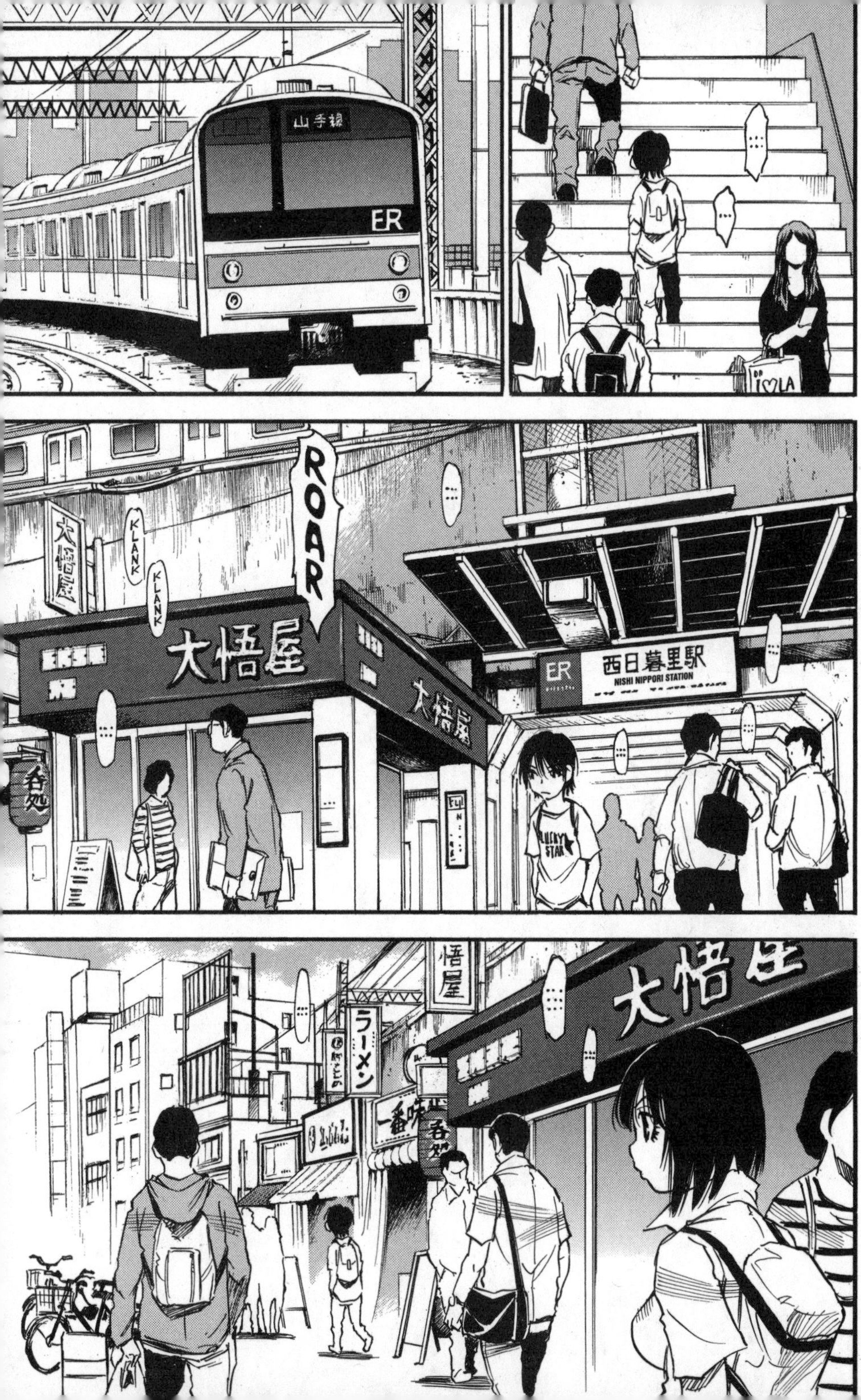

....
....
山手線
ER
ROAR
KLANK
KLANK
....
....
....
....
....
大悟屋
大悟屋
大悟屋
ER
西日暮里駅
NISHI NIPPORI STATION
呑処
LUCKY STAR
....
....
大悟屋
大悟屋
ラーメン
一番味
呑処

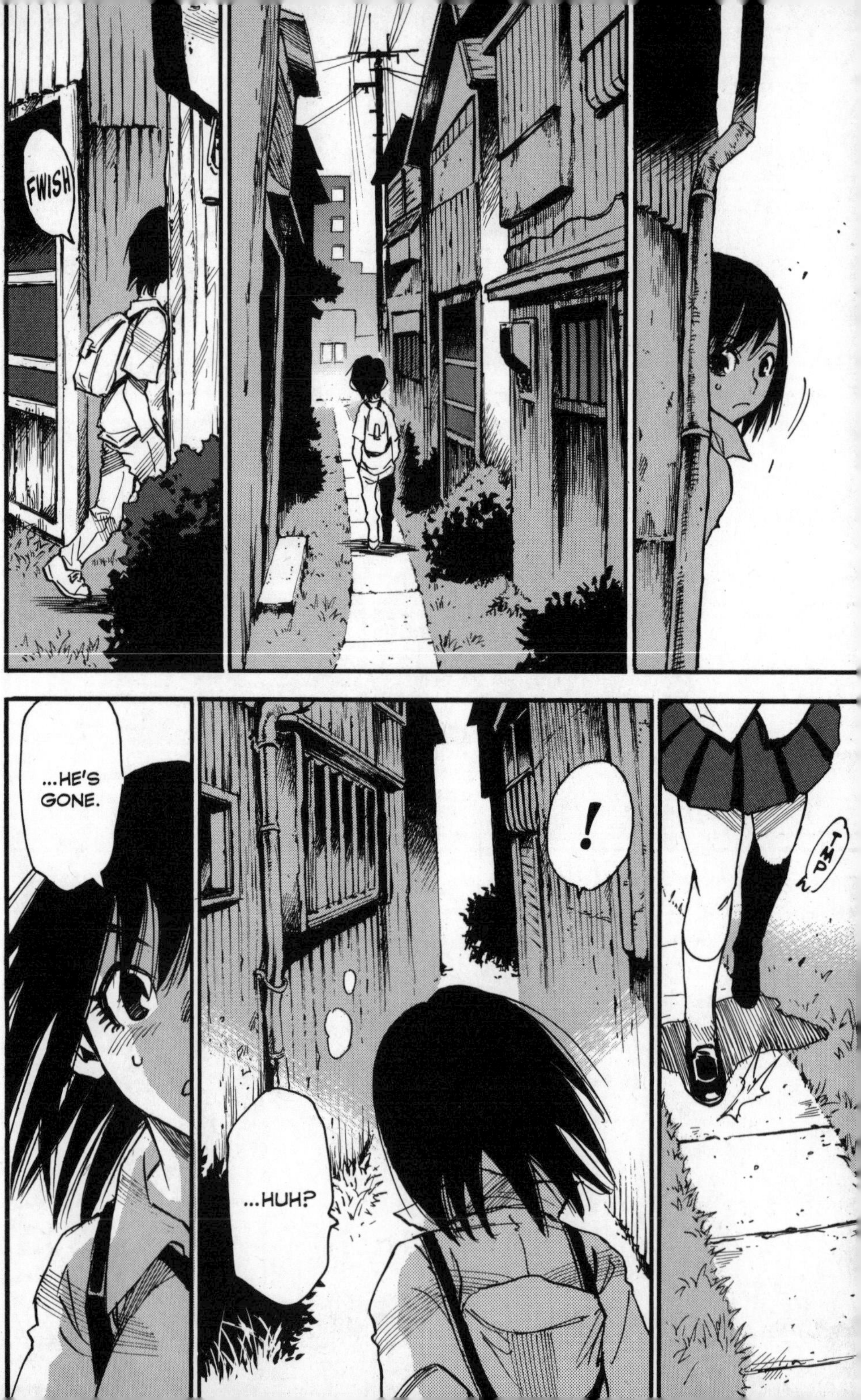
FWISH
TMP
!
...HUH?
...HE'S GONE.

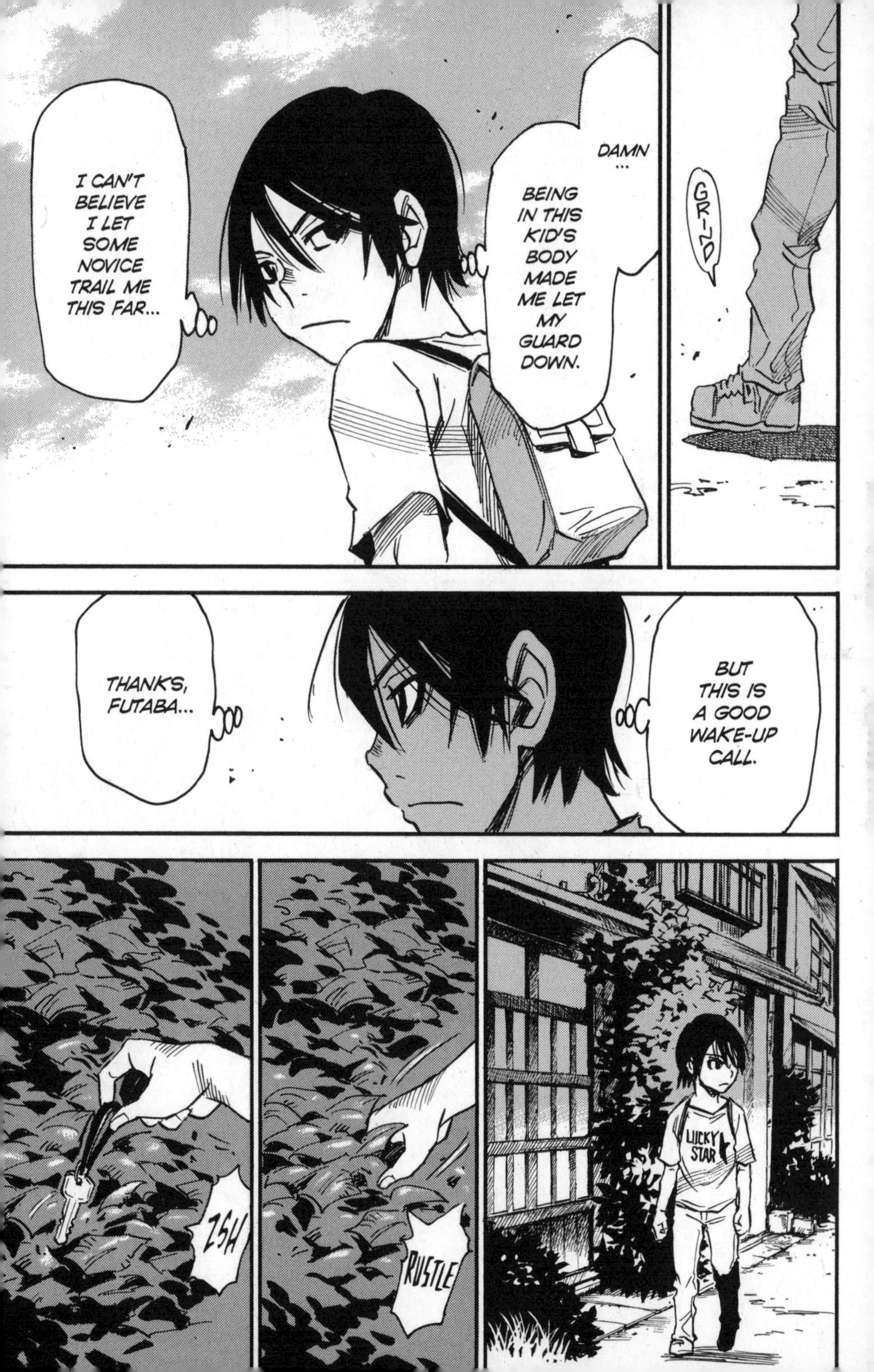
GRIND
DAMN... BEING IN THIS KID'S BODY MADE ME LET MY GUARD DOWN.
I CAN'T BELIEVE I LET SOME NOVICE TRAIL ME THIS FAR...
BUT THIS IS A GOOD WAKE-UP CALL.
THANKS, FUTABA...
LUCKY STAR
RUSTLE
ZSH

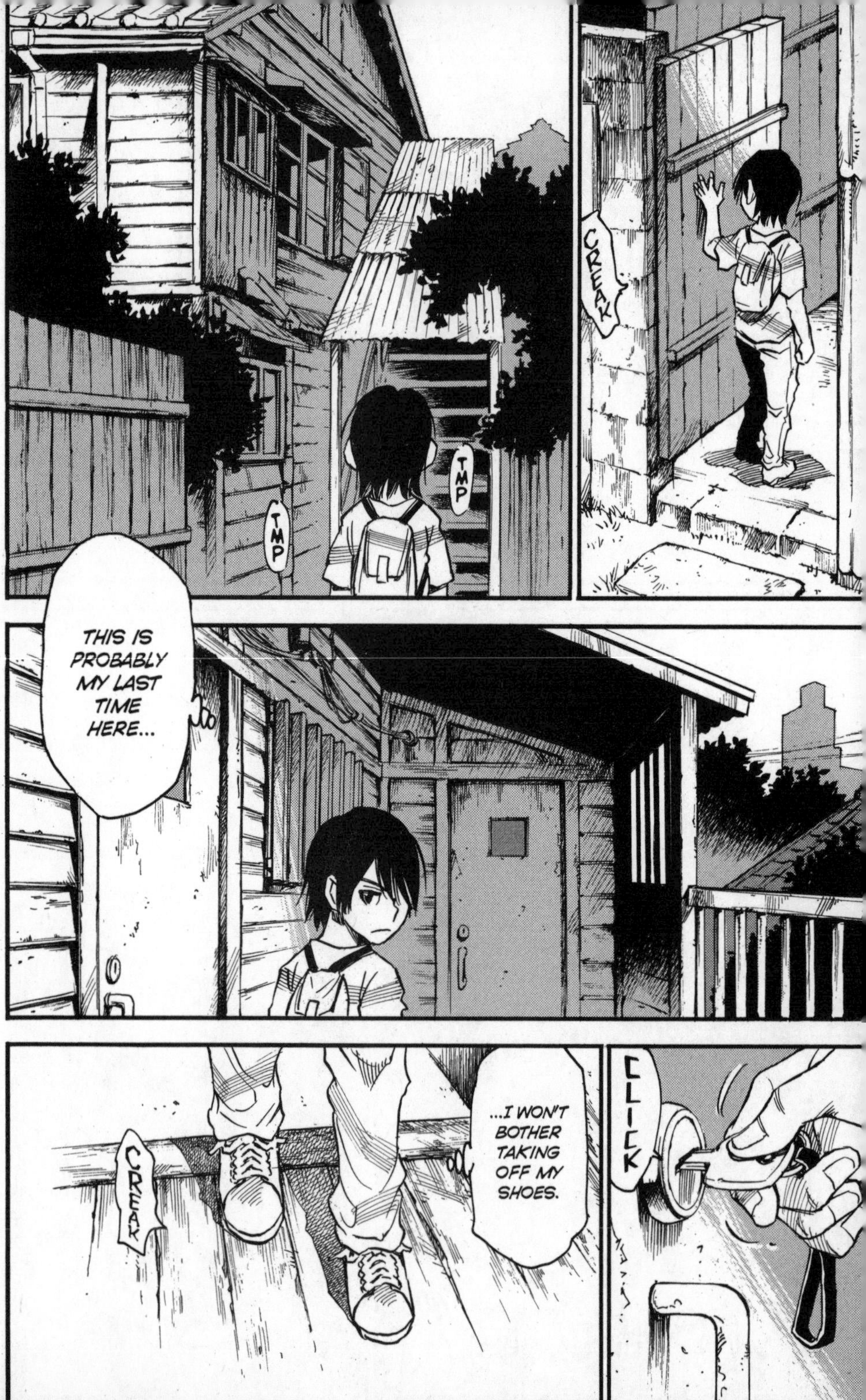
CREAK
TMP
TMP
THIS IS PROBABLY MY LAST TIME HERE...
CLICK
...I WON'T BOTHER TAKING OFF MY SHOES.
CREAK

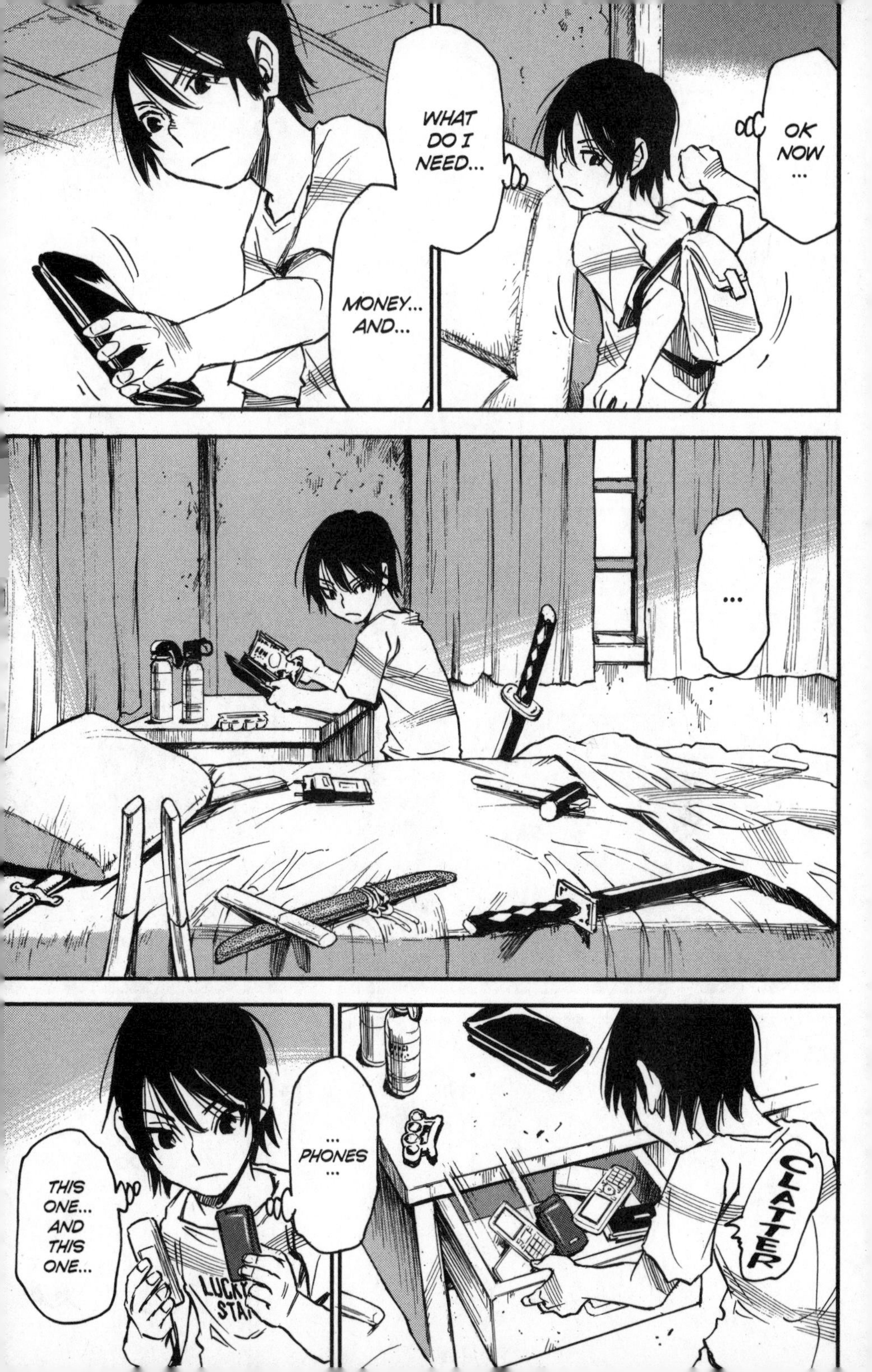
OK NOW ...
WHAT DO I NEED...
MONEY... AND...
...
CLATTER
... PHONES ...
THIS ONE... AND THIS ONE...
LUCKY STAR

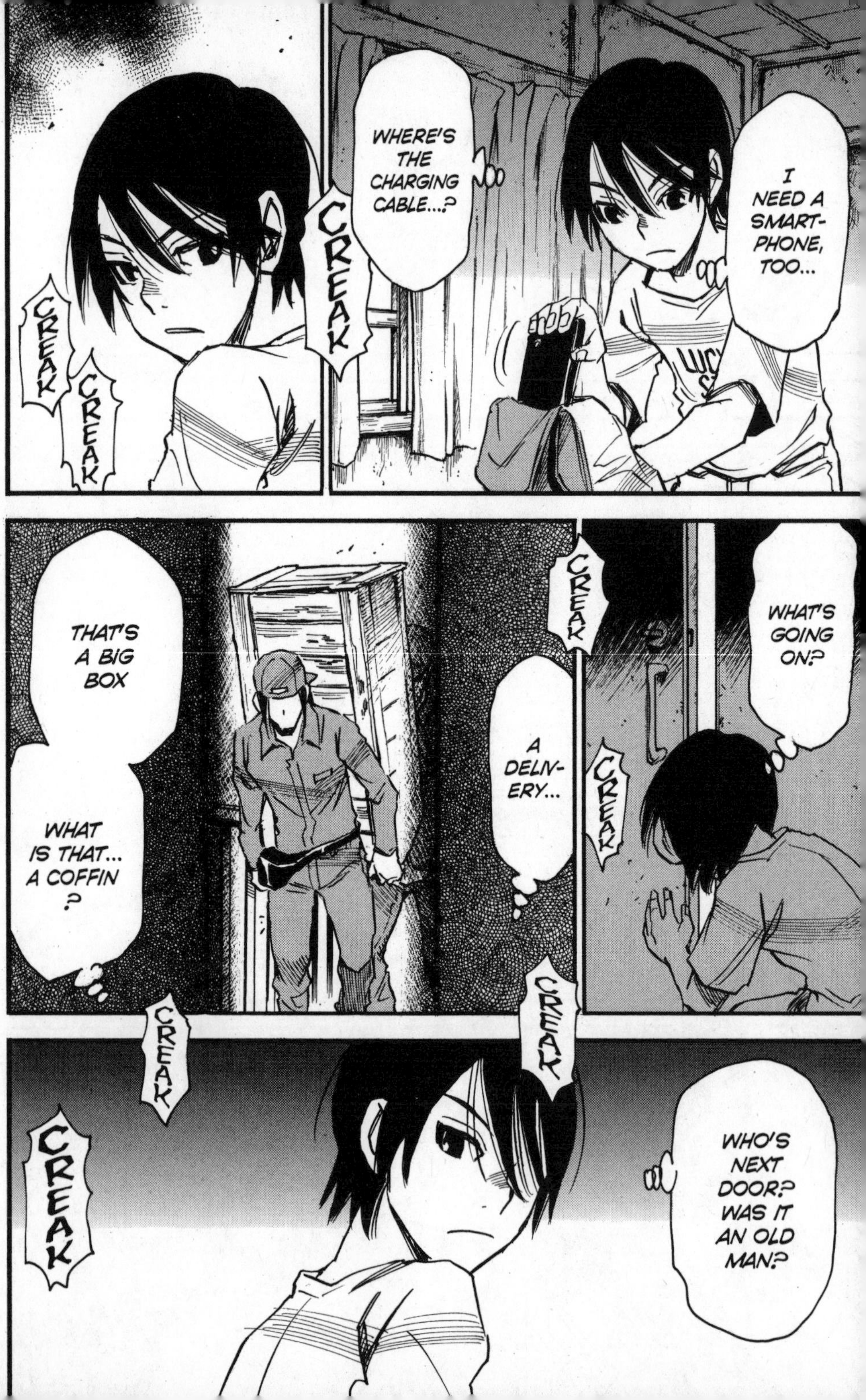
I NEED A SMART-PHONE, TOO...
WHERE'S THE CHARGING CABLE...?
CREAK
CREAK
CREAK
WHAT'S GOING ON?
CREAK
CREAK
A DELIV-ERY...
THAT'S A BIG BOX
WHAT IS THAT... A COFFIN ?
CREAK
WHO'S NEXT DOOR? WAS IT AN OLD MAN?
CREAK
CREAK

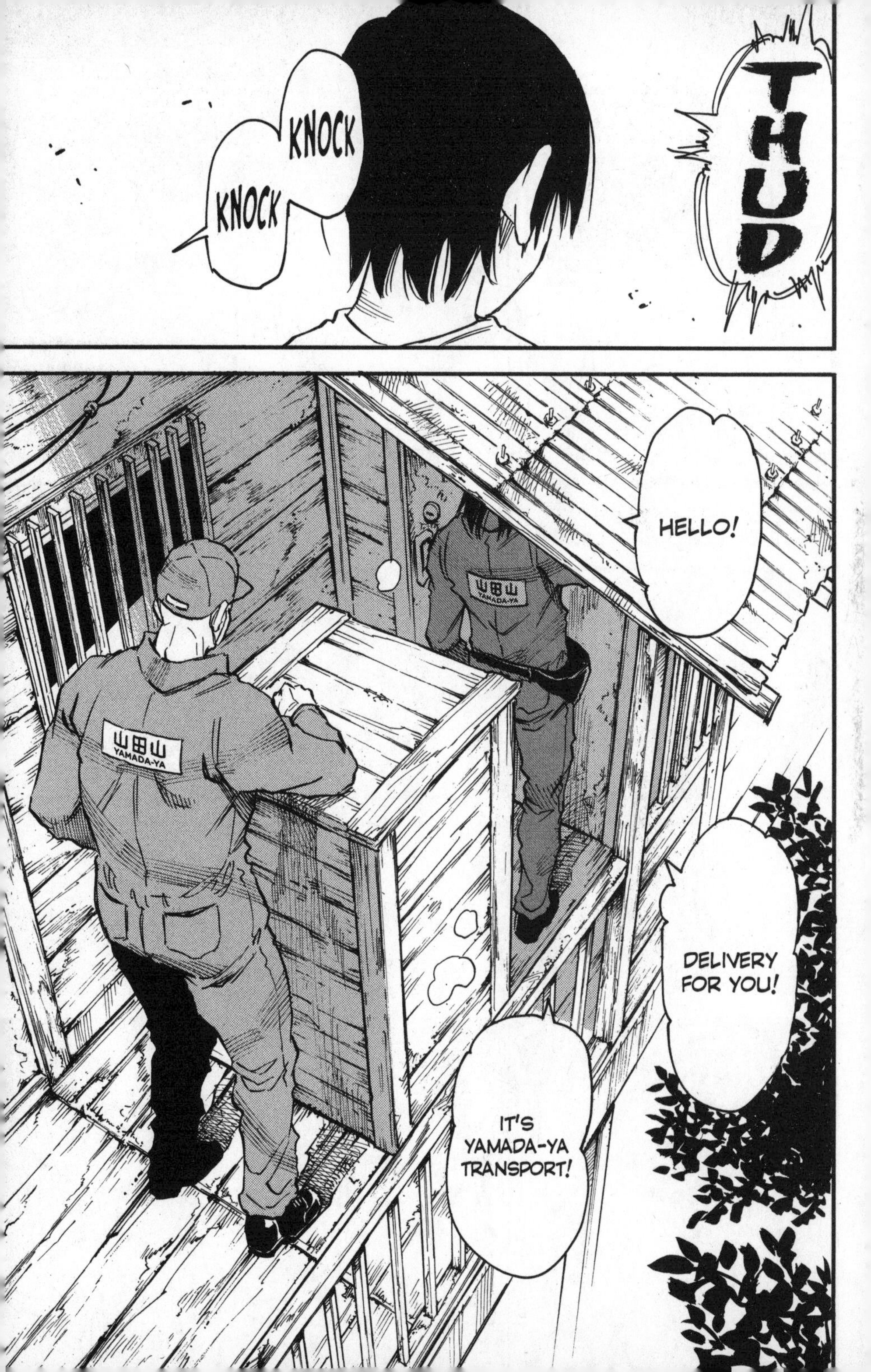
THUD
KNOCK
KNOCK
HELLO!
DELIVERY FOR YOU!
IT'S YAMADA-YA TRANSPORT!

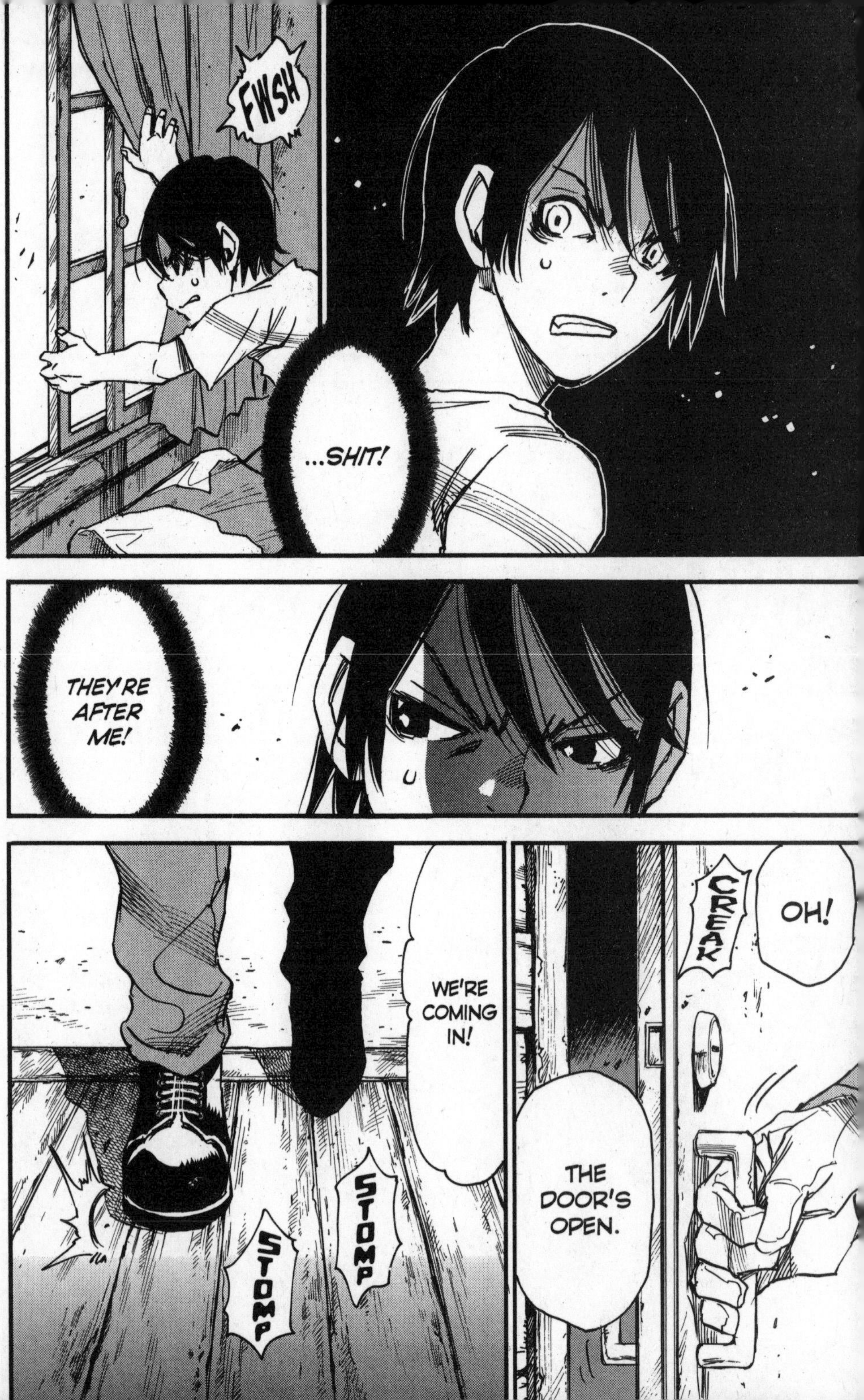
...SHIT!
FWSH
THEY'RE AFTER ME!
OH!
CREAK
THE DOOR'S OPEN.
WE'RE COMING IN!
STOMP
STOMP

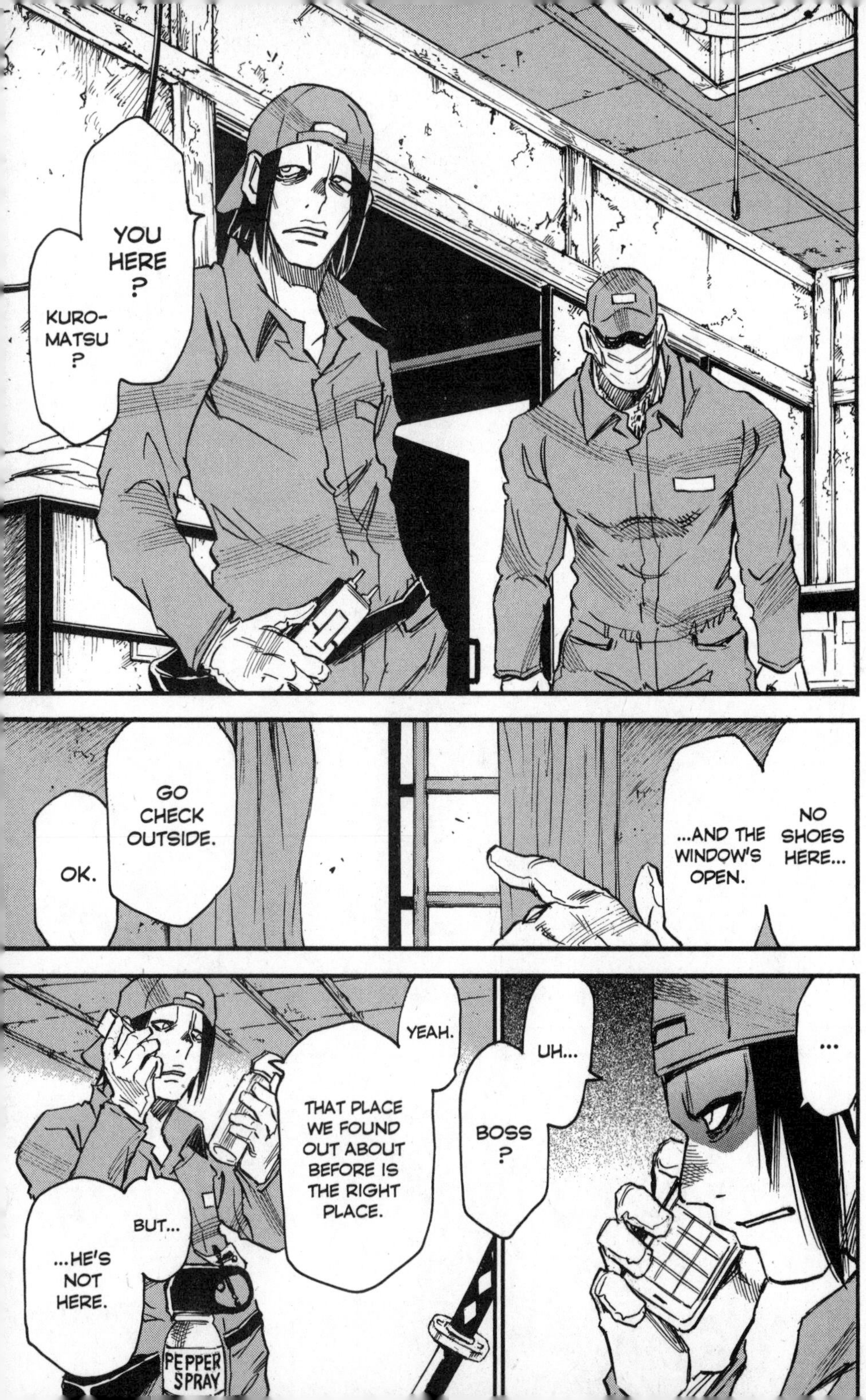
YOU HERE?
KURO-MATSU?
NO SHOES HERE...
...AND THE WINDOW'S OPEN.
GO CHECK OUTSIDE.
OK.
...
UH...
BOSS?
YEAH.
THAT PLACE WE FOUND OUT ABOUT BEFORE IS THE RIGHT PLACE.
BUT...
...HE'S NOT HERE.
PEPPER SPRAY

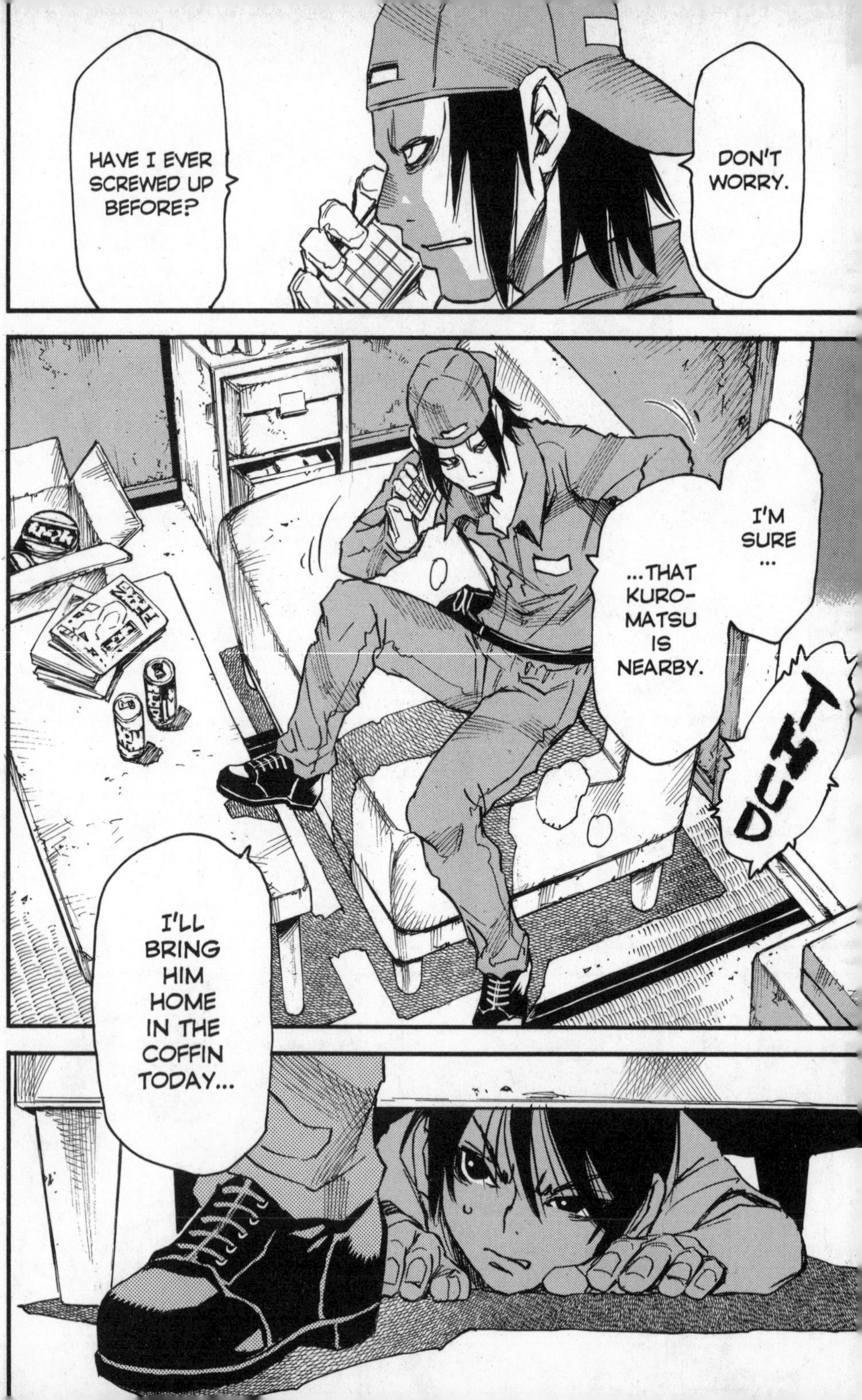
DON'T WORRY.
HAVE I EVER SCREWED UP BEFORE?
I'M SURE ...
...THAT KURO-MATSU IS NEARBY.
THUD
I'LL BRING HIM HOME IN THE COFFIN TODAY...

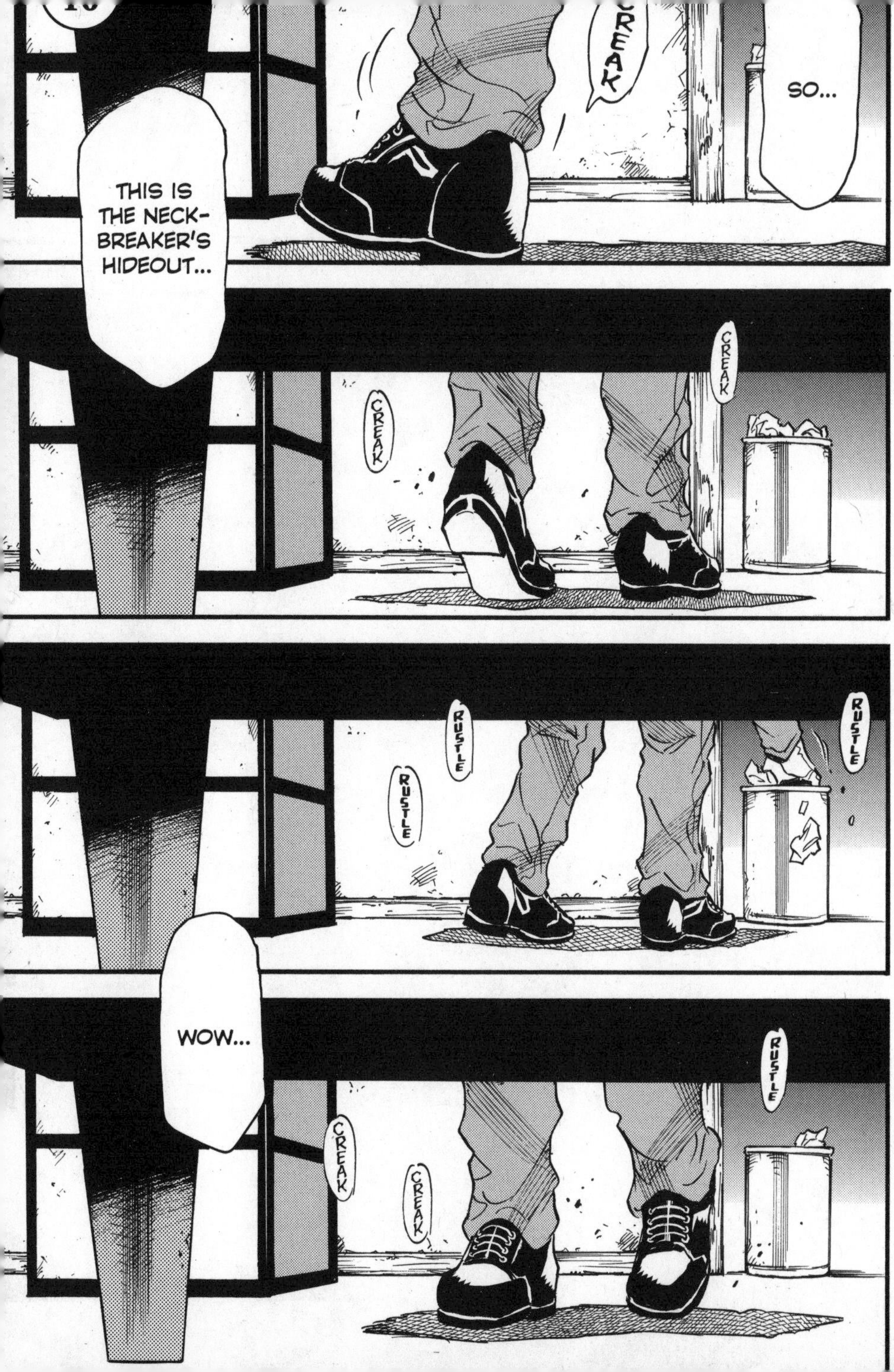
SO...
CREAK
THIS IS THE NECK-BREAKER'S HIDEOUT...
CREAK
CREAK
RUSTLE
RUSTLE
RUSTLE
RUSTLE
WOW...
CREAK
CREAK

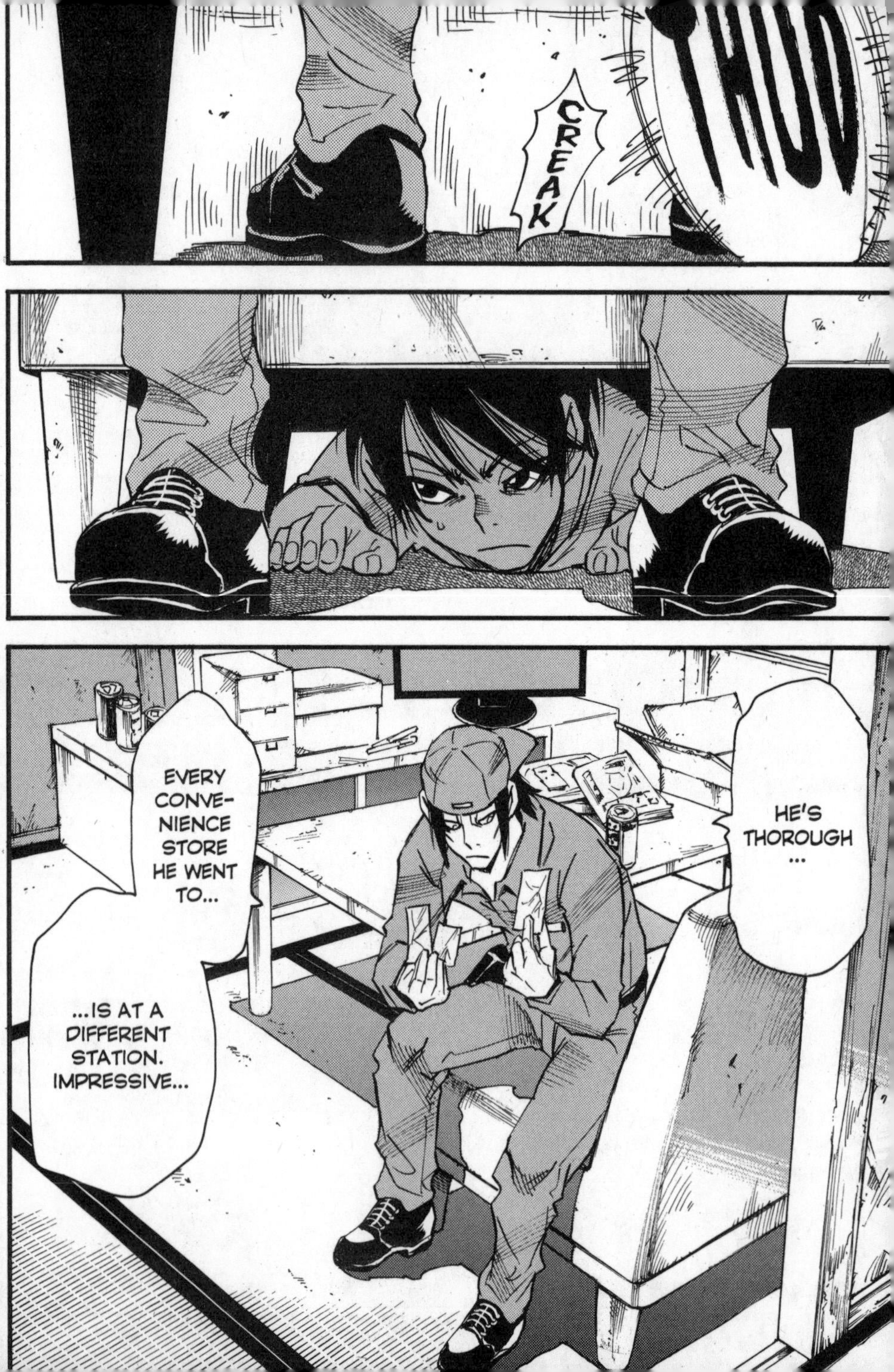
THUD
CREAK
HE'S THOROUGH...
EVERY CONVENIENCE STORE HE WENT TO...
...IS AT A DIFFERENT STATION. IMPRESSIVE...

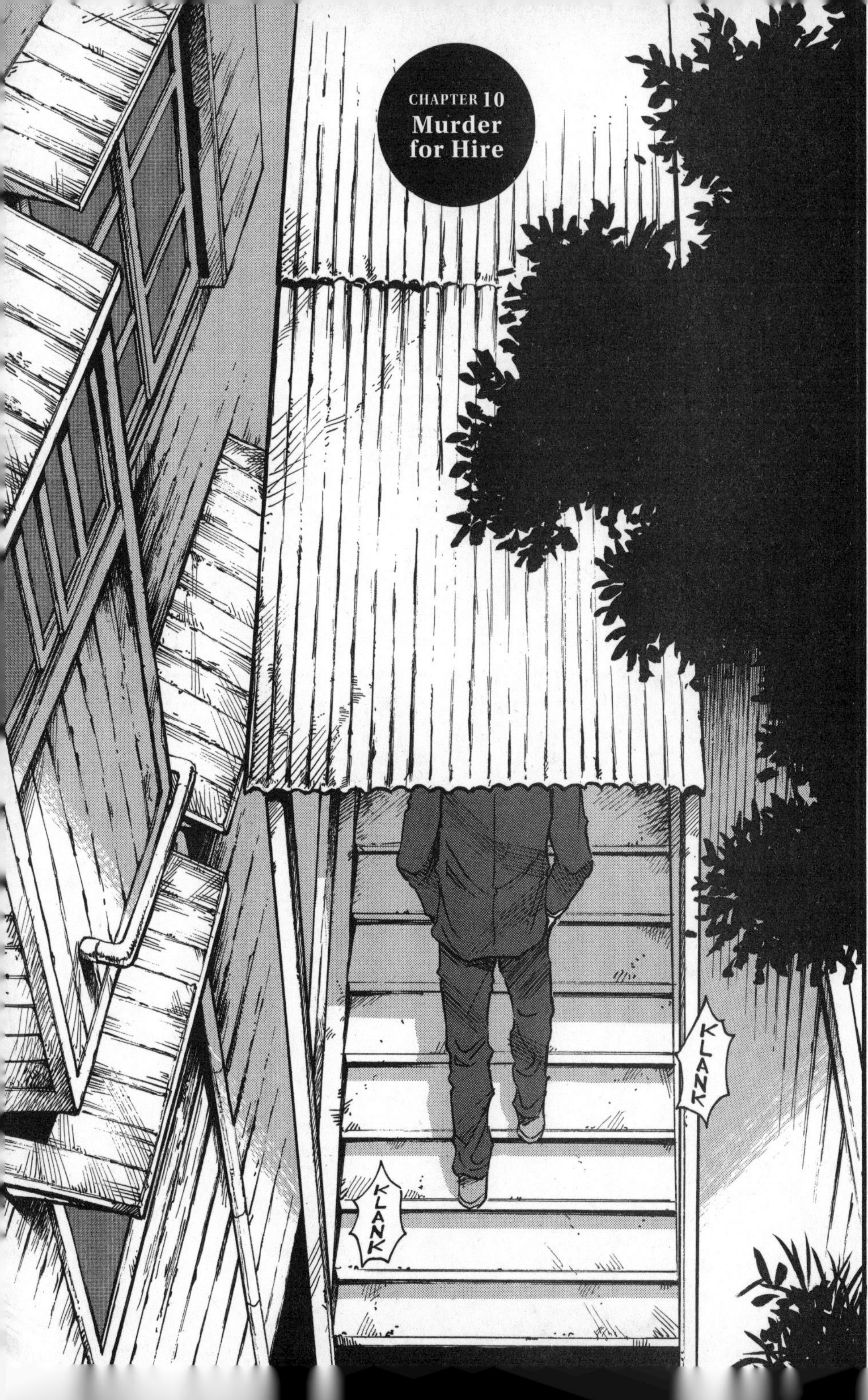
CHAPTER 10
Murder for Hire
KLANK
KLANK

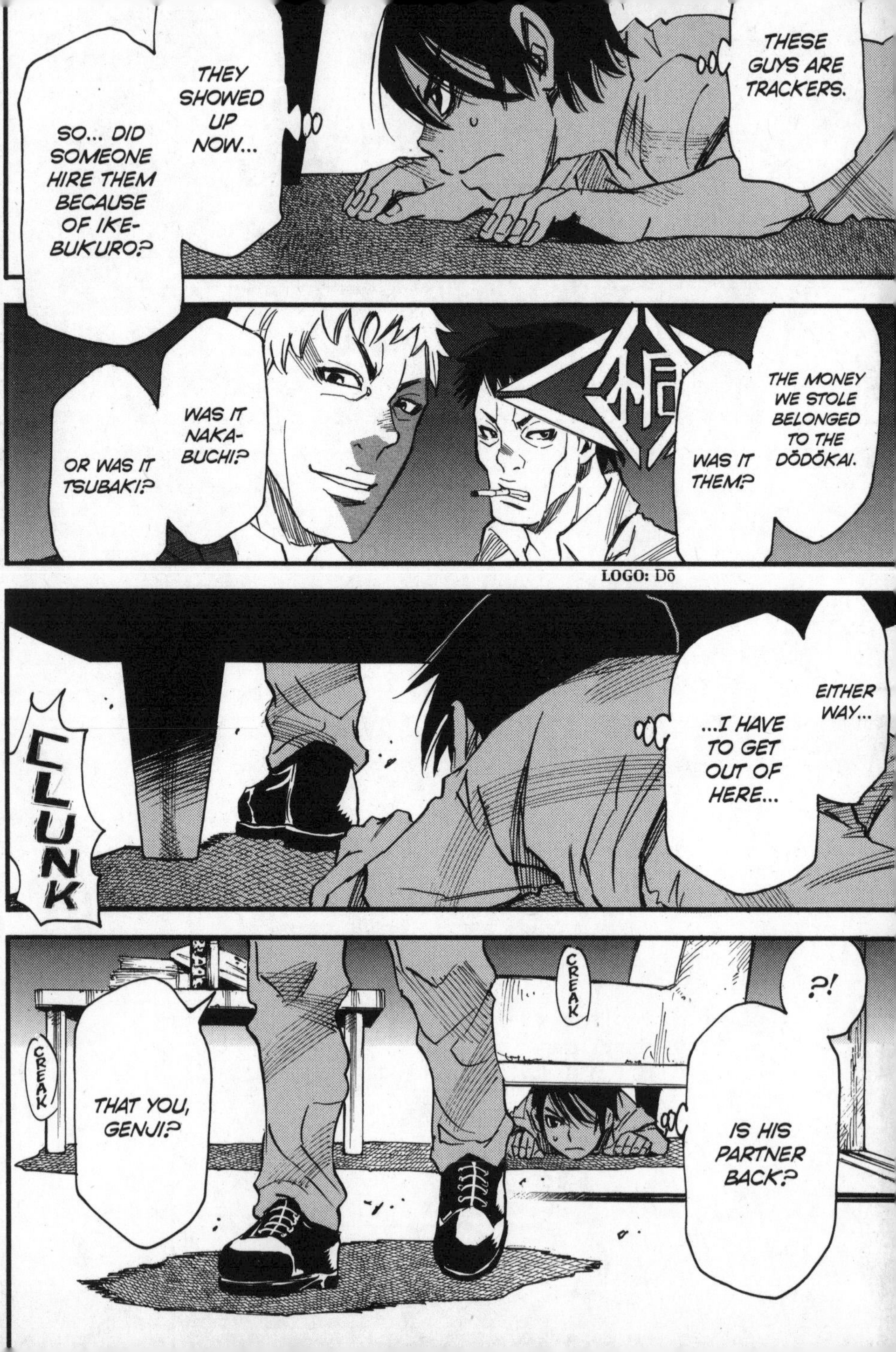
THESE GUYS ARE TRACKERS.
THEY SHOWED UP NOW...
SO... DID SOMEONE HIRE THEM BECAUSE OF IKE-BUKURO?
THE MONEY WE STOLE BELONGED TO THE DŌDŌKAI.
WAS IT THEM?
WAS IT NAKA-BUCHI?
OR WAS IT TSUBAKI?
EITHER WAY...
...I HAVE TO GET OUT OF HERE...
CLUNK
?!
IS HIS PARTNER BACK?
CREAK
CREAK
THAT YOU, GENJI?

LOGO: Dō

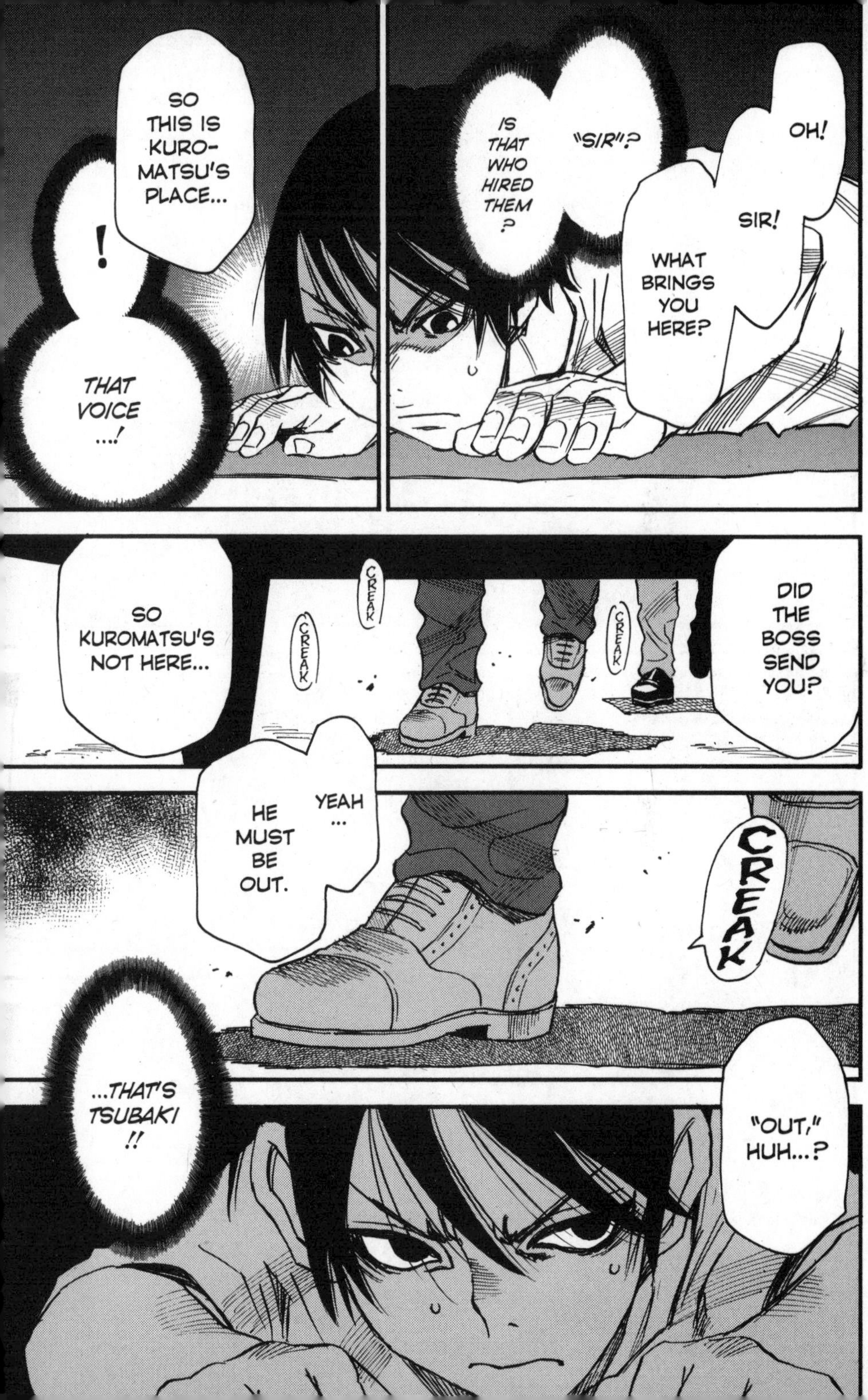
OH!
SIR!
WHAT BRINGS YOU HERE?
"SIR"?
IS THAT WHO HIRED THEM?
SO THIS IS KURO-MATSU'S PLACE...
!
THAT VOICE ...!
DID THE BOSS SEND YOU?
CREAK
CREAK
CREAK
SO KUROMATSU'S NOT HERE...
CREAK
YEAH ...
HE MUST BE OUT.
"OUT," HUH...?
...THAT'S TSUBAKI !!

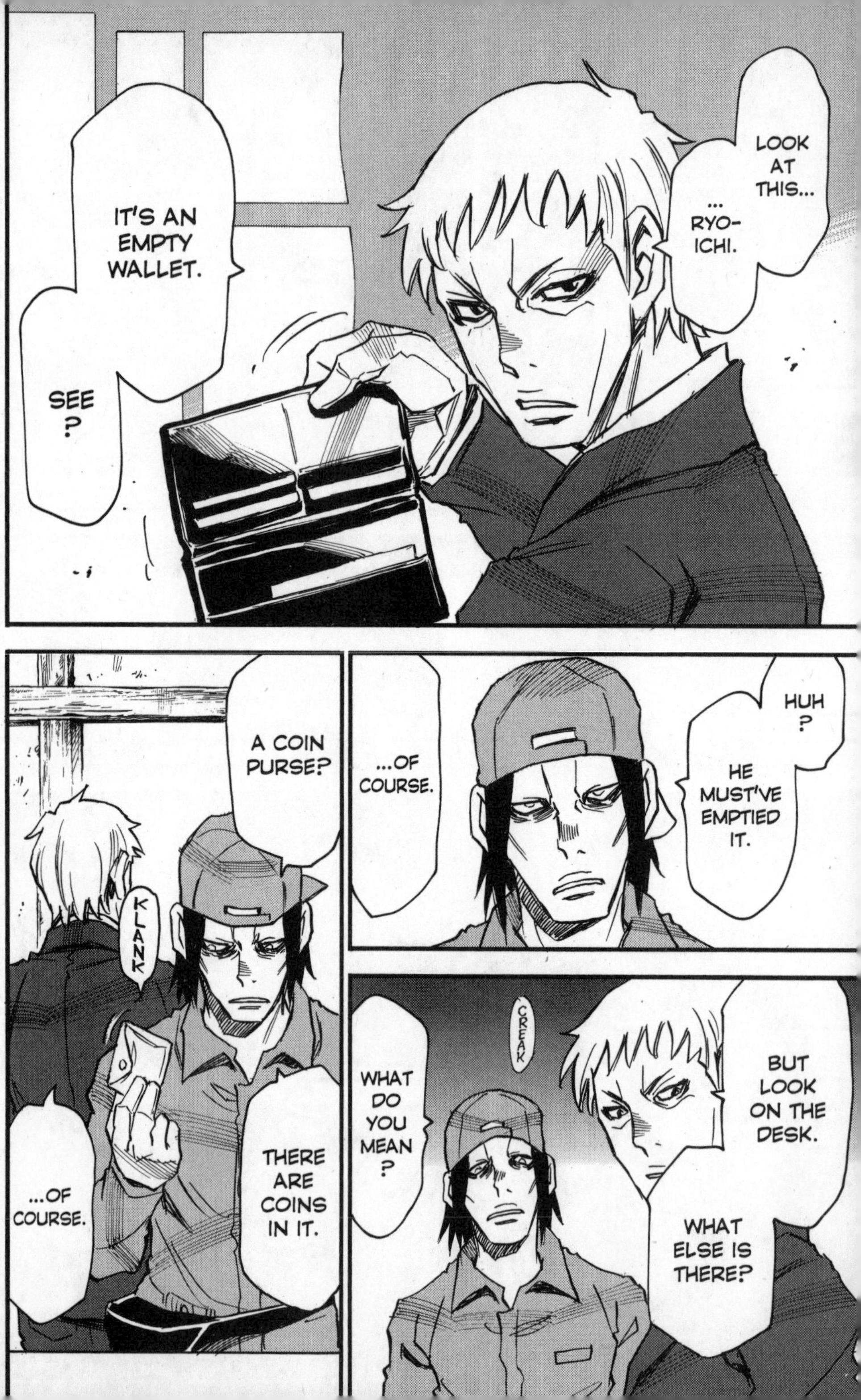
LOOK AT THIS...
...RYO-ICHI.
IT'S AN EMPTY WALLET.
SEE?
HUH?
HE MUST'VE EMPTIED IT.
...OF COURSE.
BUT LOOK ON THE DESK.
WHAT ELSE IS THERE?
CREAK
WHAT DO YOU MEAN?
A COIN PURSE?
KLANK
THERE ARE COINS IN IT.
...OF COURSE.

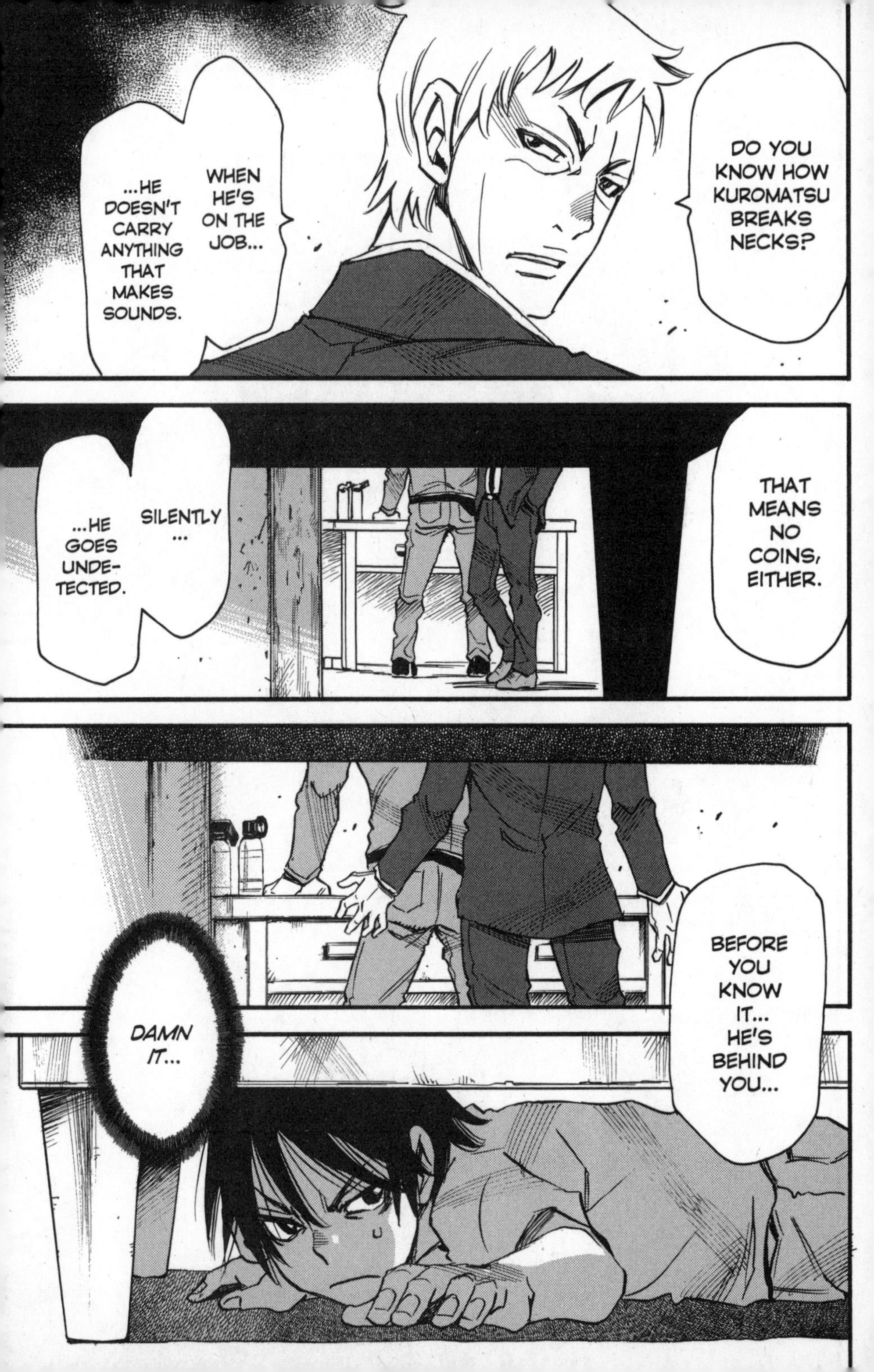
DO YOU KNOW HOW KUROMATSU BREAKS NECKS?
WHEN HE'S ON THE JOB...
...HE DOESN'T CARRY ANYTHING THAT MAKES SOUNDS.
THAT MEANS NO COINS, EITHER.
SILENTLY...
...HE GOES UNDE-TECTED.
BEFORE YOU KNOW IT... HE'S BEHIND YOU...
DAMN IT...

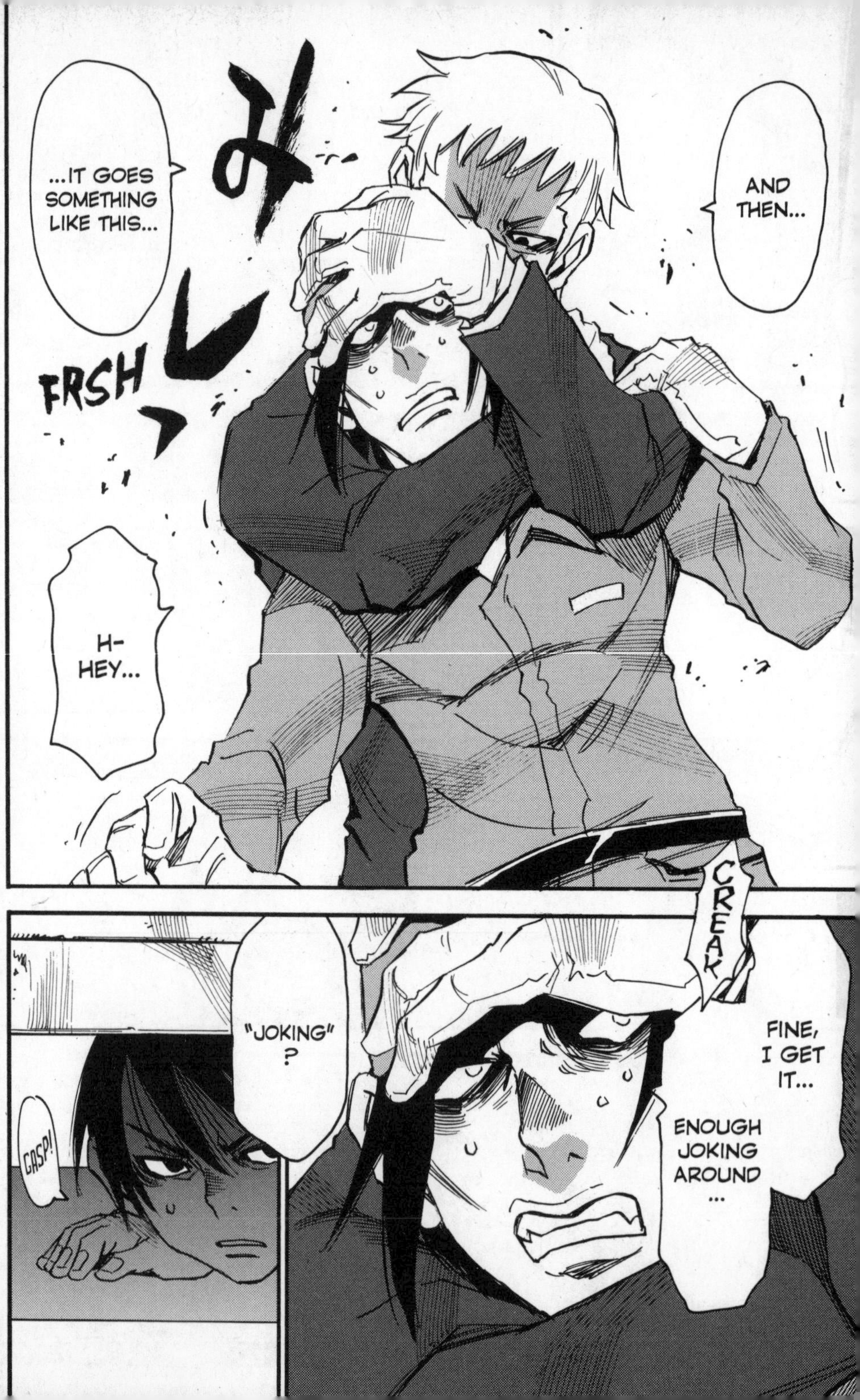
AND THEN...
...IT GOES SOMETHING LIKE THIS...
FRSH
H-HEY...
CREAK
FINE, I GET IT...
ENOUGH JOKING AROUND ...
"JOKING" ?
GASP!

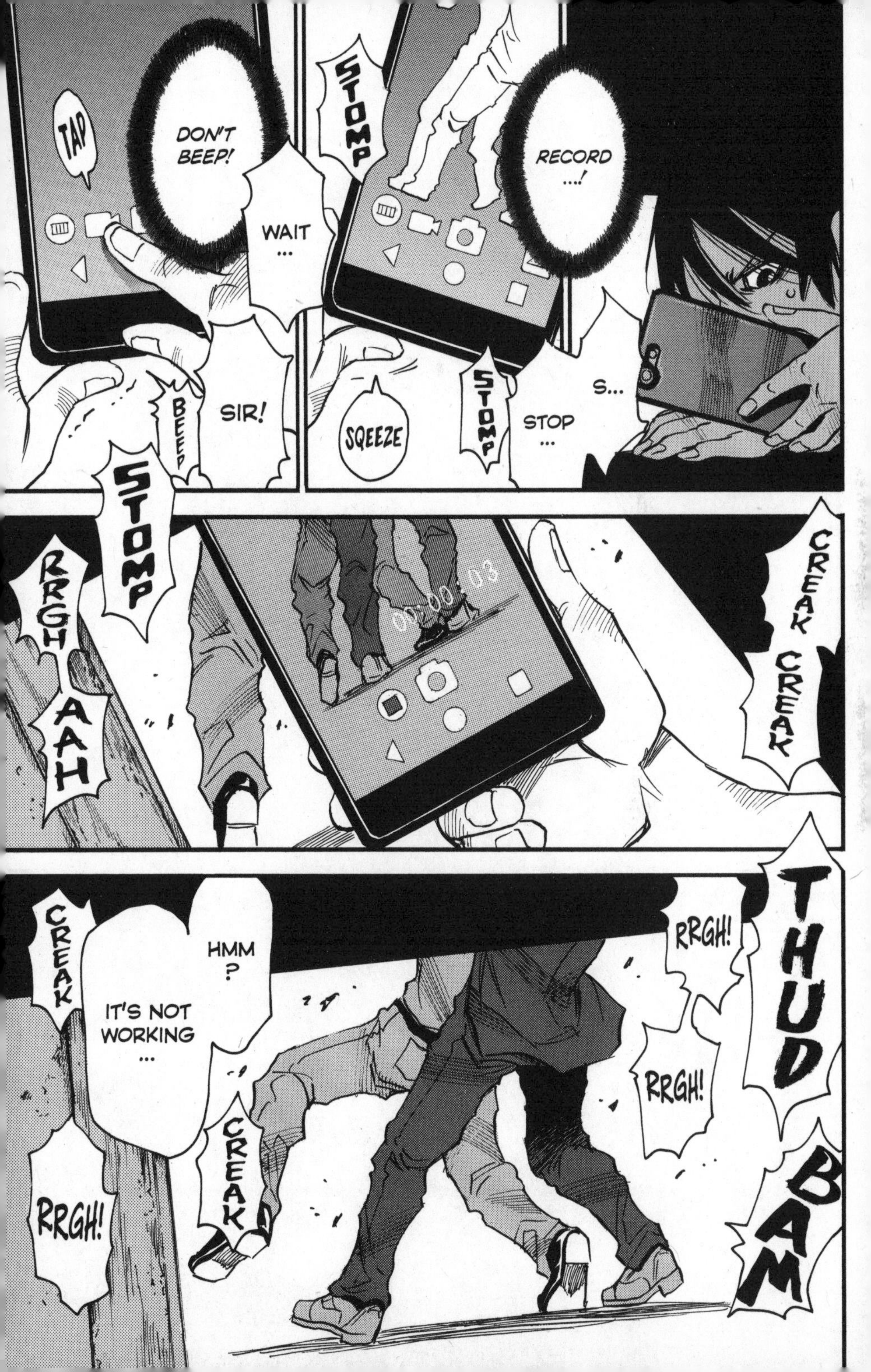
S...
STOP ...
RECORD ....!
STOMP
STOMP
SQUEEZE
DON'T BEEP!
TAP
WAIT ...
SIR!
BEEP
STOMP
CREAK
CREAK
CREAK
STOMP
RRGH
AAH
THUD
RRGH!
RRGH!
BAM
HMM ?
IT'S NOT WORKING ...
CREAK
CREAK
RRGH!

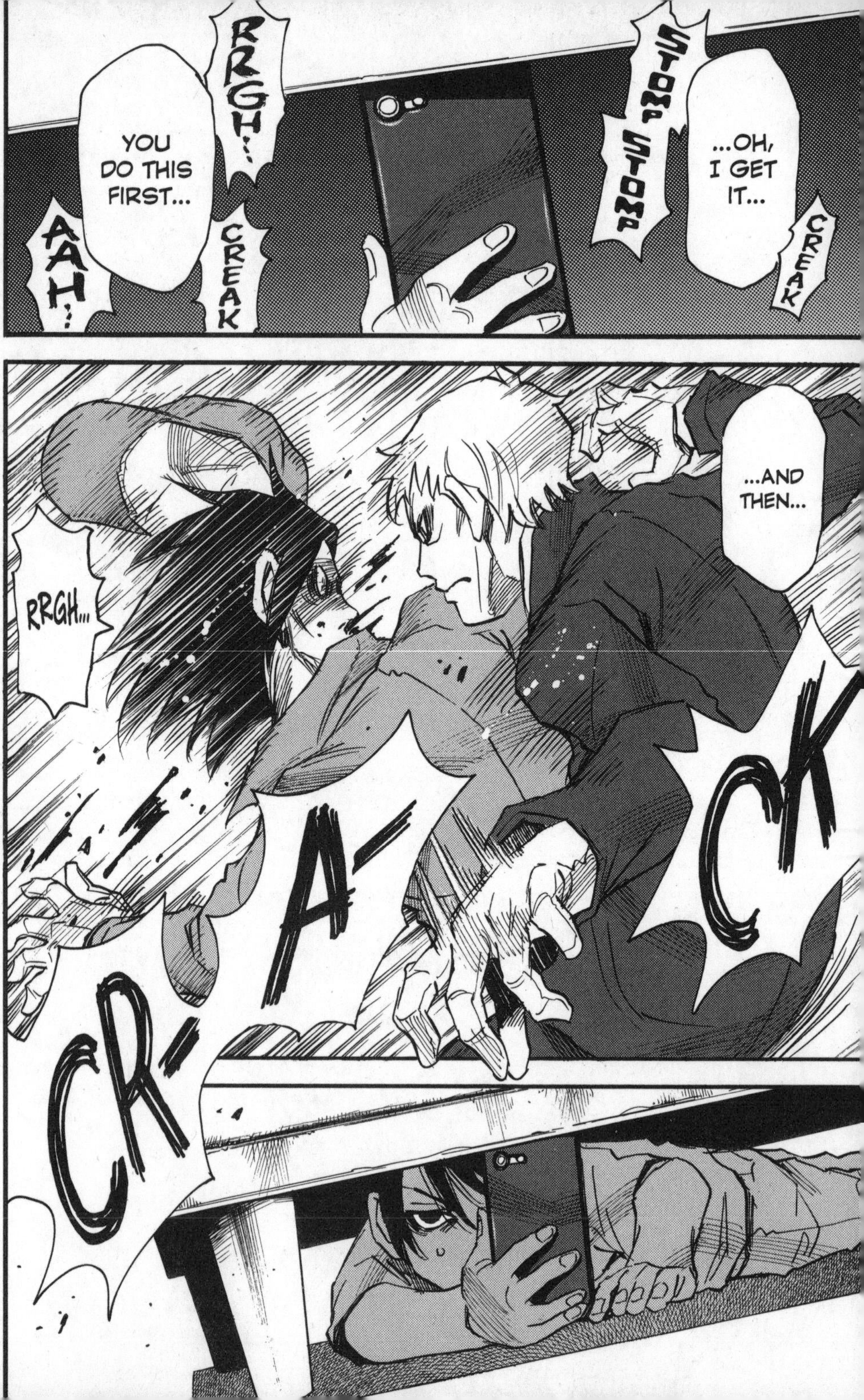
...OH, I GET IT...
CREAK
STOMP STOMP STOMP
RRGH...
YOU DO THIS FIRST...
CREAK
AAH...
...AND THEN...
RRGH...
CR-A-CK

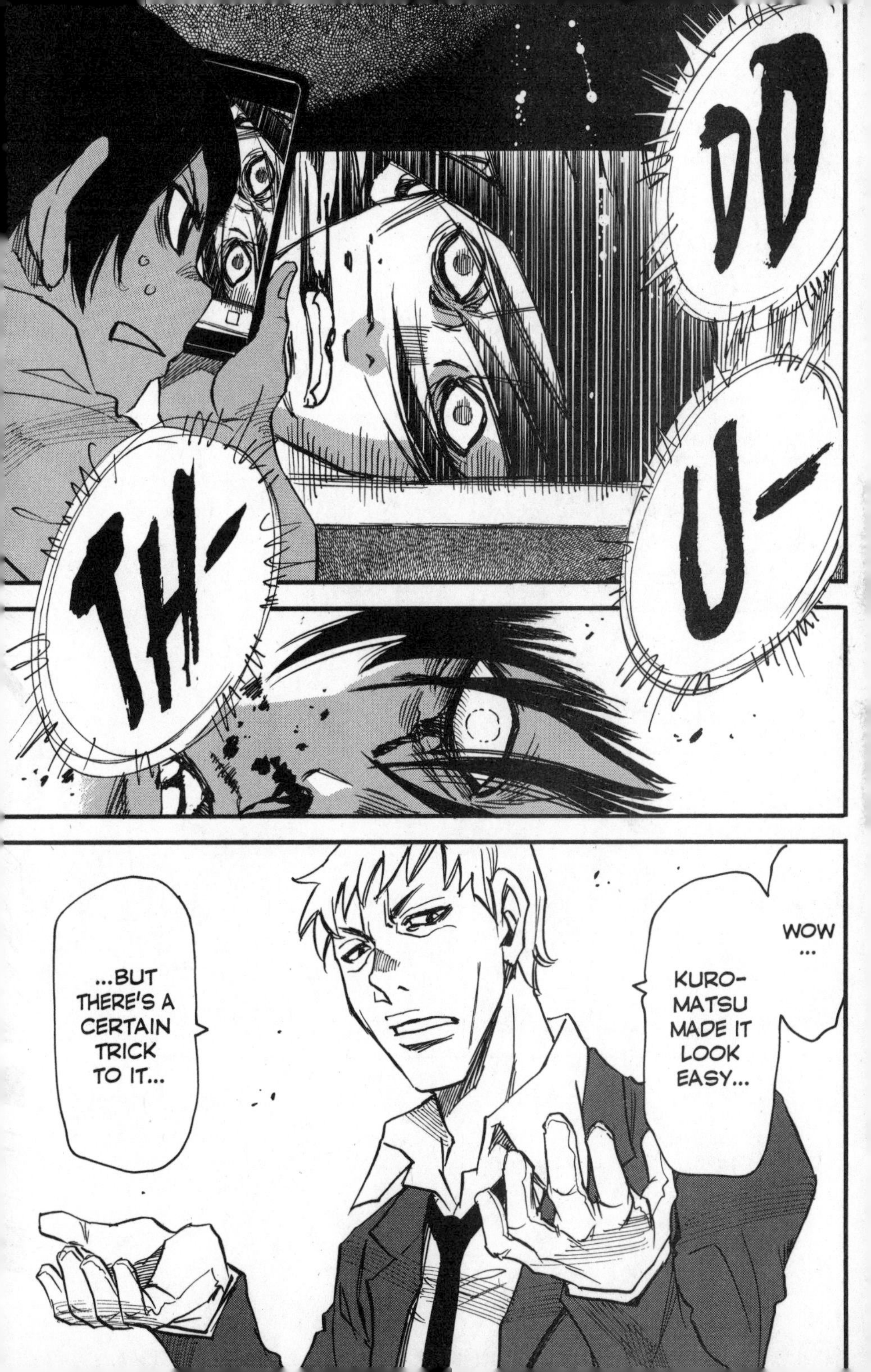
DD
U-
TH-
WOW ...
KURO-MATSU MADE IT LOOK EASY...
...BUT THERE'S A CERTAIN TRICK TO IT...

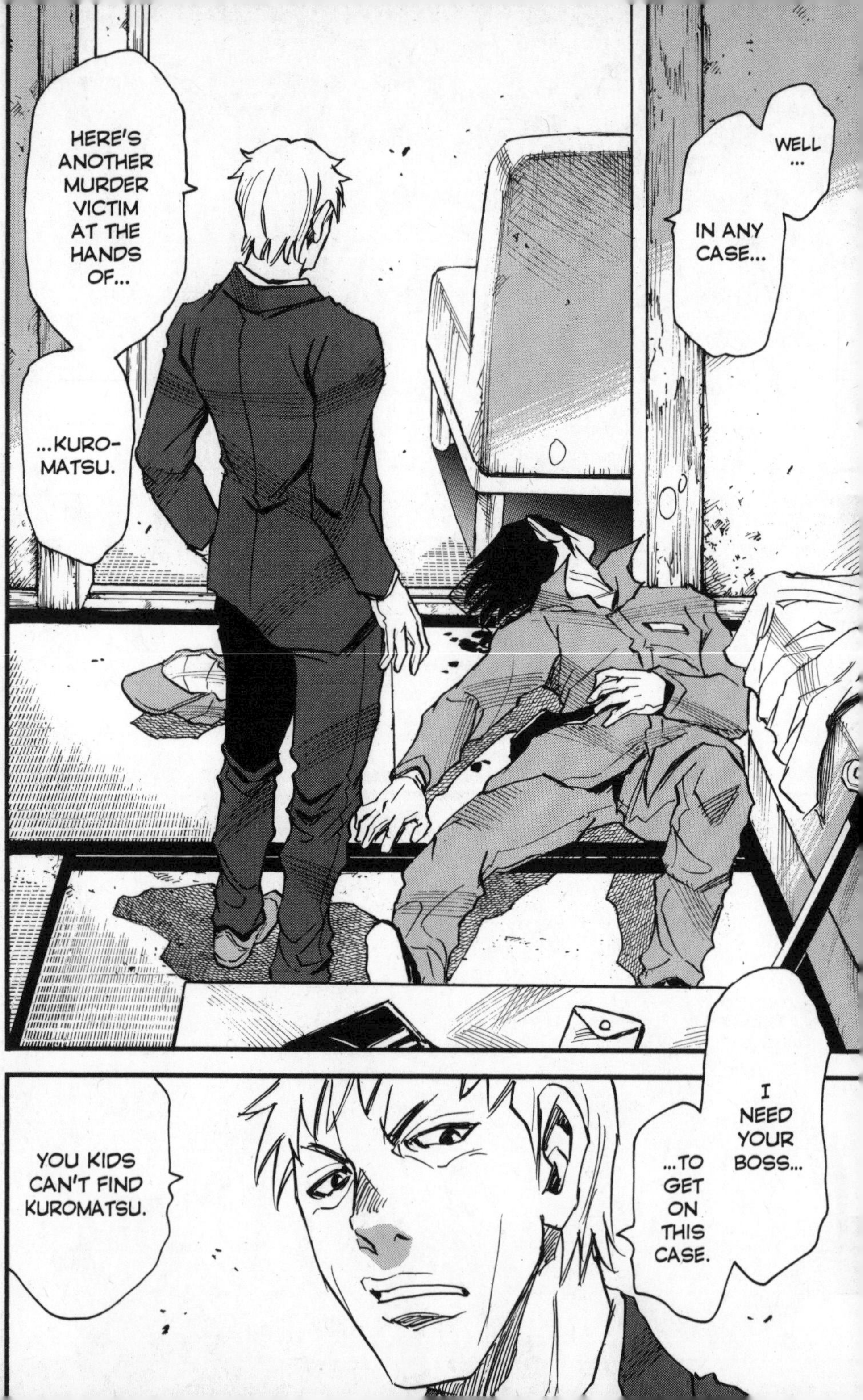
WELL...
IN ANY CASE...
HERE'S ANOTHER MURDER VICTIM AT THE HANDS OF...
...KURO-MATSU.
I NEED YOUR BOSS...
...TO GET ON THIS CASE.
YOU KIDS CAN'T FIND KUROMATSU.

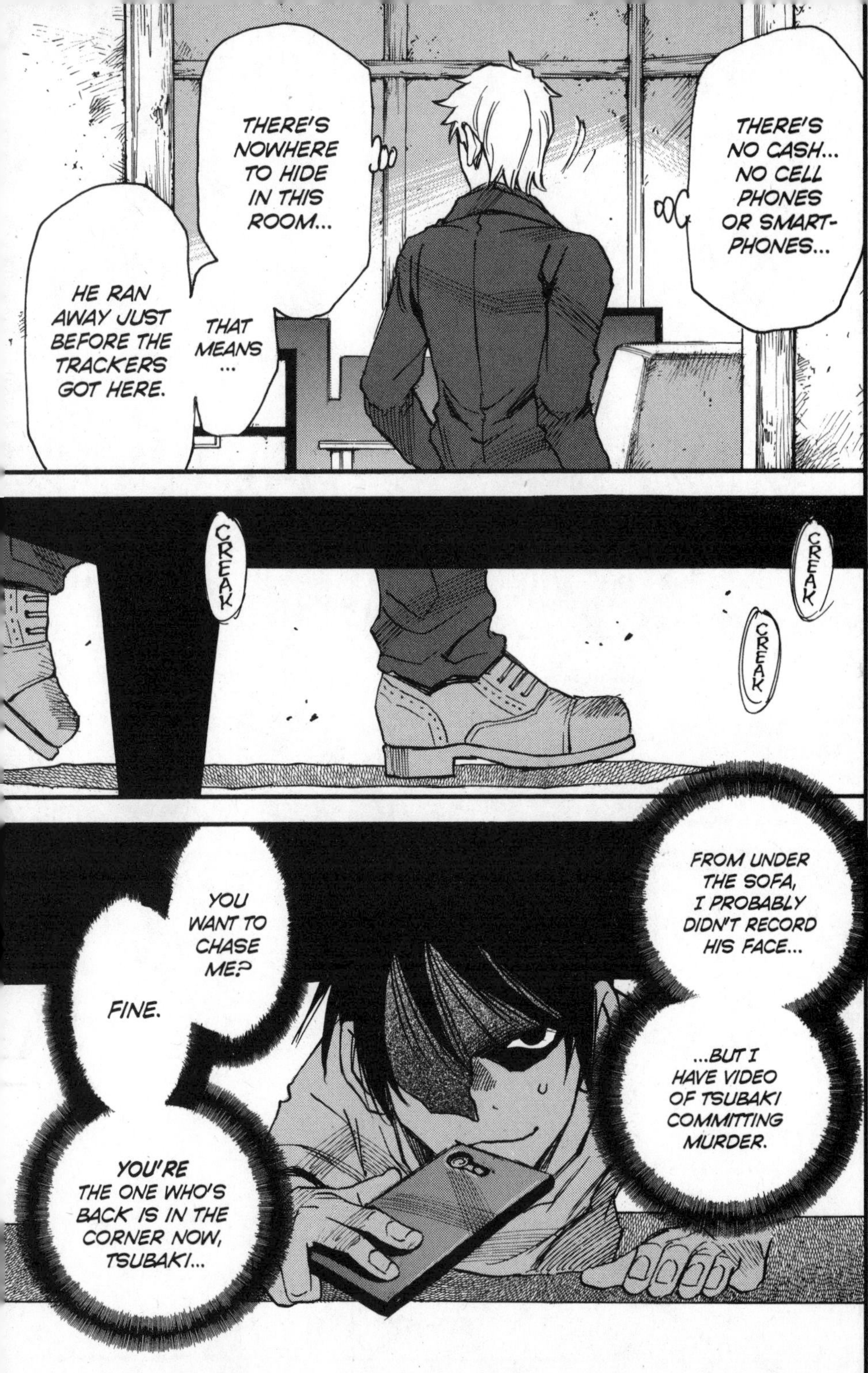
THERE'S NO CASH... NO CELL PHONES OR SMART-PHONES...
THERE'S NOWHERE TO HIDE IN THIS ROOM...
THAT MEANS ...
HE RAN AWAY JUST BEFORE THE TRACKERS GOT HERE.
CREAK
CREAK
CREAK
FROM UNDER THE SOFA, I PROBABLY DIDN'T RECORD HIS FACE...
...BUT I HAVE VIDEO OF TSUBAKI COMMITTING MURDER.
YOU WANT TO CHASE ME?
FINE.
YOU'RE THE ONE WHO'S BACK IS IN THE CORNER NOW, TSUBAKI...

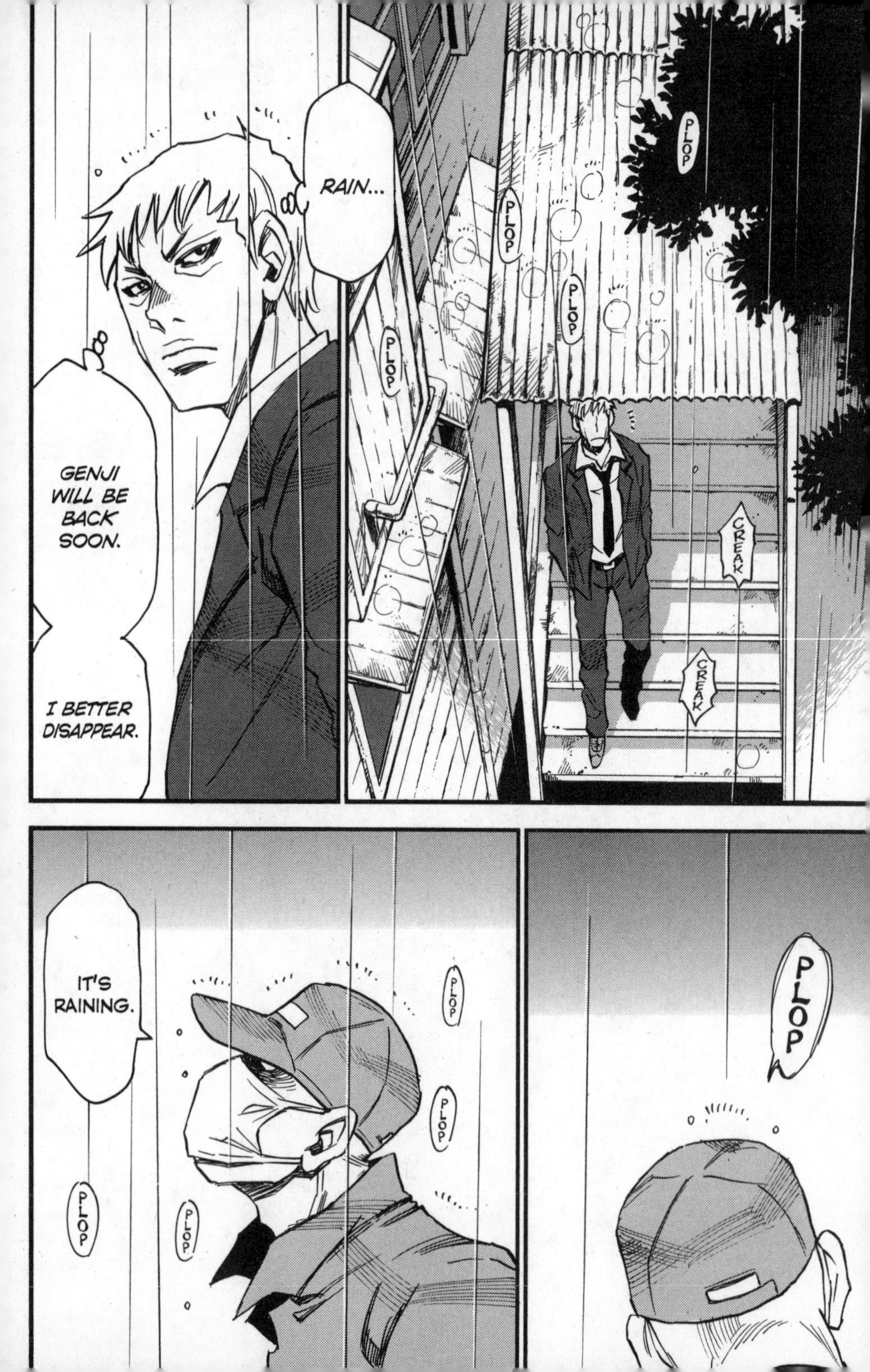
PLOP
PLOP
PLOP
PLOP
CREAK
CREAK
RAIN...
GENJI WILL BE BACK SOON.
I BETTER DISAPPEAR.
PLOP
IT'S RAINING.
PLOP
PLOP
PLOP
PLOP

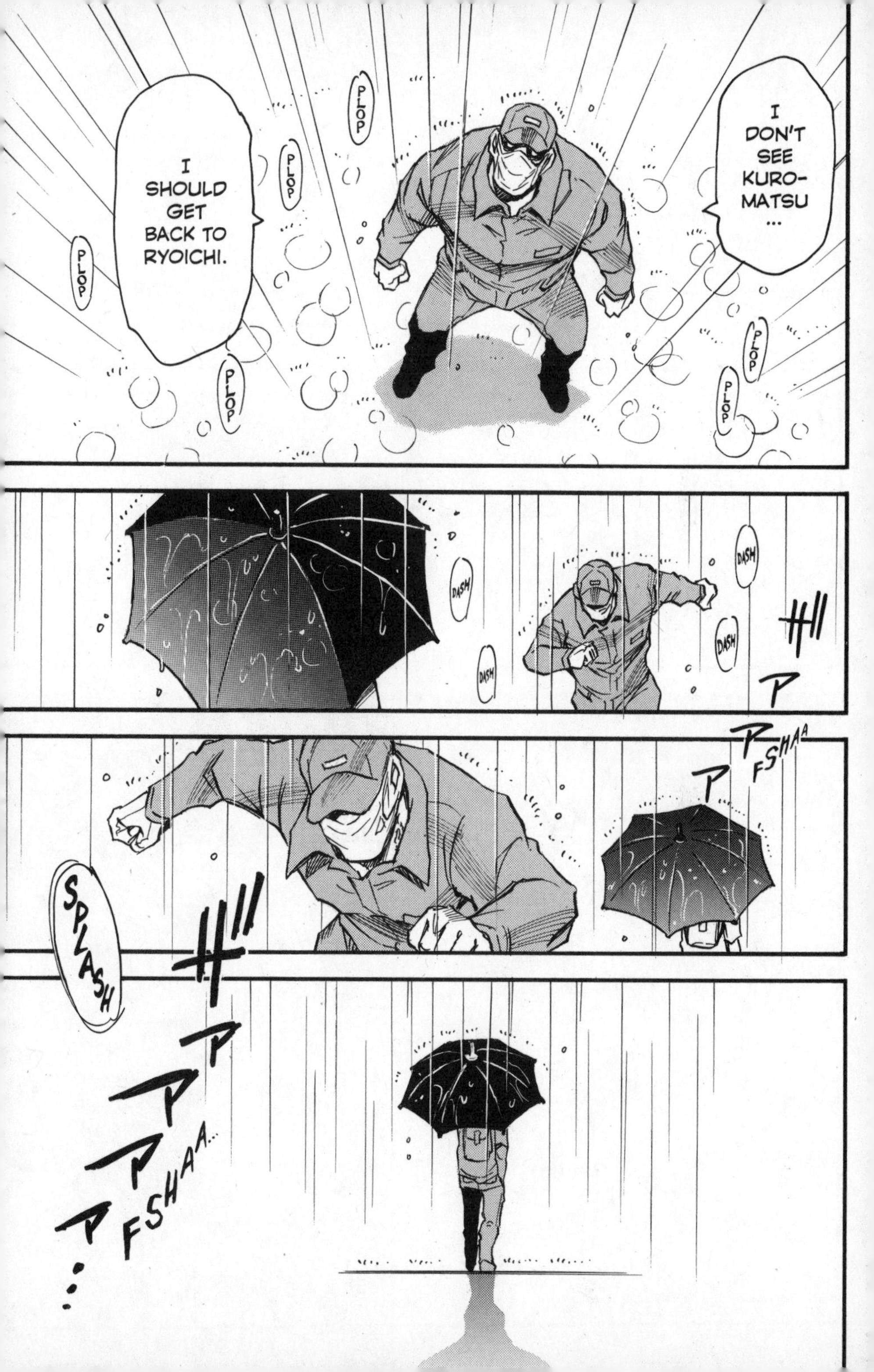
I DON'T SEE KURO-MATSU...
PLOP
PLOP
I SHOULD GET BACK TO RYOICHI.
PLOP
PLOP
PLOP
PLOP
DASH
DASH
DASH
DASH
FSHAA
SPLASH
FSHAA...

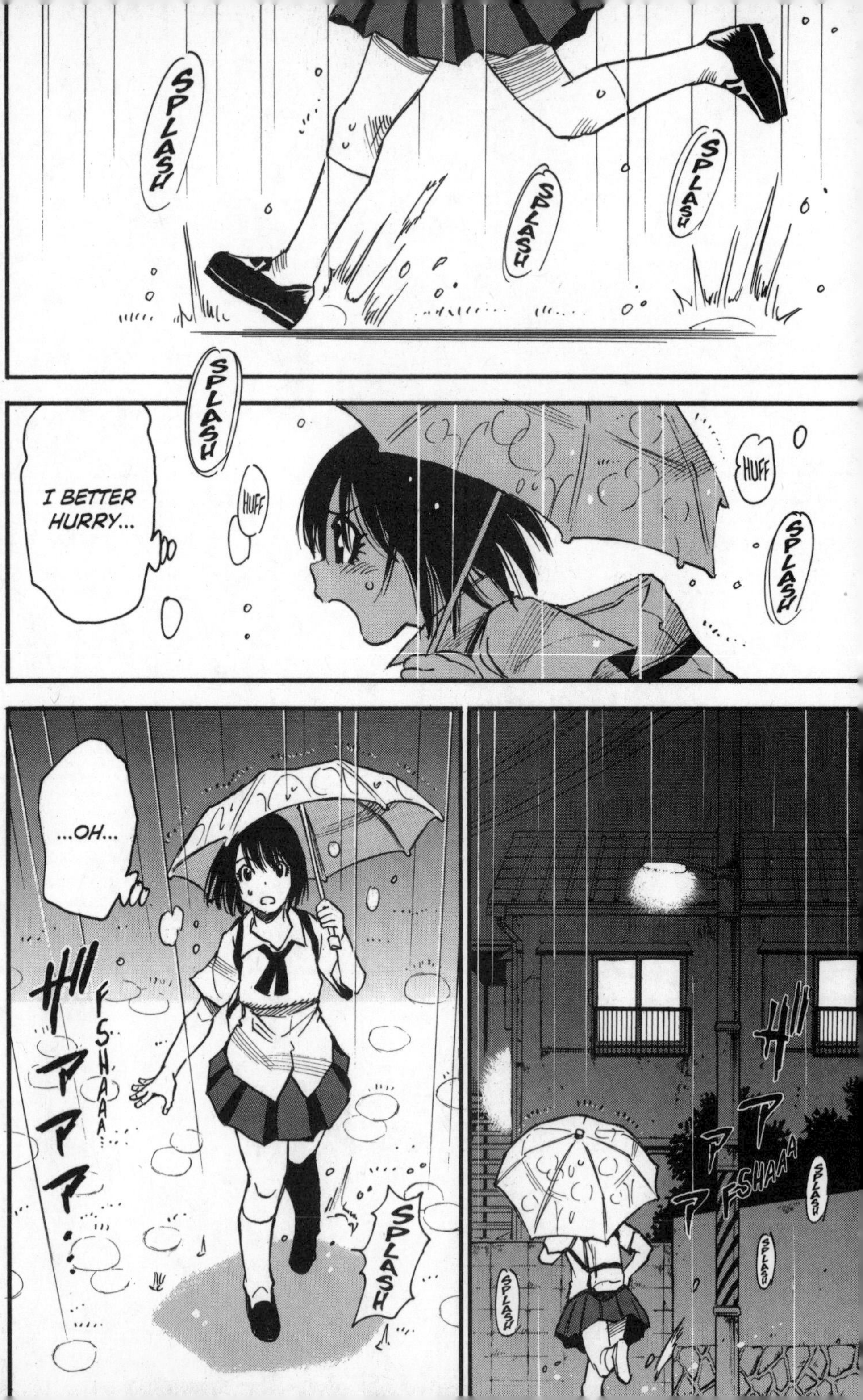
SPLASH
SPLASH
SPLASH
SPLASH
HUFF
HUFF
SPLASH
I BETTER HURRY...
FSHAAA
SPLASH
SPLASH
SPLASH
...OH...
SPLASH
FSHAAA...

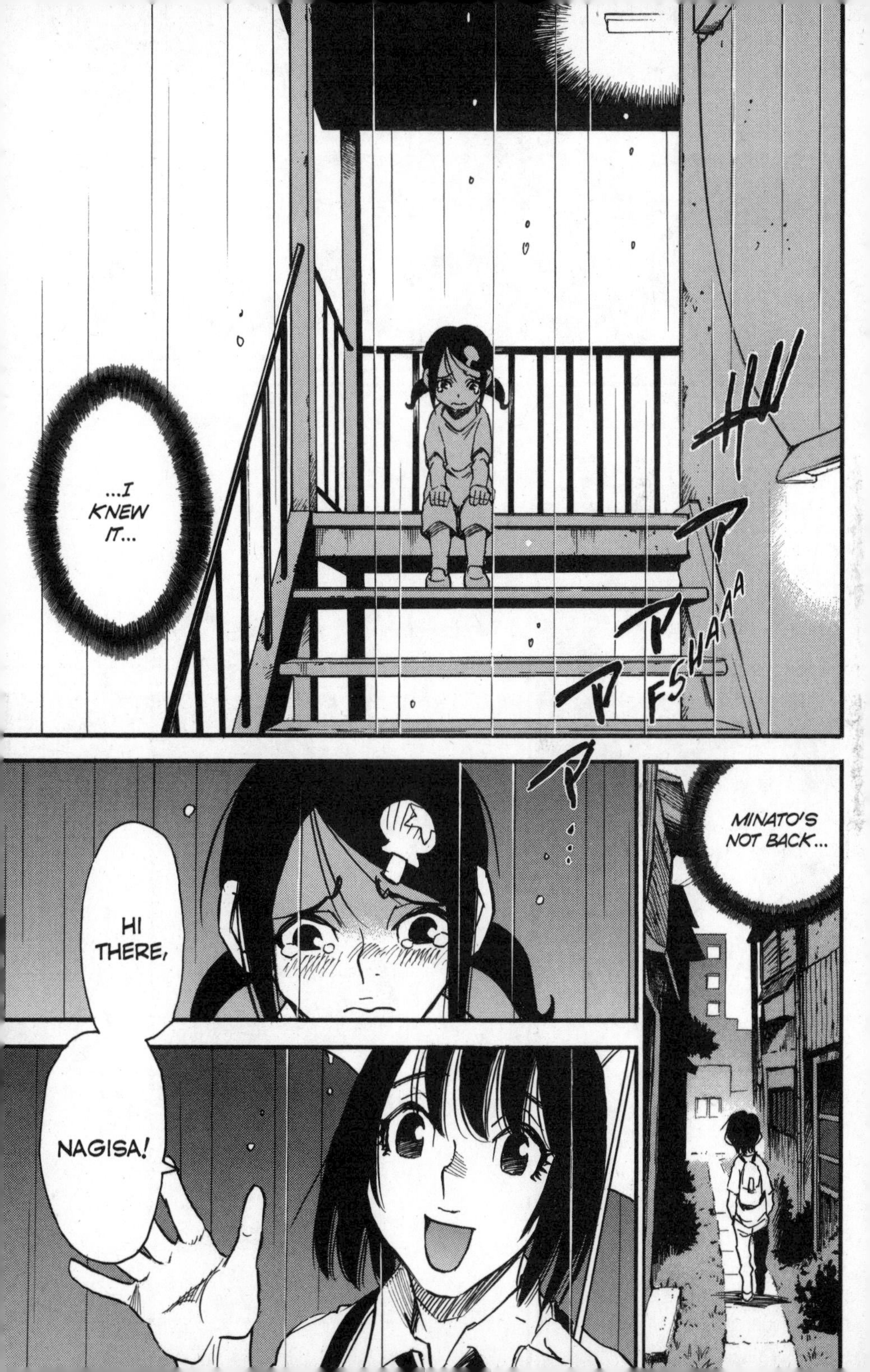
...I KNEW IT...
FSHAAA
MINATO'S NOT BACK...
HI THERE, NAGISA!

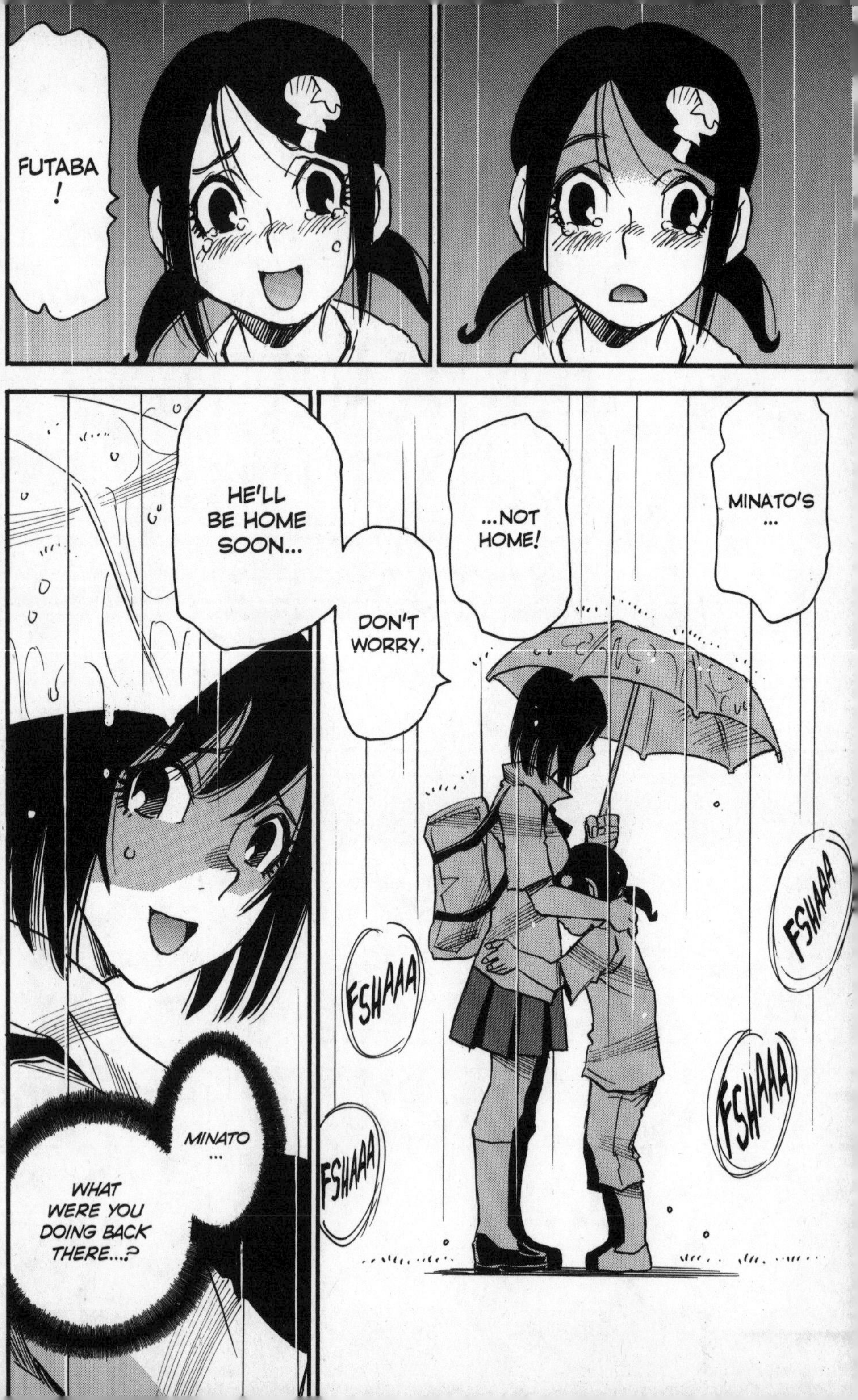
FUTABA !
MINATO'S ...
...NOT HOME!
FSHAAA
FSHAAA
FSHAAA
FSHAAA
HE'LL BE HOME SOON...
DON'T WORRY.
MINATO ...
WHAT WERE YOU DOING BACK THERE...?

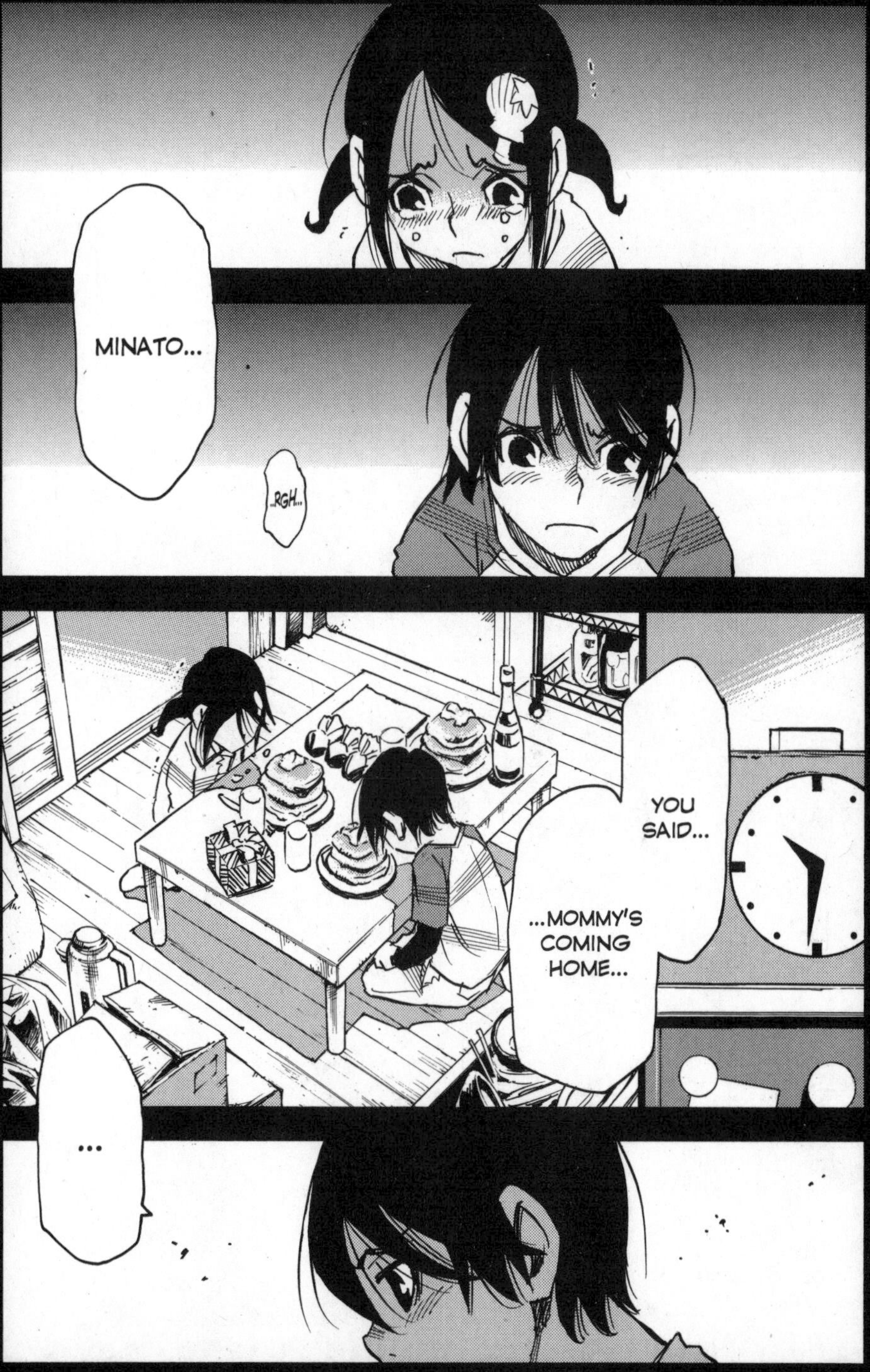
MINATO...
..RGH...
YOU SAID...
...MOMMY'S COMING HOME...
...

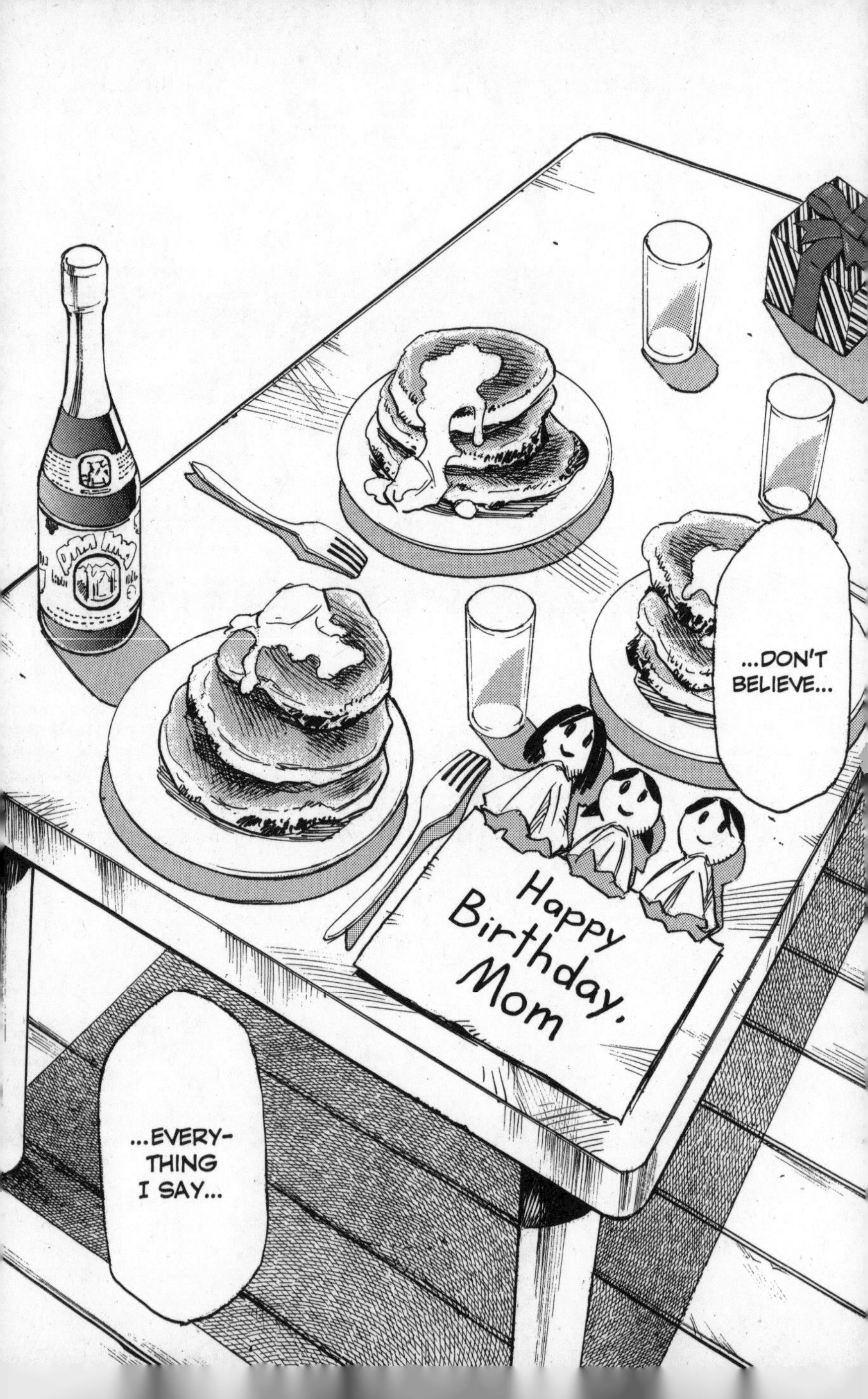
...DON'T BELIEVE...
Happy Birthday, Mom
...EVERY-THING I SAY...

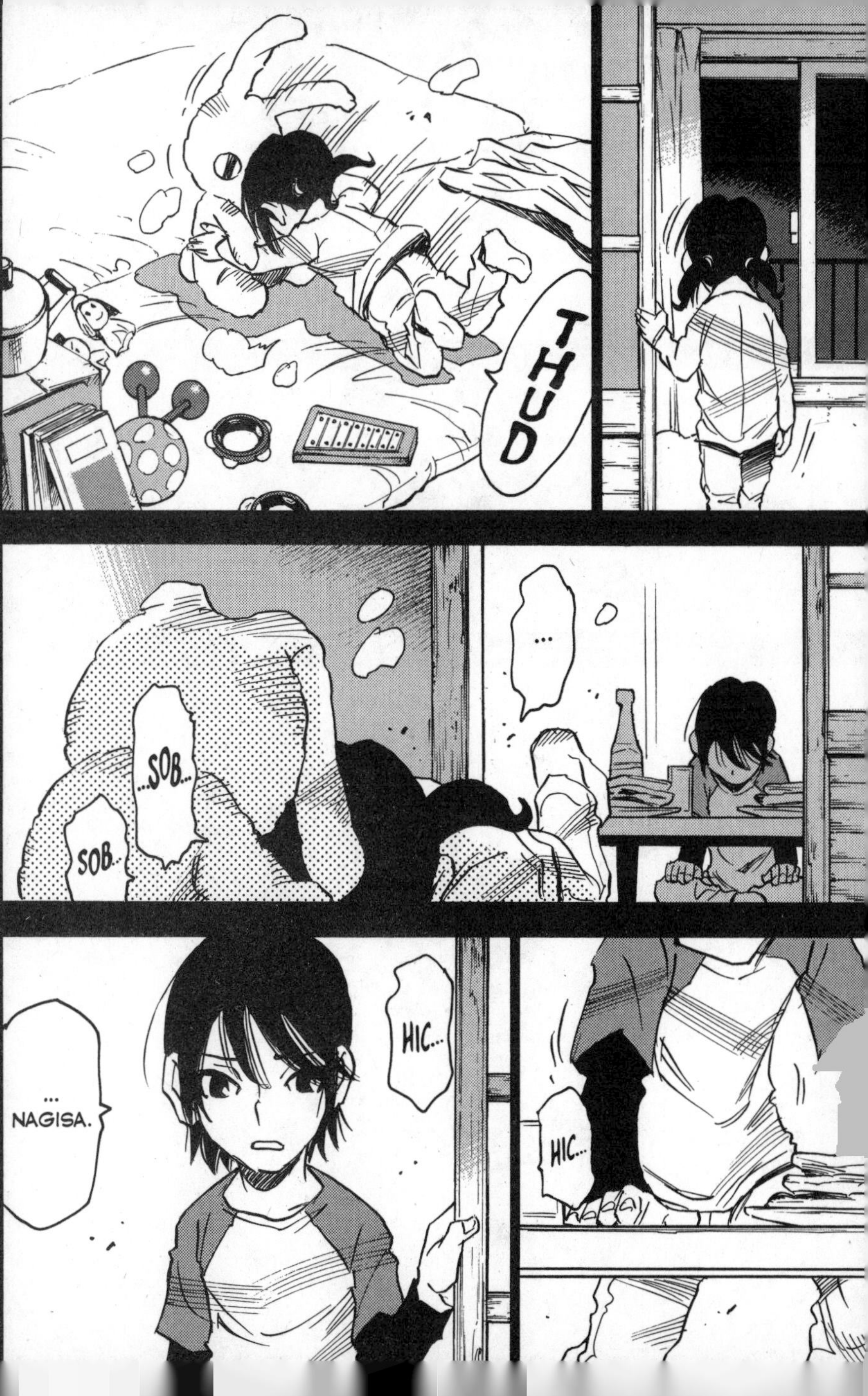
THUD
...
...SOB...
SOB...
HIC...
HIC...
... NAGISA.

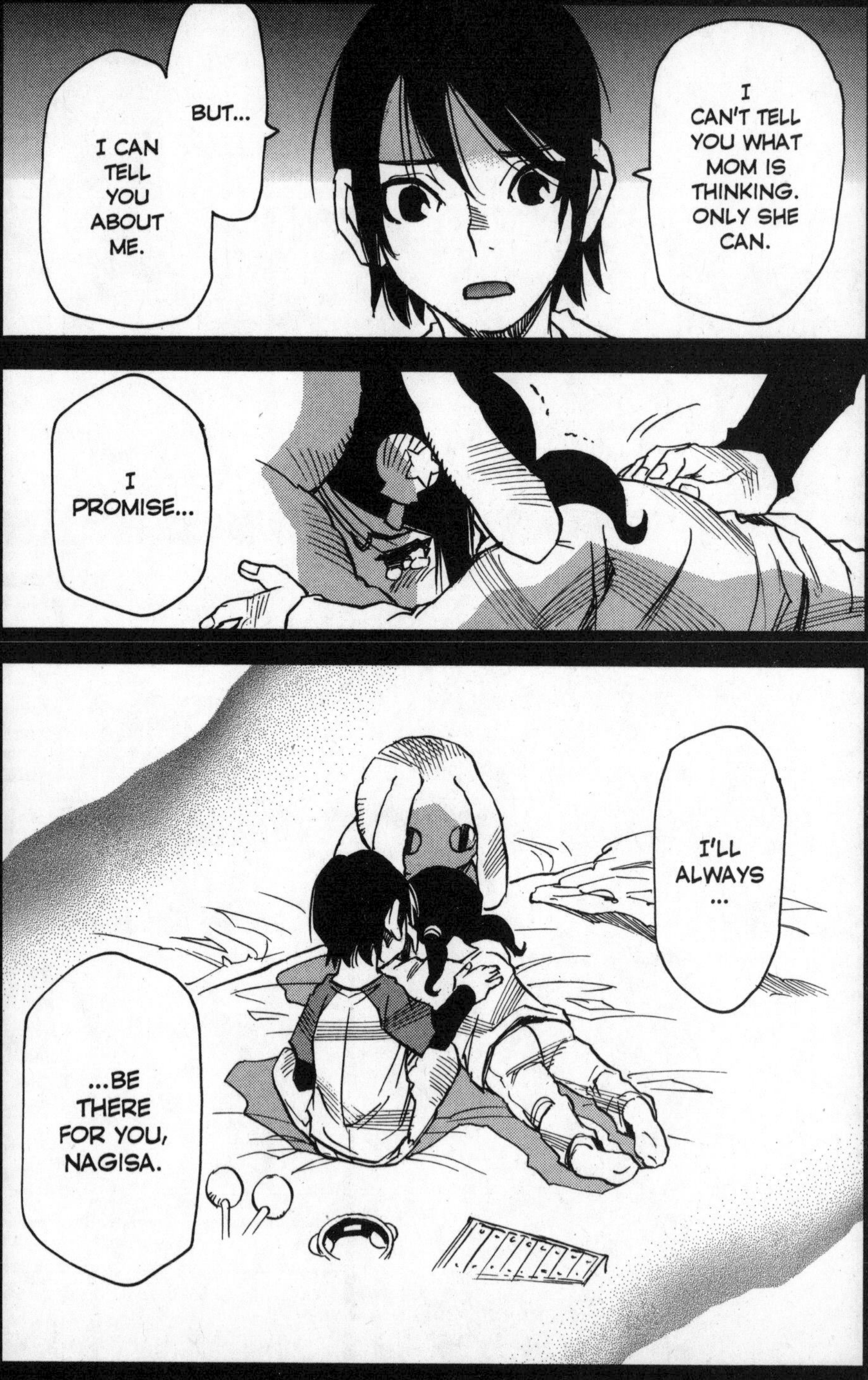
I CAN'T TELL YOU WHAT MOM IS THINKING. ONLY SHE CAN.
BUT...
I CAN TELL YOU ABOUT ME.
I PROMISE...
I'LL ALWAYS ...
...BE THERE FOR YOU, NAGISA.

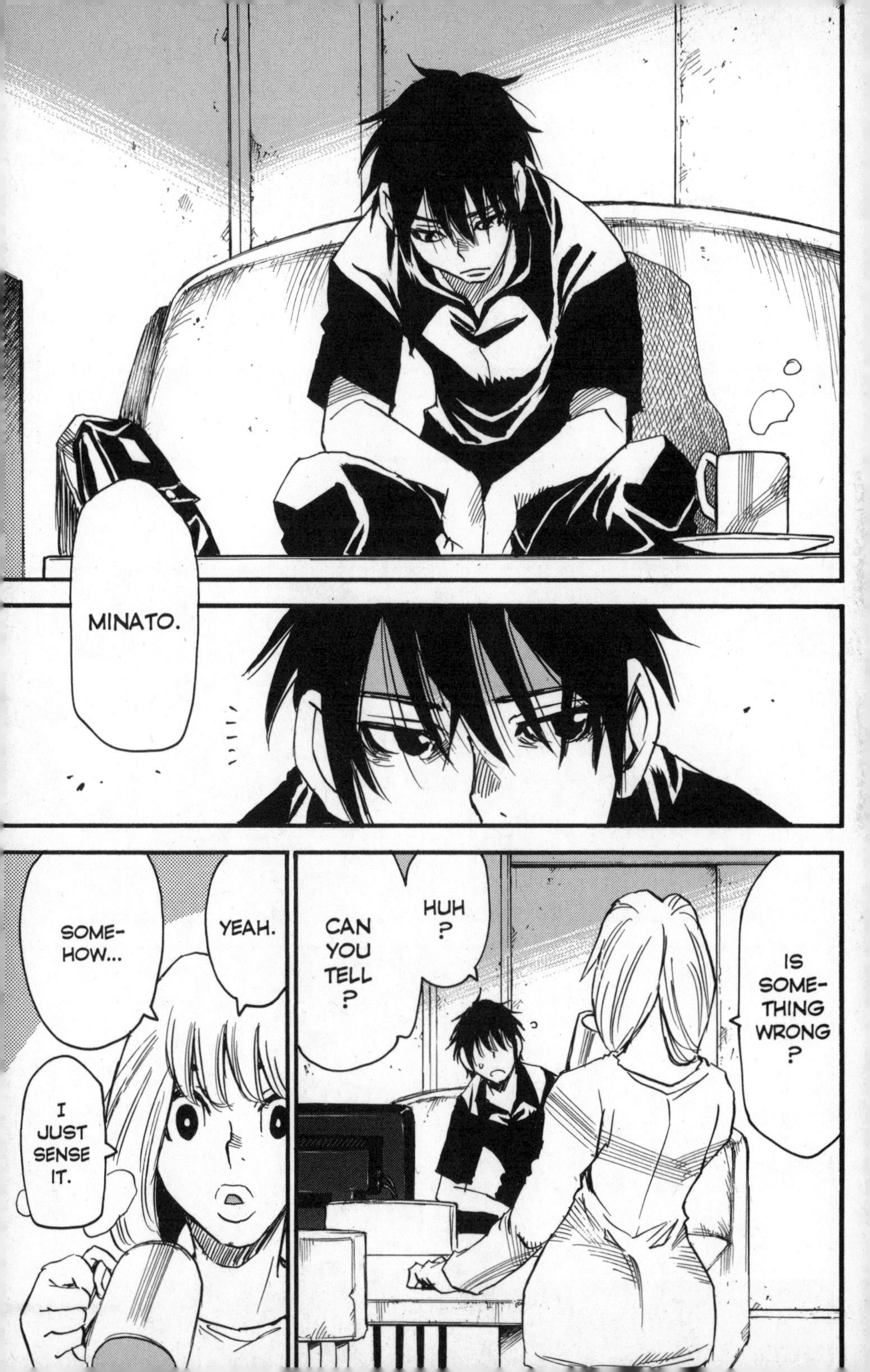
MINATO.
IS SOMETHING WRONG?
HUH?
CAN YOU TELL?
YEAH.
SOMEHOW...
I JUST SENSE IT.

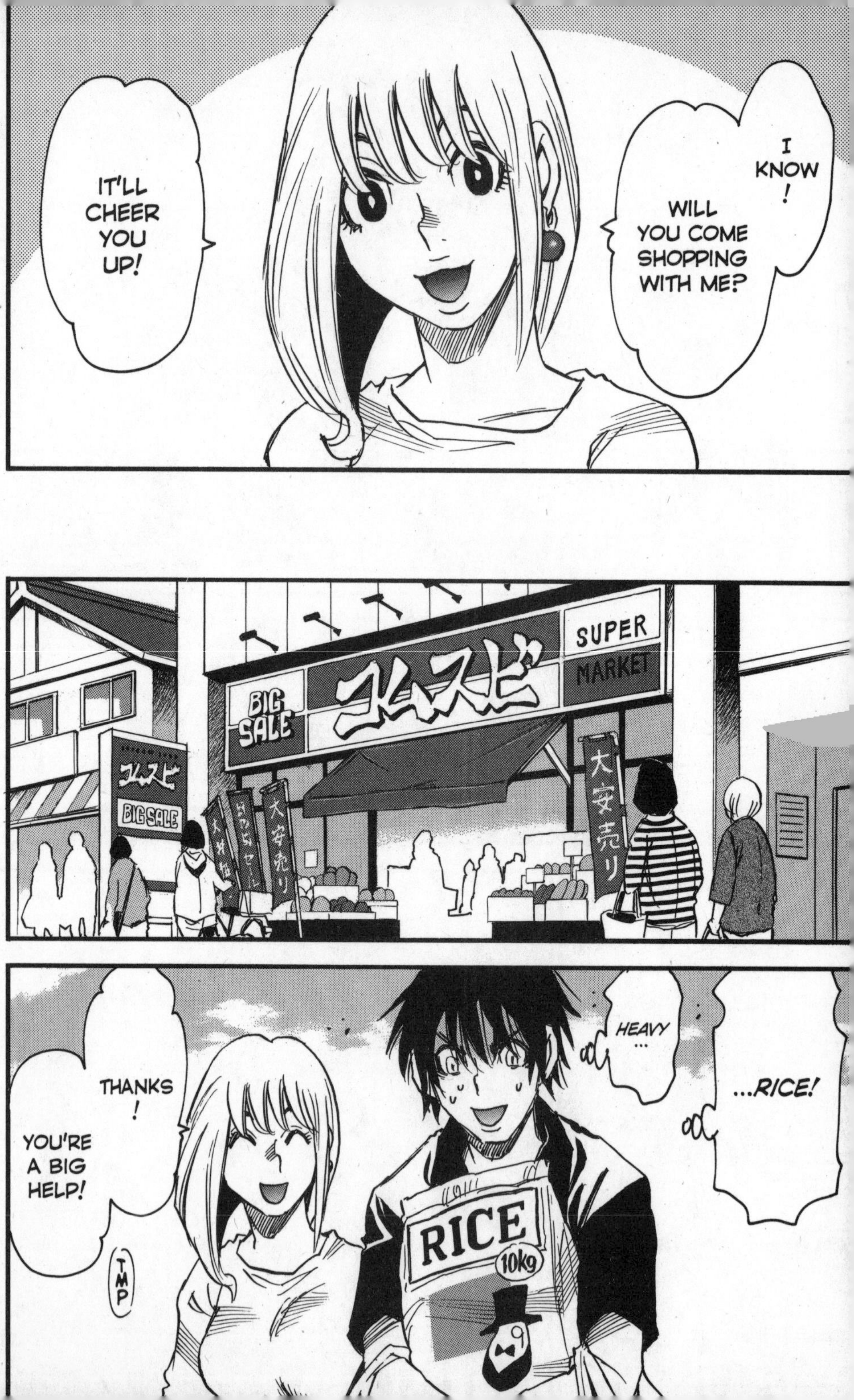
I KNOW! WILL YOU COME SHOPPING WITH ME?
IT'LL CHEER YOU UP!
SUPER MARKET
コムスビ
BIG SALE
大安売り
大安売り
コムスビ
BIG SALE
...RICE!
HEAVY ...
THANKS! YOU'RE A BIG HELP!
TMP
RICE
10kg

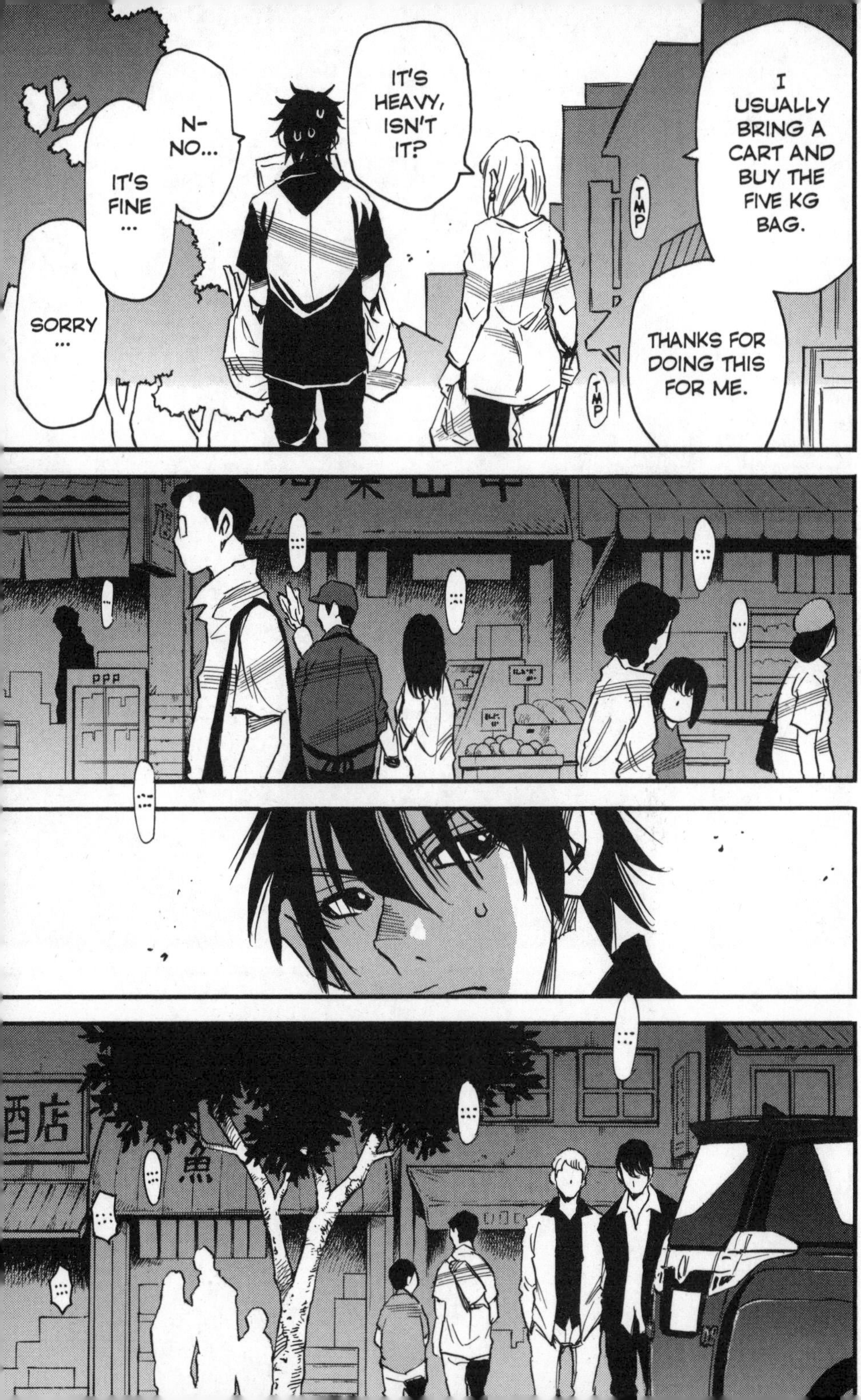
I USUALLY BRING A CART AND BUY THE FIVE KG BAG.
THANKS FOR DOING THIS FOR ME.
TMP
TMP
IT'S HEAVY, ISN'T IT?
N-NO...
IT'S FINE...
SORRY...

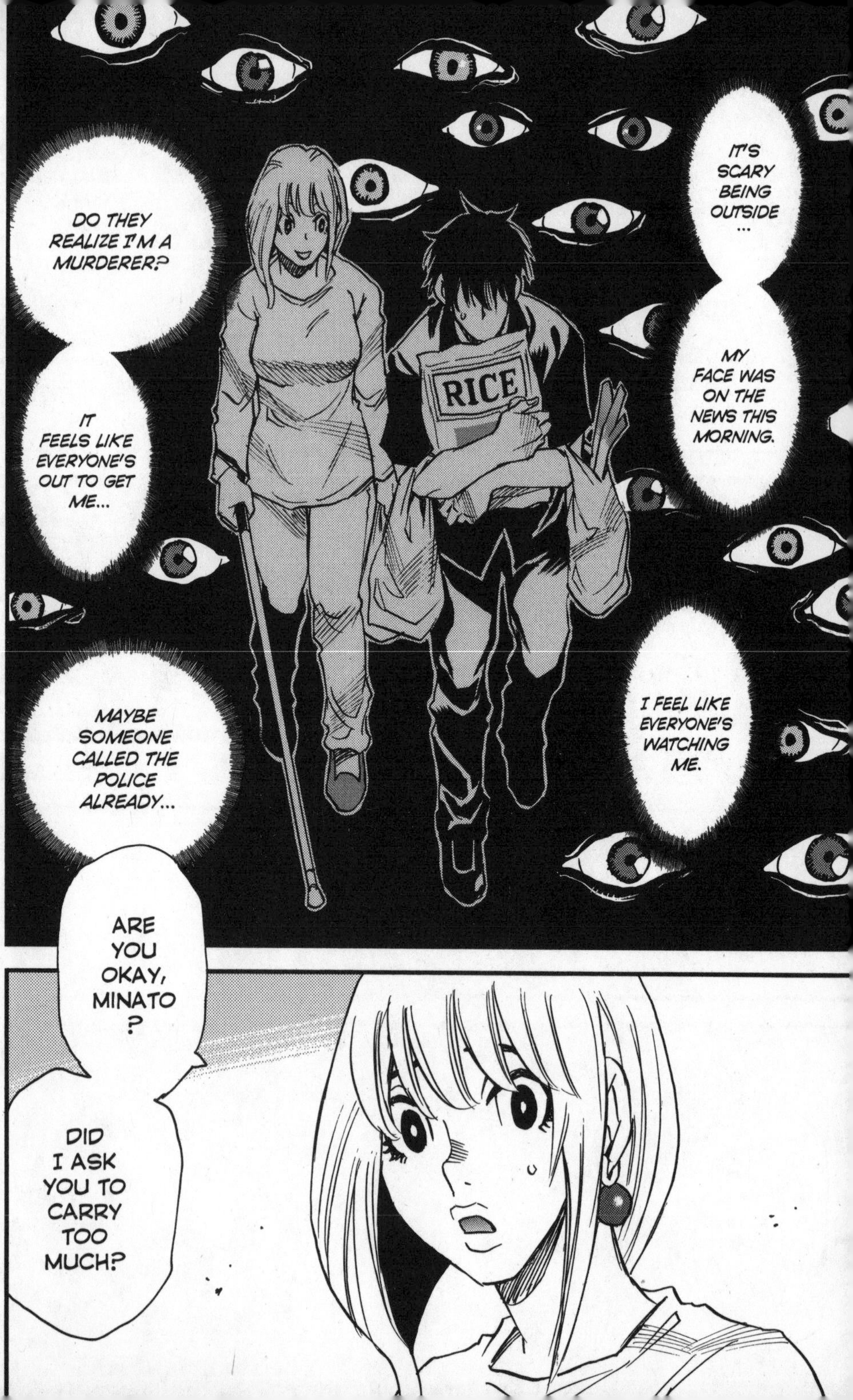
IT'S SCARY BEING OUTSIDE ...
DO THEY REALIZE I'M A MURDERER?
MY FACE WAS ON THE NEWS THIS MORNING.
IT FEELS LIKE EVERYONE'S OUT TO GET ME...
RICE
I FEEL LIKE EVERYONE'S WATCHING ME.
MAYBE SOMEONE CALLED THE POLICE ALREADY...
ARE YOU OKAY, MINATO?
DID I ASK YOU TO CARRY TOO MUCH?

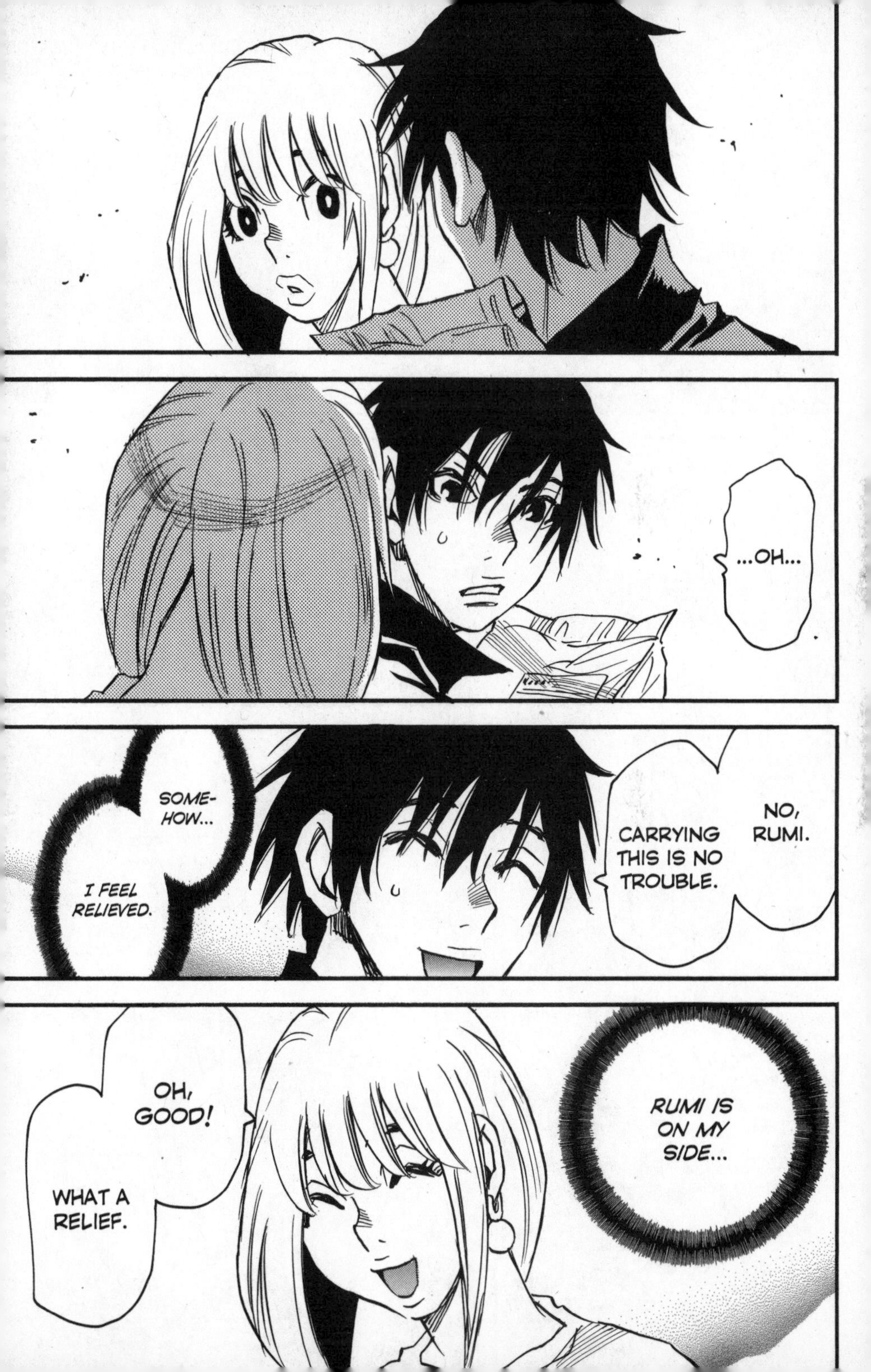
...OH...
NO, RUMI.
CARRYING THIS IS NO TROUBLE.
SOME-HOW...
I FEEL RELIEVED.
RUMI IS ON MY SIDE...
OH, GOOD!
WHAT A RELIEF.

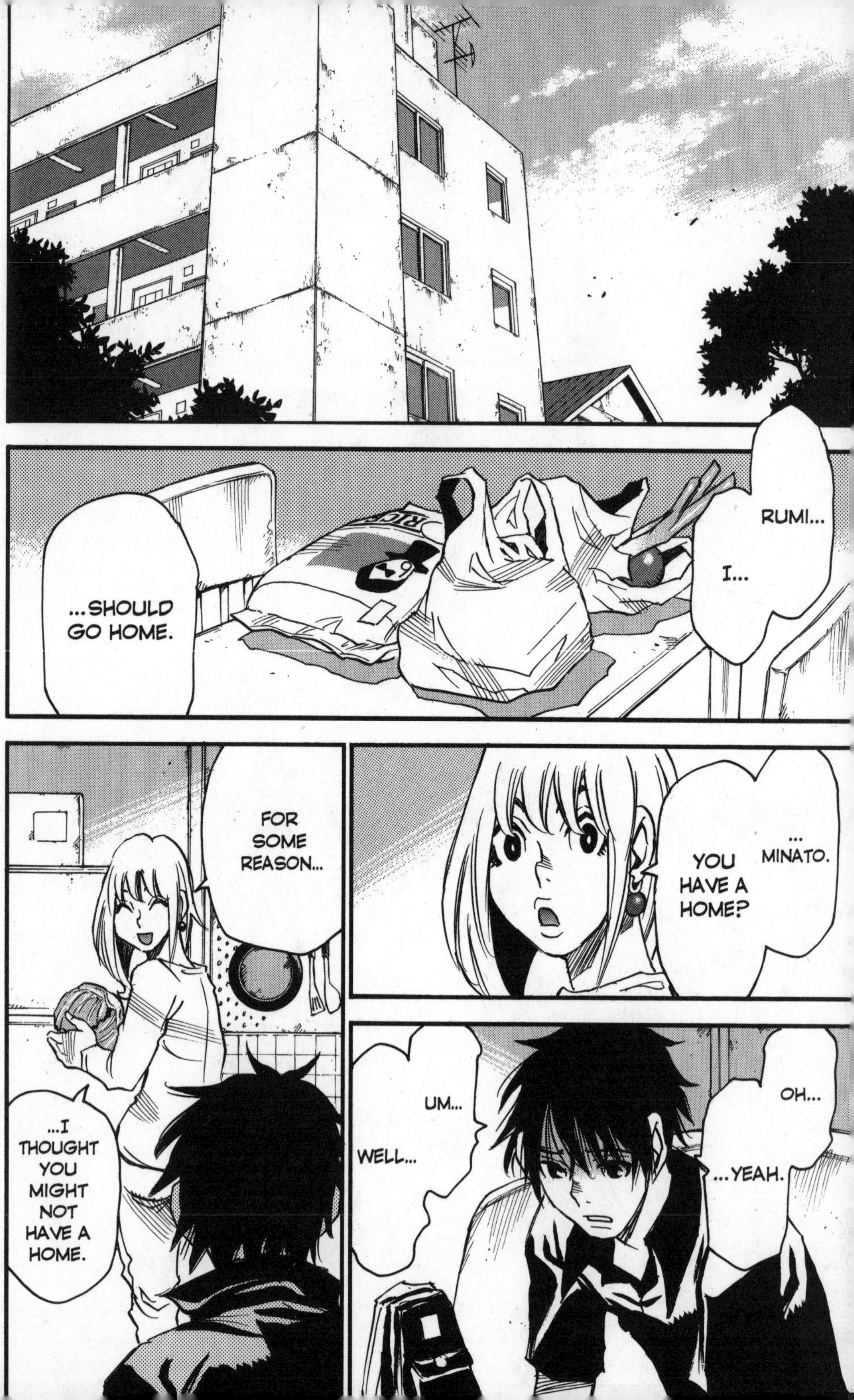
RUMI...
I...
...SHOULD GO HOME.
... MINATO.
YOU HAVE A HOME?
OH...
...YEAH.
UM...
WELL...
FOR SOME REASON...
...I THOUGHT YOU MIGHT NOT HAVE A HOME.

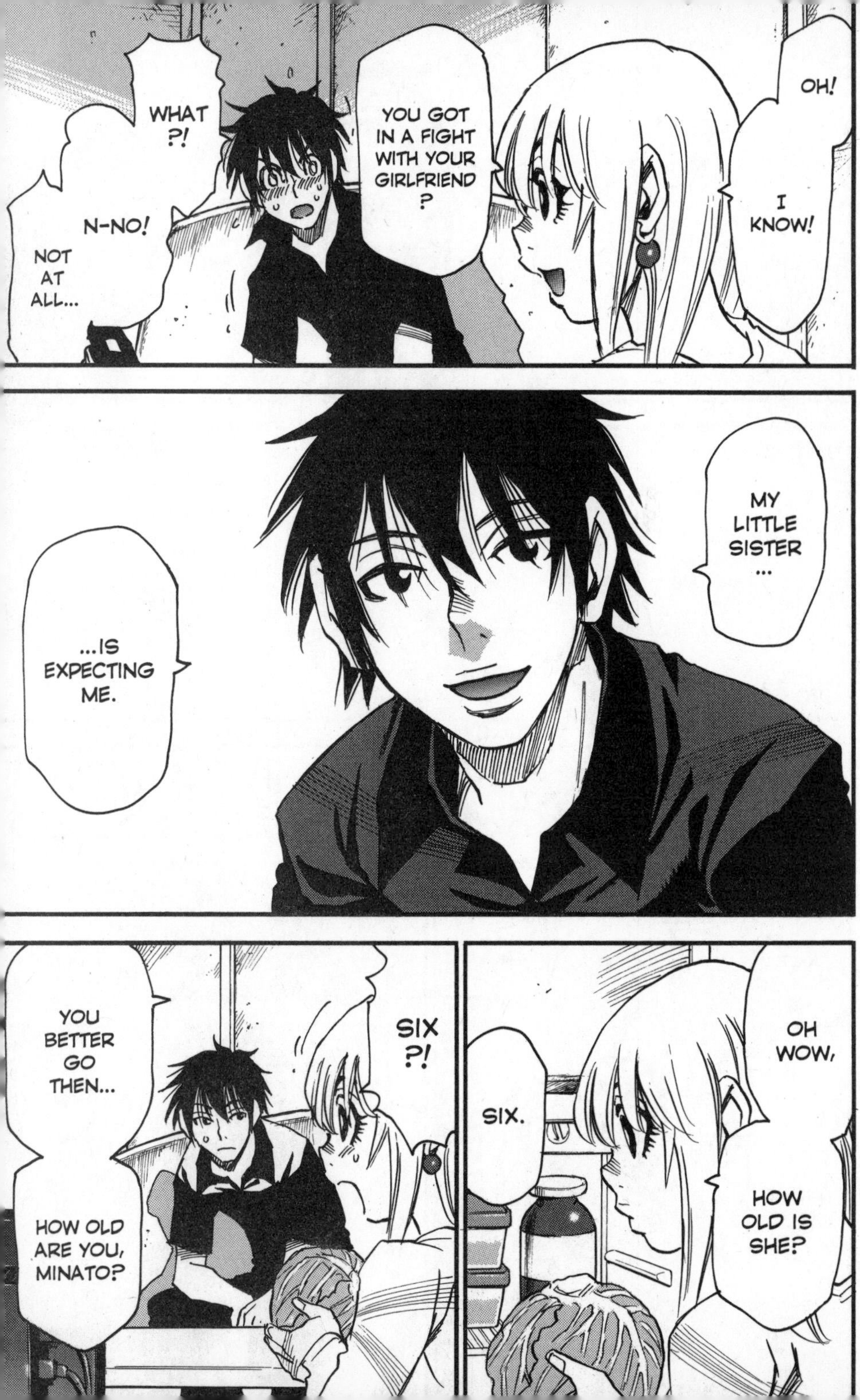
OH!
I KNOW!
YOU GOT IN A FIGHT WITH YOUR GIRLFRIEND?
WHAT ?!
N-NO!
NOT AT ALL...
MY LITTLE SISTER ...
...IS EXPECTING ME.
OH WOW,
HOW OLD IS SHE?
SIX.
SIX ?!
YOU BETTER GO THEN...
HOW OLD ARE YOU, MINATO?

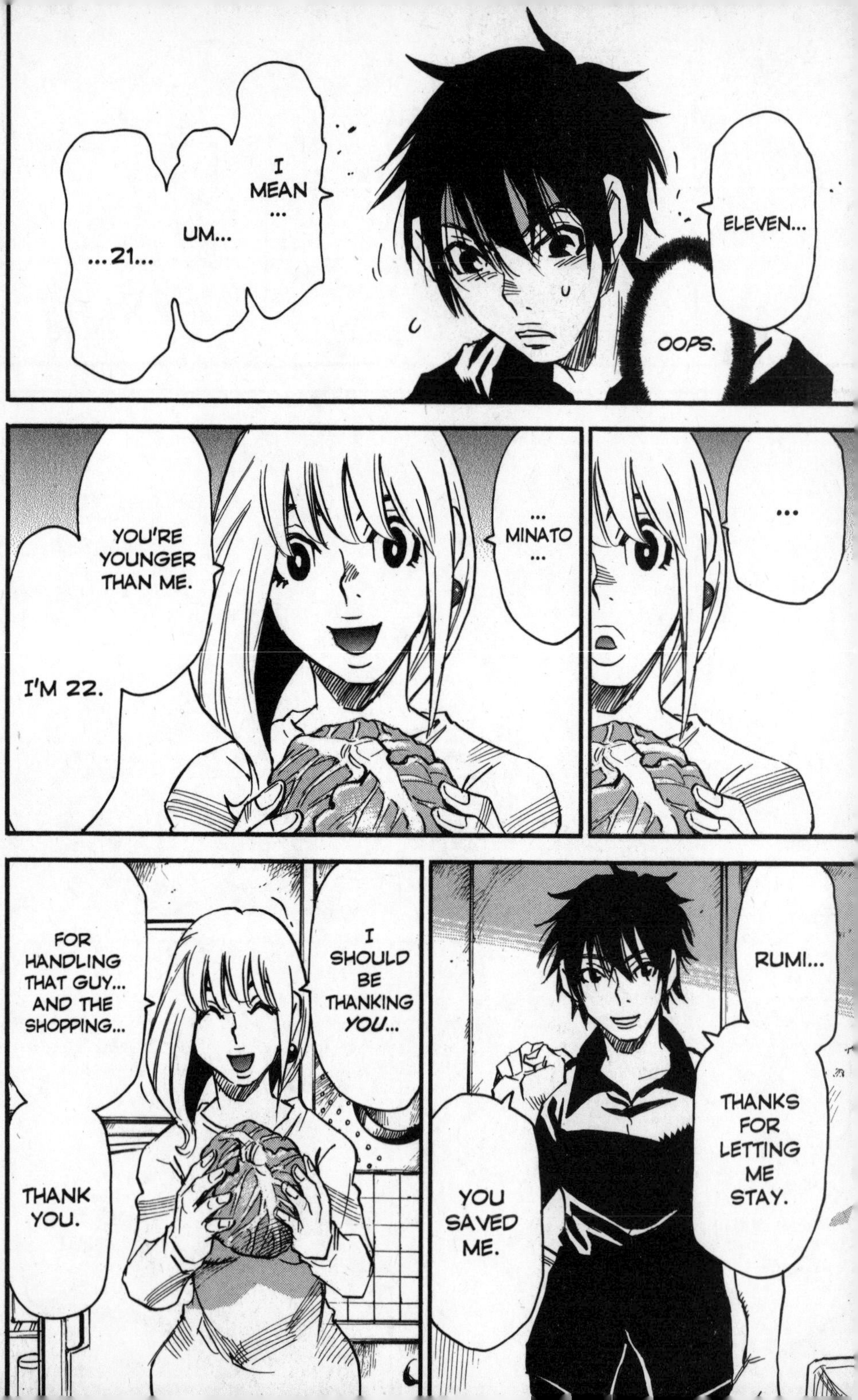
ELEVEN...
OOPS.
I MEAN ...
UM...
...21...
...
... MINATO ...
YOU'RE YOUNGER THAN ME.
I'M 22.
RUMI...
THANKS FOR LETTING ME STAY.
YOU SAVED ME.
I SHOULD BE THANKING *YOU*...
FOR HANDLING THAT GUY... AND THE SHOPPING...
THANK YOU.

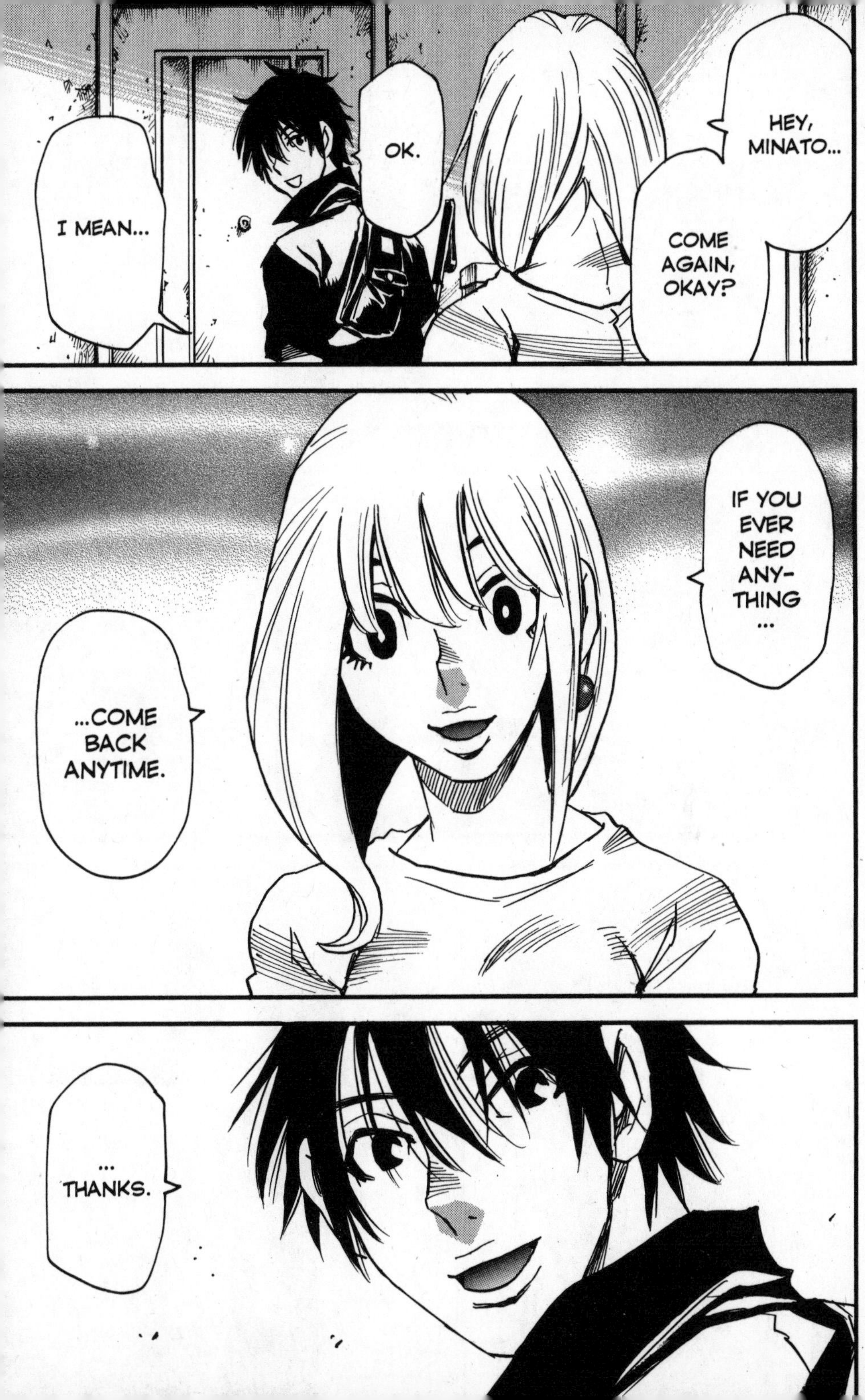
HEY, MINATO...
COME AGAIN, OKAY?
OK.
I MEAN...
IF YOU EVER NEED ANY-THING...
...COME BACK ANYTIME.
... THANKS.

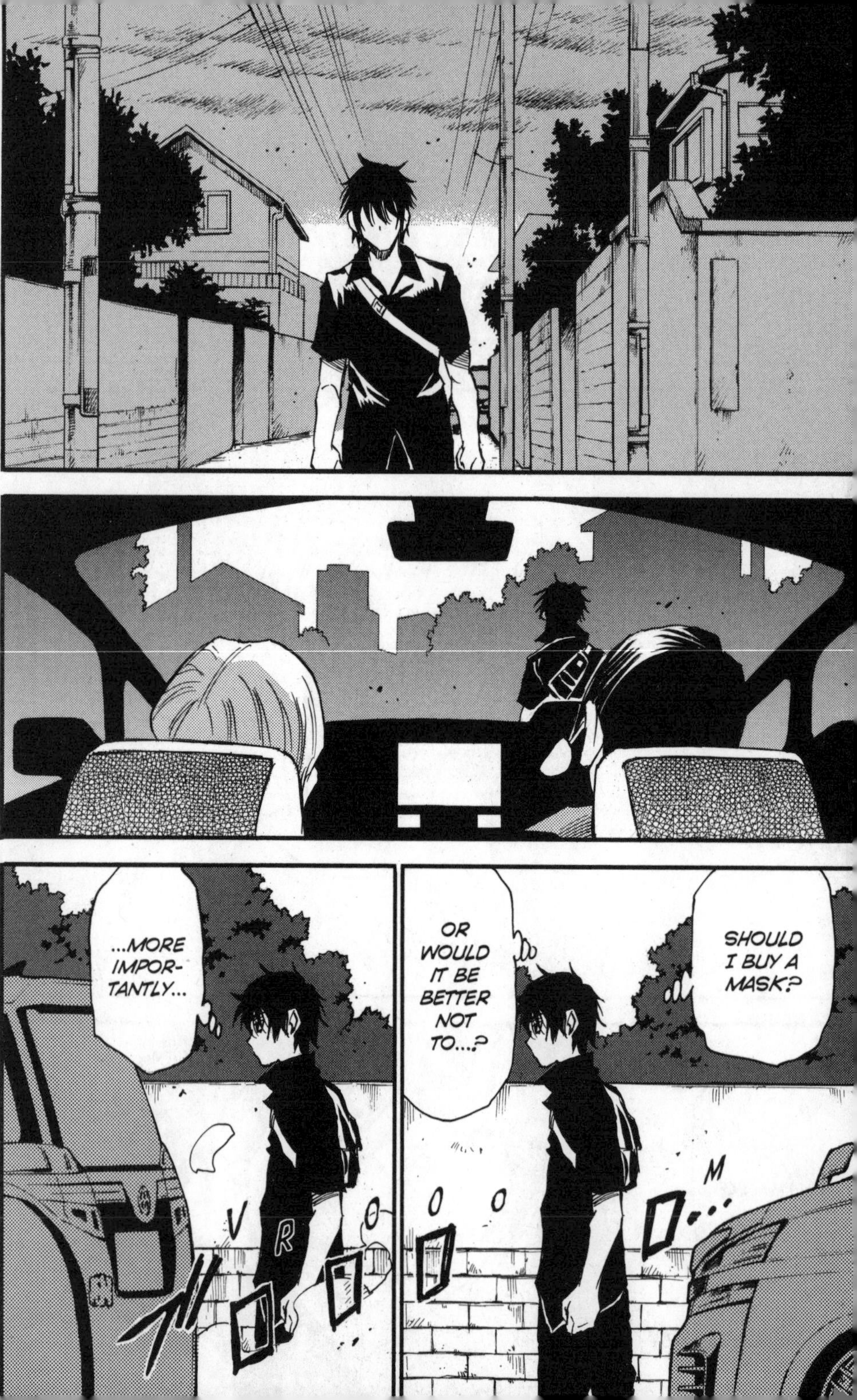
SHOULD I BUY A MASK?
OR WOULD IT BE BETTER NOT TO...?
...MORE IMPORTANTLY...
VROOOOM...

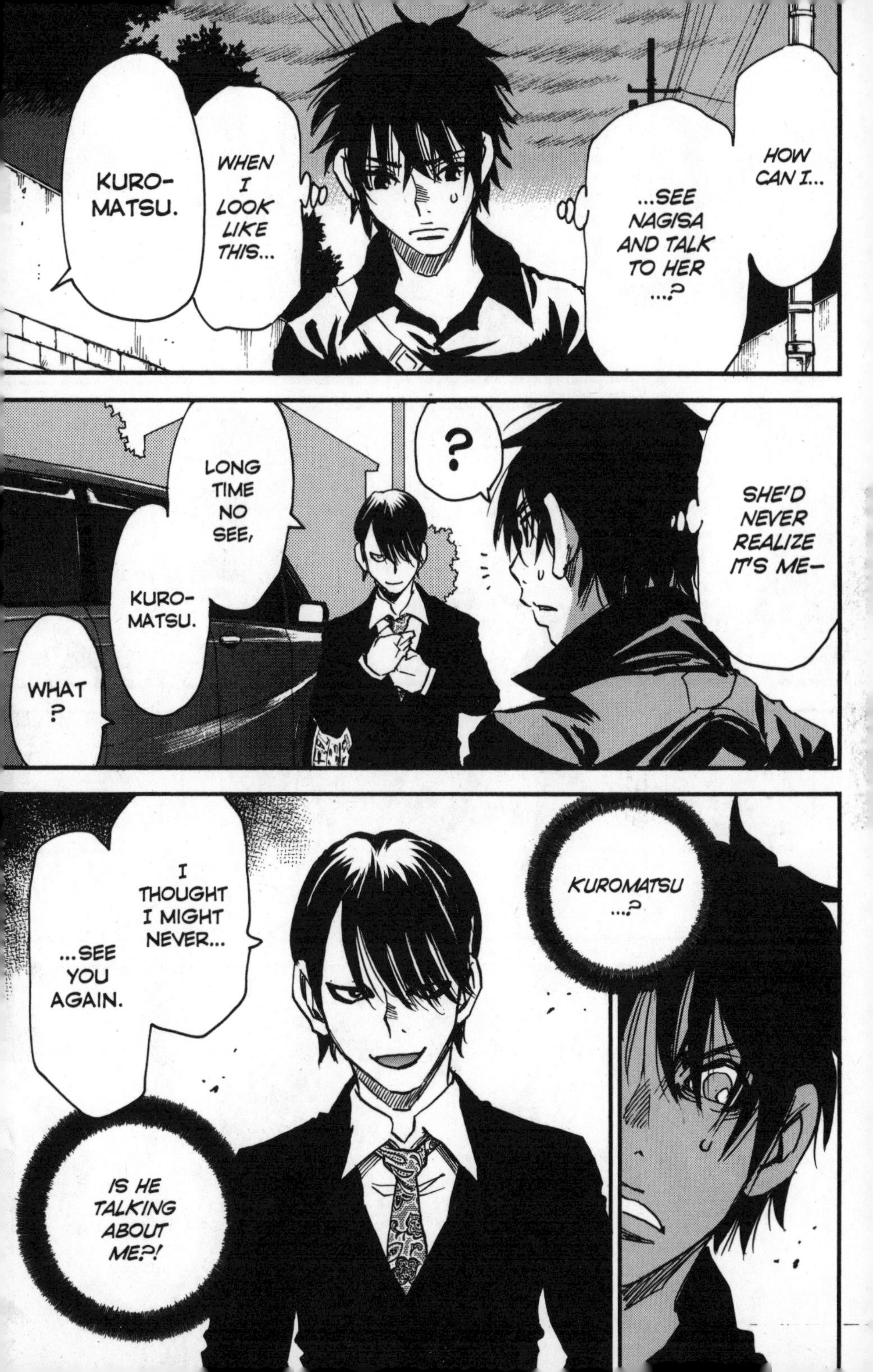
HOW CAN I...
...SEE NAGISA AND TALK TO HER ...?
WHEN I LOOK LIKE THIS...
KURO-MATSU.
SHE'D NEVER REALIZE IT'S ME—
?
LONG TIME NO SEE,
KURO-MATSU.
WHAT?
KUROMATSU ...?
I THOUGHT I MIGHT NEVER...
...SEE YOU AGAIN.
IS HE TALKING ABOUT ME?!

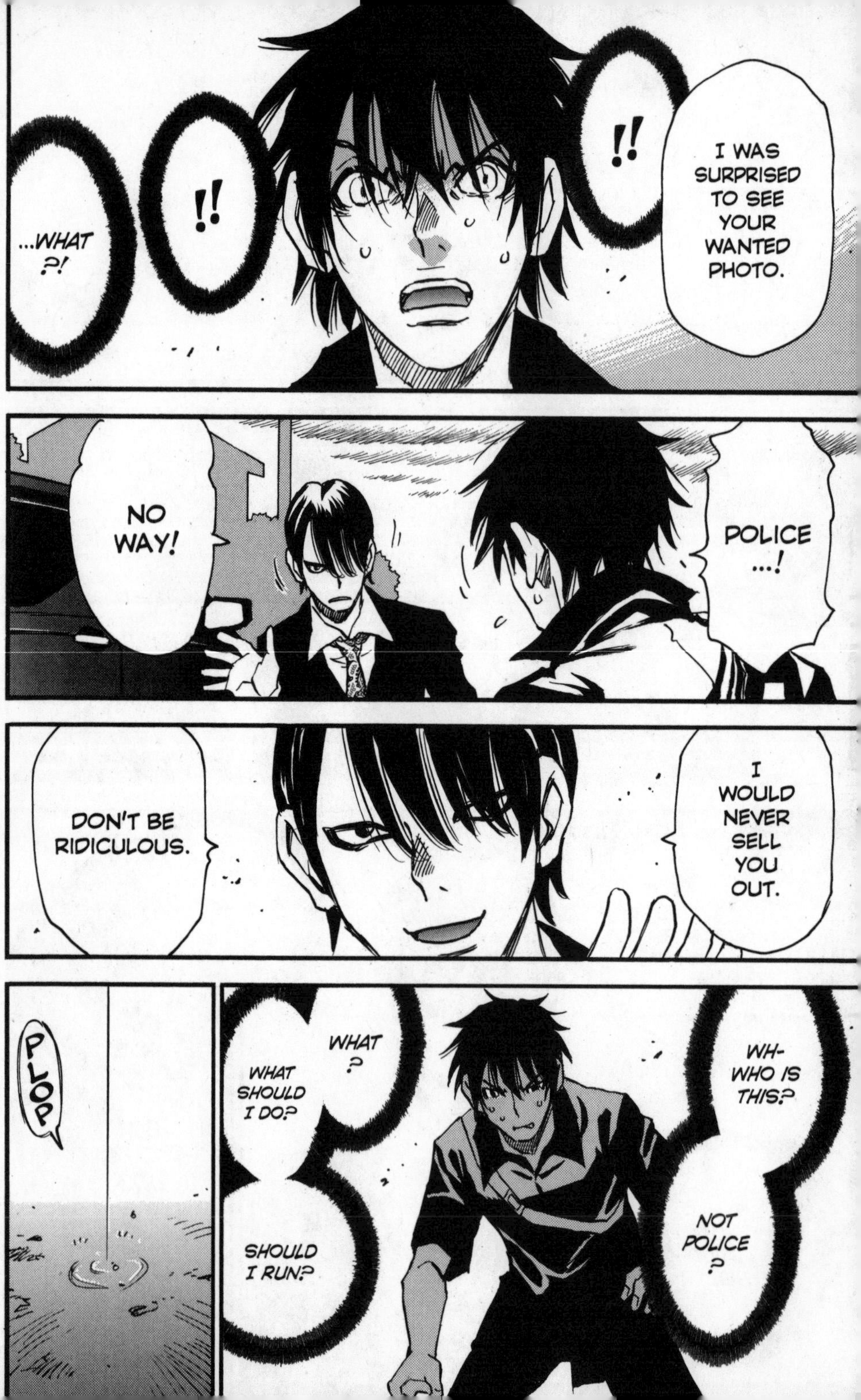
I WAS SURPRISED TO SEE YOUR WANTED PHOTO.
!!
!!
...WHAT ?!
POLICE ...!
NO WAY!
I WOULD NEVER SELL YOU OUT.
DON'T BE RIDICULOUS.
WH- WHO IS THIS?
NOT POLICE ?
WHAT ?
WHAT SHOULD I DO?
SHOULD I RUN?
PLOP

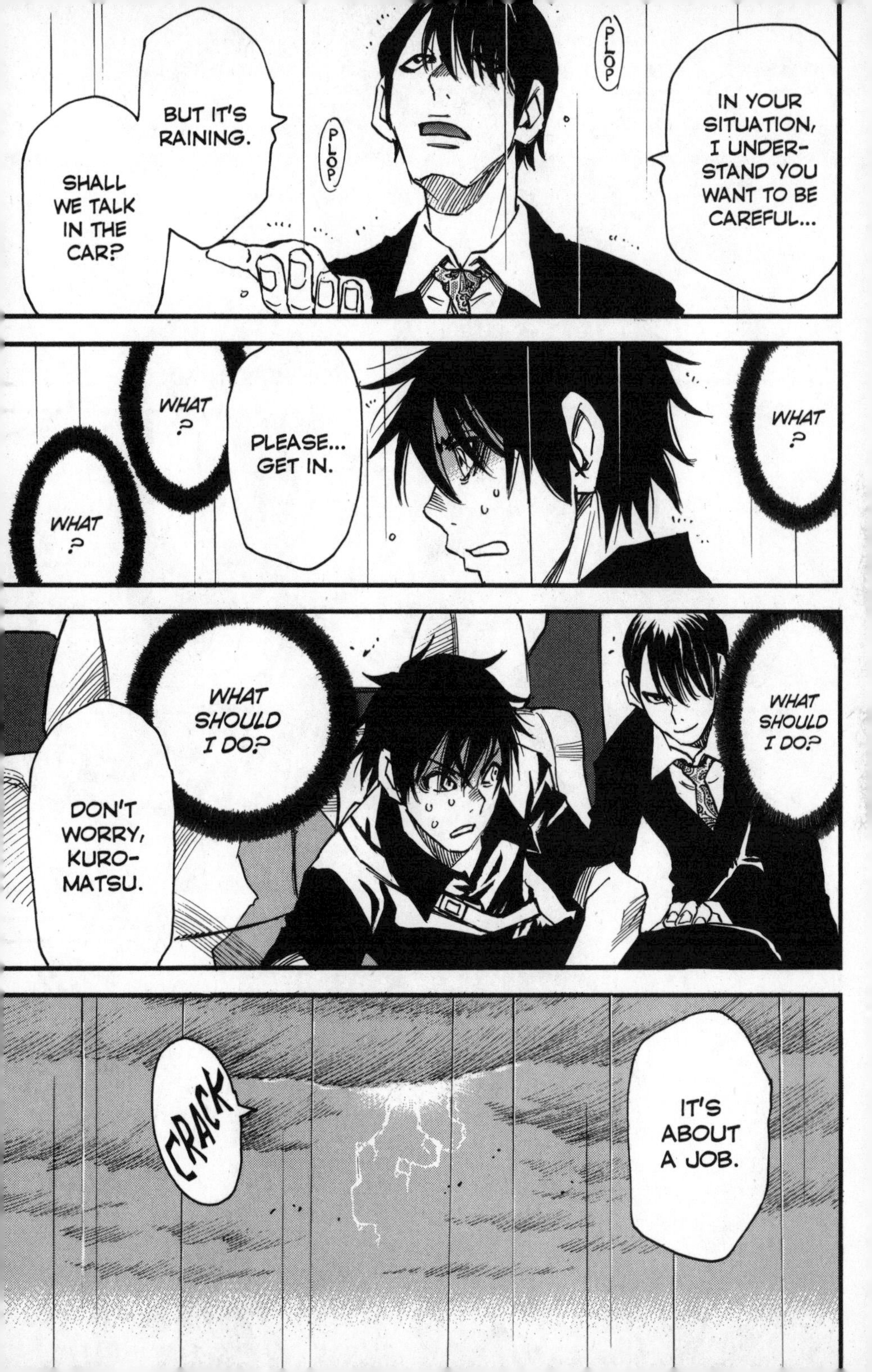
IN YOUR SITUATION, I UNDER-STAND YOU WANT TO BE CAREFUL...
PLOP
BUT IT'S RAINING.
PLOP
SHALL WE TALK IN THE CAR?
WHAT?
PLEASE... GET IN.
WHAT?
WHAT?
WHAT SHOULD I DO?
WHAT SHOULD I DO?
DON'T WORRY, KURO-MATSU.
IT'S ABOUT A JOB.
CRACK

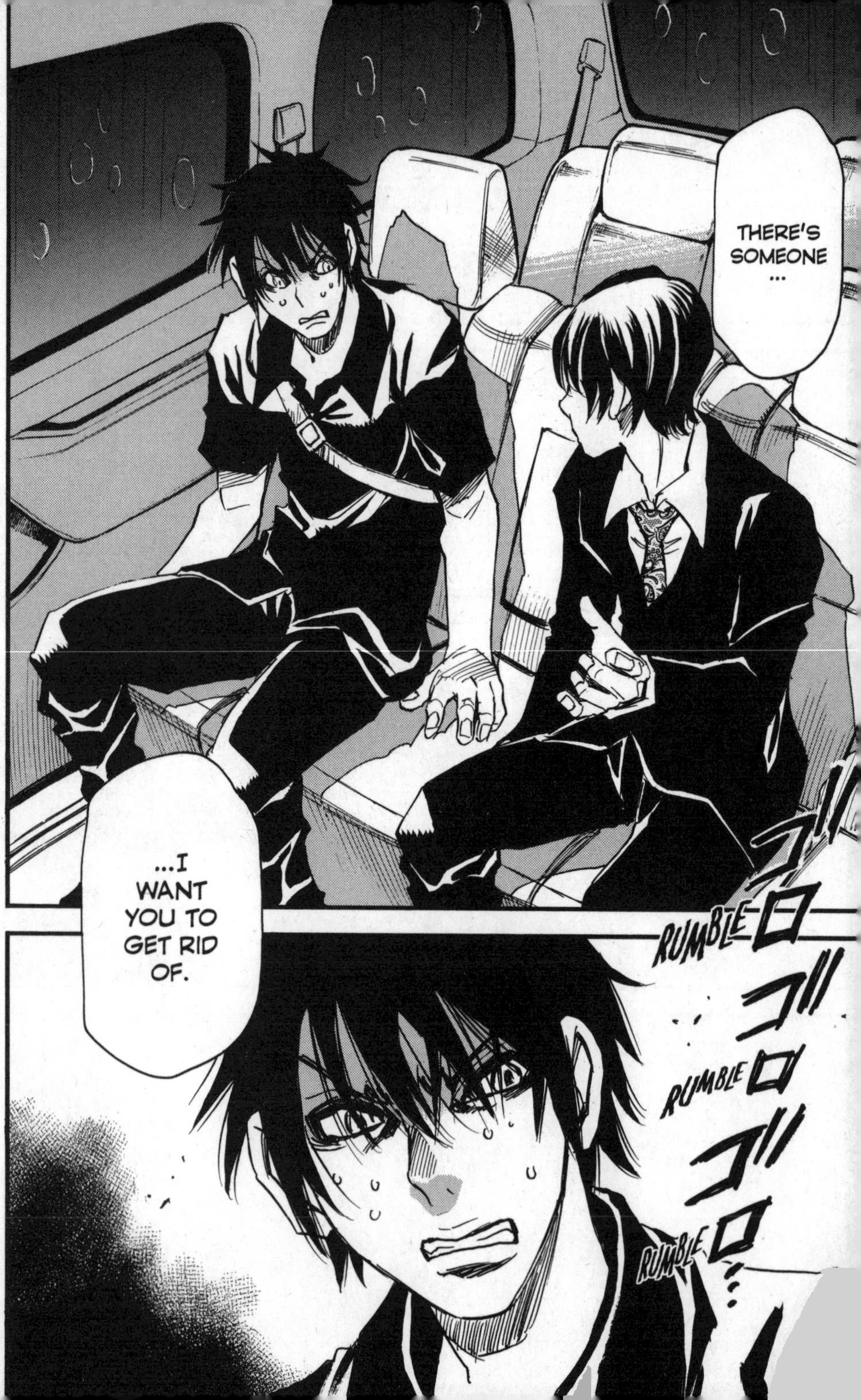
THERE'S SOMEONE ...
...I WANT YOU TO GET RID OF.
ゴロ RUMBLE
ゴロ RUMBLE
ゴロ RUMBLE

STAFF
Kei Sanbe

Yoichiro Tomita
Manami, 18 years old
Koji Kikuta
Yasunobu

Keishi Kanesho

SPECIAL THANKS
Naginyo

BOOK DESIGN
Yukio Hoshino
VOLARE inc.

EDITORS
Naofumi Muranaka
Takuya Nagao
Hiroshi Nishimura
Toshihiro Tsuchiboshi

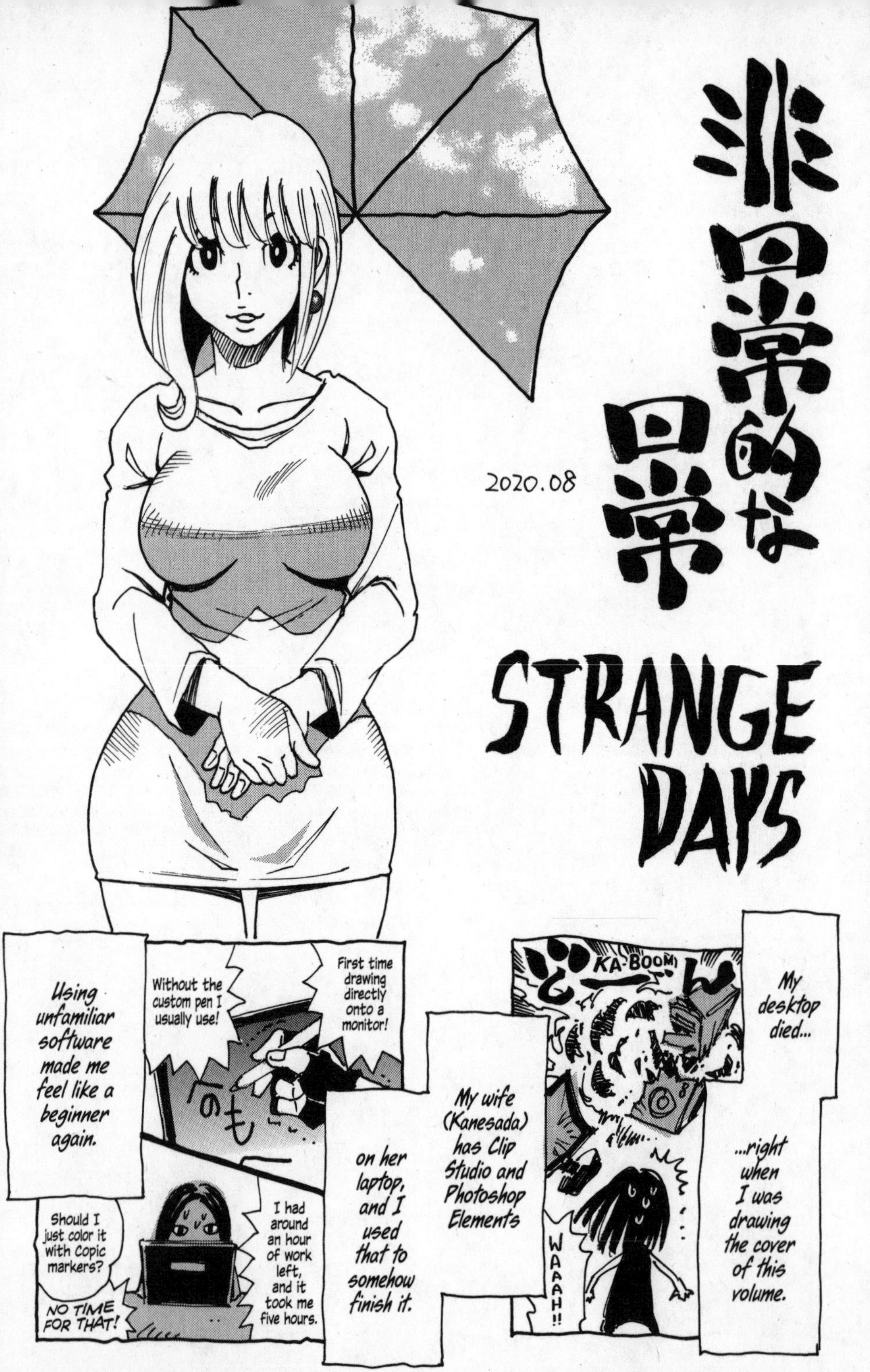

非日常的な日常
STRANGE DAYS
2020.08
My desktop died...
...right when I was drawing the cover of this volume.
KA-BOOM
WAAAAH!!
My wife (Kanesada) has Clip Studio and Photoshop Elements
on her laptop, and I used that to somehow finish it.
First time drawing directly onto a monitor!
Without the custom pen I usually use!
I had around an hour of work left, and it took me five hours.
Should I just color it with Copic markers?
NO TIME FOR THAT!
Using unfamiliar software made me feel like a beginner again.

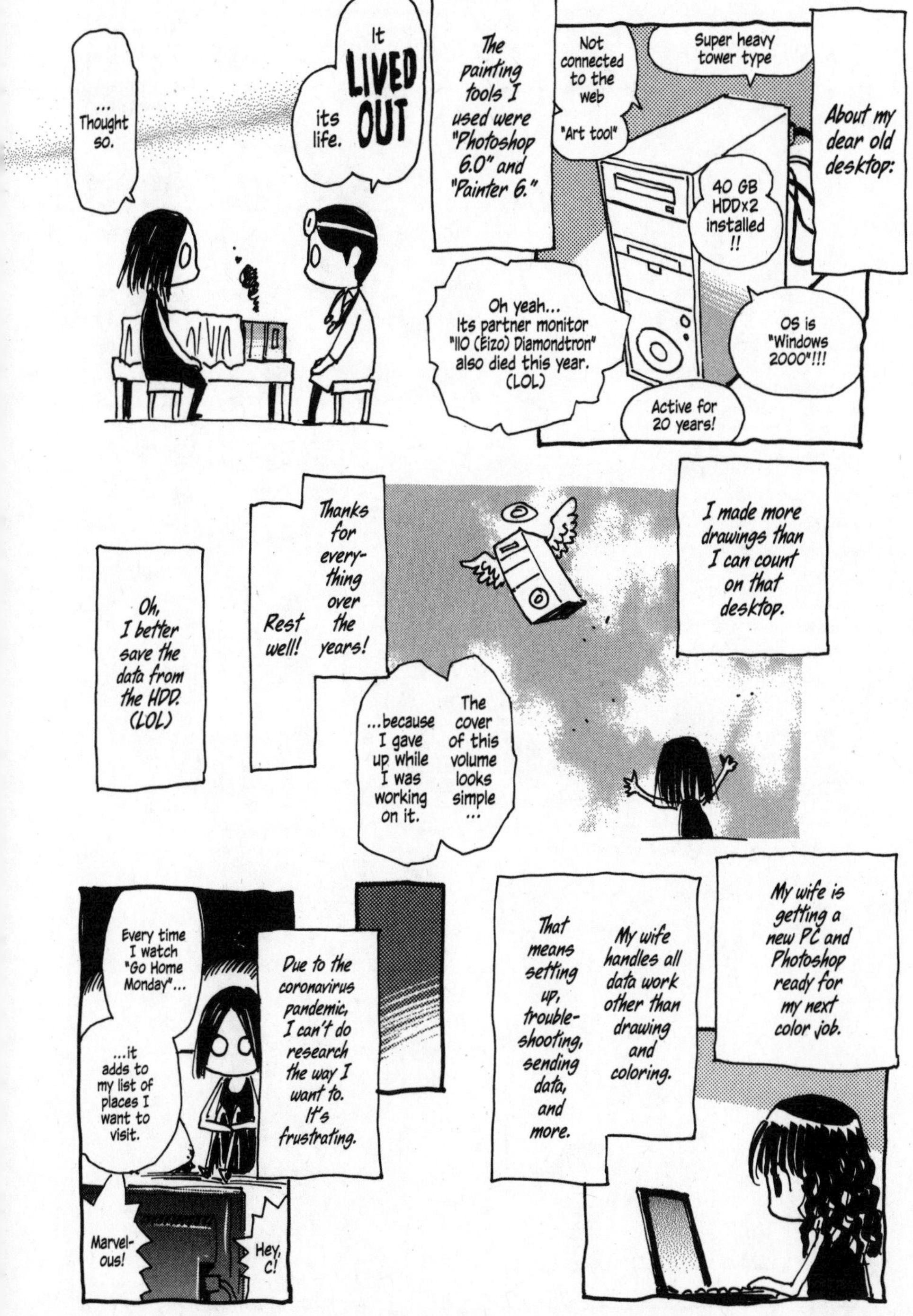
About my dear old desktop:
Super heavy tower type
Not connected to the web
"Art tool"
40 GB HDDx2 installed !!
OS is "Windows 2000"!!!
Active for 20 years!
Oh yeah... Its partner monitor "IIO (Eizo) Diamondtron" also died this year. (LOL)
The painting tools I used were "Photoshop 6.0" and "Painter 6."
It LIVED OUT its life.
... Thought so.
I made more drawings than I can count on that desktop.
The cover of this volume looks simple ...
...because I gave up while I was working on it.
Thanks for everything over the years!
Rest well!
Oh, I better save the data from the HDD. (LOL)
My wife is getting a new PC and Photoshop ready for my next color job.
My wife handles all data work other than drawing and coloring.
That means setting up, trouble-shooting, sending data, and more.
Due to the coronavirus pandemic, I can't do research the way I want to. It's frustrating.
Every time I watch "Go Home Monday"...
...it adds to my list of places I want to visit.
Hey, C!
Marvel-ous!

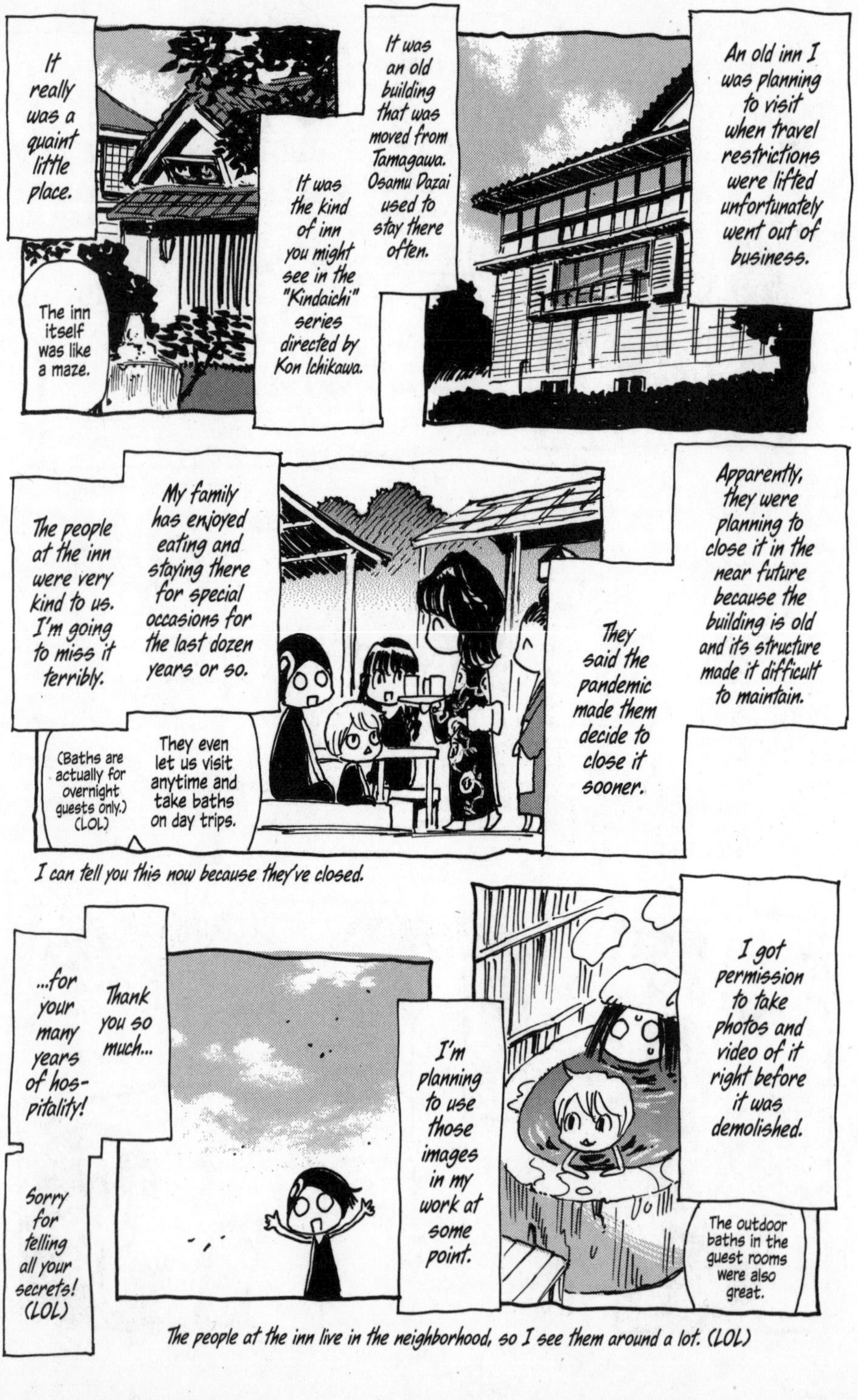
An old inn I was planning to visit when travel restrictions were lifted unfortunately went out of business.
It was an old building that was moved from Tamagawa. Osamu Dazai used to stay there often.
It was the kind of inn you might see in the "Kindaichi" series directed by Kon Ichikawa.
It really was a quaint little place.
The inn itself was like a maze.
Apparently, they were planning to close it in the near future because the building is old and its structure made it difficult to maintain.
They said the pandemic made them decide to close it sooner.
My family has enjoyed eating and staying there for special occasions for the last dozen years or so.
The people at the inn were very kind to us. I'm going to miss it terribly.
They even let us visit anytime and take baths on day trips.
(Baths are actually for overnight guests only.) (LOL)
I can tell you this now because they've closed.
I got permission to take photos and video of it right before it was demolished.
The outdoor baths in the guest rooms were also great.
I'm planning to use those images in my work at some point.
Thank you so much...
...for your many years of hospitality!
Sorry for telling all your secrets! (LOL)
The people at the inn live in the neighborhood, so I see them around a lot. (LOL)

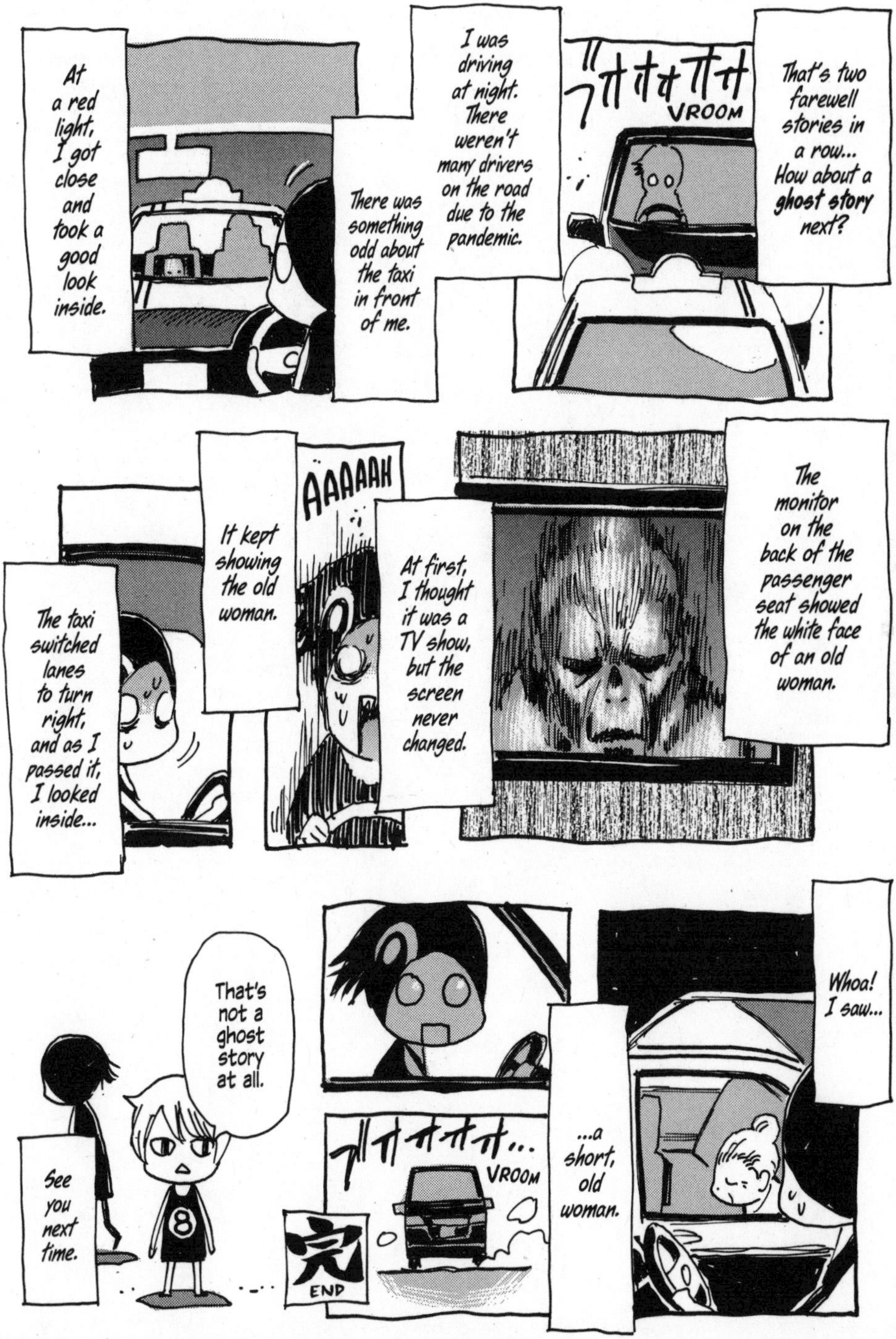
VROOM
That's two farewell stories in a row... How about a **ghost story** next?
I was driving at night. There weren't many drivers on the road due to the pandemic.
There was something odd about the taxi in front of me.
At a red light, I got close and took a good look inside.
The monitor on the back of the passenger seat showed the white face of an old woman.
AAAAAH
At first, I thought it was a TV show, but the screen never changed.
It kept showing the old woman.
The taxi switched lanes to turn right, and as I passed it, I looked inside...
Whoa! I saw...
...a short, old woman.
VROOM
完
END
That's not a ghost story at all.
See you next time.

A Kodansha Trade Paperback Original

Island in a Puddle 2 copyright © 2020 Kei Sanbe
English translation copyright © 2022 Kei Sanbe

Published in the United States by
Kodansha USA Publishing, LLC, New York.

Publication rights for this English edition arranged through
Kodansha Ltd., Tokyo.

First published in Japan in 2020 by Kodansha Ltd., Tokyo
as *Mizutamari ni ukabu shima*, volume 2.

ISBN 978-1-64651-457-1

Printed in the United States of America.

1st Printing

Translation: Iyasu Adair Nagata
Lettering: Evan Hayden
Kodansha USA Publishing edition cover design by Adam Del Re

Publisher: Kiichiro Sugawara

Director of Publishing Services: Ben Applegate
Director of Publishing Operations: Dave Barrett
Associate Director, Publishing Operations: Stephen Pakula Publishing
Services Managing Editors: Madison Salters, Alanna Ruse Production
Managers: Emi Lotto, Angela Zurlo

KODANSHA.US

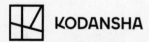